WELSH SURNAMES

WELSH SURNAMES

by

T. J. Morgan
and Prys Morgan

CARDIFF
UNIVERSITY OF WALES PRESS

www.uwp.co.uk

British Library Cataloguing-in-Publication Data
A catalogue record for this book is available from the British Library.

ISBN   978-0-708-30936-0

Printed and bound by CPI Group (UK) Ltd, Croydon, CR0 4YY

Contents

Preface

THE PRIMARY aim of this work is not to explain the 'meanings' of Welsh names: rather it tries to provide a historical survey of how the distinctive Welsh surnames came about. To take one instance, the earliest version of the name *Griffith* is *Grippiud*; this version as a result of natural changes became *Gruffudd, Gruffydd,* and eventually ends up as *Griffiths* and on the way, especially in colloquial usage, produces a large number of variant forms such as *Griffies, Grephies,* etc. more markedly in the records of the English border counties. In addition there were the 'hypocoristic' or pet forms, *Guto* and *Gutyn* which change to *Gittoes, Gittings,* etc.

The sources used, although not exhaustive, are I believe a wide and fair representation. Texts which have a colloquial quality are particularly valuable since they often record versions which are corrupt: these in many instances are clues to versions not found in places or at levels more literary or formal, for instance, texts of pedigrees. Ideally, of course, one would wish to quote examples which in their printed form exactly reproduced the original, without any or with the bare minimum of alteration or editing, so that one could feel quite confident that one was looking at the unaltered 'original' even though they were glaring examples of corruption. One has to realise that early texts are not in many cases edited and published for the sake of someone whose interest is concerned with the linguistic aspect and in the actual form of the text, but quite often for the sake of historians. For instance, Mr Peter Bartrum in the construction of his massive work on pedigrees has naturally made use of a number of variant sources, both in manuscript form or printed, and it is proper that he should use recognised standard forms of names and make no attempt to reproduce the several versions of the different texts which would result in a jungle of variants.

Some texts are translations of the original Latin, for instance the Caernarvon Quarter Session Rolls, and the Caernarvon Court Rolls, and the names generally appear in modern edited forms although at times the actual MS version is given in brackets if it is judged to be of interest. In a publication such as the *Star Chamber Proceedings* the names are given for each reign so that the names of each county are kept together. It should therefore be understood that in a fair proportion of the texts from which examples have been taken, the forms of names may not be the actual manuscript version and allowance must be made for this. Certain other texts have the original with an English translation, e.g. *The Record of Carnarvon* and *The Black Book of St David's.* Caution of another sort is needed when use is being made of some of these texts: the editors of the two books mentioned seem to have no knowledge of Welsh so that they were at times liable to confuse women's names with men's names, especially if *fil.* or *f.* is used for *filius* and for *filia*; and since they frequently print forms such as *Hona* for what should be *Houa (Hwfa)* one has to conclude that they were misled by the medieval script in which *n* and *u* are difficult to make out. Modern Welsh scholarship enables us, generally speaking, to make the necessary adjustments and to suggest what the proper reading should be. Other documents requiring the same kind of corrective are the official government publications of the 'Letters and Papers'. class. It is one of the main concerns of this work to provide evidence that an unexpectedly large number of names in use outside Wales are Welsh in origin, much altered and corrupted, so that it was an enormous advantage to have the Shropshire Parish Registers in printed form, generally fully indexed: those yielded a great quantity of valuable evidence, not only valuable in its amount, for in the entries over the years concerning the same persons and the same families, one often witnessed the process of decay and corruption. The bibliography will show that a small number of Welsh parish registers have been published; the registers of certain Gwent parishes published by Bradney are very valuable but one must be very wary, even sceptical, concerning explanations of names offered by Bradney. The parish registers of Cumberland and Westmorland are also available in published form. The possibility had occurred to my mind at an early stage that vestiges of North British names might be found in these areas; representative documents of the medieval period were examined, such as Lay Subsidy Rolls, the published parish registers, the present-day parliamentary lists of voters covering the area as far north as Penrith and the Border. The investigation although not entirely fruitless, did not provide much that could be confidently used; a few remote possibilities remain in my mind which would require a good deal of philological repair work, and this book is not the place for conjecture and suggestions.

A considerable amount of material covering the border area of England and Wales was examined: a thesis on the ancient documents of the lordship of Clun, the extent of Bromfield and Yale, the Lordship of Oswestry, the records published in the *Transactions of the Radnorshire Society*, the parish registers already mentioned, a number of books published in recent years include the Marches in their survey. From the point of view of this work, the English-Welsh border area is the most productive because many names which disappeared from Wales were there retained, virtually if not completely. More importantly, colloquial versions and nicknames were retained, and one sees the sound changes coming about when Welsh forms were subjected to the pronunciations of an English dialect. The names and versions of names which survived or were developed in the area now being considered would sooner or later spread into England generally, and also back into Wales in spellings quite often different from their Welsh originals or sounds.

To make a fairly comprehensive survey of the modern period nothing could be more complete than the registers of parliamentary and local elections for these include virtually everybody. Returning officers agreed to make me a present of recently obsolete lists of electors: the first batch were in force in 1959, the second in 1976. Altogether I scrutinised the registers of the whole of Wales, and every constituency following a line southwards from Penrith to Stroud, though I could not manage the task of covering the whole of Lancashire. I was of course not interested in finding conventional names such as *Evans* and *Morgan*, but a look out was kept for names less obviously Welsh in origin or form although obviously Welsh in origin such as *De Vonald* in Penrith which is just *Devonall, Devonald* (from *Dyfnwal*) made to look French; or *Vellins* in Cheadle which comes probably from the lenited form *Felyn, Velin,* as compared with *Melling, Mellings* which stand for the unlenited versions. Although a considerable amount of valuable evidence was collected from these registers of electors I am sure that many valuable forms and versions were passed by unnoticed; as the work progressed one came to realise that certain names, previously unsuspected, were of Welsh origin and that examples had been seen somewhere in an earlier scrutiny and allowed to slip by unrecorded. For instance, at a certain stage I happened to see and consider the name *Gwriad* in Lloyd Jones's *Geirfa* and realized that the name without its initial *G-* was the origin of *Wyriot,* examples of which I had seen in present-day electoral registers when I had no reason to pick them up. That is why I made so much use of telephone directories, as a kind of 'repair service' hoping that I could recover some of these possible losses. The name *Gladdis*, from *Gladys* or *Gwladus*, is a good example.

Electoral lists vary a good deal in the way they are set out; to give the precise location of a surname makes a very cumbersome source reference and I have here dispensed with details giving ward and street names. It has been my habit to scrutinise the lists of names in newspapers and I have not hesitated to record examples taken from *The Times, The Daily Telegraph* and *The Western Mail*. It was pleasing to see instances of *Cundell, Cundall* in various parts of England, versions of the name *Cynddelw* which fell into disuse and did not produce a surname in the Welsh-speaking community: finding *Cundelu* in *The Daily Telegraph* was like bringing up the coelacanth in the fishing net.

It will be realised by readers who stand at a distance outside Welsh scholarship that for much of the content of this work it is entirely unnecessary to provide references to authorities. To those who are familiar with the language and with contemporary Welsh scholarship, such statements would correspond to the tables of simple arithmetic. There is no failure, I hope, to give references where really necessary.

I am particularly grateful to Professor G.O. Pierce who readily gave me a number of valuable references; Mr Barry Davies (Lisvane, Cardiff), the local historian, deserves my especial thanks for replying to my enquiries, as does Major Francis Jones, Wales Herald Extraordinary, concerning his native county of Pembroke. I repeat my appreciation of the kindness of chief executives or returning officers who sent me copies of registers of electors free of charge. There are two archivists who did me a good turn; Mr B.C. Jones, archivist of Cumbria County Council, who gave me much help regarding the parish registers, published by the Cumberland and Westmorland Antiquarian and Archaeological Society and other early documents such as the Poll Tax for Carlisle (1377) and the Lay Subsidy for Cumberland, 6th Edward III; and the archivist of Shropshire who arranged to send me a microfilm copy of Miss G.E.A. Raspin's thesis on the Marcher Lordship of Clun (ADClun).

I have had in mind in the composition of this book that it would be consulted by readers with no knowledge of Welsh and have explained certain matters which the native speaker can afford to disregard, and explained in a way that the intelligent reader who is not a language specialist can follow. I have also had in mind that a book of this kind will be consulted at odd times by persons interested in the origins of their own name or those of ancestors and, at risk of repetition, have avoided an excess of cross-references. Providing an index for this kind of work would require another complete volume. Instead, a 'guide' has been provided whenever it was thought necessary, e.g. to enable a reader to find the section which included the name or version or corruption of that name falling outside the obvious heading that might concern him. For example, the guide will show that versions of *Bedo* may be found under the heading *Meredith*.

I am deeply grateful to Mrs Gwyneth Hughes, my former secretary in the University College of Swansea, for providing the typewritten copy. No words of gratitude can adequately express my indebtedness to Mr John Rhys, the director of the University of Wales Press and to his assistant, Mr Iwan Llwyd Williams. Finally I owe thanks to the Leverhulme Trust for their grant towards my travelling expenses and other costs involved in the preparation and composition of this book.

It will not require much detection to see that the original manuscript of this book was very much longer and that I had to find means of reducing its length. I have thus omitted a large number of names which are well-known or self-explanatory, for example, the surnames based on well-known place-names, on an 'English' pattern, such as Cardiff, Swansea, Anglesey, Mold, Moldsdale, Radnor, etc. A small number of such names have been retained where they provide a link in my evidence, e.g. Brychan, Brecon, Brycheiniog, Brecknock, Breconshire. I also omitted detailed treatment of most of those surnames, adopted chiefly in the Tudor period, and mostly in North Wales, derived from estates or residences, for example, Almer, Bangor, Bodvel, Brynkyr, Bodwrda, Coetmor, Yale, Llifon, Nanney, Madryn, Quellyn, Saethon, Trevallyn, Trefor, Trygarn, and so on. A few such surnames, which illustrate specific points, have been retained, such as Blayney, Carreg, Gower, Lougher, Maesmor, Mostyn and Pennant, for detailed examination in the classified list. I have also retained in the classified list a few Welsh place-name surnames such as Barry, Cogan, Taafe, which arose during the Norman conquest of Ireland. In any case, I have appended a fairly full list of place-name surnames in chapter four of the introduction.

My son, Dr Prys Morgan, furnished me with many examples he came across in the course of his researches. At some time during the actual compilation of the book I was forced by circumstances beyond my control to rely on his cooperation to such an extent that it required more than acknowledgement to indicate the amount which the book owes to his contribution, and bringing his name into the authorship is the only sensible thing to do.

T. J. MORGAN
Bishopston
Swansea

Introduction

1. THE ORTHOGRAPHY OF WELSH SURNAMES

THE ORTHOGRAPHY of Welsh has a number of peculiarities which need to be explained if the content of this work is to make sense to readers who are not familiar with the language and are conditioned by the spelling systems of their own language. Using an approved phonetic script would make the book unreadable to ordinary readers, and at the risk of appearing too elementary I propose to use in this section a method of transposing Welsh sounds into a system of English values. Using Welsh place-names as examples will have the advantage that the pronunciation of well-known place names is familiar through broadcast news bulletins. The system of consonantal mutations will come later on; in the first place it is necessary to deal with the way Welsh makes use of the letters of the alphabet to represent sounds, and only to the extent that explanation is deemed necessary and helpful. The vowels *a, e, i, o, u* are stable, representing one sound only, but the sound which *u* represents needs special attention. In medieval Welsh the vowel represented by *u* was like French *u*, the 'roundness' coming from the pouting lips as it were. It later moved so that the 'roundness' is produced between the hard palate and the tongue which is pressed against the upper teeth and given a spoon-like shape. This move made it identical with the 'clear' sound of *y*, WG13: the sound is described by Morris Jones in these words, 'the Welsh *y* is an *i* pronounced further back but with open lips', WG14. This *u/y* sound remains in the speech of the greater part of North Wales, but it is not heard at all in the natural speech of South Wales, and the rhymes of popular verse composed in South Wales show that South Wales long ago lost the distinction between *u/y* and *i* (i.e. English *ee*). Standardized written Welsh continues to write *du* 'black' and *tŷ* 'house'; and the Welsh speaker of South Wales uses these spellings although his natural pronunciation has the sound of English *dee* and *tee*. The medieval English scribe found it difficult to express the *u/y* sound or sounds by means of the symbols known to him, and *du* is generally written *dye*, e.g. *Pwll-du/Puldye*. If in the late medieval period he took the sound heard in South Wales speech, the scribe would use *dee* for the *ee* of English writing properly to represent the South Wales sound, and in any case it is a reasonable approximation of the sound heard in North Wales. A man with the epithet *Du* attached to his name becomes *Dee; Guto* becomes *Gitto (Gittoes), Gutyn* becomes *Gittin(s). Gruffudd*, of which *Guto* and *Gutyn* are hypocoristic versions came, in Welsh, to be written *Gruffydd*, the use of *y* in the final syllable making no difference; the change to *Griffith* represents the vowel sound heard in South Wales and the nearest that English spelling can get to that peculiar vowel sound.

The other peculiar sound is the sound of *ll* heard in Llan- place-names, *Llanelli, Llandeilo*, etc. The tongue is held in the *l* position and breath is forced out between the side of the tongue and the upper teeth on the side kept open, either right or left, the tongue being raised on one side to close the passage; Morris Jones, WG19 calls it the 'unilateral hiss'. It will be seen later when the mutations are described that *l* is the lenited form, or the 'soft mutation' of *ll*, and in certain constructions, initial *ll* becomes *l*, e.g. 'to *Llanelli*' becomes '*i Lanelli*', just as 'to *Cardiff*' becomes '*i Gaerdydd*'. But one may be misled by seeing 'English' versions or transcriptions of certain names. Welsh

Llywelyn (and the permitted variant *Llewelyn*) is oftener than not written *Llewellyn; Hywel* is written *Howell* (*Howells, Powell*); *Cydweli* is known to most in the form of *Kidwelly*, and the *ll* of *Caerphilly* is misleading if one has learned that *ll* in Welsh stands for the 'unilateral hiss'. Another thing that might mislead the stranger and uninformed is a tendency amongst the Welsh themselves to substitute *l* for initial *ll* and to say *Landaff, Lanelli, Landudno*. The outstanding example of this substitution is the way *Lloyd* is pronounced, for this stands for *llwyd*, with no mutation.

It is more necessary in fact to know about the orthographic devices which are used in Welsh for sounds not necessarily peculiar. Double *d*, i.e. *dd* stands for voiced *-th-* as in breathe, e.g. *Caerdydd, Pontypridd, Rhuddlan, Rhondda*. Single *f* in modern Welsh stands for *v* and double *ff* is needed for English *f*, e.g. *Caernarfon*; Aberdovey is *Aberdyfi* = 'mouth of R. Dovey', the Cardigan river is generally seen in the form of Tivy or Teivy; in Welsh *Teifi*. The Welsh use of *ff* is seen in *Ffestiniog, Trefforest*; Caerphilly should be *Caerffili*. These various orthographic devices, and others, are standardized in modern Welsh; medieval Welsh texts lack standardization and one has to use one's knowledge of modern Welsh to switch over to interpret systems of writing which are different from modern Welsh writing and different from each other. These differences are increased by the texts written or copied by scribes who were not themselves Welsh, or not familiar with the native Welsh system. This means that one must expect to find a great variety in the 'unstandardized' versions in the examples quoted, but it will not be necessary to explain every departure from the norm. The native Welsh scribe generally uses *d* for *d* and for *dd*; the Anglo-norman as a rule uses *th*. Uncertainty arises from the use of *u* for the single *f* (v) sound. The letter *v* which is no longer regarded as a constituent of the Welsh alphabet is often used in medieval Welsh by native Welsh scribes, but that will cause no difficulty, any more than *k* (for *c*) which is also excluded as unnecessary. Difficulty may arise from the use of *u*, for it may stand for *v* or *w*, in addition to being the symbol of the vowel sound; but the main difficulty is the inability to distinguish clearly between *u* and *n* in certain MSS especially if the writing is faded. The native Welsh scholar generally manages for he knows what ought to be there. An editor of a Latin text lacking native Welsh scholarship is liable to be deceived by *u* and *n* when transcribing Welsh names in the text and one finds a name such as *Hwfa, Hofa* (*hwua, houa*) printed as *Hwna, Hona*, or *Gweiruul* (= *Gweirful*) as *Gweirnul*. Quite often the MS is itself a copy, and the kind of misreading now being described is often the failure of the copying scribe, not necessarily of the modern editor. The name *Ieuan* and the superlative adj. *ieuaf* (written *ieuau*, 'youngest') which is sometimes used as a personal name, get badly mixed up in the medieval texts, e.g. the Chronicles edited by the late Professor Thomas Jones, Peniarth 20 (Translation) p.9; P. 20 Welsh text p.84, compare the versions in the text and of other copies in the footnotes. In the printed text of the *Record of Carnarvon*, the name is sometimes *Hova*, at others *Hona*, arising probably from an original *Houa*.[1]

The sound of Welsh *ch* in a name such as *Dafydd Goch* was generally transposed by means of the spelling used in English *cough, rough, enough*. (The equivalence of the

---

[1]   *v.* T.P. Ellis, editor of *The First Extent of Bromfield and Yale*, AD 1315, Explanatory Note X. The editor uses certain personal names to point to the pitfalls. The text quite definitely gives *Hona*, and not *Hova* or *Houa*, and there is no instance of *Houa* at all; comparison is made with the RecCa and the Survey of Denbigh both of which have *Hona*. The second example is *Eigion*; the third is *Ienna*, common also in RecCa and S. Denbigh. 'In eight instances in the text it is written *Ienaf* or *Iennaf* . . . In one case only is the name written *Ieuan* – see p.68 of text, and in fifteen instances it is spelt in full unmistakably as "*Ienna*" '. The editor may not have realized that *Ienaf* could be a miscopying of *Ieuaf* ('youngest', not necessarily of Ieuan) and that *Ienna* was a colloquial version of *Ieuan*.

symbols will be best understood by seeing the process in reverse: a borrowing of the English *laugh* in certain South Wales dialects is *lach* with very little awareness that it is the English word.) *Gough* was pronounced 'Goff', and still is, and this 'phonetic' version of the surname is occasionally used. Sometimes an attempt was made to represent the long *o*, leaving the *ch* unaltered as far as the spelling went: this gave *Gooch*, and in course of time this produced a new pronunciation. There were other ways of transposing the -*ch*- sound, e.g. using *h* only, *Goh* or *Gohe*. The reader must be prepared to see the symbol *z* and *Goch/Gough* written *Goz* or *Goze*. The *zed* symbol was not needed in Welsh writing and it could be put to other uses, as it was in the writing of Irish and Scots Gaelic; cf. names such as *Mackenzie, Menzies, Dalzell*, in which the *z* is now pronounced as if it were the English *zed*. In Welsh records the *z* is seen oftenest in the written abbreviation of 'verch' (daughter), *vz*, which had to be used so often in pedigrees.

The sound of *ll*' (i.e. 'the unilateral hiss') was much more difficult: *chl, thl* were sometimes used; *fl*, as in *Fluellen*, was also used; and these 'symbols' represent attempts to pronounce *ll*'. In some texts no attempt is made to find a way of writing the *ll*' sound and it is left as *l*. This may mislead modern editors of medieval texts. If the text is printed in a diplomatic reproduction, deciding what the *l* stands for is left to the reader, but if the text is edited for the sake of a modern reader, or if the Welsh or Latin as the case may be is translated, the editor must determine when the single *l* represents the *ll*' sound and when the *l* sound. The editors of the Caernarvon Court Rolls and Quarter Session Rolls, in their English translations with modern Welsh versions of the names that occur, have been misled by the single *l* more than once and have treated it as if it were necessarily the lenited form of *ll*'. In the appropriate places the single *l* should have been converted into *ll*; for instance, the adj. *llwyd* 'grey, brown hair' retains the radical consonant (i.e. does not lenite) when it means 'grey, brown hair', even after a feminine personal name, *Morgan Llwyd, Morfudd Llwyd*. In a translation or modern version of a text that uses *l* at all times, failing to adjust the single *l* when necessary implies that it stands for a lenition every time: in other words, proper name + *loyt* should become . . . *llwyd*. (The editors may have been misled also by the assumption that the adj. underwent soft mutation after a personal name, which on the whole is correct; *llwyd*, though, is an exception.)

The reader to whom Welsh is completely new will be puzzled by the frequent references to the initial mutations. There are three kinds of consonantal mutation, lenition or 'soft mutation', aspirate, and nasal. Lenition is the only form of mutation involved in the subject matter of this book. The mutation takes the following form: *c > g; p > b; t > d; g* is removed, not sounded or written; *b > f; d > dd; ll > l; m > f; rh > r*. What is meant is that these consonants as initial consonants are liable, for a great number of reasons, to undergo the changes indicated; for instance, a fem. sg. noun after the def. art., *cath* 'cat' becomes *y gath*; a noun following the numeral *dau* 'two', or the fem. *dwy*, *pen* 'head' becomes *dau ben* 'two heads'; *dafad* 'sheep' becomes *dwy ddafad* 'two sheep'; *gwraig* 'woman, wife' becomes *y wraig, dwy wraig; glaw* 'rain' can change to give *cawod o law*, 'shower of rain'.

In the context of personal names lenition will be seen mainly in the epithet which is attached to the personal name (and which might eventually become a surname). *Coch* 'red' becomes *Iolo Goch*. The mutation of *coch* is also seen in the compound adj. *pengoch* 'redhead': The *p* is lenited in *Dafydd Bengoch*. *Tew* 'fat' sometimes retains the radical, *Gwilym Tew*; there may also be examples in which it is mutated, *Gwilym Dew*. The mutation of *g* is seen in the adj. *gwyn* 'white'; fem. *gwen, Eifion Wyn, Margaret Wen. Bras* 'fat' becomes *Adda Fras*, and in a compound adj. *Adda Benfras. Du* 'black', becomes *Dafydd Ddu*; *llwyd* as already explained remains unmutated in this construction except when it means 'holy', e.g. *Dewi lwyd*, referring to St David. *Llygliw* 'mouse-coloured' was sometimes attached as an epithet, *Einion Lygliw*; *mawr* 'big' mutates in *Llywelyn Fawr*, 'Ll. the Great'; *melyn* 'yellow' in *Hywel Felyn*.

These paragraphs are intended to help the reader identify the tools being used on the job. The consonant *r* is always trilled and in the initial position it is an aspirated *r*, e.g. *Rhuddlan, Rhuthun, Rhos, Rhys, Rhydderch*; and names borrowed from English or French, *Robert, Richard, Roger*, are given this aspirate although it often may not be shown in the written version. (In fact the writing system of native Welsh texts was defective in this respect, that *r* was generally used for *rh*.) The consonants *g b d* followed by the aspirate or by *rh* undergo a 'hard mutation' and change to *c p t*, and *dd* (voiced) becomes -*th*- (unvoiced). This converse of lenition is called provection, WG181; and there will be reason to refer to provection frequently as it comes about when the *b* of *mab/ab* 'son of', preceding the father's name is changed to *p* if the father's name begins with an *h* or *rh*, and brings about eventually surnames such as *Prys (Price), Prydderch, Probert, Prichard, Parry, Powel* (as compared with *Bevan, Bowen*). Provection comes about if a final *b* combines with the initial *b* of the word following, so that *ab-Bleddyn* becomes *Pleddyn/Plethyn*. Another cause of provection is the contact of *s* and *dd*: the best known example is *nos da* 'good night' (for 'nos + dda', *nos* being fem., the adj. ought to have a soft mutation): *Rhys Ddu* may remain, but it is also liable to change to *Rhys Du*, and *Gwladus Ddu* to *Gwladus Du*. A final *n* could also affect *dd* and produce *Ieuan Du*.

Originally the native Welsh were not able to pronounce the sounds of English *j* ('jug, John') or English *ch* ('cheek') or *sh* ('shop'). These three sounds occurring in borrowed words were generally treated as if they were the same, and came (at first) to be sounded as *s* or *s* with the quality of consonantal *i*, written *si* : *siaced* 'jacket', *siars* 'charge', *sialens* 'challenge'; *siop, siom* (from sham, shame). Welsh speakers in time managed to pronounce the sounds of *sh* and *j* and English *ch*; and in colloquial speech, native Welsh words with *s* possessing the quality of *i, si*, or *is*, changed to *sh*, e.g. *eisiau* 'want', pronounced *ishe* or *isho*, *llais* 'voice', often pronounced *llaish*. But as Welsh had no alphabet symbols for English sounds *j, ch* and *sh*, Welsh *si* continued as a symbol for the sound or sounds, e.g. *siec* 'cheque'. When names such as John, Jenkin came direct from English, they went through a stage of being *Siôn, Siencyn* (and count as *s* in the system of Welsh prosody): we continue to use these forms and pronunciations although fully capable of pronouncing *j*; i.e. we use *John, Jones, Jenkin(s)*, pronounce them as in English and regard them as normal; colloquially we use the *sh* sound for the written versions *Siôn, Sioni, Sionyn, Siencyn*. These, put back into English spelling, become *Shone, Shenkin*.

The kind of change exemplified by *guard* and *ward* came to apply to Welsh names beginning with *Gw-* in the speech of anglicised or completely English areas and in the writing of medieval English scribes. Names such as *Gwenllian, Gweirful (Gweirfil)* are often found as *Wenllian, Weirfil*, with no grammatical cause or syntactical reason to justify it, and this continued into the early modern period, e.g. PRLlantrithyd 32.1575, *Wenllia' Gitto*; 35.1597, three examples of *Wenllia'*; 37.1612, *Gwe'llian*. The surnames *Wogan, Wargen(t), Wyriot* are examples of this. The converse is seen within Welsh when names such as *Watkin* and *Walter* become *Gwatkin* and *Gwallter*. When words with initial *gw-* undergo soft mutation, they become *w-*, i.e. *gwin, gwenwyn, gwair*, will at times be *win, wenwyn, wair*, in the appropriate constructions: this change makes a pattern so that a borrowing beginning with *w* will be treated as if it were the lenited form of the word, and *warrant* becomes *gwarant, wanton/gwantan*.

2. THE PATRONYMIC SYSTEM

A PERSON is known by his name, and it helps to identify him to say whose son he is : in its simplest form, *Adda + mab + Einion*, 'A son (of) E'. Welsh has no case endings and the normal genitive construction requires no preposition, corresponding to 'of'; the genitive relationship is expressed or implied in the mere juxtaposition of the two nouns (and by what is 'understood' in the context): the 'son of Einion' is just *mab Einion*. *Mab*, in old and medieval Welsh written *map*, is cognate of Irish *mac*. A common noun in apposition to a personal name undergoes lenition, e.g. *Dafydd frenin, Dafydd feddyg*, ('David the King, or King David; David the doctor'), showing the lenition of the nouns *brenin, meddyg*. The construction *Adda + mab + Einion* therefore becomes *Adda fab Einion*. There are many, many instances in the medieval period of adding the grand-father's name, and even of adding the great-grandfather's.

The Welsh *f* sound was probably bilabial and therefore more easily lost, e.g. *Rhiw-abon* for *Rhiwfabon, Bodorgan* for *Bodforgan*; and a good example of this loss in the initial position is the way, in natural speech, the possessive pronoun *fy* 'my', is invariably *'y*, e.g. *y nhad* 'my father'. Thus *fab* becomes *ab*.

The effect of the aspirate of *Hywel, Rhydderch*, so as to change *ab* to *ap*, (*Powel, Prydderch*) has been mentioned above, and the result of combining *b + b*, *ab Bleddyn* giving *Pleddyn*. It would therefore be 'incorrect' to use *ab* in these contexts; it would be contrary to a natural phonetic law which required provection. There is no provection before a vowel, *ab Owen*; but these illustrations of *ab* and *ap* do not cover all contin-gencies and uncertainty remains about the use of *ab* or *ap* in certain other contexts. One finds provection in a variety of combinations of consonants; adj. *dig* 'angry' with the abstract ending *-der* becomes *dicter; gwlyb* 'wet' and *-der> gwlypter*; the compound of *gwlyb* and *tir* (or strictly the lenited form *dir*) is *gwlyptir* 'wet ground', *v.* GPC 1687; and this is the kind of provection which changed the *b* before *g* in *Dafydd ap Gwilym*. One cannot expect writers of the language to decide upon *ab* or *ap* in the several possible combinations of consonants and it has become fairly common practice to use *ap* before consonants. In spite of the relatively regular working of the phonetic law affecting the *b* of *ab*, one comes across examples which do not appear to conform, e.g. ADClun 193, *John Peian* (three times), 194, ditto, which no doubt is 'ab-Ieuan' in origin.

The forms *Broderick, Brobert* and *Bowel* we found very puzzling. *Bowel* need not in fact concern us for this name can be traced to the name of an English river. But the absence of provection in the case of the other two names is more difficult to account for. We have a suspicion that *Broderick* was of Irish origin, made through the processes of 'approx-imation' to have the appearance of a Welsh or British name. One major difficulty in this theorising is the unstableness of the vowel *o*, e.g. *Broderick*, Meole Brace 216, *Brederick*, St Chad's Index; and the variations of the consonants, i.e. *Brod -, Bretherick*; and the interchange of *-d-* and *-th-*; so that the *Bretherick* follows the pattern of *Retherick*. A further variation is the deliberate change of *Brotheroe* into *Brotherwood* in one parish register.

The other surname presenting difficulty comes from the entries in the PR of Wem, 63-1672, John *Brobbin*, which becomes *Brobyn, Brobin, Broben*. Assuming that *Robin* should in fact stand for *Rhobin* one naturally expects the *ab + Rhobin* to give *Probin*, but

the forms *Brobin, Broben,* occur in positions which cannot possibly represent *ab +
Rhobin.* The PR of Whittington gives two instances of *Br-* , 132-1636, *Thomas Rydlas*
alias *Bropen* of Porkington; 137 -1639, *Anne Broper* als *Anne Rydlas,* widow.

The forms classified with *Rhys* etc. below, namely *Breeze* (typical of Monts.) and *Brice,*
can be explained really without reference to *Prys,* etc. The *zed* sound of *Breeze* rules it out,
and the occurrence of *Brice* in contexts which are completely English make this surname, although pronounced to rhyme with *Rice,* entirely unrelated.

In the case of a woman the word meaning girl and daughter, *merch* would be fixed after
the personal name, so that with lenition, it would have the same pattern, *Lleucu ferch
Einion.* [2] As the personal name in the genitive following a fem. sg. noun would lenite,
the construction in medieval Welsh would be Lleucu ferch *Dd*afydd. As already
explained *verch* is very often written in the abbreviated form of *vz.* In colloquial speech it
would be influenced by the masc. pattern and became *ach.* Theoretically *ach* preceding
the father's name could produce versions corresponding to *Bevan, Powell, Prichard*; there
is very little evidence to show that this happened but there may be a trace of it. Theoretically, *ach-Richard* could become *Chrichard*: this could be expected to change to have
the sound of *Crichard*; the name *Richard* is pronounced *Richet* or *Ritchet,* hence *Pritchet,
Pritchette*; in the colloquial speech of South Wales, the hypothetical *Chrichard* or *Crichard*
would be *Crichet,* and this, spelt *Critchett* actually exists; there are three examples in the
Cardiff and S.E. Wales TD. There is also a *Crichard* in the Bristol TD with an address in
Bath; this could, conceivably, be from *Mac-richard*; but the *Critchett* version is strongly in
favour of a Welsh origin for *Crichard* also.

As the patronymic system or pattern gradually fell into disuse, the *ab/ap* element,
where it was retained as a 'sound', would cease to serve its original purpose, that is, of
denoting the son of B; and this loss of meaning or function is easily demonstrable by
quoting instances which have *ab/ap* after a daughter's (or girl's) name, and instances of
using *ab/ap* between son and grandfather's name, by which time of course the grandfather's name has virtually become a fixed surname. For examples, *vide* **Classification**
Roger, Proger. Where the *ab/ap* element could attach itself to the father's name it would
tend because it was unaccented to lose its vowel, leaving just the consonant *b/p,* as in
Prys, Parri, Bowen etc. In rare cases the vowel was kept, that is, the surname became
fixed with the vowel of *ab/ap* still there, and this would be possible if the name to which
ab/ap was attaching itself was a monosyllable, for the *ab/ab,* especially in an English
context, could receive the stress of the penult.

It is difficult to say in certain instances whether it was merely a matter of writing, for
instance, Star CP 4, Robt ap Price = 5 Robt Aprice. For further examples of *Aprice,
Apreece,* etc. *vide* **Classification** *Rhys.* For further examples of *Apoell, A Powell, A
Prichard,* etc. *vide* **Classification** *Howell, Richard.*

There is an *Up-* element in certain English names, e.g. *Upthorpe,* and this may be the
influence which turned *Ap-* into *Up-* in certain cases (one occasionally sees *Apthorpe*). It
is certain that *Upjohn* is a variant of *Apjohn* for one finds the *Up-* spelling in *Upgruffydd,
Uprichard,* etc. For further examples of *Upjohn, Uprise, Upgriffith, Uprichard,* etc. *vide*
Classification *John, Rhys, Gruffydd, Richard.*

---

[2]   In Latin documents *fil.* or *f.* is used often for *filius* and *filia.* Sometimes editors with no knowledge of Welsh
fail to identify a girl's name because the abbreviations *fil.* or *f* does not help, and give 'son of' in the translation, e.g. BBStD 238 Liwelyth fil Blethery, trans. 'son of . .'; 262 Wladus fil Eynon, trans. Waldus
[sic]the son of Eynon; 262, Perwer fil Ieuan, = Perwer the son of . .'.

The following are representative examples of the various forms of *ferch* in the patronymic pattern:

> Lp Oswestry 160. 1393 Tanno verch David ap Ithel; PRClunbury 18. 1619. Katherine verch Thomas; PRSannan 1666 Maria ach Richard; 1667, Lowria ach Voris (lenition of genitive after fem. sg.); ALMA 235 (= p.261) Anne ach Risiart.

It is no surprise to find instances in documents written outside Wales of a failure to distinguish between *ab* and *ach*; and such instances are probably evidence of a tendency in Wales to use *ab* for son and daughter:

> InvECP 121 Flints 1547, Margaret ap Yevan, daughter and heir. . .; 146, Monts 1547 . . . the will of Maly alias Mary ap David; PRSelattyn 202. 1688 Elizabeth ap Thomas; 209.1688 Mary ap William; AnglPleas 19, Margaret verch ap Llewelin.

In the following one sees the clerk of the court giving the wife the *ap* form of her husband's name: InvECP 133, Flints 1549 Elizabeth ap William, alias Elizabeth verch Ellys ab Tona, of the city of London; (the notes show she was married to a man named Howell ap William).

Examples of dropping *verch* and of *ap* after the daughter's name so that father's name is surname:

> PRAlberbury 36. 1609 Catherina Edwards als verch Edwards; 50. 1613 . . . et Elizabeth ap Edwarde als Edwards.

It deserves to be mentioned that originally the wife continued to be known by the name she had before marriage and this custom continued well into the eighteenth century. Any part of Wales can supply examples. The diary called *Y Cwtta Cyfarwydd* is set in St Asaph and the surrounding area:

> 45. 1613, Evan Thomas ap John Gruff' . . . Margaret Hughes his wief; 48. 1613, Ellen Lewes the wief of Rondle Lloid; 48. 1613, Ellen Lloid the wief of John Ffoulke of Vaynol; HBr, 143. 'Another anomaly prevailed with respect to names and still continues in the Western parts of Breconshire, particularly in Ystradgynlais and Ystradfellte. The wife retains her maiden name and should the husband be called Thomas David and her father William John, she subscribes Margaret William formerly written Margaret vz William, Margaret verch or the daughter of William and as late as the beginning of the eighteenth century this custom prevailed even in the *town* of Brecon, for in the Chapel of the men of Battle in the priory church we have ''here lieth the body of Elizabeth Morgan the wife of Lewis Price of this town who died 1704, aged 70'' '.

This only appears curious and anomalous because we view the custom from our end: we ought to ask 'What is to be expected in a period and society using the patronymic system of naming?' If the husband is A son of B, and the wife is C daughter of D, the wife after marriage does not become daughter of B; she remains daughter of D.[3] After centuries of this usage it will take many generations even after changes in the legal or official system, and the omission of *ab* and *ach* from individual names, for the custom or idiom to die out. It is also worth recording an explanation I once heard given by the late Professor J. Lloyd Jones (in conversation) of the fairly common usage in Gwynedd of

---

[3] Cf. PRLlCrossenny 9. 1623. 'Jane pye, vidua de lanvayre, relict' Jacobi harry Morice, sepult.', footnote, 'At this period it was unusual for women in Welsh districts to assume their husband's surname, their husband so seldom having one'.
Cwtta Cyf. 131. 1630, 'John Ffoulkes killed Jane Wen his own wief . . . the said Jane Wen al's Ffo' . . .

having a double surname, not necessarily using hyphen, such as *J. Lloyd Jones, T.H. Parry Williams, R. Williams Parry, John Morris Jones*, to take the names of four distinguished men of letters as examples in our time. The inclusion of the mother's name together with the father's patronymic was in use as much and as naturally as the father's. The usage of the double surname of the upper classes is no doubt genealogical in origin and motive, to make the compound name evidence of the confluence of two families or two pedigrees; this gives to the hyphenated name the associations of social class and distinction, but it would be wrong to believe that the double surname of Gwynedd was intended to be a mark of social superiority.

Over and above the individual names of Welsh origin which have gone into the sum total of names in general use in Britain, such as *Rees, Owen, Llewelyn, Bevan*, something of greater importance is the structure based upon the patronymic pattern and the names which became surnames as a development of the pattern or as by-products of the system and its break-down. This is the process which produced *Jones* and *Davies* and *Williams* and *Evans*. These surnames do not qualify to be considered Welsh in *origin*: the root or embryo is Jewish or Greek or Germanic, and even *Evan*(s) is derived from *Johannes*; but these names, and many others, became surnames largely through the patronymic system, especially through the second stage of the decay and development of the system. Put in simple terms, the father's christian name at a certain point in the sequence became the son's surname, and continued as the grandson's and great-grandson's as it had become fixed in the particular family concerned, so that there is, as it were, a Welsh quality in those names, no matter what their linguistic origins may be, which are baptismal names used as surnames, in a form unchanged or possibly with a slight alteration – *Robert* becoming *Roberts* (in addition to *Probert*), *David* becoming *Davies* (or remaining *David*), *John* becoming *Jones* (or remaining *John*). The use of the genitive *'s* is not a Welsh construction, but it is still true to say that *Jones* developed because *John* was in the position of the father's name in the patronymic pattern.

Before considering the process of halting the movement of the patronymic system and the establishment of the fixed surname, it is interesting to observe the reverse of this happening in earlier periods, that is, instances of families of non-Welsh origin with a fixed surname, becoming identified with the Welsh social system and allowing the patronymic system to replace their fixed surname. Theophilus Jones, HBr, remarks on this more than once, for instance p.143, second footnote, 'Thus the Norman name of Bullen after being discontinued [sic] from Laurence downwards was resigned by the family, and the name of Williams substituted by Thomas Williams in 1613, who was the son of William ap Phillip ap Richard ap John ap Laurence Bullen. These are the present Abercamlais and Penpont families. So also the names of Boys, after ringing the changes of Jenkin William Boys and William Jenkin Boys is now steadied into Williams of Velinnewydd, though the name of Jenkin still continues to be known among them as a Christian name'. The pedigree of Bois is given on p.324, 'Now Williams of Velin newydd': after several generations of *Bois* the children of a *William Bois* become *Williams*, and in another branch the son of a *Thomas Bois* becomes *Hugh Thomas*.

On p.380 the name of *Turberville* disappears in a particular family, the son of *Thomas Turberville* becoming *William Thomas* and his son assuming the father's name in the form of *Gwilym*, v. pedigree p.390. On p.467 there is an example of *Awbrey* succumbing to *Morgan*. Bradney has a number of instances; HM, i.60, the family named *Willey* becomes *James*, a *John ap David Willey* has a son called *James ap John*, the children of this *James* retain the father's name as their surname. Part 2.183, Abergavenny, 'For three centuries the occupiers of the Hardwick ... were a family whose surname was Perious or Peres. Though by their name they may have been of Norman origin, they soon forsook it, and after the changes usual in Welsh families, finally settled into Jones'; *v.* pedigree p.185. The pedigree of *Wallis* alias *Valence* 'and afterwards Lewis' is given on p.285, and shows *Wallis* and *Valence* giving way to the patronymic pattern and eventually becoming *Lewis*: the father of *David Lewis*, first principal of Jesus College, Oxford, was *Sir Lewis ap John*, and his three sons retained the name *Lewis* as surname. Families derived from *Herbert* stock lose the name as such but remain aware of their ancestry and original name, and readers may at times be baffled by the difference between the 'stock' name and the one in actual use, which is, or is derived from, the christian name of a descendant in a certain generation. In Part 1. Skenfrith p.31, the pedigree of the family of *Powell* of Perth-hir is given, with *Herbert* in brackets; it shows how *Powell* became the fixed surname as follows: Howell ap Thomas ap Gwilym → William ap Howell (slain in Battle of Banbury 1469) → William Powell, and from then on Powell remaining fixed. On p.47 there is another Herbert family, *Evans* of Llangattock Vibon Avel, and it is instructive to show the name that branches from this family: Ievan ap Thomas Herbert – his sons, Thomas ap Ievan; William Evans, clerk, Ll.B, vicar of Ll. Vibon Avel and Treasurer of Llandaff Cathedral, ob. 5 Jan. 1589-90; John Evans, clerk, vicar of Cwmdu ... John ap Ievan, James Evans. Another branch of the Herbert stock became *Proger v.* p.94, LlCrossenny. The family identified with Llanarth and Treowen became *Jones* when the patronymic changes were halted; p.302 'William ap John Thomas ... This last was the first to assume a surname being known as William John Thomas alias William Jones ... standard bearer to King Henry VIII.'

The adoption of the fixed surname is exemplified in the families and pedigrees referred to above: it is not difficult to see what happened. When the *ab* element is dropped the patronymic connotation of the second name (i.e. the father's) does not disappear all at once: the patronymic pattern may continue without the use of *ab* or *ach*.

> PRLlanbadog, 1596, William Richard supposed son of Richard Dicwon; 1599 Howell Walter, son of Watter Jon Morice; 1600 John Watter, son of Watkin Edward; 1606 Jane William, dau' of Williankin Jenkin. [4]

Compare with these entries the following: 1538, Alse Morgan, dau' of Lewis Morgan; i.e. she is not entered as *Alse Lewis*.

The register of Conwy within a space of a quarter of a century illustrates the use of *ap*, the omission of *ap* and the retention of the patronymic principle, the attachment of ab/B to the father's name, and the use of a fixed surname in the case of the two girls:

> PRConway 1583 John ap Retherech fil Rether ap Robert; 1586 Elena Davies fil Thomas Davies; 1586 Williemus Lewis fil Lodovici Owen; 1594 Williemus Bowen; 1597 Johanes Gruffith filius Gruffini ap Hugh; 1607 Elizabeth ver' Owen filia Owini Plethine: 1608, Elizabeth Plethine filia Owini Plethin.

In 1607 Elizabeth is named in the old style; in 1608 the entry belongs to the new style. Peter Roberts the diarist of *Y Cwtta Cyfarwydd* is in the following entry referring to his own child, p.81, 1619:

> My eldest daughter Grace vz Piers being then XII yeres of age lacking 11 days died (Piers = Peters).

---

[4] If the printed version Williankin properly reproduces the text, this entry is a fine example of the scribal error called 'error of anticipation'. If the entries can be relied on, two of them show the equivalence of Walter, Watter and Watkin.

Another entry will illustrate the use of a surname, p.96, 1623: one Richard Price M'cer son of John ap Rees (i.e. Richard is not *ap John* or *Jones*).

Many, many examples could be quoted to show the change over from the patronymic pattern to the new style of the fixed surname: they would also show the co-existence of the old and new styles[5] and the belatedness of the change in the areas geographically removed from anglicising influences, and among the classes who were socially removed from these influences. William Bulkeley of Brynddu, Anglesey, in his diary covering the period 1734-1760 is able to refer to persons of his own class by means of a surname or by naming the residence which in the case of so many had become normal: *Meyrick Bodorgan* or *Bodorgan*; when he refers to servants or craftsmen or peasants, he frequently uses *ap*, or just uses the christian name; the surname does not seem to exist. To illustrate the continued and unselfconscious use of the patronymic pattern: Professor W.J. Gruffydd's father was John Griffith; John Griffith's eldest brother was a *Jones*, their father (W.J. Gruffydd's grandfather) being named *John*: this remnant of the patronymic system in Arfon is as recent as 1850. Even in Gwent the old style, even the use of *ap*, lingered on in some families well into the eighteenth century. Bradney, HM,i, 259 gives the pedigree of the family of Arnold of the Hendre: 'The pedigree is noticeable in that the family was the last in the neighbourhood to use the *ap*, adhering to the old Welsh style of nomenclature ...' e.g. Arnold ap Arnold ... bapt. 5 Jan. 1739-40, living at Dorstone 1807.[6]

It is impossible to say when precisely the new style of the fixed surname began and who were the first examples, for all the evidence cannot be assembled. It would not be relevant to regard as evidence examples occurring outside Wales. A man and wife with children moving to England could not continue for long to use the patronymic system in an English community for it would make no sense; and one is not surprised to find early instances in the bilingual society of the English borders of a fixed surname and dropping 'ab': e.g. ADClun 41, Adam Dygan (1328, several similar examples). In lawsuits from Wales heard in the London courts there is inevitably an urge to bring the Welsh names into line with the English habit: there seemed to be a process of transposing into English, for not only is there a halting of the patronymic principle with the omission of *ab* but a conversion also in such names as *ap Ievan* into *Evans* and even into *Jones*:

Star CP 172, William Evans als ap Ievan; 186, Ricd ap Robert ap Ievan; Ievan ap Ricd, his son, alias John Robts; 200, Jno ap Dd als Davies. InvECP 32, Merioneth 1556, William ap Ieuan alias William Jevans 'a pore prentice in the city of London'; 83, Denbs. 1533, Thomas ap Ieuan ap ... alias Thomas Jones, of London.

It is not implied by using these examples that the law courts were responsible for the move towards the fixed surname: the process was taking place within Welsh society, at

---

[5] The PR of Llantrithyd in the first decade of the seventeenth century has a number of examples. As expected the gentry classes, i.e. the Bassets, Aubreys, Nicholls, have the fixed surname: the contrast of the old and new is to be seen in the entries representing the lower orders:
2.1601, Mary Penry the d. of Wm. Penry; Mary Myrick ye d. of Myrick Eva'. 2. 1602, Jenkine Richard the son of Richard Rice. 3.1603, Mary Harry d. of Richard Harry; Katherin David d. of David Willie'. Katherin Edwards d. of Willia' Edwards; Elizabeth Yeavan d. of Roger Yeava'; Joan Thomas d. of Thomas ap Evan. 3.1605, Elizab. Rosser d. of Mathew Rosser. 3.1606, Ann Rosser d. of Roger Evan.

[6] Mary his grand-daughter married Robert James of Bedwellty 1837; their son was Ivor James, first registrar of the University of Wales. He called himself Ivor Barnold James although he was not christened with this name.

first amongst the gentry, and later through imitation amongst the lower strata. One cannot prove or disprove the statement made by Bradney, i.302, concerning William ap John Thomas, standard bearer to Henry VIII, that 'he was the first to assume a surname, being known as William John Thomas alias William Jones'. Something similar is said about the Lewis family of St. Pierre, Part 4, Caldicot, p.75, '. . . Thomas ap Lewis, the son of Lewis ap Sir David, was killed at the battle of Banbury in 1469 . . . His son was the first to adopt Lewis as a permanent surname and in 1487 was lord of the manor of Raglan. . . .'.

Earlier examples, no doubt, could be found of families using a permanent surname, especially among the families of men serving the Crown, and in towns and garrisons which had families of English origin. Bradney means *assuming* a permanent surname in the case of families which had traditionally adhered to the patronymic style. More important than searching for the earliest examples is to understand the movement as a whole. The movement towards the fixed surname gathered momentum during the Tudor reigns, and in the seventeenth century covered most of Wales despite the evidence of the survival in the eighteenth century of remnants of the older system. Long before the Tudor period Wales was not unaffected by English influences, and it would be helpful to remember that great stretches of the English border area would be Welsh-speaking or bilingual: this bilingual society would be the ford through which English influences penetrated into the monoglot Welsh society. The first great Vaughan family is located in Bredwardine, Hereford. The name of this family has its origins in the epithet *Fychan*, attached to the name of *Rhosier* who married *Gwladus*, daughter of *Dafydd Gam*: Dafydd and Rhosier were both killed protecting the body of Henry V at Agincourt, 1415. This *Rhosier*'s father was *Rhosier*, therefore the father had to be *Rhosier Hen*, 'the Old', and the son *Rhosier Fychan*, i.e. 'Little Roger'. Rhosier's sons (not all) are called *Fychan* or *Vaughan*, and it is fairly clear that Vaughan in this generation had become their surname. Many of the Vaughan families of Brecknock, Radnor, Gwent and Carmarthen received their name from this source. Other examples of the same process came about later in the great families of North and West Wales so that Vaughan as a name has the associations of the gentry social class. This example represents one of the means of fixing upon a permanent surname, i.e. choosing the epithet identified with the father or grandfather, possibly in an anglicised version.

Two other epithets which came to serve the same purpose were *llwyd* as *Lloyd*; and *gwyn* or *wyn*, as *Wyn, Wynn, Wynne* (or *Gwynne*). The alterations in form and pronunciation of *Fychan, Llwyd*, and in the spelling of *Wyn/Gwyn*, helped the process, for *Vaughan, Lloyd* and *Wynne/Gwynne* are removed from the proper meaning of the original epithets. JEG 291, in a cross-reference from the family of Golden Grove, Carmarthenshire, mentions Agnes who married Meyrick Lloyd of Llangernyw, and then has a quotation, 'of whom are descended the Lloyds of Llwyn-y-maen, Llanforda, being "ye antientest families that bear ye name of Lloyd in North Wales" '. Llanforda is over the border in Shropshire. *Lloyd* is less exclusive than *Vaughan* and *Wynne*, for it is found in reasonable numbers as the name of ordinary families; but it is worth noting that the indexes of county histories largely concerned with the great families have a surprising number of *Lloyds*. The family that best represents the use of *Wynn* is the family of Gwydir, Caernarfonshire. John (Wyn) ap Maredudd, who died in 1559, had the epithet *Wyn* attached to his name, his son Maurice Wynn, who died in 1580, was the first to use the surname *Wynn*. The Wynn of Berth-ddu and Bodysgallen is a branch of Wynn of Gwydir, and among the members of this family the forms *Wynn, Wyn, Gwyn,*

Gwynn, Gwynne, are used in some form or other. The *Wynn* in the name of Sir Watkin Williams Wynn, of Wynnstay, Rhiwabon, is also derived from Gwydir. The *Wynne* of Peniarth has an origin unconnected with Gwydir, and the *Wynne* of Voelas has an origin of its own.

Another method of deciding upon a permanent surname was to use the name of one's residence and estate. In the sixteenth century it was a a mark of one's social class, more especially in North Wales to adopt a residential surname. There may be instances which are much earlier, for it is said that the name *Carreg* was taken as surname as early as 1396 (*v* p.68); but on the whole the adoption of *Mostyn, Pennant, Bodvel, Nanney, Glyn, Tannat* etc. belongs to the sixteenth century and early seventeenth. It may appear pretentious to those of us conditioned by the twentieth century who are judging these changes, but at that time the permanent surname was becoming a necessity and the gentry families adopted a pattern already in use among their counterparts in England. In the chapter below on place-names as sources there will be a few instances of clergymen adopting the names of their parishes as surnames. Vicars and rectors were usually sons of influential families of landed estates so that they were just following a style which their origins and social standing justified.

The number of instances of 'translating' a Welsh name or using -*son* for *ab* compounded with the father's name is very small. JEG 23 has one example, the son of *Robin Norris* becomes *Henry Robinson*, but it is not a Welsh name in the first place, cf. InvECP 96, Denbs. 1551, William Robynson, alias Roberts of London; 128, Flints. 1553, John ap John alias Johnson of London. The name of the Catholic martyr Richard White, translated from *Gwyn*, is also very exceptional, with a special explanation of its own connected with his religion. There seems to be an earlier example, PWLMA 334, Dafydd White [Entry 1388. Dafydd Gwyn ab Ieuan ap Morys, 'Dafydd Gwyn may be identified with Dafydd White: the latter was a burgess of Old Carmarthen too'.] The following explanation does not sound very convincing, JEG 130, Friars, Llanfaes: 'John Wynn, alias Whyte, was servant to the Earl of Pembroke, AD 1555. The said Earl having another servant of the same name, desired this John Wynn to assume the name of "Whyte" which he and his posterity did ever afterwards'. *v.* Arch. Camb. iv, 163, 284. Cf. also JEG Neugwl Ucha' in Lleyn. John Wynn alias Whyte of Trefan, cross-ref. pp.130, 163. One son is *Wynn*, the others are *Whyte*. Many of the descendants are from one of the *Whytes*.

At some point or other in the sequence of generations of each family, the patronymic method was made to settle and the father's name was treated as surname so that it was passed on to the grandchildren. The *ab/ap* element is dropped entirely if the father's name (initial vowel or consonant) provides no grip which the *b/p* can hold on to, such as *Gruffydd* or *Morgan*.[7] There were names which enabled the *b/p* to survive, such as *Bevan, Powell, Probert*: this was a linguistic change; the elision which in natural speech made *ab-Evan* into *Bevan* would not be perceptible and there would hardly be an awareness that a syllable was missing. In many instances the *ab/ap* was omitted before *Owen, Evan, Harry, Rhydderch, Robert* etc., leaving the father's name to become surname in its usual form, or with the -*s* ending, *Evans, Harries, Roberts*. It is impossible to say why it should be *Bevan*

---

[7] This statement is correct in spite of the occasional examples of 'Upgriffith'; after all there are no examples of 'Bgriffith'. The following appears to be an exception, RadsSoc XLVI, 36, temp. Eliz. *John Besteven* . . . St. Harmons. This is 'ab-Steven', the -st- having a prosthetic sound (as in *Esteban*) to which the *b* could attach itself. There are two entries of Estevens in the Swansea TD (in Glyn-neath and Penrhos).

in some cases, *Evans* in others; why *Parry* in some, and *Harry* or *Harris/Harries* in others. JEG 60 has a family which summarises the variations: the three sons of *Owen ap Hugh* (seventeenth century) are (1) *Thomas ap Owen* (whose son is William ap Thomas ap Hugh), (2) *Edmund Owen* who died without issue; (3) *Hugh Bowen*.

The change represented by *ab Owen/Bowen* was quite common in the sixteenth century and Bowen, Price etc. were becoming standard forms.[8] For instance, Cwtta Cyf. 76-7, 1619, '. . . one Will'm Price eldest son and heire of John Price the younger sonne and heire of John Price the elder son and heire of Cad'dr Price Esq'e sonne and heire of John Wyn ap Cad'dr late of Rhiwlas deceased was xristened'. This takes the name back four generations; the name starts with Rhys ap Meredydd who fought in the battle of Bosworth; his son Robert ap Rhys held the office of chaplain in the court of Henry VII and Henry VIII: his heir was Cadwaladr; other sons were Dr Ellis Prys and Thomas Vaughan. The John Wyn ap Cad'dr of 1619 was the son of this Cadwaladr.

Hugh Price (1495-1574) founder and patron of Jesus College, Oxford, born in Brecon, was the son of Rhys ap Rhys. The most famous *Prys/Pryse/Price* was Sir John (1502-1555) of Brecknock, most famous because he published the first book in Welsh in 1546; he was the son of Rhys ap Gwilym ap Llywelyn ap Rhys Llwyd ab Adam. The following are quoted to show the process in other names:

> B 13.93, Pembs Plea Rolls 1560, Llewellin Badam; L & P 552, Hereford, Sir Richard Badam; Surveys GK, Millwood 1584, 171, John David Batha; WPortBooks 62, Philip abenon = 63 Philip Bynan = 67 Philip ap Eynon; 62, Griffin abenon = 103 Griffith ap Beynam; InvECP 87, Denbs. 1538, David ap Enyon ap Madock; 96, Denbs. 1551, Howell ap Bynyan; 117, Flints. 1538, Ralph Benyon; Glam Cartae 1543, John Bevyn; Star CP 73, Flints. John Bythell; HM i. Abergav. 161. Names of vicars, 1589, William Prichard . . . son of Thomas ap Richard.

Theophilus Jones, HBr 143, must have seen examples in records of the anomaly of two surnames in the same family: 'When this custom was first introduced, two brothers frequently adopted different surnames; for instance, John Thomas had two sons, Griffith and William; Griffith subscribed himself Griffith John, and the other brother wrote "William Thomas" '. The change of style obviously could not be clear-cut and there must have been a period of uncertainty as to when the old style should be abandoned.[9] Examples have been quoted of persons being known by two surnames at different times; sometimes it is the father's christian name, at others it is the grandfather's. During the period of uncertainty, finding two brothers with differing surnames is not entirely unexpected. Many examples could be given: I choose to quote from the letter of a correspondent, Mr Barry Davies of Lisvane, Cardiff, a local historian who has examined records of families with great thoroughness: 'My own ancestors looked as if the second Rees Eustance and his descendants were set to adopt it (i.e. the name Eustance as their surname) but he had no male heirs. His father was named Morgan Rees and his sons, as named in his will, afford an interesting example of surname formation and how typically it happened in this area – in the 16th century for gentry, in the 17/18th century for yeomen and later in the 18th century for lower

---

[8] John Price (*c.* 1600-76), distinguished scholar and theologian, who spent part of his life in Rome, latinized his name and used Pricaeus, *v.* DWB 787.

[9] Cf. an example of changing what had become a fixed surname with a lapse into the old style, which in turn, provides a new fixed surname: JEG 321, Isaacs of Llanfrothen; Isaac Robert Morris, his children at the beginning of the eighteenth century take the surname Isaac; in the middle of the century, the children of Evan Isaac become Evans.

orders... Morgan Rees names his three sons as Rees Eustance, Joseph Rees and David Rees. Elsewhere but not in my memory, I have other instances of the pattern, sometimes more complicated than this. It seems not to have been uncommon for the eldest son to take his grandfather's name. Of the above three sons only David Rees had male heirs and their surname was firmly established as Rees. Their descendants were farming in Llanmaes and Llantwit Major down to the last century...' (letter dated Jan. 9, 1978). The family tree (v. Clarke 549) is:

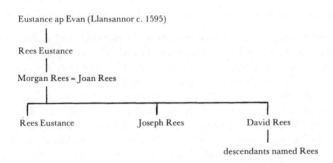

Eustance ap Evan (Llansannor c. 1595)

Rees Eustance

Morgan Rees = Joan Rees

Rees Eustance   Joseph Rees   David Rees

descendants named Rees

Early records have frequent examples of having the mother's name, as if there were no father who could be named in the pedigree; this may be due to posthumous birth, or early death of father so that the child gets his identity through his mother:
B 13. 227, SR 1292 Duthegu ver' Erdylad; 228 Adam ap Erdylad; 223 Philip ab Isot; B 15. 287. Aberystwyth-Cardigan. Hugyn ap Weyrvil; B 4. 159. Ardudwy 1325. Iorwerth ap Ieuan ap Wenllian; CalACW 49. Ereward ap Leuca (end of 13c.); RecCa 22 Jeuan ap Eweryth; B 6. 256, Lleyn 1350 ... de David ap Neste; B 15. 43, AS 1406 Deikws ap Tegau; CatAncDeeds V. 13604, Anglesea, 8th Henry IV. David ap Weirwyll vergh Tuder ap Rys; 111. C.3486, Merion. Gwenllean vergh Angharat vergh Mally; CaernHS 26, Bolde Rental 36, Anght vz Eden ap Detheg (= Angharad...Dyddgu); 37, Margaret vz hoell ap Tangwistil vz grono; 37, Gruf ap Tanno vz Tuder ap Atha.
Examples of this kind show how the mother's name might become a surname, e.g. BBStD 18, Steph'as Nest; 40, Robertus Nonne; 186, Thomas Gweyruyll. The names *Angharad, Gwladus, Gwenllian, Nest*, are given in the classification as sources of surnames.
The period of the adoption of the permanent surname had one other form of change, namely the replacement of native Welsh names by names of English or French origin which may be called approximations of the names they replaced. The obvious examples are *Lewis* for *Llywelyn/Llewelyn; Hugh* for *Hywel/Howell; Edward* for *Iorwerth*. This change has two stages, first the substitute name as christian name, and later as surname. These names will be discussed in detail in the classification. *Lewys/Lewis* is used as a 'translation' of *Llywelyn* as early as the thirteenth century, in documents not of Welsh authorship, but this is not proof of adopting the name by the persons or the families concerned, e.g. CAP 505, Lewys the son of Griffin [1277-78] = Llywelyn, son of Gruffydd ap Gwenwynwyn, which reference also shows *Gruffydd* being 'translated' by the use of *Griffin*.

There is no lack of evidence in the fourteenth and fifteenth centuries of the use of *Lewys*, either as the man's proper name or as an alternative for *Llywelyn*. For example, *vide* **Classification** *Llywelyn*. The evidence in the article below will show how in the fifteenth and sixteenth centuries *Lewis* came to be adopted by poets whose proper name was *Llywelyn*, so that a sort of interchangeability was set up by this usage. The really significant move came when families who had favoured *Llywelyn* throughout the generations, as their pedigrees show, use *Lewis* instead; when therefore the time came to halt the patronymic millwheel, *Lewis* became surname in several of the great families. Their example was followed by other classes so that *Lewis* became one of the very well-known surnames of Wales, and winnings for *Lewis* meant losses for *Llywelyn*.

One noted during the scrutiny of records of the fifteenth and 16th centuries how often *Hugh*, especially in North Wales, displaced *Hywel*. The note jotted down after scrutiny in B 6 of the Lleyn Ministers Accounts was 'with so many names in these papers, although Howell and Llywelyn of uncertain spelling occur, there are no instances of Hugh or Lewis'; the note on B 10, 158, – Anglesey Crown Rental, sixteenth century – 'Absence of Hywel, frequency of Hugh', and the note after examining the Anglesey Muster Book 1574 was 'Growing number of "Lewis"; taking christian names only, three "Hugh" to every one "Hoell" '. The pedigrees of JEG show *Hugh* coming in to displace *Howel*, e.g. pp.31, 83, 86. On p.165 the name 'Howel alias Hugh Nannau' is given and the entry on p.292 summarises the changes: 'Llangian in Lleyn, Margaret, d. of Hugh ap Lewis ap Howel ap Llewelyn'. The displacement of *Howel* by *Hugh* did not take place to the same extent in N.E. Wales, and hardly at all in S.Wales: the memorandum after scrutiny of *Y Cwtta Cyfarwydd*, set in St Asaph, was as follows: 'Howell and Powell occur with reasonable regularity, fairly clear Hugh did not displace Hywel to any great extent'. Compared with the numbers in Gwynedd, the number of surname *Hughes* is not high, and any lists of names such as telephone directories will show that *Howells* and *Powell* are abundant in all parts of the South, and relatively rare in Gwynedd. It is probably true to say that *Hugh* and *Howel*, or *Hughes* and *Howells*, became separated, yet some awareness remained of a connexion: a minor poet in Anglesey, Hugh Evans, 1767-1841, called himself 'Hywel Eryri'; and Hugh Williams, 1843-1937, well-known as Baptist minister and hymn-writer called himself 'Hywel Cernyw'.

The substitution of *Edward* for *Iorwerth* is not as easily demonstrated as the two substitutions dealt with above, although the relationship of *Edward* and *Iorwerth*, or the alleged connexion, is better known, for it is still a commonly held belief that *Iorwerth* is a 'translation' of *Edward*, or the other way around, and kings named *Edward* are called *Iorwerth* in Welsh. (*Gervase* in the medieval period was sometimes used for *Iorwerth*, but this usage was 'literary' or documentary, and did not flourish). *Edward* came to be used with frequency, together with *John, Henry, Richard, Robert*, in the fourteenth and fifteenth centuries: Bartrum 1350-1415 has a total of 32 examples of Edward, compared with three in period 1215-1350, and there is one example at least to show that the connexion or equivalence goes back to the period 1350-1415, Bartrum 559, Edward Trefor ap Ieuan ap Adda Goch; cross-reference, 'see Iorwerth ab Ieuan ab Adda Goch'. In the CaernQSR there are not many instances of *Iorwerth*; there is a grandfather on p.202 and a great-grandfather on p.200; there are several examples of the hypocoristic version *Iolyn*, and there are eight examples of *Edward* as first name, according to the index. In the eighteenth century the connexion was well established: Edward Hughes in ALMA 864 ends a letter by signing 'Iorwerth ap Hywel a elwid yn gyffredin Edward Hughes' (= 'generally known as E.H.'), which has two bits of evidence. The hypocoristic form that had been oftenest used in South Wales was *Iolo*, so that Edward Williams was able to provide himself with the literary name of 'Iolo Morganwg'.

When the father's name became the surname of the family and descendants, it would in many cases remain unaltered; some had to remain unaltered, *b* or *p* could not grip and hold on to them. The anglicising tendency or the 'official' influences would add genitive *'s* not only to names which were not of Welsh origin, such as *Williams, Jones, Roberts, Richards, Edwards*, but also to native Welsh names, giving *Evans, Howells, Griffiths*. The matter now being discussed is not one of derivation, but of usage and idiom, and these vary widely. *John* and *David* are fairly common (as surnames), in Pembrokeshire and the Vale of Glamorgan;[10] *Morgan, Owen, Tudor, Llewelyn* are usually unaltered although there are a few examples of *Morgans* and *Owens*. *Howell, Harry, Griffith, Richard, William*, are all found without the genitive *-s*, but in most cases they are *Howells, Harris/Harries, Griffiths, Richards, Williams*. Examples of *Evan*, occurring naturally as a surname are hard to find: B 7. 308, N Pembs 1599, Meylir Ieuan, = probably Ievan or Evan; and the poet Edward Evan(s) 1716-88 was called Edward Evan very often by his contemporaries. Names which have initial *b* or *p*, the vestige of *mab/ab*, are used in the Welsh-speaking community without any genitive *'s*: it is unidiomatic to have *Bevans, Bowens, Proberts, Prichards*; when such forms occur they are usually found outside the Welsh-speaking areas, or context:

DLancaster, (Kidwelly 1609) 181, Aubrey Bevans; CRHaverford 149, Mr. Beavans *c.* 1656; 130, Mrs. Beavans (the index has other examples); PRShipton 23. 1625, Johannes Bevans; PRHughley 6.1611, Catherina Beevans; Present-day registers: Knutsford, Hale-West Ward, Bevens; Over-ward, Bevins; South Pembs, St. Issells South, Bevans; Preseli, Camrose, ditto, Goodwick ditto; Cheadle, Marple, Central-West, Bowins; South Worcs., Malvern East-Langland, Proberts.

There is probably good reason for this feeling that *Bevans* etc. is contrary to idiomatic usage. The name to which *b* or *p* is prefixed is already in the genitive case, since it follows the original *mab*: it would be an absurdity to add the English genitive ending to the Welsh construction. When there is no part left of the original *mab*, there is no grammatical or rational hindrance to the adding of E genitive *'s*; in one sense the genitive *'s* takes the place of *ab/ap*.

The use of the genitive *'s* occurred with such frequency in the names of Welsh people as a result of the change from the patronymic style to the fixed surname, that names with the genitive *'s*, whatever their original derivation, came to be identified with the Welsh people and to be regarded as a sign of Welsh nationality, not only *Evans* and *Howells* and *Griffiths*, but *Jones* and *Williams, Roberts* and *Richards, Rogers* and *Harries*. Reference has already been made to William John Thomas alias William Jones, standard bearer to Henry VIII, said by Bradney to be the first to assume the surname. JEG 186, dealing with the pedigree of *Williams* of Cochwillan and Llandegái states that William Williams, the grandson of William ap Gruffydd who was high sheriff

---

[10] The PR of Llantrithyd represents the vale. The index shows that there are far more examples of the unaltered name than examples with *'s*, in the case of David, Evan, Griffith, Harry, Hopkin, Howell, Jenkin, John, Mathew, Philip, Richard, Robert, Watkin, William.

1485-1500, was 'the first of the family who assumed the name of Williams'. An extensive investigation would be needed to discover the first Jones and the first Williams; it would not be safe to accept claims as to who were first.

Examples of *Davies* can be found in Wales in the fourteenth century but in an English context, e.g. B 10. 69, Oliver Daveys nuper Constablarium Castri de Kermerdyn (= Minister's Accounts, Crown Lands 1352). The early instance in Bartrum is puzzling, 1350-1415, 533, Dafydd Davies ap Gwilym ap Dafydd.

Examples of *Davies, Jones, Evans, Harries* are plentiful in the early periods of the Star Chamber and other courts of the period.

> Star CP 141, Jno Davys, of London, poor, true and faithful. 15, Robert Johans . . . Robt Johns (Monm); 78, Jno ap Jones (Glam); 99, Thomas ap Jones als Du (Monm); 172, Wm Evans als ap Ievan; InvECP 63, William Davys (Narberth 1518); 102, John Davies Denbs, 1556. 49, Margaret Harreys, Carms 1544.

These Exchequer papers abound with examples of the following kind: *Jevans, Evaunce, Jones, Johns, Johans, Joanes, Jhonys, Johnez.*

The examples above represent the spread of the genitive '*s* surnames in Wales. It may be possible to supplement the reason for associating these genitive '*s* surnames with Wales. If a census of christian names could be conducted for the fifteenth, sixteenth and seventeenth centuries, it would undoubtedly show a decline by the seventeenth in the frequency of many names that were commonly used in earlier periods, not their disappearance but their relative infrequency; and in contrast there would be an increase in the frequency of names which were popular in England; a small group of native Welsh names retained their popularity. *John, William, Hugh, Thomas, Lewis, Robert, Richard, Henry, Edward*, would be the names showing extended use; the native *David* (for *Dafydd*), *Evan, Rhys*, would also show an increase: *Gruffydd, Morgan, Hywel, Owen*, would be holding their own; but there would be a decline in the use of such names as *Goronwy, Maredudd, Bleddyn, Madog, Rhydderch, Cadwaladr, Cadwgan*. If new names are being increasingly adopted, they must be taking the place of older names, and some native Welsh names virtually fell into complete disuse in the Welsh-speaking community, names like *Urien, Cadell, Gwion, Gwgan, Gwrgant, Gwythyr, Cynfyn*, although these might survive among the English-speaking population of South Pembrokeshire or in the anglicised parts of Gwent and in the English border counties. If there is a concentration on the small group of names mentioned above, *John, David, Thomas, Lewis*, etc. during the period of abandoning the patronymic system, the result will be great numbers of families with surnames derived from these first names, in their unaltered form, as *b/p* forms, or as genitive '*s* forms.

The census or survey mentioned above would show a similar change in the names given to girls, a great decrease in the use of native names such as *Angharad, Gwenllïan, Nest, Dyddgu, Lleucu*, the virtual disappearance of certain names, *Perweir, Hunydd, Hoen*; and a great increase of a small group, *Elizabeth, Margaret, Mary, Catherine, Ann*. One surmises that association with royalty was a great influence in the spread of such names. The adoption of biblical names, especially Old Testament names,[11] extended the range

---

[11] Biblical names, especially O.T. names, are found in all parts. During the scrutiny of the electoral register of Cardigan, the following were noted (the list omits the frequency): Iago, Enoch, Benjamin, Jacob, Abraham, Ishmael, Isaac, Jeremiah, Esau, Emanuel, Joseph, Elias, Jonathan, Joel, Japheth, Jehu, Levi, Tobias; Ebenezer, which in fact is not a personal name, should be added to the list above. Gwent has a large element of O.T. names and we observed when going over the registers of Gloucestershire that the Forest of Dean had a marked fondness of such names. The name Jeremiah stands out in Gwent and it is remarkable how many examples there are of Israel.

of first names, for men and women, but this vogue came later, in the wake of seventeenth century puritanism and eighteenth and nineteenth century evangelism, and these biblical names are evidence to show how long the patronymic system survived or lingered in certain places and families, for after becoming baptismal names, it was not too late for them to become surnames. They have not the high density of the commonplace *Jones-Davies-Williams*, but there is a fair scattering of families named *Samuel, Moses, Jacob, Enoch, Elias, Jeremiah.* Without going any further into the causes of the restricted range of baptismal names we thought it would be instructive to show the results statistically. During the examination of present-day electoral registers we decided, now and again, to count the numbers of the commonplace surnames: the count and comparison will confirm some of the observations made above.

Anglesey, Pentraeth: Hughes 60 (no Howell or Powell); Jones 111; Lewis 6; Owen 52; Parry 35; Roberts 32; Williams 43.

Llanddona: Evans 12; Griffith 2; Griffiths 6; Hughes 22; Jones 38; Owen 21; Parry 5; Roberts 38; Williams 38.

Llangoed: Davies 30; Owen 32; Parry 18; Roberts 64; Hughes 53 (no Howell or Powell); Jones 152; Williams 65.

Llanidan: Jones 154; Hughes 33; Owen 21; Roberts 51; Williams 113.

Denbigh, Cerrigydrudion: Jones 152; Roberts 81.

Llanrhaedr-yng-Nghinmeirch, Llanynys: Jones 117; Roberts 45.

Caernarvon, Llanddeiniolen – Deiniolen Ward: Jones 230; Hughes 61; Lewis 28; Roberts 68; Williams 180.

Llanberis, Peris Ward: Jones 271.

Llanllyfni, Talysarn Ward: Hughes – whole column, no Hywel, Howell, Powell; Lewis 21; no Llywelyn.

In Blaenau Gwent, we chose the Llanelly-Gilwern area, within the Brecon – Radnor constituency:

Davies 52; Edwards 40; Griffiths 17; Howell/Howells 16; Jones 139; Lewis 45; Morgan 27; Powell 50; Watkins 24; Williams 94.

It is really remarkable, considering how many other kinds or classes of names existed in the medieval period and how much naming equipment there was, that all that should have contributed a relatively small amount to the surnames of the modern period in the Welsh-speaking parts of Wales. It is still more astonishing when one reviews the names of the border counties and finds the neglected names surviving, together with names making use of the naming equipment, in Shropshire, Cheshire, Herefordshire. Much use was made in the earlier period of hypocoristic and colloquial forms, and many of these are still used colloquially, *Guto, Gutyn* for *Gruffydd, Ianto/Ifan, Evan, Dai, Deio*, etc. Many of these hypocoristic and 'familiar' forms became surnames in the English counties, but they remained as unofficial, colloquial versions in Welsh-speaking Wales and were not made into surnames during the formative period.[12] It helps to explain this difference to bear in mind the illiteracy of the period when names first came to be entered, for example, in parish registers. Peasants and craftsmen with names which had their origin in colloquial usage in the Welsh-speaking community would take the colloquial versions into communities which had no awareness that the names by which the newcomers were known were colloquial versions, so that the colloquial versions prevailed; the illiterate bearer of the colloquial name, or corrupted version, could not

---

[12] Allowance must be made for the possibility of exceptions; Cf. PRLlantrithyd 32.1575, Wenllia' Gitto . . . buried. 34.1592, Christian Dio; 35.1598, Jonn Dio.

put right the entry in the register or make known to the community that there was another, proper version of his name.

Occupational names, place-names, nicknames, although as much used colloquially in Wales as in England, as distinguishing epithets attached to personal names, play only a small part in the system of Welsh surnames. There is evidence below showing a great variety of surnames in the border counties, derived from these epithets, often in corrupted or mis-spelt forms. This really is negative evidence which shows that very little use was made of the sources and materials which could have given range and variety to Welsh surnames: if the other sources and materials had developed into surnames there would not be 271 people named Jones in the Peris ward of Llanberis, out of a total of 1421. If we look for the positive reason for the predominance of Jones, Williams, etc. it is the underlying patronymic principle. Put briefly, the children of a man named *John Dew* ('the Fat') or *Wil Felyn* ('the Yellow = Fair-haired') could receive the surname *Dew/Tew, Felyn/Melyn*, and this took place quite often in the anglicised areas of Wales and in the English border counties; in the Welsh-speaking community the chances were that they would have the surnames Jones and Williams.

There may be reasons of a sociological nature in the range and choice of names. Is it possible that the Welsh-speaking community, which, deprived of its gentry class, was almost completely peasant, had no right to go beyond a certain list of conventional names? Two later developments have the quality of emancipation, of breaking out of the narrow range, and a quality of self-assertion. A time came when the peasantry acquired a biblical culture which brought with it a new motivation in the choice of names and a great range of virtuous names to choose from. At a later stage this peasantry, or many of them, acquired a literary culture and this made available new names which had become known and attractive because they had been adopted by their new cultural leaders, the poets and preachers who had themselves sprung from the peasant class. The poets and preachers gave themselves bardic and middle names as evidence of their distinction and accomplishment. Their gifts had lifted them into prominence, above the level of their origins, their success justified the adoption and use of the bardic or middle name. In succeeding generations these special names of the bardic and ministerial class were added to the range of names from which parents could choose for their children.

3. Descriptive Surnames

THE READER who lacks familiarity with the language may be bewildered by the erratic behaviour of the adj. which follows, and becomes attached to the personal name: in some cases he sees the lenited form, after the masc. name as well as the fem. name; in others unlenited or radical consonant. It may be sufficient to say that the reader can expect to see two inconsistent usages, *Wyn/Gwyn; Felyn/Melyn; Fawr/Mawr; Dew/Tew*; and that the reader may skip the attempt that follows, to explain – partly – the grammatical confusion.

There appear to be two reasons (which quite often are not easy to tell apart) for attaching an adj. to a person's name. One feels that in certain instances the adj. was used as an appropriate or fitting description because the person concerned deserved it; the description existed in its own right. In other instances one can infer that the adj. was needed to distinguish between two persons with the same name living in close proximity, or spoken of in the same context. Despite the difficulty of identifying the two motives and in spite of the exceptions which are at times difficult to explain away, there are good reasons for thinking that there were a number of early examples of the simple description, with no intention of making a distinction between two persons, and that originally the adj. used in this way retained the radical consonant, after the masc. name. In other instances, for example, father and son with the same name, the adj. would come to be applied to make the distinction between them: when used for this reason the adj. would undergo soft mutation. [13]

The retention of the radical consonant has persisted in the case of a few adjs in the idiomatic usage of certain dialects, but the occasions of using the distinguishing adj. would occur far, far oftener than the occasions of using the simple descriptive adj. and this greater frequency would almost amount to a rule that the adj. placed in apposition to a proper noun should lenite, so that the simple descriptive adj. would tend to lenite because of the influence of the major construction. In spite of the influence of the major construction, examples are still found of adjs remaining unlenited; this seems to be the persistence in certain dialects of the ancient usage of the descriptive adj. – *Twm Gwyllt* ('Wild'), *Dafydd Tew* ('Fat'), *Twm Mawr* ('Big') are actual examples of present-day usage.

Certain adjs may have reasons of their own for retaining the radical. Because *llwyd* had the meaning 'sacred, holy', as well as 'grey, greyish brown' it required two usages; it retained the radical for the second meaning (after masc. and fem. alike) and lenited when it had the other meaning, e.g. *Dewi lwyd*, referring to St David. There may be instances, especially in medieval bardic verse, of provection: the combinations *-ndd-* and *-sdd-* could change to *-nd-*, *-sd-*, converting a lenited consonant back to its radical form, e.g. *Ieuan Du, Gwladus Du*. The adj. *bach* 'little, small' is even more exceptional: following a common noun, its usage in South Wales is regular, i.e. unlenited after masc. noun, lenited after fem., and in South Wales the same applies when it follows a

---

[13] A powerful argument in favour of this interpretation is the way the adj. is used to distinguish between two, sometimes, three farms with the same name: even though the common noun of the farm name is masculine, the adj. mutates, e.g. y Garth Fawr, y Garth Fach; and if there were another farm between them, it would be 'Y Garth Ganol'.

proper noun; in North Wales it remains unlenited even after the fem. sg. noun, and this applies to its usage after a fem. pers. name.

Many examples will be seen in this work of the two different usages (lenited and unlenited) in the case of the same adj. and with no syntactical reason to account for the difference. This may reflect difference of usage in dialects: *gwyllt, mawr, tew* in certain dialects could retain the ancient usage of the descriptive adj.; in other dialects they could have succumbed to the influence of the distinguishing usage, so that it would be possible to have *Gwilym Tew* and *Gwilym Dew*. But there can be little doubt that the main reason is the deliberate restoration of the radical consonant (going contrary to natural usage) when the epithet was felt to be functioning as a surname; and this would be more inclined to occur in a context which was beginning to lose the instinctive idiomatic usage, so that the version which was contrary to natural usage would not offend the sense of correctness, i.e. the context of social class or a locality that was more anglicized than bilingual. This probably is the reason for having *Wyn (Wynn, Wynne)* and *Gwyn (Gwynn, Gwynne)* as forms of surname coming from the same adj.

Adjs describing physical characteristics would be the kind chosen oftenest, for the simple description or for the purpose of distinguishing – colour of hair or complexion, physical dimensions, defect or infirmity or deformity, something in one's personal character or behaviour, such as pride or docility or talkativeness. It would be very necessary within the family to distinguish between senior and junior; at times, between son and father and grandfather. This need gave rise to the use of *bychan* 'small = junior', on occasions *bach* 'little', *hen* 'old', *ieuaf* 'youngest', *lleiaf* 'smallest'. Some of the adjs are compounds, e.g. *pen* 'head' + colour, curliness, shape; or *tâl* meaning the same. Sometimes *mwng* 'mane' would be used, in a compound, with the intention of poking fun. It may strike us now as very strange that descriptions which are very unpleasant and positively nasty to the person concerned should be fixed to a name. Maybe it should not shock us that such epithets were applied; what is so strange is that the person concerned had to bear the label permanently, not only adjs such as *cam* 'bandy or squinting', but words far more unpleasant and offensive, *hagr* 'ugly', *mantach* 'toothless', *salw* 'plain', *chwerw* 'bitter', *crach* collective noun 'scabs'. Only a small number of the epithets picked up in the scrutiny of medieval texts became surnames, and it is possible that some in the list below were just single instances of usage.

The kind of description which developed into regular labels and sometimes surnames was the description of appearance, especially colour of hair or physical characteristics, and also the adj. needed within the family to make distinctions, as between senior and junior. The thought has crossed my mind more than once that the colour adjs might have had a significance of rank or priority. The adj. *annwyl* 'dear', probably meant 'the favourite'; the adj. *gwyn* 'white', can be used, just as 'white-headed' can, to express affection and mean the favourite child of the family; for 'white-headed', *v.* Wright, *English Dialect Dictionary*. If this was the case, *Gwyn/Wyn* might have been used to describe something other than fair hair or complexion, but the formation of the compounds, *penwyn, talwyn* 'white-headed', etc., and the use of these as epithets make it reasonably certain that the head or hair is really meant. There will be examples below of . . . *Wyn ddu*, i.e. '. . . white the black': in such a context and period, *Wyn* had long ceased to be an adj. and had become a naming device, with the original literal meaning abstracted from it.

4. PLACE-NAMES AS SURNAMES

THE USAGE of attaching a place-name to a personal name is very common at the colloquial level and always has been. It is probably the practice in all areas for farm-names to be used in this way: I recall that the name of every farm around my home was attached to the names of its occupants, *Wil Cwmcyrnach, Llew'r Garth*, etc. If a man moves to another district to work or reside it is usual, colloquially, for the place-name of origin to be attached. The word 'colloquial' is emphasized because although the usage is very prevalent, place-names have only in special conditions become surnames, and the proportion of official surnames originating in place-names is extremely small, this being so different from the proportion of English surnames. The domination of the patronymic system and the permanent family surname which emerged from it and replaced it, is no doubt the reason for the exclusion of the place-name as an official surname in the early-modern and modern periods. Mention has already been made of the social changes of the fifteenth and sixteenth centuries amongst the influential classes, which included the adoption of permanent residential or estate names, a change that was part of a larger whole, namely the movement towards adopting an English system and following English manners and patterns. One naturally associates these social changes and this particular move with the Tudors and the political changes of the period, and there can be no doubt that the rapid transformation (in respect of nomenclature and in other respects) belongs to the sixteenth century, but there is evidence that pushes the start of the tendency or vogue a good deal further back than Bosworth and the Acts of Union, that is, the fashion of adopting the estate name as fixed surname. One expects the change to take place first near the border, in Welsh families within the English border and the Marches: there was no dyke or wall to cut off all contact with England in the medieval period, long before 1485; but, if the evidence is reliable, there are instances just as early as the border examples in families far removed from the border.

Thomas Pennant's explanation of the adoption of his family name is given below, p.176; it is noteworthy that the locale is Flintshire, and that *David ap Tudur* who became *David Pennant* was the first of the family to marry an Englishwoman from just across the border. He also provides an explanation of the adoption of the estate name by the Mostyn family, p.169. There is an example from within the Marches going back as far as 1406, although there is a good deal of wavering for some time, between the traditional usage and the new fashion. The name *Evan Blayney of Tregynon* is recorded in a list of burgesses of Welshpool: his patronymic was *Ieuan ap Gruffudd ap Llywelyn Fychan*. The name *Blayney* is an English scribe's version of *Blaenau*, a name aptly describing the locality of the family home in the hills. There was some hesitation in the style of the sons: they did not automatically receive and use *Blayney* as a surname, and it was descendants in later generations who removed the doubt and adopted the name permanently.[14]

There are likely to be special reasons to explain instances of the above kind – closeness to the English border, marrying an English wife, 'playing safe', possibly, after the wars of Owain Glyndŵr. In the absence of any known special reason it is

[14] Prys Morgan, 'The Blayney Period' in *Gregynog* pp.25-6.

surprising to find an instance far away in Lleyn, in the pedigree of *Carreg*, near Aber-daron, JEG 179, 181. The statement is made concerning *John Carreg Bach* that he was 'the first who took the name of "Carreg" ' in 1396. The pedigree shows a large number of descendants bearing the name, but it virtually disappears amongst the names on p.181, in the nineteenth century, so many being 'o.s.p.' or girls.[15]

The episcopal context provides another early instance of the residential name, e.g. H Asaph 1.216, The Bishops, AD 1346, *John Trevor I = Ieuan ap Llewelyn o Drefawr*, the Welsh name merely indicating that he was 'from Trefawr' or 'Trefor'; he is called 'John de Trevaur' in papal petitions, *v.* footnote. Next, 1.218, *John Trevor II*, 1395. As the kind of cleric who got the high offices came from the influential landowning families, it is not unusual for them to assume residential or estate names, especially when the fashion spread. Another example of a later period is the family who took the name *Glyn*, (*Glynn, Glynne*), from Rhosfawr near Pwllheli: according to JEG 239 the surname started with John Glynn, rector of Hen Eglwys, 1514. His son William Glynn became Master of Queen's College, Cambridge and Bishop of Bangor. The official papers of the Tudor period abound with references to persons named *Glynn*, as clerk or archdeacon or dean of Bangor, or as 'yeoman of the Chamber' in the Queen's court. The family of Neuadd Wen, Monts took the name of the river *Tannat* (Tanad) to be their surname; the name is found in the church, e.g. H Asaph 1.488, *Griffith Tannatt*, M.A., Jesus Coll. Oxford (of Glantanat, date 1589); ibid V. 253, named as vicar of Llansantffraid-ym-Mechain, 1579. To go back to the *Blayneys*, their name is also found amongst the vicars and rectors, e.g. ibid V. 320, *Richard Wynn Blaene*, Rector of Manafan. There are examples also of vicars and rectors adopting the name of their parish as surname, e.g. ibid V. 206, Sinecure rectors of the parish of Whitford, 1537, *Whitford* (alias Price), *Dns Hugh* (i.e. Dominus Hugh Whitford).

The place-name is used most often when a person or family moves to another district; there is then a very strong motivation to attach the place-name of origin to the pers. name. If the move takes place in an English-speaking neighbourhood there is a good chance (in the early or formative period) that the place-name will become a surname; cf. PRWhittington 126. 1633, Elizabeth verch Griffith, a poor woman, the mother of one *John Trawsfynydd*; PRWrockwardine 28. 1647, *John Karnarvon*. It is fairly obvious that it was much easier to regard this sort of name as official in South Pembrokeshire or the Gower peninsula than in Welsh-speaking Wales, because it was easier to disregard the patronymic style; e.g. B 7. 288, *Roger Marychurch of Lawhaden*; the names such as *Narberth, Nash, Lanyon, Scourfield, Carew, Laugharn, Picton*, and their frequency are evidence of the difference between the Welsh-speaking and non-Welsh-speaking districts. Movement over the border will take *Gwent (Went), Brecon, Radnor, Denby, Flint*, etc. into English counties, and note especially *Magor* and *Caerleon* from Gwent. The name *Loughor* (from the Welsh Casllwchwr and the river Llwchwr) became established with no need of emigration to England; proximity to Swansea and Gower Anglicana may be the explanation. The surname *Gower* has more than one source, the Gower of West Glamorgan can be shown to be one of them, *v.* p.101. Other names of considerable importance are *Powys (Powis)* and *Gwynedd*, especially the latter because of its frequency and its variant forms, *Gwinnutt, Winnet*, etc.; cf. Star CP 2. Henry VIII, *Jno Gwyneth*, provost of Clynnog Fawr; InvECP, 5, Anglesey 1533, *John Gwenethe*; Caerns 1533, *John*

---

[15] Mr. R. Carreg, Carreg, was a magistrate in Pwllheli in 1887, *v.* Emyr Price, *Prentisiaeth Lloyd George a Phwllheli*, pp.7-8.

Gwyneth, parson or provost of Clenockvaure, and vicar resident of Luton; p.22, 1556, *John Gwynett*. The registers of Shropshire have many examples of *Powys* and *Gwynedd* and variants; and also of *Clwyd*: PRChelmarsh 66, 73, *Cluet*; and to prove this is Clwyd, cf. PRChurch Preen 15. 1724, . . .p. of Clanver Daffry Cluet, co. Denby, i.e. Llanfair Dyffryn Clwyd; PRClaverley 340. 1773, *John and Mary Clewett*; PRWrockwardine 1. 1591, *Thomas Cludd*.

As the movements and destinies of individual persons are often uncharted and unknown, finding their names in far away places is a matter of chance, not of design. What could be more unexpected than the following examples of *Kidwelly* and *Cyfeiliog*? (1) Census of Calais 1540, f. 506, *Walter Kydwale* (born in Wales), seven children at Calais; also appears in other documents of the time as *Walter Kidwalley*, e.g. PRO E 315/371-2, Survey of Pale of Calais 1556, *Walter Kidwellie*, of Pepling nr Calais; (2) Leycester and Mainwaring, *Tracts . . . respecting Legitimacy of Amicia, daughter of Hugh Cyveliok 1673-79*, edited by W. Beaumont, Manchester, Chetham Society 1869.

One suspects sometimes that surnames which appear to be derived from personal names are really the personal name component of the name of the parish, that is to say, that *Dewi/Dewey* stands for *Llanddewi* and *Deiniole* for *Llanddeiniol*. Take the following example as proof: CaernCR17 *Ieuan Deusent*; this must be a reduction of Llanddeusaint, for it cannot be anything else. Cf. PWLMA 510, Gruffydd ap Dafydd Llwyd ap Dafydd *Dewi*; 1429, Reeves, Mabwynion: Dewi is in a position requiring *ap* if it here stands for a person, so that it is fairly certain that it is a reduction of the parish name. Moreoever, although it is inferential evidence, *Dewi* was not much used, if at all, as a personal name in the medieval period, and examples of *Dewey* on the Welsh border probably come from some *Llanddewi* or other; cf. PRDiddlesbury 29. 1688, *Abraham Dewie*; Oswestry, electoral reg. Whitchurch Urban; City of Hereford, Holmer; South Gloucs, Sodbury-Wickwar, examples of surname *Dewey*.

In the following the parish of *Llanfeuno* is represented, PRTasley 22. 1730, *George Vainow*. The parish of Llanfeuno is within the diocese of Hereford = 'the church of Beuno', and *Vaino(w)* is an acceptable version in English spelling of the mutated form. The mutated version of the following is fairly certain proof that the source is a *Llandeilo*, PRTasley 4. 1604, *Jane Dylowe*; there is a Llandeilo in Elfael, not far from the Hereford border; *v.* below for further examples of *Teilo/Deilo*.

The examples of *Blodwell*, of which there are a good number, represent without doubt *from Llanyblodwell*, and are not direct representatives of the original pers. name seen in B 13.224, SR 1292, 'Oswaldestre', *Yareword ab Madoc ab Blodewal*; cf. H Asaph 1.318, Deans of St. A., 1418, *John Blodwel* a native of Llanyblodwel; 319, *David Blodwell* 'succeeded his brother'; Star CP 167, James 1, Denbs, *Ricd Blodwell*; 221, Misc-ellaneous, *John Blodwell*, Oswestry. Further examples, PRMyddle 298, *John and Margaret Blodwel*; West Gloucs, Tidenham 1., *Blodwell*; West Flint. Rhyl, S.E. ditto.

The subject of the presence of Welsh names in Ireland has not been given much attention although many examples are mentioned in the books of MacLysaght.

Individual persons or families from Wales could have settled in Ireland at any time for any one of several reasons but the main movements which took men and names from Wales were the Norman invasion of Strongbow, who took with him many followers from Wales, both Norman and native Welsh, and the wars and oppressions and land seizures of the seventeenth century. The name *Walsh* is an Irish pronunciation of *Welsh*, and means a man who came from Wales in the Strongbow invasion. The name *Wogan* (*v. Gwgawn, Gwgon*) was taken over from Pembrokeshire by one or more of Strongbow's followers, and the best examples of taking territorial names are *Prendergast* and *Carew*: cf. *Families* 248, 'Maurice de Prendergast, whose name was taken from a village in Pembrokeshire, came to Ireland with Strongbow . . . Some families of Prendergast assumed the name Fitzmaurice at an early date. . . The name Prendergast has been widely corrupted to Pender'; Guide 168, 'Pender, Pendy, Pinder. These were abbreviated forms of Prendergast'. In fact, these 'abbreviated forms' are more likely to be English surnames.[16] The Guide 38 says of *Carew*, 'Of Norman origin, formerly *de Carron*, this family is long associated with co. Tipperary'. 'Norman' may be correct but the etymology is bogus. The Norman family of Gerald of Windsor in Pembroke probably took their territorial name from the neighbouring fortress of Carew or Caeriw, which apparently was the family seat; Lloyd, HW 423.[17]

The Guide 45 says of *Cogan, Coggan*, 'The first of this family came to Ireland with Strongbow and settled in co. Cork. Later the name became Gogan and Goggin. It is also synonym of Coogan'. *Gogan* is a different name, being *Gwogan/Gogawn*, of which *Wogan* is a version (*v.* p.112); *Cogan* is a place-name of the Cardiff area. Clark 378 has the genealogy of 'Cogan of Cogan', starting with Sir Milo de Cogan 'who . . . gave name to the parish and manor of Cogan near Cardiff . . . Sir Milo took part in the conquest of Ireland, and some of his descendants settled in that country'. The explanation of the place-name Cogan is probably the wrong way round: Professor G.O. Pierce disregards the explanation but does not question the assertion as to the connexion between the Cardiff *Cogan* and the presence of the name in Ireland.[18]

In *Irish Families* 272-3 it is said that *Taaffe* is originally a Welsh name 'signifying David' and compares the name with the colloquial *Taffy*. The *Taaffe*'s settled in co. Louth soon after the invasion. The connexion with *David/Dafydd* is highly improbable and it is much more likely that the source is the river-name, *Taf (Taff)*, either the Cardiff *Taf (Taff)* or the Dyfed *Taf*: it looks as if the *-aa-* is meant to keep the vowel long as it should be in the river-name.[19] Further study might well demonstrate that place-names of the Cardiff area or of Pembrokeshire are the clues to other personal names or surnames in Ireland; the name *Barry* could come from either the Glamorgan *Barry* or

---

[16] Unfortunately the author fails quite often to identify the most obvious names or families of Welsh origin, not to mention the less obvious; or does not take the trouble to distinguish Welsh from English, e.g. *Irish Families* 160, *Mac Gilfoyle*, 'It is sometimes disguised under the form Powell, an English surname adopted in its stead during the period of Gaelic depression'. Appendix E has 'The best known of the Norse, Norman and English names which have become "naturalized" by long association with Ireland'; the list includes Arthur, Blaney, Cogan, Fagan, Flood, Prendergast, Rice, Rothe (or Ruth), Taaffe, Wogan. Elsewhere in the text most of these are said to be Welsh or from Wales. The exact source of Blainey remains unknown in the *Guide to Irish Surnames* 28, 'The Blaneys or Blaineys came from England at the end of the sixteenth century and settled in co. Monaghan where they gave their name to the town of Castleblayney". Again 147, Mathew, 'A family of repute of English origin'; they are certainly a family of repute: they are known in Wales as the Mathews of Llandaff and Radyr.

[17] Cf. the following sentence from Lloyd's chapter on the Norman invasion setting out from Pembrokeshire; p.539, 'In the spring of 1170 another of the great clan came over in the person of Raymond the Fat, son of William Fitz Gerald of Carew . . .'. The *Gazetteer* gives *Caeriw*; if the name is in origin *Caer* + *rhiw* 'fortress on hill', the *h* would be lost in the unaccented position when the two elements became a compound.

[18] *The Place-names of Dinas Powys Hundred* 30-35.

[19] *Taff* (the anglicized version of the Cardiff *Taf* = Tav) is not known as a surname in Wales: examples are given in the classification from the Shropshire registers and these probably represent people from east Glamorgan who moved over the English border; there are also present-day examples of Taaffe, found e.g. in Worcestershire; these may represent immigrants from Ireland.

have gone from Manorbier in Pembrokeshire, the seat of Odo of Barry; in any case the name in the first place comes from the Glamorgan *Barry*, HW 423. A list of some length could be drawn up of individuals and families named *Bowen, Evans, Griffith, Lloyd, Mathews, Glynn, Gwynn, Blaney* etc. settling in Ireland, through appointments or marriage or as colonists; this information would not help to explain the origins of the names, but it is a matter of interest and importance that descendants bearing these names may return as Irish people to live in any part of Britain, including Wales. This has undoubtedly happened in the case of *Wogan, Duggan, Taaffe*, and amongst the *Blaneys* now living in England or Wales there are likely to be Irish *Blaneys*.

Some place-name surnames which illustrate some particular point have been treated fully in the alphabetical classification. The great majority of these names require no explanation since they simply denote place of origin or of residence, and most of the names the reader is likely to come across are listed briefly here.

Allatt, Allett : River Aled, Denbs. **Almer, Almore** : Allmere, Denbs. **Bangor** : Bangor, Caerns. **Barry** : Barry, Glam. **Berwen** ? Berwyn Mts., Denbs. **Blainey** : Blaenau, 'headwaters' or 'hill country'. **Blodwell** : Llanyblodwell, Monts. and the borders. **Bodvel** : Bodfel, Caerns. **Bodwrda** : Bodwrda, Caerns. **Brangwyn** ? Bryngwyn, Gwent. **Broughton** : Broughton, Denbs. **Brymor, Brynmor** ? Bryn-mawr, Caerns. **Brynker, Brunker** : Bryncir, Caerns. **Cain** : River Cain, Flints. **Carew** : Caeriw (Carew), Pembs. **Carlyon** : Caerleon, Gwent or Caerleon (Chester). **Carreg** : Carreg, Caerns. **Cluett, Cludd** : River Clwyd, Denbs. **Cogan** : Cogan, Glam. **Conway** : Conwy, Caerns. **Coytmore** : Coetmor, Caerns. **Cyvelioke** : Cyfeiliog, Monts. **Deythur** : Deuddwr, Rads. **Elvett** : Elfed, Carms. **Emlyn** : Emlyn, Carms. **Erwood** : Erwood, Brecs. **Eyrthig** : Erddig, Denbs. **Eyton, Eutun** : Eyton, Denbs. **Ffachnalt** : Ffachnalt, Flints. **Glais** : Penglais, Cards. or Glais, Brecs. **Glynn/Glynne** : Glynllifon, Caerns. **Gower** : Gŵyr (Gower), Glam. **Gwinnutt, Gwinett** : Gwynedd, North Wales. **Hanmer** : Hanmer, Flints. **Hargest** : Hergest, Rads. and the borders. **Hope** : Hope, Flints. **Keelan, Kellan** : Cilan, Denbs. **Kennifeck, Kenfig** : Cynffig (Kenfig), Glam. **Kemeys, Kemys** : Cemais (Kemeys), Gwent. **Kerry** : Ceri (Kerry), Monts. **Kidwelly, Kidwalley** : Cydweli (Kidwelly), Carms. **Kyffin** : Cyffin, 'border-land'. **Kyrinion, Karenion** : Caereinion, Monts. **Lamphey** : Lamphey, Pembs. **Landimore** : Landimore, Glam. **Lanyone** : Lanyon, Pembs. **Laugharne** : Talacharn (Laugharne), Carms. **Llifon** : Glynllifon, Caerns. or Llifon, Anglesey. **Lougher** : Casllwchwr (Loughor), Glam. **Madryn** : Madryn, Caerns. **Marychurch** : Marychurch, Pembs. **Maysmore** : Maesmor, Denbs. **Mostyn** : Mostyn, Flints. **Myvod** : Meifod, Monts. **Nanney** : Nannau, Meir. **Narberth** : Arberth (Narberth), Pembs. **Nash** : Nash, Pembs. **Pembrey** : Pen-bre, Carms. **Pembro** : Pembroke, Pembs. **Pennant** : Pennant, Flints. **Penrice** : Pen-rhys (Penrice), Glam. **Picton** : Picton, Pembs. **Pill** : Pill, South Wales coastal creek. **Powis** : Powys, Mid-Wales. **Prendergast** : Prendergast, Pembs. **Quellyn** : Llyn Cwellyn, Caerns. **Raglan** : Rhaglan, Gwent. **Saethon** : Saethon, Caerns. **Scourfield** : Scourfield, Pembs. **Scurlock, Scurlage** : Scurlage, Glam. **Skeyvioke** : Ysgeifiog, Flints. **Stackpoole** : Stackpool, Pembs. **Sully** : Sili (Sully), Glam. **Taafe** : River Taf, Carms. or Glam. **Tannat** : River Tanad or Tanat, Monts. **Tenby, Temby** : Tenby, Pembs. **Trevallyn** : Trefalun, Denbs. **Trevor** : Trefor, Denbs. **Trygarn** : Trygarn, Caerns. **Vainow** : Llanfeuno, Gwent/Hereford border. **Yale** : Iâl (Yale), Denbs. **Went** : Gwent. **Whitford** : Whitford, Flints. **Winston/Winstone** : Trewyn, Gwent.

5. HYPOCORISTIC NAMES

THESE NAMES are not only interesting in themselves but will be found also to be most productive of surnames: in fact a great variety of surnames found mainly in the English border counties have their origin in the pet forms of familiar christian names such as *David, Gruffydd, Ieuan, Iorwerth, Llywelyn*. Usually this description is applied to the forms which have either *-o* or *-yn* as an ending, and extensions of these endings, e.g. *-to, -tyn, -cyn*; but it is intended here to widen the application so as to include other versions which express, or in origin expressed, the same feeling of affection or familiarity, for instance, the versions using the terminations *-ws, -w, -i, -ach, -an*, and some of the colloquial versions of names which are just abbreviations of the proper name, such as *Dai* for *David/Dafydd*.

Colloquial speech still uses some of these hypocoristic forms instead of the proper name, although usage varies from place to place. In my own dialect *Evan* may become *Ianto* in the language and usage of schoolboys and young men, and *Gruffydd/Griffith* may become *Guto*; Rhys may become *Rhysyn*, Lewis/*Lewsyn*; but I cannot be sure whether these versions are 'active' in other dialects; they may not, perhaps other dialects have different hypocoristic names. The form *Deio* appears to be largely confined to certain parts of North Wales, [20] and *Deian* is still more restricted to parts of Gwynedd (and used for a younger age-group than *Deio, Ianto* etc.); the use of *Bilo* (*William*) seems to be used only in parts of Carmarthenshire. One is speaking now of the natural, idiomatic, unself-conscious use of these colloquial, familiar forms, and of a usage that has survived unbroken in natural speech from a much earlier period: this is emphasized for the recent vogue of ensuring that children are given good Welsh-sounding names, instead of the commonplace, the borrowed and the biblical, has made parents choose hypocoristic names known to them through their learning, to give to their children as baptismal names. *Iolo* has ceased to be used colloquially for *Iorwerth* (for the simple reason that *Iorwerth* had fallen into disuse), but it is now chosen as a baptismal name, and I could mention instances of boys, now grown men, registered at birth as *Guto* and *Ianto*. Boys registered as *Iolo* or *Guto* or *Ianto* are not *Iolo, Guto, Ianto* in the school playground and *Iorwerth, Griffith, Evan* in the classroom; they are *Iolo, Guto, Ianto* at all times and everywhere, and in these cases, they are not colloquial versions of other more formal names. A small number of girls' names have hypocoristic forms. *Gwenllïan* had the form *Llio*, but this fell into disuse although the alternative *Gwenno* continued to be used. These two versions are now chosen as registered, official names. *Nanno* for *Ann* is still used colloquially, and until quite recently, forms using *-w*, and *-ws* were heard (and may still be in certain dialects), *Nanw, Begw*, and *Catws* (for *Catherine*).

Those to whom all this is new may wonder and ask how the hypocoristic version ever came into use as a synonym for the full name seeing how very different they are from each other, e.g. *Bedo* for *Maredudd* (*Meredith*), and especially the variant *Bedyn*; or *Guto* and *Gutyn* for *Gruffydd*. It helps to explain the disparity if one realizes that some of these familiar, pet versions, probably had their origin in baby language and in the babble of mother and child. We must leave unexplained why some names have two endings, *Guto/Gutyn; Iolo/Iolyn*, but it is right to say that these various hypocoristic formations

[20] Note however examples in PRLlantrithyd, 34. 1592, Christian Dio; 35. 1598. Jonn Dio.

influenced each other and the ending -*yn* which belonged originally to a certain class of colloquial names could spread to affect the class using -*o* and replace it. On the whole *Gutyn, Iolyn* etc. came to be used mainly in Gwynedd and Powys, and only rarely in South Wales, so that the surnames derived from *Gutyn* and *Iolyn* are found in the English counties which are over the border from North Wales. The use of *Bedyn*, as variant of *Bedo*, belonged to Gwynedd. *Deio* was largely North Wales usage, especially the extensions *Deicws, Deicyn*. It is difficult to perceive a consistent pattern of usage that fits in with the broad divisions of dialect and it would be safer not to be influenced by a search for a pattern. Usage varied greatly, from name to name, and place to place, and it is possible that in some instances, usage might be confined to a relatively small or narrow band of territory and escape unnoticed in other localities, with the result that the sources of certain surnames could be missed. Although there are doubts in the mind, it does appear that in certain parts of the overlap of Powys/Shropshire the form *Ienno/Ienna* was formerly used, which is almost certainly the origin of *Genno, Gennah*, etc. There may be a connexion with *Ieuan*, and with the colloquial *Ienn/Jenn* of Radnorshire; it is also possible that it is connected with *Iennyn (Jennings*, etc.) which would mean ultimately a Breton-French origin, and if this is the case it is quite possible that *Ienno* is derived as an 'extension' of *Iennyn*, to make a pair like *Guto/Gutyn*. In any case the available evidence seems to show that the range of usage of *Ienno/Ienna* was confined to the area of the Powys/Shropshire overlap.

To provide further illustration of the way the different types of pet and colloquial names influenced each other: there is no -*t* in the structure or origin of *Ieuan* to account for *Ianto* and it is a reasonable inference that the -*to* ending was taken from *Guto*. A still more striking example of the extension of -*to* is *Deito* even though *Deio* was already available. The suffix -*cyn* may be a cognate of English *kin* or a borrowing: this added to *Dai* produces *Deicyn*, and this with *Deio (Deito)* makes a 'pair', like *Guto/Gutyn*. If -*yn* is regarded as the suffix, this makes *Deic* to be stem, and this makes possible a further variant, that of adding to *Deic-* the ending -*ws* seen in *Conws* (from *Cona, Cwna, Cunnah*), *Einyn/Einws* (from *Einion* or *Einon*). The forms *Iancyn, Ioncyn* may not be Welsh in origin, but English; but having become part of the Welsh system, they produce *Iencws, Ioncws*. The examples of *Bedyn* mentioned above seem to indicate that its usage was restricted to Gwynedd, and mainly to Anglesey, and this limited range means it was an extension (and displacement) of *Bedo*. Although only one example happens to have been collected, it indicates that there was another hypocoristic of *Maredudd*, evolved from the stem *Mared-* and *Guto/Deito*, namely AnglPleas 4, *Gwilym ap Hoell Mereitto*.

Madog appears to have had a variety of hypocoristic versions, firstly *Madyn*, occasionally *Medyn* with vowel affection. The version using suffixed -*o*, was *Mato* – the -*to* might have come from *Guto*. Examples of *Matw* and *Matws* are quoted below, and these make one hesitate much in case they are forms of *Mathew*, which is *Matto* quite often in dialect. (One finds *Madws* for *Madog* in the Morris Letters but these may be due to the facetious style of writing and may not be evidence of general, natural usage). There is a curious variant in CaernCR 99, *Dafydd ap Madowgyn*. There is some evidence also that *Bady* (*Baddy*) stands for *Madog*, but the evidence, or the interpretation of it, is not beyond doubt. The forms *Bado* and *Bato* might also be versions of *Madog*, one on the pattern of *Bedo*, the other following *Guto, Deito*. The initial *b* for *m* need not be an obstacle to accepting this suggestion: the interchange of *b* and *m* is fairly common in Welsh. *Madwyn* also occurs: this may be *Baldwin*, for versions such as *Bodwyn* are found. It is quite possible, though, that -*wyn* is here a hypocoristic suffix, also found in *Deiwyn*. This suffix may be the English *win*; it may also be the Welsh adj. *gwyn*, since 'gwyn' is used to express affection. *Hwlyn* (*Hullin*) and *Hwlcyn* were used for *Hywel* although it is doubtful whether the basic *Hwl/Hull* is in any way connected with *Hywel*, in origin. The name *Hullah* is not found in a Welsh context (although *Hulta, Pulta, Hulka* are found) but the examples of names which have final *-a*, *-ah*, with variants *-yn* or *-cyn*, justify the view that *Hullah* and *Hullin* are variant forms in the sense that they make a 'pair'. These names are treated separately in Reaney with no suggestion that they were connected. Although they are not names of Welsh origin, they were merged with *Hywel* (especially *Hullin/Hwlyn*) and with the name which displaced *Hywel*, namely *Huw* (*Hugh*); and *Hulta, Pulta, Hulka*, as well as *Pwlkyn*, seem to be developments which took place in Welsh.

The range of usage of these versions, *Hulta, Pulta, Hulka*, was not widespread as the texts of the examples found will show. The development may be set out as a theorem: as *Hullah* is to *Hullin, Hulka* is to *Hwlcyn*;[21] and in the case of *Hulta*, the forms which have *-to* provide a pattern. It is plain to see how they influenced each other for *Guto* is found in the form *Gutta*, and further examples of the *-o/-a* variation are *Deio/Deia*; *Deito/Deita*; *Llelo/Llela*; and probably *Ieuan* had *Ienno/Ienna*.

The hypocoristic forms of *Iorwerth* are fairly straightforward, *Iolo, Iolyn*, (*Biolin, Boylin, Boyling*), *v.* p.140. The name that displaced it, *Edward*, came to have its own pet forms. It had the colloquial *Ned* in English, and this in certain parts of North Wales became *Nedw* with the *-w* ending or with the *-w-* of the original *Edward* remaining in the formation of the rounded lips. It was usually *Edw* as the examples will show, but in the jocular style of the Morris Letters one finds *Iedwarth, Iedwarts, Iedws, Iedw*:

> 1.320, Iedw ap Risiart ap Iedw; 1.422, Iedw o Fodedern; 1.453, Iedws: 2.77, Dr. Iedwarts; 2,185, Iedw Llwyd (= Edward Lhuyd); 2.582, Ned Nedws; cf. InvECP 112, Philip and Roger *Edo*, of Worthenbury, brothers of Geoffrey ap *Edward* ap Howell, Flints 1515; 115, Richard Edo, Flints 1529; Thomas Eddowe of Hanmer, 1529; 117, David Edoo, Flints 1538; Richard Edow, Flints 1553; PRMyddle 50, 1596, sep. Davidis ap Griffith ap Eddo.

This is the form from which the surname *Eddowes* is derived, found in large numbers in Montgomeryshire and quite often in Shropshire, e.g. Shrewsbury, Abbey Ward; Wrekin, Edgmond; Oswestry, Great Ness.

Although it plays no part in the development of surnames it will be of interest to scholars to observe the tendency to use the def. art. before some of these pet names. It was not a rule to use the def. art.; in most instances there is no art., but the examples that do occur are reliable, and it is difficult to account for the usage (*v. Welsh Syntax* 12 for examples of *y Gutto, y Bedo*, occurring in bardic verse).

> Dwnn 1. 45, y Gyto; 1. 49, Harri ap Ieuan ap y Bedo; cf. examples of y Dai, y Deian; B 5. 58, Lleyn 13 century. y dei duy; B 5. 145, Caerns 1293, y dai du; B 6. 268, Lleyn 1350, jorwerth ap y dyan; Bartrum 1350-1415, 585, Gutun ap y Dai ap Madog Llwyd. ibid 599, Hywel ap y Dai ap Madog Llwyd; H Asaph V. 206, Sinecure rectors 1484, Howel ap y Dai ap Ithel.

Feminine personal names can be the source of surnames although the examples of this development are not many, *v.* p.19; hypocoristic forms of fem. names are still less

---

[21] Other examples of a version with *-cyn* producing a complementary or doublet version with *-co* are *Siencyn/Sianco*, i.e. *Shenkin/Shanco*, *v.* p.138 and *Huwcyn/Huwco*. An example of *-yn/-a* is *Belyn/Bela*. The art. on Hywel will deal with the use of Hwlyn and Hwlcyn as pet forms of Hywel, and give examples of the assumption that Hwlcyn is derived from Hywel; cf. Dwnn ii. 142, Footnote, '. . . Hwlcyn . . . contraction of Hywelcyn, the diminutive of Hywel'.

likely to become surnames; but we consider that the following forms justify inclusion in this chapter as interesting in themselves.

Alsod, derived from *Alice, Als*, is found in the pedigrees, e.g. Clark 186. The ending is the English dimin. *-ot, -od* found also in certain other names; *Catws*, for Catherine, was used colloquially in West Glamorgan in the first half of this century; *Dwgws*, Bartrum 1215-1350, 448, Dwgws f. Madog Llwyd ap Gruffudd; 1350-1415, 772, two instances. This stands for Dyddgu. *Elissod*, PWLMA 345, Elissod Penri of Carmarthen; Ex Pro James I. 35, Elissed vz Jevan (context Llywel, Brecs.).

One assumes these are pet or diminutive forms of *Elizabeth*. Withycombe's list of versions of *Elizabeth* does not include [E]*lyzod* but does include French *Lisette*. *Lysod* was at one time fairly common in Glamorgan, e.g. Clark 101; cf. also Bradney HM i.305, Ped. of Herbert of Llanarth names Lyzod; PRCaerwent 1587, lissode, dau. of John Griffin; PRLlCrossenny 1621, Lizod verghe Thomas.

The diminutive *-an* ending changes *Betsi* into *Betsan*.

Gwenllian had the hypocoristic *Llio*; The more modern *Gwenno* is probably derived from the abbreviated form *Gwen*, which might be *Gwenllian* or *Gwenhwyfar*. Certain examples one finds of *Gwena* might be just latinized versions of *Gwen*, e.g. PRSannan 1666, Gwena Williams uxor Johannis Anwyl (cf. 1668, Dows filia David ap Morris. Dowsa filia Ricei); but in the following examples *Gwenna* is the actual name and probably represents the hypocoristic version: PRAlberbury 11. 1570, Gwenna Hill, Gwenna Foulke; 13. 1572, Gwenna Weaver.

Margaret has a number of pet forms including *Meg* and *Peggy*. The *-an* dimin. suffix gave *Megan*; Lloyd George regarded *Megan* and *Margaret* as synonymous and also used the form *Beggan Bach*, v. John Grigg, 2. p.54. In the following the suffix *-yn* is added to Peg: B 15.50, AS 1406, *Dd Peggyn*; the version of the variant text has an Irish appearance, *David ap Peggine*.

Mary, Mari; Withycombe 93-4 says that *Mally* was formerly much commoner than *Molly*, but it fell into disuse at the end of the eighteenth century. *Mali* is still used colloquially in Welsh-speaking families; cf. B 11.70, Broniarth 1429, Malli uxor Will(yn); Bartrum 1350-1415, 835, Mali f. Ieuan; CaernHS 26, Bolde Rental 35, Mally vz y Coz ap Atha; 43, Mally vz Mad(og); InvECP 146, Monts. David Amathewe Gough, executor of the will of Maly alias Mary ap [sic] David. The *-an* termination makes the variant form *Malan*; FC 362, Mali; 361 Malan.

CaernHS 26, Bolde Rental 36, Mabot vz Wyn; ADClun 214, Mawod vergh Willim.

Mayzod, not mentioned by Withycombe, seems to be a derivative of *Mary*, using *-zod* of *Lyzod* as if it were a suffix; it occurs quite often in Glamorgan pedigrees, e.g. Clark 89, 173, 165, *Mazod* (twice).

Tanno which is found quite often in North Wales records one surmises to be a form of *Tangwystl*: AnglPleas 22, Angharat verch Llewelin ap Nest verch Tanno verch Ievan Gogh; CaernHS 26, Bolde Rental 37, Gruf ap Tanno vz Tuder ap Atha; 41, Gruff ap Tanno vz Tuder ... Tanno ap [sic] Tuder...; CaernCR 54, Tannow, servant of Einion ab Adda; 60, 'Tannow ferch Teg'.

ABBREVIATIONS

AB	Edward Lhuyd, *Archaeologia Britannica*.
ADClun	G.E.A. Raspin, 'Transcript and descriptive list of the Medieval Court Rolls of the Marcher Lordship of Clun' (Unpublished University of London diploma thesis, August 1963).
ALMA	Hugh Owen (editor), *Additional Letters of the Morrises of Anglesey (1735-86)*, Cymmrodor, xlix, 1947-9.
AMCC	*Ancient Monuments of Caernarfonshire, ii, Central*.
AN	Anglo Norman
AnglCourt 1346	G. Peredur Jones, 'Anglesey Court Rolls 1346', TAAS, 1930, 33-49.
AnglMuster Book	E. Gwynne Jones, 'An Anglesey Muster Book', TAAS, 1946.
AnglPleas	Hugh Owen, 'Plea Rolls of Anglesey 1500-1516', TAAS (Supplement), 1927.
AnglRent	T. Jones Pierce, 'An Anglesey Crown rental of the sixteenth century', TAAS, 1951.
Ann Camb	J. Williams ('Ab Ithel') (editor), *Annales Cambriae*, Rolls Series, 1860.
Arch. Camb.	*Archaeologia Cambrensis*, the Journal of the Cambrian Archaeological Association (London etc. 1846 ff).
Arthurian Legend	John Rhŷs, *Studies in the Arthurian Legend*.
B	*Bulletin of the Board of Celtic Studies* (Cardiff 1921 ff).
Bardsley	C.W. Bardsley, *English Surnames*.
Bartrum	P.C. Bartrum, *Welsh Genealogies*.
Bartrum (1)	P.C. Bartrum, *Early Welsh Genealogical Tracts*.
BBC	J. Gwenogvryn Evans (editor), *The Black Book of Carmarthen*.
BBStD	J.W. Willis-Bund (editor), *The Black Book of St David's*.
B Dewi	D. Simon Evans, *Buchedd Dewi*.
Bennett Pedigree Book	Welsh pedigrees, especially of Gower, by William Bennett of Penrice, mid-seventeenth century (MS at Royal Institution of South Wales, Swansea).
Bolde Rental	C.A. Gresham, 'The Bolde Rental', CaernHS, xxvi, 1965.
BrRadnor	Brecon and Radnor (electoral rolls).
Br Saes	Thomas Jones (editor), *Brenhinedd y Saesson*.
BT	J. Gwenogvryn Evans (editor), *The Book of Taliesin*.
B Tyw Pen 20	Thomas Jones (editor), *Brut y Tywysogion*, Peniarth MS 20.
B Tyw RBH	Thomas Jones (editor), *Brut y Tywysogion*, Red Book of Hergest.
Bulkeley	Hugh Owen, 'The diary of William Bulkeley of Brynddu, Anglesey', TAAS, 1931.
BYale	T.P. Ellis (editor), *The First Extent of Bromfield and Yale*.
CA	Ifor Williams (editor), *Canu Aneirin*.
CaernHS	*Transactions of the Caernarfonshire Historical Society* (1939 ff).
Caern CR	G.P. Jones and Hugh Owen (editors), *Caernarvon Court Rolls*.
CaernQSR	W. Ogwen Williams (editor), *A Calendar of Caernarvonshire Quarter Sessions*.
CalACW	J. Goronwy Edwards (editor), *A Calendar of Ancient Correspondence*.
CatAncDeeds	*A descriptive catalogue of ancient deeds in the Public Record Office* (6 vols. London 1890-1915).

CalInqu Edw III	*Calendar of Inquisitions post mortem and other analogous documents preserved at the Public Record Office* (vols. 7 to 14, London 1904-54).
Cal Pat Rolls	*A Calendar of Patent Rolls : Elizabeth I, vol. V, 1569-72* (London 1966).
CAP	William Rees (editor), *A Calendar of Ancient Petitions Relating to Wales*.
Carms	Carmarthenshire
Castell Gorfod MS	Early eighteenth century MS of South Wales genealogies (Castell Gorfod MS 8 at NLW).
Census 1861	General Register Office, Census Returns for England and Wales, 1861 (MSS at PRO, London).
Census of Calais	Census of the Pale of Calais, *c.* 1540, Longleat MS 60 (MSS of the Marquis of Bath, Longleat).
CD	John Morris-Jones, *Cerdd Dafod*.
Clark	G.T. Clark, *Limbus Patrum Morganiae et Glamorganiae*.
CLlH	Ifor Williams (editor), *Canu Llywarch Hen*.
CRHaverford	B.G. Charles (editor), *A Calendar of the records of the borough of Haverfordwest*.
CRW	T.H. Parry-Williams (editor), *Carolau Richard White*.
CRhC	T.H. Parry-Williams (editor), *Canu Rhydd Cynnar*.
CT	Ifor Williams (editor), *Canu Taliesin*.
Cumberland	Whenever a parish register is referred to, or exchequer lay subsidy roll, 'Cumberland' will be included.
Cwtta Cyf.	D.R. Thomas (editor), *Y Cwtta Cyfarwydd*.
Cy	*Y Cymmrodor* (occasional publications of the Society of Cymmrodorion, London).
Cymm Trans	*Transactions of the Honourable Society of Cymmrodorion* (London 1893 ff).
Denbs	Denbighshire
DGG	Ifor Williams and Thomas Roberts (editors), *Cywyddau Dafydd ap Gwilym a'i gyfoeswyr*.
DLancaster	William Rees (editor), *A Survey of the Duchy of Lancaster lordships*.
DNB	*The Dictionary of National Biography* (63 vols. London 1885-1900, with later supplements).
DPO²	Theophilus Evans, *Drych y Prif Oesoedd*. 2nd ed.
D. Tel	The Daily Telegraph newspaper, London.
DWB	*The Dictionary of Welsh Biography down to 1940* (London 1959).
Dwnn	Lewys Dwnn, *Heraldic Visitations of Wales and Part of the Marches* (1846).
E	English
EANC	R.J. Thomas, *Enwau afonydd a nentydd Cymru*.
EEW	T.H. Parry-Williams, *The English Element in Welsh*.
Ekwall	Eilert Ekwall, *The Concise Oxford Dictionary of English Place-names*.
ELlSG	J. Lloyd-Jones, *Enwau lleoedd Sir Gaernarfon*.
ELS Cumberland	*Exchequer Lay Subsidy of Cumberland*.
E.R.	Electoral Rolls
Exch Proc Wales	Emyr Gwynne Jones (editor), *Exchequer Proceedings concerning Wales*.
Ex Pro James I	T.I. Jeffreys-Jones (editor), *Exchequer Proceedings concerning Wales in tempore James I*.
F	French
FC	O.H. Fynes-Clinton, *The Welsh Vocabulary of the Bangor district*.
Fenton	Richard Fenton, *A Historical Tour through Pembrokeshire*.

Flints	Flintshire
Flintshire Place-names	Ellis Davies, *Flintshire Place-names*.
G	J. Lloyd-Jones (editor), *Geirfa Barddoniaeth gynnar Gymraeg*.
Gazetteer	Elwyn Davies (editor), *A Gazetteer of Welsh Place-names*.
GDG	Thomas Parry (editor), *Gwaith Dafydd ap Gwilym*.
Geiradur Mawr	H. Meurig Evans and W.O. Thomas (editors), *Y Geiriadur Mawr*.
GGl	Ifor Williams and J. Llywelyn Williams (editors), *Gwaith Guto'r Glyn*.
Glam	Glamorgan.
Glam Cartae	G.T. Clark, *Cartae et alia munimenta* . . . .
Glam Hearth Tax	Glamorgan Hearth Tax, *circa* 1671 (various MSS in section E179 at the PRO).
Gloucs	Gloucestershire
Gower Manorial Rolls	Various Gower manor rolls of the seventeenth century (MSS at the Royal Institution of South Wales, Swansea).
Gower Survey	Gower Survey of 36 Elizabeth I, 1594-5, Badminton Manorial Papers 2628 (MS on deposit at NLW).
GPC	*Geiriadur Prifysgol Cymru* (Caerdydd 1950 ff).
GTA	T. Gwynn Jones (editor), *Gwaith Tudur Aled*.
Guide	Edward MacLysaght, *A Guide to Irish Surnames*.
H	J. Morris-Jones and T.H. Parry-Williams (editors), *Llawysgrif Hendregadredd*.
H Asaph	R. Thomas, *A History of the Diocese of St Asaph*.
Hanes Eg. Anni	Thomas Rees and J. Thomas (editors), *Hanes Eglwysi Annibynol Cymru*.
HBr	Theophilus Jones, *History of Brecknockshire*.
Herefs	Herefordshire
HM	J.A. Bradney, *A History of Monmouthshire*.
H Rads	Jonathan Williams, *A general history of the County of Radnor*.
HW	J.E. Lloyd, *A History of Wales*.
I	Irish
IGE	Henry Lewis, Thomas Roberts and Ifor Williams (editors), *Cywyddau Iolo Goch ac eraill*.
IGE[2]	*Cywyddau Iolo Goch ac eraill* (second edition).
InvECP	E.A. Lewis (editor), *Inventory of Early Chancery Proceedings*.
JEG	J.E. Griffith (editor), *Pedigrees of Anglesey and Caernarvonshire Families*.
L	Latin
L'Estrange Ewen	C.H. L'Estrange Ewen, *Surnames of the British Isles*.
Leycester and Mainwaring	W. Beaumont (editor), *Tracts . . . respecting the Legitimacy of Amicia, daughter of Hugh Cyveliok*.
LGC	J. Jones and W. Davies (editors), *Gwaith Lewis Glyn Cothi*.
LHEB	Kenneth Jackson, *Language and History in Early Britain*.
LL	J. Gwenogvryn Evans (editor), *The text of the Book of Llan Dâv*.
LP	Henry Lewis and Holger Pedersen, *A Comparative Celtic Grammar*.
L & P	*Calendar of Letters and Papers, foreign and domestic, of Henry VIII, 1509-1547* (London 1862-1932).
Lp Oswestry	W.J. Slack (editor), *The Lordship of Oswestry*.
MA	Owen Jones, William Owen and Edward Williams (editors), *The Myvyrian Archaiology of Wales*.

Matthews	C.M. Matthews, *English Surnames*.
med	medieval
Mer LSR	Keith Williams-Jones (editor), *The Merioneth Lay Subsidy Roll 1292-3* (Cardiff 1976).
ML	J.H. Davies (editor), *The Letters of Lewis, Richard, William and John Morris*.
ML Index	Hugh Owen, 'Index to the Morris Letters', TAAS (supplements) 1942, 1944.
MLSW	T.B. Pugh (editor), *The Marcher Lordships of South Wales*.
mod	modern
Monm	Monmouthshire
Mont Coll	*The Montgomeryshire Collections; the Transactions of the Powysland club* (London etc. 1868 ff).
Monts	Montgomeryshire
NLW	National Library of Wales, Aberystwyth.
NLWJ	*The National Library of Wales Journal* (Aberystwyth 1939 ff).
NLW Plymouth	MS Deeds in the Plymouth Collection at the NLW.
NW	North Wales
OE	Old English
OFr	Old French
OIG	*Orgraff yr Iaith Gymraeg*.
OG	J.E. Lloyd, *Owen Glendower*.
ON	Old Norse
OW	Old Welsh
Paroch	Edward Lhwyd, *Parochialia*.
Pembs	Pembrokeshire
Phillimore	Henry Owen (editor), *The description of Pembrokeshire*.
PKM	Ifor Williams (editor), *Pedeir Keinc y Mabinogi*.
Pre-conq Domesday	Olof von Feilitzen, *Pre-Conquest Personal Names of Domesday Book*.
PRCaerwent	J.A. Bradney (editor), *Parish Registers of Caerwent*.
PRConway	Alice Hadley (editor), *Parish Registers of Conway*.
PR Llanbadoc	J.A. Bradney (editor), *Registrum Antiquum de Llanbadoc*.
PRLlanddewi Rhydderch	J.A. Bradney (editor), *Parish Registers of Llanddewi Rhydderch*.
PRLlanfighangel Ystern Llewern	J.A. Bradney (editor), *Registrum Antiquum de Llanfihangel Ystern Llewern*.
PRLlantrithyd	H. Seymour Hughes (editor), *The Registers of Llantrithyd*.
PRLlCrossenny	J.A. Bradney (editor), *Parish Registers of Llantilio Crossenny*.
PRO	Public Record Office
PRSannan	R. Ellis (editor), *The Parish Registers of Llansannan*.
PRWhicham	J.F. Haswell (trans.), *Parish Register of Whicham*.
PWLMA	R.A. Griffiths, *The Principality of Wales in the Later Middle Ages*.
Rads	Radnorshire
RadsSoc	*Transactions of the Radnorshire Society* (Llandrindod 1930 ff).
RB	John Rhys and J. Gwenogvryn Evans (editors), *The Text of the Bruts from the Red Book of Hergest*.
RCA	E.A. Lewis and J. Conway Davies (editors), *Records of the Court of Augmentations*.

Reaney	P.H. Reaney, *A Dictionary of British Surnames*.
RecCa	Henry Ellis (editor), *The Record of Carnarvon*.
Rec Denb Lp	John Williams (editor), *The records of Denbigh and its Lordships*.
Richards 1753	Thomas Richards, *A British or Welsh-English Dictionary*.
RP	J. Gwenogvryn Evans (editor), *The Poetry in the Red Book of Hergest*.
RM	J. Gwenogvryn Evans (editor), *The Text of the Mabinogion . . . from the Red Book of Hergest*.
Shrewsbury BR	H.E. Forrest (editor), *Shrewsbury Burgess Roll*.
Shropshire Parish Registers	(various editors) Shropshire Parish Register Society.
St David's Diocese	Index of Marriages, Archdeaconry of Carmarthen, Diocese of St David's (Church in Wales MSS records deposited at NLW).
Star CP	Ifan ab Owen Edwards (editor), *A Catalogue of Star Chamber Proceedings*.
StTG	D.J. Williams, *Storïau'r Tir Glas*.
Surveys GK	C. Baker and G.G. Francis (editors), *Surveys of Gower and Kilvey*.
Survey of Pale of Calais	Mid-sixteenth century MS survey of the Pale of Calais (E315/371-2 at PRO).
SW	South Wales
SWMRS	*South Wales and Monmouthshire Society Publications* (Cardiff 1951).
TAAS	*Transactions of the Anglesey Antiquarian Society* (1927 ff).
Taxatio	*Taxatio Ecclesiastica, Angliae et Walliae, auctoritate P. Nicholai IV c A.D. 1291* (Record Commission, London 1802).
TC	T.J. Morgan, *Y Treigladau a'u Cystrawen*.
TCWAAS	*Transactions of the Cumberland and Westmorland Antiquarian and Archaeological Society*.
TD	Current telephone directories
TDW	Samuel Lewis, *Topographical Dictionary of Wales*.
Theater du Mond	Thomas Parry (editor), *Theater du Mond*.
Thomas	William Thomas of Michaelston-super-Ely, copy by D. Jones of Wallington of mid-eighteenth century diary (MS at Cardiff Public Library).
Times	The Times newspaper, London.
TLlM	G.J. Williams, *Traddodiad Llenyddol Morgannwg*.
TYP	Rachel Bromwich (editor), *Trioedd Ynys Prydein* (1st edition).
v.	*vide* (see).
Val Ecc	*Valor Ecclesiasticus tempore Henr. VIII*.
Val.Norwich	W.E. Lunt (editor), *The Valuation of Norwich*.
W	Welsh
WATU	Melville Richards, *Welsh Administrative and Territorial Units*.
W. Mail	The Western Mail newspaper, Cardiff.
WG	John Morris-Jones, *A Welsh Grammar*.
WM	J. Gwenogvryn Evans (editor), *The White Book Mabinogion*.
Worcs	Worcestershire
WPortBooks	E.A. Lewis (editor), *Welsh Port Books*.
WS	William Salesbury, *Dictionary of English and Welsh*.

Alphabetical Classification

[Note: Cross-references are given below, thus **Jones** *will be found discussed under* **Ieuan, Davies** *under* **Dafydd**, *but in some cases the minute variations of the surname spellings are so many that in those cases it has been necessary to give only a representative sample in the cross references.]*

A

Adam, Addaf, Adda, Badda, Batha, Bathaw, Batho, Badam etc.

The Biblical name entering the language in the Roman period would become *Addaf*, through the internal lenition of *d* and *m*. Early Welsh orthography generally had no separate symbol for the *dd* sound and used *d* for *d* and *dd*. English or Anglo-Norman scribes would be inclined to use *-th-* and this practice continues in the registers of Shropshire. Final *-f* is easily lost in colloquial speech, e.g. in the ending of the superlative adj., *trymaf/tryma*, and therefore *Adda* can be expected; there is no lack of *Ada* or *Atha* (for *Adda*) in medieval texts, alongside Adaf; in the early modern period, Adda became the standard form.

A knowledge that Adda stood for an original Adam might be the reason for the use of Adam in certain early texts; a more likely explanation is that the English version came to be used in Wales just as John and David came to be used instead of, or in addition to Ieuan and Dafydd, with the result that 'ab Adam' could occur as easily as 'ab Adda'. In the early modern period when fixed surnames were being established, the father's official name in many cases would be Adam which in turn became the surname Adams.

Adda in an English-speaking community, especially over the border, would be affected by English speech (in sound and spelling) and become *Athaw, Bathaw*, later *Atho, Batho*, and with *'s* added, *Athawes, Bathawes*. The final *-a* could also produce the neutral sound represented by *Bather* in the Shropshire registers.

'ab Adam' would of course give *Badam* or *Baddam*, and *Baddams*. The inn Abadam Arms, Porth-y-rhyd, Carms. takes its name from a 19th century Adams who changed his name to Abadam. Examples of *Battams* occur (Oswestry electoral reg. below), and this form could, theoretically, be explained as the 'hardening' which changes *g, b, d* into *c, p, t* in certain positions in S.E. Welsh dialects, but this is very doubtful. Another change is largely a matter of spelling, namely, changing *Badam* into *Badham*, through false analogy with -ham place-names. There could well be an authentic Badham derived from a place-name; e.g. in Bishops Froome, Leominster, the address 'The Badhams' occurs, but one may be fairly certain that many instances of Badham in the border counties and in S. Pembs are the result of the false analogy.

SELECTED EXAMPLES

Addaf: B13. 142, 1283 Bonds for peace, Adaf fil Anyan; B4. 154, 1325, Adaf ap Adaf. BBStD 154, Iuliana Adaf, ...Iohes Adaf. ADClun 12, Ieuan ap Adaf; 68, Athaf ap Griffit. *Adda*, (in some cases alongside *Addaf*) B5. 59 late 13c. Ada ap Kenric. B5. 143, 1293, Ada ap y puys; 147, Adaf ap arthur. B6. 358, Iorwerth ap Atha, Atha grun; 360, Atha Duy. *Adam* (early examples) B13. 216, SR 1292, Iuor ap Adam, Yuan ap Adam ap Kneytho, B24. 191, Adam Fras, abbot of V. Crucis, 1240.

The BBStD in addition to *Adaf* as shown above has *Adam* distributed throughout the text. It also has examples of the derivative which uses the ending -od, as in Mayzod, Lysod etc., p.78, Claricia Ademot ... Adam Ademot.

EARLY MODERN

RadsSoc V1. 13, Will, 'Glascomb' 1557, ...ap John Attheo of Kevenllis (? for 'Athoe'). XXVIII. 16, Old Radnor, 1560, William Bathow. XXX. 52, William Bathowe. XXXV. 34, 1593, Ednoll, John Bathoe, Hugh Bathoe, Thomas Bathow. StarCP 212, Thos ap Thos Abatha of Llanboidy. InvECP 72, Denbs. 1518-29, ... ap Eden Apatha. Surveys GK (Millwood 1584) 171, John David Batha. L & P 552, Sir Richard Badam, Hereford. HM i. 45, Ll. Vibon Avel, list of tenements in 1606 includes name of 'William Badam'. ibid 91, Llangiwa, Iohn Badham, date 1763. ibid iv. 31, Caldicot, 'Badam's Court took its name from Sir John ap Adam ... Some of the family became after the Welsh fashion Badam and some Hopkins. Hopkin Badam was living at Chepstow at the end of the eighteenth century'. Note: The name Thomas de Badham occurs in CalInqu Edw III, 244, p.186. context Sussex; this appears to be a place-name but examples are found of using *de* before personal names because using 'de' was a French or Norman pattern of naming, e.g. p.177, Philip de Rees.

SHROPSHIRE REGISTERS
Selattyn 107. 1633, Thomas ap John ap David ap Adda. Whittington 154. 1631, Johan Badain (misreading of Badam). 429. 1733, Sarah Badda. Oswestry 59. 1569, Annes vz Atha. 462. 1628, Katherin the daughter of Seeth ap Atha. Stanton Lacy 4. 1563, Katherine Bathewe; 17. 1586, William Bathewe; 48. 1631, Edward Batho; 80. 1663, ... Batho; 31. 1606, Mary Baddam; 32. 1608, John Baddam. Bitterley 163, 1779, Thomas Batthews (? Mathews). [This is the editor's query. The -tth- suggests that the person who entered the name regarded it as a form of Matthew. The assumption may be correct for the interchange of *b* and *m* does take place in some words, especially in dialect. On the other hand the forms Bathaw, Bathow, and the uncertain quality of the vowel or diphthong of the final syllable are good reasons for treating this as a form of Batha.] Bromfield, Index, Baddam, Badam, Badham. Cleobury Mortimer, Index, Baddam, Badham. Pontesbury 4. 1540 ... Bathawe; 14. 1551 ... Bathow. Diddlesbury 106, Bathow. High Ercall, 2. 1585, Bathaw. Great Ness 128. 1737, Benj. Bather; it is also written Batho and Bathur; cf. 134. 1742, Benj. and Marthur [sic] Bathur. St. Mary's Shrewsbury, Index, Badho, Bathoe, Batha, Bather. Great Bolas, 24. 1632, William Badda = Bathew, Bathaw, Batho of other entries; 38. 1660, Bathers; 29. 1641, William Bathowe; 33. 1659, William Bather, 1669, Bathoe.

SUMMARY OF PRESENT-DAY REGISTERS
Atha, South Worcs., Bretforten, Pebworth; Cheadle, Bredbury South. *Athawes*, S. Gloucs., Olveston. *Batha*, Oswestry, Osw. Urban, N.W., Ellesmere Rural, Dudleston Heath. *Batho*, Shrewsbury, Battlefield, Quarry Portion; Oswestry, Tetchill. *Bather*, Shrewsbury, Meole Brace.
Times and D. Tel 4 Jan. 1980, Adda, Shrewsbury; it would be difficult, without personal enquiry, to determine whether the version should be pronounced as Welsh Adda or as if it stood for Ada, written Adda.

Addaf *v.* Adam

Ade, Adgyn, Ady
Reaney has a large number of these E surnames, and they are only mentioned here because of an apparently hypocoristic W form

Adws, B15,50, AS 1406 Adws Of.

Occurrence of 'ap Ady, Thomas ap Addey' in Oswestry neighbourhood suggests that surname Baddy derives from Ap Ady, although the surname of Thomas Baddy, 18th cent. hymnwriter has been stated to derive from some form of Madog. For Ap Ady, *v.* Cal Pat Rolls, Edward VI, vol. iii, p.284, owner of lands around Oswestry, Trefonnen.

Aeddan

G is uncertain whether this should be *Aeddan* or *Aedan*, a name occurring rarely in early poetry and genealogies. It occurs in Aneirin, line 359, but Ifor Williams has no note on it. Thomas Jones has no doubt, and prints *Aeddan*, e.g. B Tyw Pen 20, p.12, *Aeddan ap Blegywryd*, date 1018. Bradney HM i. 102 has the pedigree of the descendants of Aeddan, Lord of Grosmont. TYP 264-5 prints 'Aedan (= Aeddan)', and the evidence in Dr Bromwich's discussion shows clearly the name came into Welsh literature from Irish sources. It must have been the name of early Irish immigrants in Wales for that is a far more likely source for the examples shown below than a mythical character in literary sources.

This is the name, with *th* for *dd*, in the following:

Glam Cartae 544, Lewelit ux. Aythan. BBStD 78, Nich'us Aythan; 84, Nest Aythan (trans. 85 has the misprint Aytham), 116, Ieuan ap Aythan, 286 . . . gwele Traharn ap Aythan.

Afel

An early borrowing of Abel would result in the form Afel. G quotes a small number of instances referring to the biblical Abel, *auel wirion* in T 54.1; *afael wirion* in H 102b 19 (M 201b 27); (he also gives one instance of Abel, in M 75b 34).

Occasional examples occur in the medieval period: BBStD 200, David ap Auel; 322 Gurgene ap Auayl; and the Gwent place-name Llangattock vibon Avel (= Feibion Afel, 'sons of A') contains the name.

The diphthong in Afael is not difficult to explain: a word such as *gafael* ('grasp') is generally *gafel* in ordinary speech and *Afael* has probably come about as a 'correction', through a false analogy. The Welsh translation of the Bible uses *Abel*. Although not often, it was given as a baptismal name when

Old Testament names came to be widely used: these O.T. names then became surnames.

Allart, Allatt, *v.* Aled

Aled, Allet, Allett

The river-name Aled is best known from the name of the poet Tudur Aled, fl. 1480-1526, traditionally connected with the parish of Llansannan. The various entries of the name 'Tuder Alet' or 'Tydder Allett' in the parish register of Oswestry are too late to be the poet, but, if connected, they must refer to his descendants, a son or grandson, e.g. Robert and Elnor, the twin children of one Tudur Aled were christened in 1565. There are many entries of christenings and burials between 1565 and 1596 which use the forms Alet, Allet or Allett.

An article concerning Tudur Aled's connexions, Cledwyn Fychan, 'Tudur Aled : ailystyried ei gynefin', NLWJ 1983, throws light on the entries in the parish register. The poet appears to have adopted the name Tudur Aled to follow the example of his father's cousin Lewis Aled. The pedigree, art. cit. 69, shows that the poet had four sons, Robert (the eldest) residing in Oswestry, and so Robert and his son Tudur or Tuder and his grandchildren are the source of the surnames in the parish register.

PRSt Mary's Shrewsbury, Index, Allart, Allott, Allet, Allett.

PRSt Chad's, Index, Allart, Allatt, Alett.

Shrewsbury BR, between 1678 and 1839 has five instances of Allart, Allatt or Allett.

Almer, Almor *v.* Introd. Place-names.

Ancred, Ancret *v.* Angharad

Andrew, Andro, Andras

G has a small number of references to Andras, derived from Andreas; the Welsh name of Presteigne is Llanandras. The form Andro would come from Andrew. The index of Glam Cartae has Andrew, Andreas, Andro; e.g. p.2000 Andro ap Res.

The following deserve to be quoted because of the *ap* forms:

PRSibdon Carwood, 7. 1675, Mathew Bandrey. PRClunbury, 43. 12. Eliz ap Andrew, Thomas ap Andrew. 43, 1645, Thomas Bandro. 80. 1703, Anne Bandra; 88, 1715, Thomas Bandra. PRStokesay, 74. 1742, Thomas s. of Benjamin and Esther Bandrew. 76. 1746, Benjamin s. of Benjamin and Esther Bandrew. 73. 1739, Benjamin Andrews and Esther Holloway, both of this p. married.

The form Bandrew occurs in the entries of this family until 83. 1759 with the entry of the baptism of James, but after this the name again becomes Andrews, e.g. the two Benjamins, father and son, become Andrews. PRHopesay, 84, Bondraw (group of three).

The following example illustrates the varying quality of the diphthong:

PRSmethcote, 8. 1661 . . . Alis Androwes = 10. 1666, Allice Andrews.

Andro, Andras v. Andrew

Angharad, Ankret, etc.

The fem. name Angharad occurs with great frequency in early documents. In many published texts the version appearing in the original document has been edited and put into a corrected form. But in the selection below there will be sufficient of the original versions to show the corruptions which became fixed names especially in the English border counties:

B4. 157, Ardudwy 1325, Angharat filia Deen.. B5. 147, CaernSubs. 1293, Angarat filia madyn. B13. 229, SR 1292, Nagharath fil Eynon. BBStD 216, Agnarath filia Dauid; 218, agnarath filia Ken; 222, Angarad fil Dauid; 222, Dauid Anchorita; 268, Angarad fil Gwasteyllan . . . (misreading, = teilaw, teilo). AnglPleas 5. Angharat verch John Llowarch. ADClun 114 . . . their mother Ancoret; CalACW 3. Angharad daughter of Madog ap Gruffydd (brackets, Angaretha). InvECP 118 (Flints. 1538-) Hangharrot verch Dauid. ibid. 147, (Monts 1547) formerly of Ingharat verch V. ibid. 164 (Breckn 1553) Hegneharad his wife. Surveys GK 269, Aughared (sic) . . . Ynghared. MLSW 138 Hangharyed ap Morgan. PRLlanbadoc 1596, Yngkarat dau' of the said William John.

SHROPSHIRE REGISTERS

Tasley 5, 6, Ancret Lewis. More, Index, Ancret, Ancrite, Anchoret, Ancrete, Anchorett – several entries. Lydham, 59, 1775. Susan Ancret (surname). Cardeston 19, Ancritt. Alberbury 634. 1797, Ankrett (surname of husband and wife). Ch. Stretton 56, 1716, Johan Ancheret = 63. 1722, Johannis Anchorite = 66. 1726, John Anchorite = 68. 1728, John Anchorett. (Index has also examples of Ankrett, of which

there are many entries.) Claverley, VII. Family of Hankerite; 281. 1750, Mary Hankerite. Worthen, Index, Ancorett, Ancerett, Ancorrets, Ancronte [sic] Ancrout. Pontesbury 143. 1642, Anchorett (as surname; Index also has Ankred). Westbury 391. 1809, Ankritt (surname); Index gives Ancret, Ankritt, Ankrift. Stokesay 22. 1613, Ankereta uxor Johannis Ockeley. Wistanstow 95. 1739, John Anchoret, p. Hopesay. ibid. 136. 1778, Sarah, d. of John and Mary Ancaret = 138. 1780, Ancoret. = 141. 1782, Anchor = 144. 1784, Ankorett, 1785, Anchoret. Abdon 1. 1567, Enchorat [?] Reynolds [editor's query]. Smethcote 37. 1734, Thomas Enkret . . . Enkrett = 39. 1739, Ankrett = 40. 1741, Ankrit. Cressage 10. 1782, Ann, fil[a] of Abraham and Ann Hankred. Condover 51. 1610, Dorothy, d. of Thos. Ancreryte, [sic] of C. bap. St. Martins 85. 1609, Enharad vz Edward; Oswestry 26. 1561, Angharad vz Hugh Laken. 91. 1583, Yngharad vz Owen or Mynydd.

The aspirate in Hankerite, seen above, is probably due to a transfer of the *h* of the second syllable.

The form Ankaret still survives as a christian name, e.g. S. Pembs 1975, Slebech: Ankaret Edwards, with an address in Rhos. It also survives as a surname, e.g. Shrewsbury 1959, Westbury – Yockleton, Ankritt.

Anian v. Einion

Annwyl, Anwyl

This surname is simply the epithet *annwyl* meaning 'dear'. The correct spelling is *annwyl*. The use of this adjective (as a naming epithet) is confined to North Wales, with only a few stray examples in southern counties, and most of the examples collected are located in the north east. To remove possible misunderstanding, the adjective is used after personal names in South Wales as much as in North Wales, to express endearment or vague feelings, but it must have had some other function or element of meaning in North Wales to have made it a fixed epithet, the additional element, we believe, was the sense of being the favourite child; St John is often described in Welsh as 'y disgybl annwyl' with this particular meaning. The first quotation from Gwent expresses the sense of endearment and tender sympathy:

PRLlanddewi Rhydderch 14. 1694. Mary vach anwill, a pauper, was buried April 5, 1697.

The following examples with all possible variations of spelling, are of the fixed epithet acting, in almost all cases, as surname: B15. 47, AS 1406, Je(uan) ap Mad(og) Anwyll; Deikws ap Mad anwyl; ibid 57, Gr Anwill. CalAncDeeds 111. A 5653 (Flints) Gregory ap David Annoill ap Jevan ap David, ditto 5657, 5661, 5674; ibid 5664 Annoile; ibid 5667 Annwyll; ibid 5972 David Aunwill. V. 11015 (Flints) Gregory ap David Annwill ap Jevaun ap David. ibid 12678 Gregory ap David Annoill. CaernCR 55, Ieuan Anwill. AnglPleas 35, Hoell ap Res Annoyl. Lp Oswestry 168, David Annewill Egnon. Exch Pro James I. Index, Anwill, als Anwyll, 46, 231, 234, 235, 279. Cwtta Cyf. 8, John Anwyll. ibid 48, M'garet Wen al's Anwyll. Sannan, 1666, Gwena Williams uxor Johannis Anwyl. PRConway 1731, Maria fil Richardi Dantyth, ex uxore Janâ Anwyl. Bartrum (985-1215), 125, Gwyn Anwyl ap Gwaithfoed; Gwyn Anwyl ap Philip ap Hywel. JEG 83, Pedigree of the Anwyls of Caerwys, starting with Robert Anwyl, early eighteenth century down to Sir Edward Anwyl. ibid 320, Dolfriog, Nanmor, Anwyl family; Caer Ddafydd, Nanmor, Anwyl family. ibid 342, Parkia, Criccieth, Anwyl family.

SHROPSHIRE REGISTERS
Ruyton 78. 1803, Margaret Anwyl, d. of Robert S. Cumberbach and Elizabeth his wife (not the surname but as if it were a second christian name). St Mary's Shrewsbury, Index, Anwyll. St Chad's, Index, Anwell, Anwyl.

MODERN REGISTERS
Anwyl in every instance.
Monts, Llanbrynmair; Llanllwchhaearn; Newtown 3. Wrexham, Bersham South Ward. West Flints, Prestatyn North, East (B); Rhyl East (C 47); Rhyl East, Central (CA 48); Rhyl West (CC 50), Rhyl SE (CF 53), Dyserth, Rhuddlan, Caerwys, Picton.
The following example, West Gloucs, Tidenham 1. Anwell is probably a variant, and follows the examples above of the same form.

Anwill v. Annwyl
Apjohn v. Ieuan

Arawd, Arawdr
GPC gives *arawd* as a common noun, meaning 'prayer, religious poem', derived from L. *oratio*. It gives *arawdr* also as a common noun meaning 'orator', derived from L. *orator*. It is unusual to find common nouns of this kind being used as personal names, and there may be a different explanation; in the circumstances it will be best to quote examples and suspend judgement.
Madog ap Araud (1282) PWLMA 382, 383, 384, Arawdr ab Ieuan ab Gwilym; 384, Rhys ab Arawdr; ibid. William [or Gwilym] ab Arawdr; ibid. Rhys ab Gwilym ab Arawdr.

Arawn, Aron (Aaron)
Arawn occurs in the first story of the Four Branches of the Mabinogi as the name of the king of the Underworld. The locale of the story at the point where Arawn appears is Glyn Cuch; Cuch flows into the river Teifi, on the left bank, between Cenarth and Cardigan; most of the examples picked up are within fairly close range of this area, and although some examples have the spellings of the biblical Aaron, perhaps they should be associated with the name of the king in the story of Pwyll:
B10. 67, West W. 1352, Aaron ap Meredydd ap Philip, bedellus de Elved. 68, predictus Aaron; 72, Aron ap Meredith Duy. B13. 217, SR 1292, commote of Widigada, Aron ab Ener; BBStD 242, Will's ap Aron. PWLMA 402, Maredudd ap Rhys ab Aron, (1413, Widigada); 412, 413, Rhys ab Aron (1312, Widigada). Bartrum, 1215-1350, vol. 2. 205, Aron = ten examples. 1350-1415, ... Peredur ab Aron ... Aron ab Ednyfed; 838 – Ednyfed ab Aron.
The modern and contemporary instances of Aaron would appear to be the biblical name, with the same kind of frequency as Jacob, Miriam, Joseph, etc. It would be impossible to demonstrate a connexion with the medieval instances, that is to say, that the modern examples have their origin in the medieval usage. Needless to say, examples occur in early poetry and other texts, of the biblical Aaron, e.g. BBC 36. Aron a moesen; MA 377[a] 39, barf Aaron, 'Aaron's beard'.
Arnallt v. Arnold
Arnold, Barnold
Reaney has fifteen variants including Arnald

and Arnott. The former of these would account for the *Arnallt* found in pedigrees, and occasionally today as a man's christian name. HM i, 219 has the pedigree of the family of Arnold of Llanfihangel Crucorney, with Arnallt occurring frequently in the earlier generations. On p.259 Bradney has the pedigree of Arnold of the Hendre, and observes, 'The pedigree is noticeable in that the family was the last in the neighbourhood to use the ''ap'', adhering to the old Welsh style of nomenclature', and special mention is made of Arnold ap Arnold ... bapt. 5 Jan. 1739-40, living at Dorstone 1807. Cf. Bartrum (1215-1350) 477, Arnold ab Arnold ab Arnold.

Arthan, Arthen

G has early references to persons named *Arthan*, and others to persons named *Arthen*. B Tyw Pen 20, 3 names Arthen, King of Ceredigion, who died in 807; ibid 62, Henri ab Arthen, 1162. HM i, 338 has the pedigree of the descendants of Maenarch, Lord of Brycheiniog and this includes an Arthen ap Cynfyn. There is a place-name Glynarthen near Newcastle Emlyn, and JEG 4 has a place-name Trefarthen, Llanidan. Even if Arthan and Arthen were quite separate names it would in time be very difficult to keep them apart and no attempt is made here to keep them separate: B13. 227. SR 1292 Wronu ap Iuan ap Arthan. B10. 155. West W. 1352 Llewelyn ap Arthan.

The name Arthan appears to have survived in the English border counties: examples were picked up in the following places: Shrewsbury, Meole Brace; Oswestry, Ellesmere Rural Dudleston; Whittington; Prees – Whitchurch Rural; Nantwich, Chorlton; Chorlton – Cuddington; Malpas; East Flint, Halghton.

There was a fem. name *Arddun*; TYP 273-4 has two examples; the following example is quoted here because of the spelling:

CaernCR 136 Arddun [MS Arthyn] ferch Tudur Goch.

Arthur

Derived from L *Artorius*; v. TYP 274. The earliest Welsh poetry names Arthur, or an Arthur. Line 1242 of the Gododdin has the phrase 'even if he were Arthur' which implies that Arthur was a standard for comparing heroism; and in the Llywarch Hen poetry, CLlH 52, Arthur's young warriors are a model of bravery in battle. G gives early examples of adjectives derived from the name Arthur. TYP 276-277 quotes 20 separate references to Arthur from the works of the Court poets of the twelfth and thirteenth century. But, judging by the examples collected, it could not have been much in use: B5. 147, CaernSubsAcct 1293, dai ab arthur; adaf ap arthur; B6. 257, Lleyn Accts 1250, de Arthur. B7. 338, CaernSubs 1597, Arthuro ap Richard. MerLSR 81, Arthour Duy.

Note the early examples in Cumbria, ELS Cumberland, p.3. Graistok, John Arthor.

Ruyton 9. 1726, William s. of Hugh ap Arthur; 16. 1731, Eliz. ap Arthur. 37. 1754, Hugh ap Arthur. Selattyn, 22, 1570, Arthwr ap Richard, fidler; ibid. Arthur ap Roger. 35. 1589, Arthur ap Rhytherch ap Eignon.

Examples of *Arthur*, City of Chester, Chester AA, St John's Ward 1. *Arthure*, Monmouth, Llanfoist Fawr. *Arthurs*, CT Barrington; Chipping Camden – Lower; Eastleach; Longborough; Cirencester 1; Ciren. 6; Moreton-in-Marsh (several); *Arthars*, Bromsgrove, Redditch N.E.; Redditch S. Central. (As this spelling occurs more than once, in different places, it is not due to a printer's error.)

Athaf v. Adam

Athawes v. Adam

Atheo v. Adam

Atho v. Adam

B

Baagh *v.* Bach

Bach

If a count could be made this adjective meaning 'little' is the one that occurs oftenest in speech, for it not only connotes smallness in stature or quantity but expresses all kinds of feeling, ranging from endearment to contempt. The usages in North Wales and South Wales have one very marked difference. In South Wales speech, *bach* is normal, like most adjectives, retaining the radical when it follows a masculine noun and mutating after a feminine noun. In North Wales speech, *bach* remains unmutated when it follows a feminine noun.

The adj. *bach* is also different from most others in its usage after personal names. Despite the tendency, almost amounting to a rule in Modern Welsh, to use the lenited form of the adjective after a personal name, (masculine and feminine alike) *bach* following a personal name is the same as *bach* following a common noun, i.e. in South Wales, retaining the radical after a masculine name and mutating after a feminine; in North Wales, retaining the radical after masculine and feminine. [A few examples are to be found with a mutation after a masc. personal name as if *bach* followed the usage of other adjectives, but this is so unexpected that instinct forces us to look for an explanation. In some cases the apparent irregularity is a misreading or a miscopying, e.g. B15. 287 (Aberystwyth – Cardigan 14c) *Rhys vach Walter* is almost certainly an error for *vab*. In some examples it would not be unreasonable to suggest that *vach* is an abbreviation of *vachan*, very often the spelling (and the sound) of Fychan, *v.* the section on **Bychan** for examples. This is probably the explanation of

Lp Oswestry 157, Heredes Rise Vach. The other examples we have come across are: CalACW 197, Dafydd Fach; B23, Arundel Charters (Llinos Beverley Smith), reference is made p.158 to Ieuan ap Dafydd Fach; AnglPleas 25, Ievan Fagh, cf. ibid 35, Gruffith ap David ap Ieuan Bagh; ibid 48 . . . Ievan Bagh. Taking for granted that *Baugh* in origin is Bach, it is difficult to account for . . *Vaugh* in the following except by saying that it is due to some kind of error: PRClunbury 27. 1630, Edward Vaugh, who is probably the same person as Edward Baugh, occurring often about this time, e.g. 26. 1628, Edwardus Baugh.]

At first one expects to see the adj. mutating after a fem. name, e.g. HM i. 389 'Landowners etc. in Llanover in 1778', mentions 'Phillip Morgan for Elizabeth Vach'. When one comes across an example of the radical after the feminine name, it may be due to one of two things: it may be the NW usage of retaining the radical or it may be that the adjective or epithet has become a surname so that if the father is Bach, both his son and his daughter will be Bach: cf. CatAncDeeds 111, D.1219 Alice Bache (context Pembs Haver. Henry VIII); PRConway, 1578, Marrion Bache; Bartrum (1350-1415) 779, Efa Bach, f. Madog Ddu ap Gwyn; PRMelverley 9. 1738, . . . Hester Bâch of this p.

One need have no doubt that *Baugh* stands for what was *Bach*. The frequency of examples of *Baugh* in the Border counties would justify the surmise that *Baugh* came from Bach; but to make the surmise quite correct there are instances of entries in records in which a man is Bach in some and Baugh in others: PROswestry 87. 1582 . . . John Baugh Taelor. 89. 1582 Elenor vz John Baugh. 120.

1587 Thomas ap John als Baugh Taelor. 180.
1596 ... by the bodie of Lowrie vz John
Bauch tayler. 252. 1604 John Bach taylor.
495. 1633 Lowry ach Shone Bach.

Shrewsbury BR, p.11 under Bage, Baghe,
William of S. alias Gittins, s. Griffin ap
Yowkes (Juckes) of Welshpool, 1475. The
first person entered under this name (Bage,
Baghe), William Corvisor (alias Gittins)
1475, is the same person as the William
entered under *Baugh* (alias Gittins). [Records
and documents written outside Wales, e.g.
Exchequer Proceedings, show the same
orthographical variations: InvECP,
Merioneth, 29 ... Bach; 68. Pembs ...
Baghe; 150. Monts ... Baugh; 156. Monts
Bagh, 157. Baugh; 221. Monm, Buagh; 222.
Kevenbauche (place-name); Star CP 122.
Mont, Wm Bach, 219. Mon, Baugh; cf. also
WPortBooks 95, David ab Yevang-bage.]

Likewise entries in registers show the
equivalence of Batch and Bach, or put more
simply, that the Welsh *bach* came to be
pronounced *batch*:

PRHopton Castle, 36. 1722, Richard Bach,
Churchwarden = 38. 1730 Richd Batch =
39. 1735, Bach; ditto 40. 1736; 42. 1744. Cf.
also 55. 1768, Edward Batch ... of
Knighton. (The index of this volume gives
Bach, Bache, Batch as variants.)
PRMonk Hopton 18. 1762, Matthew Batch
= 24. 1791. Bache; ibid. 9. 1769, Francis and
Mary Batch = 16. 1755, Bache. PRCleobury
Mortimer, Index, Bache, Bach, Batch,
Batsh. PRBurford 73. 1664 ... Edward
Batch and Mary = 77. 1669, Edward Bach
and Mary. Cf. also D. Tel 4.9.80 Deaths,
Batch.

Another variant is Beach:
PRStanton Lacy, 160. 1762, Richd, s. of
Benjamin Bache and Betty ... 163. 1765,
Elizabeth d. of Benjn Beach and Betty. 165.
1768, John s. of Benjn Beach and Betty.
There are further entries of the baptism of
children up to Decima, and the surname is
Beach on each occasion, until 1778, p.182
when it becomes Bach again. The index puts
the forms Beech, Beach, etc. and Bache, Bach
all together. The register of Bitterley
illustrates the same equivalence of Bach,
Beech, Beach.

Early examples of attaching *bach* to
personal names:

B5. 146, CaernSubs 1293, dai bach. B6. 359,
Sheriff NW 1326, Tegwaret Bagh. B11. 60,
Court Broniarth 15c. Deio baz ap Deio ap
Ieuan. CAP 390, John Baagh. ADClun 24,
Rosser bach; 211, Huw ap Muric Bach.
RecCa. Index, Bach, Bache, Bagh. Glam
Cartae 1852, Thome Bache of Glynrotheney,
2020, Dio Bagh. DLancaster 109 (Skenfrith)
... vocatum tyre Lluelin Bache.

One can never be quite certain that the
epithet has become fixed as a sort of surname;
examples like the following show that the
attachment could be fairly loose: CaernQSR
222, William ap Robert alias Bach;
PROswestry 145. 1590, Owen ap David als
Bach. As *Bach* did not develop into a surname
amongst the Welsh-speaking population, one
may feel fairly sure that the children and
grandchildren in these two cases became
Roberts (or Probert) and Davies.

The chances of becoming a fixed surname
are far more likely in anglicised and partly
anglicised areas, PRCaerwent and Ll.
Discoed, Caerwent, 1591, Ieu'n Bagch;
1592, Wm John Bagch; Surveys GK 228.
1632, Nicholas Bennett, Wenllian Bach his
wiefe; 277. 1689, George Bach.

It should be stated that although *bach*
generally speaking is used to denote smallness
of stature, and/or to express endearment or
pity or contempt, it may in rare cases be used
to distinguish between father and son who
have the same name. This is usually done by
the other adjective meaning 'small', namely
bychan, but in the following, *bach* appears to
have this function:

B11. 60, Court Broniarth 15c. Deio baz ap
Deio ap Ieuan; Bartrum 1350-1415, 629,
Ieuan Bach ap Ieuan ap Einion Gethin.

The Shropshire registers have been used
above to show that *Bach, Batch, Beach* came
from *bach*, either as odd spellings or as changes
in pronouncing; *Bawghe* could be added to the
variations, from PRSidbury, 3. 1574, 4.
1576; cf. RadsSoc XXIV. 34, Norton,
Watkin ap Holl Baughe. It is hardly necessary
to quote any further from the registers merely
to show that the registers abound with
examples. It is possible that in some of the
cases quoted the *ch* may represent English tʃ,
i.e. the English names Ba(t)ch and *Beech*.

It would be tedious also if the notes were
reproduced of the places in the several

constituencies surveyed in which examples of *Bach, Bache, Baugh* were found. They are to be found in all constituencies, especially Salop and Ludlow. In Ludlow, Highley, *Bache* is found in abundance; in Wrekin, Dawley, *Baugh* occurs frequently, and throughout the constituency. It may be worth giving details concerning the few instances in Wales: Newport, Allt-yr-yn 2. *Bach*; Monmouth, Abergavenny, Castle & Priory, *Baugh*; West Flints, Rhyl South West (CD) *Bach*; Rhuddlan, ditto. One is tempted to believe that these are instances of the name returning to Wales from outside.

Bachan *v.* Bach

Bache *v.* Bach

Badarn

Star CP 115. Monm, Elizabeth: ... Eliz Badarn, late wife of Jno Evans of Llanfihangel Ystum Llywern. This appears to be the lenited form of Padarn, taken from the parish name, Llanbadarn.

Baddam, Badham *v.* Adam

Baddy *v.* Ade, Madog

Bage, Baghe *v.* Bach

Balch

This adjective has a range of meanings, 'fine, splendid, proud, arrogant, glad', but the predominant meaning is 'proud'. The following appear to be examples of *balch* fixed after the personal name:

B3. 151. NW Boroughs, Criccieth Castle 1295, Lewell' Walch. ADClun 140. David ap Iorwerth Valgh. CaernCR 76. Ieuan Vallagh (?).

The following may be examples:
PRFord 36, Balch, (single family, late 18th century). St Chad's, Index, Balch (Balsh), six entries. Shrewsbury BR Index, Balch, Balke – John of S., s. Thomas of Oswestry 1475. (two other entries).

PRESENT-DAY REGISTERS

Preseli, Goodwick, Balch; (Nevern, Morfa, Boalch).

Reaney gives *Balch, Baulch, Boalch* under Belch, and links the meanings of *belch*, '*eructatio*', and *stomach, pride, arrogance*. Welsh *balch* cannot be a borrowing from English into Welsh, because *balc'h* is found in Breton, and the cognate *balc* in Irish. It is quite possible, however, that some of the examples of *balch, Balch, Balsh* found in Wales are of English origin.

Baldwin

This Anglo-Norman name which is found in the Welsh name of Montgomery and the county of Montgomery, namely, *Trefaldwyn, Sir Drefaldwyn*, became *Maldwyn* in Welsh, and this form is often used as a rather stylish name for the county. Earlier in this century *Maldwyn* became a fairly popular christian name for boys.

It is worth recording that the name is found in the form of Bodwyn (Bodwen), which probably represents a natural pronunciation of Baldwin; CaernQSR 58, Baldewyn Wik; 64, Bodwyn Wyke; 128, Bowdwen Wyke; PRConway 1597, Hugo filius Davidi Bodwen.

Balsh *v.* Balch

Bandry *v.* Andrew

Bangor *v.* Introd. Place-names

Bardd

This noun, meaning 'bard, poet', generally mutated when fixed as an epithet after a pers. name. Ieuan Fardd, cf. ML, Index, various names of John Owen, 'sometimes called Ioan Fardd...'. It is also possible to use the def. art., e.g. a local example, Lewis y Bardd: AnglCourt 1346, 34, Dafydd ap Barthe. (= y bardd). MerLSR 34. Ithel Warth. (probably = Fardd). ADClun 23. David barth. Star CP 108. Monm, Ricd Jenkin als varthe; 218. Rads. Lambard Bard. B Yale 82. David Barth (? 84. David Birth, David Byrth).

Barnold *v.* Arnold

Barry

This name is generally the surname of Irish families, or of families whose ancestors have come over from Ireland. In the first place it was taken to Ireland by the Norman family of *de Barri*. The mistaken idea that the Norman family gave their name to Barry Island (in the present S. Glam.) is dealt with by Phillimore Pt.3, 307 and EANC 105; in fact it is the other way around. Phillimore points out that the name before the coming of the Normans was *Barren*, the final *n* being dropped as in other names adopted by the Normans. R.J. Thomas quotes the evidence of the most famous of the family, namely from Giraldus himself: and Lloyd, HW 423 note, has one sentence, to set it right.

It is well known that the de Barri Normans were amongst the most prominent of the invaders of Ireland – Gerald's own brothers,

Robert and Philip (*v.* above p. 30).
Barth, Barthe *v.* Bardd
Batch *v.* Bach
Batham, Battams *v.* Adam
Bathawes *v.* Adam
Bathewe *v.* Adam, Mathew
Batho *v.* Adam
Baugh *v.* Bach
Baughan, Baughn *v.* Bychan
Baulch *v.* Balch
Bawghe *v.* Bach
Baynham *v.* Einion
Beach *v.* Bach
Bealing, Bealy *v.* Belyn
Beavin *v.* Ieuan
Bedard, Bedart *v.* Edward
Bederd *v.* Edward
Bedding, Beddis *v.* Maredudd
Beddoe, Bedyn, Beddyn *v.* Maredudd
Bedward *v.* Edward
Beevers, Beevor *v.* Ifor
Bel, Bela, Beling, Belling, Bellyn *v.* Belyn
Belch *v.* Balch
Bellis, Bellison *v.* Elis
Belyn
G 55 gives a small number of early references to a Belyn who one infers from the poetry was a great military leader in the early period; he probably is the Belyn referred to in the earliest annals under the year 627: Belin moritur, Harl. 3859, Cy, IX, 157; *v.* also Lloyd, HW, 184 who treats him as a historical, not mythical, person; similarly, Phillimore, 550. There is no suggestion of a double *-l* in the early texts of the annals or of the poetry and one reads the name to rhyme with *telyn, celyn*; but later texts which have the name vary, sometimes it has a single *-l*, and sometimes double *-l*, as if it were the same as E *telling, dwelling*. There seems to be a tendency for the accented single *-l* in Welsh to become *-ll-* in English: *melyn* 'yellow' becomes *Melling*. Anyhow, the examples show that the name was in use; and after *ap* the initial *b*, naturally, would become *p*.
RecCa 91. Bellyn ap llowarch. B15. 43, AS 1406. Variant text (for . . . ap Blethin) = llewelyn ap Ieuan Belyn. ibid 54. Bellyn fr. eius. CaernHS 26. Bolde Rental: 36, Bellyn ap llin ap Atha; 44, ditto; CaernQSR 13. List of Jurors, Ric'us ap D'd ap Pellyn; Rys ap Lli' ap Gruff ap Pellyn; further examples of Pelyn and of Bellyn without *ap* preceding: 69,

Hoel ap John Bellyn; 225, ditto; R. ap R. ap Gruffydd Pelyn = 105 . . . Gruffydd ap Pellyn. PRConway 1606, Johnes ap dd ap Pelline, alis Jn Barker; 1620, ffoulke ap Wm Pellin. L & P 3, 1523, p.203, Grant to John ap Pellyn, Rhuthyn; 233, Grant to David Lloyd ap Pell. Rhuthyn. Bartrum 300-985, no examples; 1215-1350, 208, two; 1350-1415, fifteen.

[Bartrum 1350-1415 also has examples of Bela: 860, Gruffudd ap Bela ap Dafydd; 869, Bela ap Dafydd ap Iorwerth. One other source showing this form, InvECP 133, Katherine verch Rees ap Griffith ap Pella, Flints 1549. Does this represent an *-a* suffix, a sort of 'complement' of the *-yn* suffix? *v.* p.34. One also finds in Flints the form Bel (Bell): e.g. Bartrum 1350-1415 has three; cf. 526, Dafydd Anwyl ap Bel Llwyd; 767, Bel ap Tudur ap Belyn; 861, Dafydd ap Bel ap Tudur. InvECP again has this form, located in Flints: 116, 1533, Howell ap Bell ap Toly; 120, 1544, Griffith and Edward ap Bell Lloyd.]

SHROPSHIRE REGISTERS
These have many instances of names derived from *Belyn* (*Bellyn*): it is difficult to summarize the variations: the variation in some respects is due to the differing quality of single *-l* and the quality of double *-l* and the nature of the preceding vowel, and one expects forms which show the neutral quality of the vowel in the final syllable.
Pontesbury 290. 1728. William Belling, of West Felton p. (cf. 324. 1743 William Peling: the former's wife is Ann, the second is Jane; they are not the same William). 444. 1794 . . . Richard and Abigail Belins. 516. 1806 Ann Bellion (?)
Myddle, 269. 1793; 271. 1796, William and Elizabeth Bealing. 285. 1760 . . . Jane Belling. 285. 1762. . . . Elizabeth Billing; 286. 1767, Mary Billing. 289. 1779. Ann Balling; 290. 1781, Elizabeth Balling (?) [Note that this register has examples of Boyling: 290. 1783, William Boyling; 314. 1805, *v.* Iorwerth p.140 and Hypocoristic.]
Great Ness 231. 1809, William Belling, b. of Ruyton . . . Loetitia Belling. Fitz 4. 1570, John Bellon, p. St. Marie's Shrewsburie, chr. 30. 1676; Thomas Bealing . . . of this parish; 34. 1684; 35. 1687, ditto. 66. 1756; Mary d. of Thomas and Elizabeth Belin; 66. 1758; 67.

1760; similar entries. Ruyton (Marriage Reg.) 87. 1760, John Beling and Elizabeth Griffiths. 44. 1761. Anne d of John and Elizabeth Bealing; 51. 1775. Elizabeth Bealing. 55. 1763. John s. of John and Elizabeth Beling. 57. 1766 —— Beling. 60. 1770 —— Beling. 63. 1772. Thomas s. of John and Anne Beling, alias Bely. 66. 1777. John s. of John and Anne Bealy. 70. 1782. William s. of John and Sarah Beling. 72. 1785. Margaret d. of John and Sarah Belin. 73. 1788. Lettice d. of John and Sarah Bealing. 75. 1794. ... John and Sarah Bealin. 81. 1812. Sarah, d. of William and Alice Belling.

[If one assumes that the entries from 1763 to 1794 refer to the same John, it is difficult to explain the three different names of his wife: it would be less difficult if Elizabeth was Elizabeth Anne, or if Sarah was Sarah Anne.] Montford 22. 1682. ... Thomas and Mary Bellin of Ensdown. 74. 1753. twin sons of Thomas and Eliz. Bealing, strangers from Hordley p. Clive 32. 1783. Mary d. of Wm Bealing, by Eliz. 33. 1787. Will. Bealing a child, bur. 34. 1791. Thos. s. of Will. Belling, by Eliz. bap. Wem. 516. 1739. Elizabeth, d. of Laurance Bellinge and Jane. [The other entries for this family, Billinge, Bellingle, Bellingley.] St Chad's, Index, Belling (one family).

An example of Peling occurring in Pontesbury was quoted above; cf. Montford 93. 1772. Mary Pealin, of Forton.

PRESENT-DAY REGISTERS
Newport, Caerleon, *Bellin*. D. Tel 18.8.79. news item, name of chess champion, Robert Bellin.

Benbow
This E name, 'nickname for an archer', occurs in RecCa after *ap*, p.75 Tud' ap Penbow.

Benet v. Ednyfed
Bengough v. Pen—
Bengry, Bengrey v. Pen—
Beniams v. Einion
Bennayth v. Pennaeth
Bennet
This name, from L Benedictus and OFr Beneit etc., was, in Reaney's words 'a common christian name from the twelfth century'. Examples in Welsh texts and contexts are plentiful, especially in the

sixteenth century; as a forename and after *ap*, but rarely do we find examples of *ap -B-* giving *P-*.
CaernQSR. 3. Jonet v'ch Ho'l ap Benet; 69, Benet ap Hoell...; Johannam ap Benet ap Hoel; 136, Owen Bened; 197, Benet ap Rhys. InvECP 31. Merioneth 1553, Yevan ap Rese ap Bened; 85. Da ... ap Benett of Llanfair, co. Merioneth, ... son and heir of Bennett Owne (alias Smyth, 1538-). 89. Denbs 1538, Benett ap Ryse ap David. 92. Denbs 1547, Griffith ap Bened of Temple Brewer, co. Lincoln. 96. Denbs. 1551, Robert ap Rice ap Penet. 112. Flints. 1518, Bennet ap Even. Star CP 14. Flints. Edw. VI; Banett ap Dd [sic].

There is one example above of *ab -B* producing *ap Penet*; it is odd that examples of a surname *Pennet* are not found in the modern period. Possibly the late arrival and usage in Welsh kept the form Bennet, as if it were not to be treated as a native Welsh name. There is a possible merging, that of the noun *pennaeth* 'chief, overlord' used as an epithet after the personal name:
PWLMA 426, Dafydd ap Gwilym Bennyth. CAP 145, Hugh Bennaythe of Pembroke ... (twice). Editor quotes refs. to Richard Bennayth of Pembroke ... and Richard Hugh of Monkton *alias* Richard Benet, and this seems to be a definite example of *Benet* taking the place of ... Bennaeth, through the process of 'approximation' possibly.

Benneth v. Pennaeth
Benwyn v. Pen—
Bergam
Compound adj. *ber*, 'leg, shank', *cam* 'bent, not straight', i.e. 'bandy-legged'.
B4. 162. Ardudwy Court 1325. Adaf Bergam. ADClun 15. Lewelin bergam; 21, 24, 26, ditto; 27. nest bergam. ALMA 301. Y Bergam (this is found in *Mynegai i Farddoniaeth y Llawysgrifau*, 391-2).
MerLSR 57. Bergam; 65. Gron(ou) Bergam. BBStD 224. Agn fil Gweythbergam, trans. 224, Agnes d. of Gweythbergam; 226. Matild' relicta Gweythb'gam (= Gwehydd Bergam, 'Weaver the bandy legged').

Berna(r)d
Mention of this name is justified by the examples with *ap*.
Bartrum 1215-1350, 309. Hugh Goch ap Pernad: cross-ref. to Llywelyn ap Pernad on

p.886 of 1350-1415.

(The saint's name is Berned in the poems of Tudur Aled, GTA, IX.17, rhyming with Bened; XVII.44; XVII.55; 84, *cynghanedd*, Barnwyd – Berned.)

Berwyn, Berwen

The surname *Berwen* occurs in PRStokesay 140. 1772 *Edward Berwen* which may be the name of the mountain range, Berwyn.

There is one noted example of the place-name being adopted as surname. It was adopted by Richard Jones, 1836-1917, who was born in Glyndyfrdwy, Denbs, and who was amongst the first contingent of the Welsh settlement in Patagonia, 1865; he continued there as a prominent leader of the settlement. This new name was adopted when he went to Patagonia and its use, instead of Jones, was no doubt an assertion, and overt sign, of his nationalism.

Bettard *v.* Edward

Betthouse, Bettoe *v.* Maredudd

Bethall, Bethell *v.* Ithel

Bevan *v.* Ieuan

Bever *v.* Ifor

Bevin *v.* Ieuan

Beynon *v.* Einion

Bibbith *v.* Pibydd

Bidder

This English name is not given in Reaney. Its explanation is straightforward, the bidder being the person who had the function of going around the neighbourhood bidding people to come to a wedding feast or funeral wake. (T.M. Owen, *Welsh Folk Customs*, 159-63.) It is found as a surname in the Swansea area, especially amongst the English population of the Gower peninsula:

B22. 375. Gower 1590. Robert Bidder.

Surveys GK, p.13. Pennard, John Bydder, Robert Bydder, 201. Jenet Bidder; 319, Bydder.

The Ieuan 'Biddir' given in PWLMA 344, 346, is probably Bidder.

Binyon *v.* Einion

Biolin *v.* Iorwerth, Iolo

Birrian *v.* Urien

Bithell, Bythell *v.* Ithel

Blaen *v.* Blainey

Blaney *v.* Blainey

Blany, Blaynee *v.* Blainey

Blainey

Sir Ifor Williams identified *Blaen* as a personal

name occurring in the Gododdin poetry, CA 113; *blaen* as a common noun means 'front', and the ode commemorating Blaen has a play upon words, that he was always in the front line.

The personal name probably fell into disuse completely, and the name *Blainey* (from *Blaenau*) comes from the common noun. One of its meanings is the source of a river or brook, as in several place-names. The locality of the river source would be upland, so that *blaen*, and especially plural *blaenau*, came to mean upland, as compared with the lowland of the valley; it occurs in the singular preceding the river name, Blaengwynfi, Blaenafon, Blaengarw, in the plural when it means uplands, Blaenau (Blaina).

There are instances of *Blaen* being used after a personal name, as if to denote the place of origin or the residence, e.g. PWLMA 456, Dafydd Blaen; 466, Ieuan Blaen (1486, Reeves, Creuddyn); 454, 455, Llywelyn ab Ieuan Blaen (1413, Perfedd); 361, Rhys ab Ieuan Blaen (1421, Mabelfyw). The surname *Blainey* (*Blayney, Blaney*) seems in all but a few cases to have stemmed from the one family at and around Gregynog, Montgomeryshire, which began to adopt it as a residential surname in the fifteenth century: *v.* p.31 for the explanation of the introduction of the name to Ireland. The proliferation is set out in S.P. Thomas, 'Branches of the Blayney Family in the XVI and XVII centuries', *Montgomeryshire Collections* 64, 1976, pp.7-38; and ibid. 'A Postscript'; *Montgomeryshire Collections* 67, 1979, pp.91-108.

The name quite naturally is found in Tregynon, Monts; Star CP 199, James I, Tregynon, Aberhafesp: Thomas Blayney, Jno Blayney; but one finds it some distance away, e.g. RadsSoc VI.12, 1545 John Blany of Stepulton; XLI.64, 1392-3, Ieuan Blaynee; 66, Jeuan Blayne; HRads. 207, John Blayney, trustee of Presteign School 1569; InvECP 179, Rads. 1538, John Blayne(y) ... London, son and heir of D ap M Hoell Blayney. In the Shropshire PRs they are found in almost every parish, e.g. Hanwood 8. 1575, Blayne; Pontesbury 8, Gwen Blane; 495, Diana Blany. The registers of Ludlow have the following versions: Blainey, Blaney, Blayne, Blayney, Blainy, and there is a large entry of Blenney.

In present-day electoral registers the name is found in very many places; the spelling Blaynee occurs in Bromsgrove, Wythall South; South Worcs, Malvern West, No. 4 or West.

Bleany v. Blainey

Bleddyn

The earliest form is seen in LL, 33, (and 44) Trev Bledgint (= Glam Cartae 62, 72), the *d* stands for *dd* and the *g* (unless it is an orthographic fossil) stands for mutated *g* which later disappeared completely, to give Bleddynt. The texts of the twelfth and thirteenth century poetry quite often retain the final -t, but final unaccented *nt* is reduced to -*n(n)*, as in *ariant/arian*, and there are plenty of early instances of Bleddyn; v. G 58-9.

There are other names with *Bledd-* as first element, the most important for the purpose of this study is Bleddri since it has the -*ri* found in *Griffri, Tutri* etc. In the texts of LL there are other names with Bled(d)-, v. Index for *Bledbiu, Bledgur,* but *e* in Old Welsh orthography quite often stood for *ei*, and these names are *Bleiddfyw, Bleiddwr*. But quite separate from this deceptive orthography, there are names of this class which show that *Bledd-* is a variant of *blaidd* 'wolf', or the other way around, that the name *Bleiddyn (Blythin)* is a variant of *Bleddyn* – as the evidence below will show, *Blythin, Blything* is the predominant form in N.E. Wales.

In view of the prominence of the element 'wolf' in early naming systems, it is to be expected that *blaidd* should be found as an epithet or surname;

CaernHS 26. Bolde Rental p.49, Table of 'Gafaelion': Iarddur Blaidd; text editor quotes 1352 Extent, Yarthur Bleythe; Bolde Rental, Iarthur Blaythe. PWLMA 403, Ieuan ap Dafydd Blaidd (1439, attorney to Beadle, Widigada). CAP 271, the house of William Bleithe in Drosloun (= Dryslwyn). BBStD 30. Moruyth Bleyth; (hardly the English *blithe* and more likely to be connected with Wolfscastle and Casblaidd). Cf. MerLSR 15. Madoco Blyoth. (Could be bloedd = 'shout', but the text is full of examples of names of animals as nicknames). Examples of *Bleddyn, (Blethyn)* are plentiful in medieval texts:

MerLSR 53. Blethint Hagor, cf. Rec Ca283. Blethyn Hagyr (for hagr, 'ugly'). B13. 143

(Bonds for keeping peace 1295) Blethin ap Gryffyd. WPortBooks 7, John Blethyn (Cardiff); 42, Ambrose Blethine. HM i (Part 2), 208. William Blethyn of Shirenewton; iv. 16. Early entry in PRChepstow Mr. Blethine.

Examples of *ap-B* giving *Pleddyn, Plethyn:*

RecCa 246. Hona ap Plethyn (correct to Houa). BYale 58, Madoc ap Plethini; 142, Eigon ap Plethyn, Griff ap Pleth, Madoc ap Pleth. HM iii, 277. Llandegveth, List of debtors mentioned in a will 1542, John ap Plethin. InvECP 112, Flints 1518-29, Griffith ap Lethyn. 124, Flints 1547, Robert Plethyn. 126, Flints 1551, Thomas Plethen. CaernCR 16, Goronwy ap Bleddyn (*Pleth* in MS).

Examples of Bleiddyn

ADClun 20; 28, Bleythyn.

DLancaster (Caldicot 1613) 135, Willim Blethyn = 144, William Blythen. CaernCR 164, Ieuan ap Bleddyn (MS Plythin).

There is evidence from an early period of the -*dd*- becoming -*v*-, as in E *mother, muvver*; this change is better known in Welsh the other way around, *rhofio* 'to shovel' becoming *rhoddio* in W. Glam.

B26. 81. Blewynum Roth ab Madoc (Fragment, Roll. Edw. I. 1294-5). [Unless it is a scribal error for *Lewelynum*; as in Lewelynum ab Yereward ab Blewyn, ibid; but the second example makes it unlikely and it is probably 'Bleddyn' heard as Blefyn/Blevyn, with a bilabial 'v' sound.] Lp Oswestry 168. *Bleuin* ap Ieuan ap Iorwerth. (This text has a number of instances in which the *l* is *ll*, but they are of *Pleuin/ Plefyn*, and one example is obviously *Pleivyn*: 145, Meuric ap plle'yn; 153, Deikws ap plleuin; 154, David ap plleiuin; 155, Ricardum ap Morgraunt ap plleu'; Iewerth ap plleu', Morgraunt ap Ieuan ap plleu'; 156, Ierworth ap plleu'; 171, David ap pelluin. InvECP 99, Denbs 1551-3. Lewes ap John ap Blevyn. Glam Hearth Tax, Llanblethian, Bliven Ritherough. It is interesting to note that Llanblethian is Llanfleiddan in Welsh; cf. Glam Hearth Tax, Siginston, Thomas Blythyan, surname derived from the parish name, the *Llan-* element being omitted.

SHROPSHIRE REGISTERS

One expects the normal version in the diocese of St Asaph:

St Martin's, Index, 81. Ann Bleddyn; 335, Lydia Blethin. 2. Whittington 128. 1634.

Blothin ap John, of Daywell (mistake for Blethin).

One also expects to see the changes which are characteristic of the Border, the addition of the 's, the neutral quality of the final vowel; and the version in Stanton Lacy 15. 1584 Elenor Plevey should be compared with Belyn becoming Bely, Bealy in PRRuyton, above. Chelmarsh 4. 1566. Wm Plethen, of Acton Round. High Ercall 625. 1770. Edward Blythen. Acton Burnell 28. 1607. William s. of William Pleven, Joiner and Dorothy. Sheriffhales 176. 1776. ... Thomas and Elizabeth Plevins, of Shiffnal Pax. 209. 1799. John Plevin, bur. 222. 1807. Ann d. of John and Mary Plevin; 224. 1809. Margaret d. of John Plevin and Mary. 244. 1773 (Marriage Book) John Plevins. St Mary's Shrewsbury, Index, Plevens. St Chad's, Index, Blevin (several fairly early examples); Plevins (one).

PRESENT-DAY REGISTERS

One naturally finds the 'normal' form Blethyn, e.g. Newport (Gwent), Bettws 3; Preseli, Wiston-Walton East, and also, of course, the version that stands for the normal Bleiddyn, namely Blythin; for example, Runcorn, Kingsley. Taking all the variants together, one may say that the distribution is widespread although not dense. It is proposed here to give one instance of each variant form and its location:

Blythyn, West Flint, Ffynnongroyw. Blything, Leominster, Bromyard. Blythen, Denbs, Llanarmon-yn-Iâl. Blevin, Copeland, Harbour Ward, Blevins, Cardigan, Aberystwyth (student). Plevin, Workington, Cockermouth. Pleavin, Northwich, Waverton. Plevins. D. Tel 4.6.84, Deaths, Torquay.

Blethine, Blethyn v. Bleddyn
Bleven, Blevin v. Bleddyn
Bleyth v. Bleddyn
Blodwell (v. also Introd. Place-names).
An early example:
B13. 224 SR 1292. Oswaldestre, Yareword ab Madoc ab Blodewal.

The examples of *Blodwell* as a surname, found in the fifteenth century and later, come from the name of the parish *Llanyblodwell* which is on the Shropshire side of the border or from the mansion named Blodwell. It was given as an example of clergymen adopting the name of the parish as origin. HAsaph 318,

Deans of St Asaph 1418, John Blodwel, 'a native of Llanyblodwel'; 319, David Blodwell 'succeeded his kinsman'.

Star CP 167. James I. Denbs, Ricd Blodwell. PR Alberbury 205. 1671. John Blodwell Esqr; 233. 1680. Mrs Mary Blodwell. further example 439. Myddle 298. 1807. John and Margaret Blodwel. Oswestry 24. 1561. Richard ap John Blodwell.

Examples are still found in today's registers: Shrewsbury Column Portion; Stalybridge & Hyde, Dukinfield West; Stalybridge No. 1. Lancashire Ward Part 2; Dukinfield Ward, Part 1; Part 2, ditto; West Gloucs, Tidenham 1.; West Flint, Rhyl South East (CF 53); East Flint, Mancot and Moor.

Blythin(g) v. Bleddyn
Bobydd, Bobyth v. Pobydd
Bodvel v. Introd. Place-names
Bodwen v. Baldwyn
Bodwrda v. Introd. Place-names
Bodwyn v. Baldwyn
Bolch v. Balch
Boliver v. Oliver
Bolver v. Oliver
Bollen, Bollin(g) v. Iorwerth
Boly, Bol, Bola (Bwl, Boul, Bool)
The word for 'belly, stomach' is derived from Britt. *bolg*-; the mutated *g* sound became a sort of half vowel indicated by the form *boly* in med W; this vocalic sound disappeared to give *bol* in NW speech; in SW it grew into a proper vowel; the same development is seen in the variants *dal, dala, hel, hela*:

B13. 223. SR 1292. Lewelyn Bola; 229. Ythel Bola. B5. 56. Lleyn late 13c., Eynion boly; 71. jok' bol. B15. 45. AS 1406. Mad ap y boly; 59. Ho(we)ll ap Jor Bol. ADClun 40. David vola; 94, David Bola; 122. Griffit ap Howel Bola. CatAncDeeds III. c. 3473. John Bola, burgess of Bala. (*temp.* Henry V). DLancaster 263 (Kidwelly) Thomas ap Gwilim Bola. PWLMA 336, 337, 338, 349. John Bernard Bola; 510. Gruffydd Fola. 289. Gwydion Bola. (1308, Beadles, Carms).

The following compound is *bol-lydan*, 'broad bellied':
CaernCR 15. Einion Bolledan.

There are examples of *bole* which are uncertain because they may well be the E Bull, Bulle, Bool, Boole, given in Reaney; it is certain that some of the following represent one or other of the versions:

B13. 228. SR 1292. Wasmer Bul, Dauid Bul. (Cf. 228. Iuan Vechan Penbul; *v.* penbwl, p.176). B15. 52. AS 1406, Dd ap Mad. bwl. B24. 189. Fasti Cist. Camb. Meredith Bool, 1336-8. B15. 49. AS 1406, Kyn Bole (?); 50, Mad Bole de Penrhos. BBStD 38. Wal(ter)us Bole; 130, Adam Bole, 300, Walt(er)i Bole (amongst names completely non-Welsh); 318, Lewel' Boul. ADClun 154, Philip *Poul* (p + b > p -p). Lp Oswestry 153 (Extenta 1393) Bole ap Hoell. Star CP 82. Glam. Lln ap Rees Bool. PWLMA 382, 388. Maredudd Boule ap Gwallter.

The following has a nickname quality:

Lp Oswestry 162. Boly Pees; (twice) occurring also in Gwely Boly Pees (BP's Holding), i.e. Peas-belly, can it possibly correspond to *Peasecod*?

The following example represents *bola-haul*, a place-name (literally 'sun's belly') meaning a place in a very sunny position; *bolaheulo* means 'to bask in the sun, sunbathe':

B13. 229, SR 1292. Lewelinus Bolahalle.

Bôn-compounds

Bôn means 'the base, lower part, bottom part, stump', and 'rump': there is a tendency to interpret *bôn* in compounds as if it applied only to the 'legs', for instance, that 'bongam' means 'bandy-legged'. The compound *bondew* with *tew* 'fat, thick' would be more suitably applied to the 'bottom', and it is possible that *bongam* meant 'stooped'.

B2. 52. West W. 1301, David Bongam. B13. 218. SR 1292, John Bongan. (? *n* and *m* interchangeable). B15. 47. AS 1406, Ho[we]ll ap gron ap Bongam. 54. Je(uan) ap y Bongam; 296. David Bougam (surely Bongam). ADClun 12. Ieuan ap Adaf vongam; 13. Lewelin bongam; 20. Adaf vongam (twice); further examples 125, 139. Lp Oswestry 161. Edwardum Vougam (read *n* for *u*).

In the following it is not certain whether the epithet is part of the 'surname': PRHopton Castle 3. 1563. John Williams, Bongam and Maud Williams.

Example of *bondew*: RecCa 70. Joz duy Bontew.

Example of Bonwen

CaernCR 70. Dafydd ap y Fonwen.

It is difficult to find a meaning for 'y Fonwen' and one may ask whether the above is a mistake for *bronwen*, 'weasel', used as a nickname.

Bona

An example of this surname is to be found in BrRads Vaynor-North. Although not of Welsh origin, it has been in Wales at least since the early eighteenth century. William Bona, (baptised Llanpumsaint, June 25, 1715) was a local poet, and better known as a collector and copyist of MSS. The parish records show clearly that the name is an abbreviation of Bonaventure, and that this complete form was quite popular in the parish in the eighteenth century. Garfield Hughes, *Iaco ap Dewi* 43. Cf. also Western Mail, July 2, 1980, Deaths, Gwladys Bona ... Port Talbot.

Bonaventure *v.* Bona

Bondraw *v.* Andrew

Bonner *v.* Ynyr

Bonnell

The place-name Bonvilston contains the name of Simon de Bonville; the Welsh name of the place contains the christian name, Tresimwn. The surname dealt with in this para. is probably not connected with the place; the surname is located in the Kidwelly region, and the Norman castle of Kidwelly may be a sufficient explanation.

DLancaster 202 (Kidwelly) William John David Bonvill; 214, Richard John Bonvill and John Richard Bonvill. Cf. later example: William Bonville (the name of the coroner in the inquest into the death of the Keeper of Hendy Tollgate). Pat Molloy, *And they blessed Rebecca*, p.242.

The name *Bonnell* occurs in the Penbre-Llanelli area and the locale suggests an identity of Bonvill(e) and Bonnell.

Bonvill *v.* Bonnell

Bool, Boul *v.* Bol.

Bougham, Boughan *v.* Bychan

Bowen *v.* Owain

Boylin, Boyling *v.* Iorwerth, Iolo

Brace *v.* Bras

Brangwyn

This name, although rare, is well known as the name of the painter Frank Brangwyn. His biographer states, p.1, 'his father belonged to an Anglo-Welsh family living in Buckinghamshire', and the footnote on p.3 tells us that the uncle, Noah, spelt the name

'Brangwin', Walter Shaw-Taylor, *Frank Brangwyn and his Work*, London 1915). Cf. the following examples:

B13. 216, SR 1292, paid at 'Bergauenny', John Brangweyn. Western Mail, Deaths, 11.9.78, Brangwynne. (Llantwit Faerdre). Cardigan Elect. Roll, Llanarth Mydroilyn, Brangwyn; (Aberarth, Brongwyn.)

Brangwyn occurs in Port Eynon, Gower, it is also found in D. Tel 24.3.84, Deaths, Folkestone.

We have been supplied with many early references to a place-name by Professor Gwynedd Pierce:

1254, Brengwein, Val. Norwich 317 (Green, Notes 157). *c.* 1291, Brangwayn, Taxatio 281. 1312-13, Brangwayne (alias Bryngweyn) 1 PM. v. 232. *c.* 1348, Brangwayn LL 320. 1349, Bryngwyn 1 PM IX. 124.

Professor Pierce believes that all these variants refer to Bryngwyn, the place, the parish and the manor described by Bradney, HM ii (Pt. 1), 103-110. One could add to the above the various references to the parish of Bryngwyn in Radnorshire, RadsSoc. VII, 14, 1651, psh of Bringwin, co. Radnor; 30, Bringwyn and Clyro; XXVII. 28, Chancery Proc. Brongwyn and Clirowe, co. Radnor; XLV. 53, Parish of Bryngwyn; XLVI. 46, Misc. Recs of 16c., Bryngweyn; 47, ditto; InvECP 187, Rads. Richard . . . parson of Bryndgwen; RCA 173, Rads. p . . . of Brengweyn; 519, Bringwyn; 526, Brongwin. There is good reason for thinking that the surname has its origin in a place-name, in Gwent or in Radnorshire.

Bras, Brace

Bras has a wide range of meanings but the dominant meaning is 'stout, thick, fat', and this is the meaning when it is attached as an epithet to a personal name. It is generally used in the mutated form but some texts retain the radical.

B13. 216. SR 1292. John Bras; 227. Maddoc Bras. B24. 191. Fasti Cist. Camb. Adam Vras, – 1240 abbot Valle Crucis. AnglCourt 1346 37. Ithel ab Adda Fras.

In compounds: the name of the poet *Dafydd Benfras*. Bartrum 1250-1415, 572, . . . ap Gruffudd Fraslwyd. ('fat and brown haired'). ML I. 393. Gwilym Rwydd-fras (made-up epithet for William Morris, 'easy going and fat').

One presumes that the surname *Brace* is a surviving version of *bras* as a fixed epithet. Its distribution is curious: in West Gloucs, Dymock, one finds many; and in Staunton-Newent Rural; in Wales, one finds occasional examples in Glam; or in places such as Crickhowell; the only area in which the numbers are large and widespread is South Pembs: Examples were collected in thirteen wards; in Carew there are 16; in the two Tenby wards, a total of 57. Because of this one had to ask at first whether *Brace* had another origin, but these doubts can be dismissed for it is consistent with other names characteristic of English-speaking S.Pembs, i.e. ancient names like Meilyr, Gwythyr, Gwriad, Gwgawn etc. surviving there, although obsolete in Welsh-speaking Wales.

Brecknock, Brecknockshire, Brecon *v.* Brychan

Breeze *v.* Rhys

Breiddin, Breithin, Breithen

Lp Oswestry 108. Survey 1586. Ed. Breiddin. The following surnames occur in the Shropshire registers:

Pontesbury 280. Breithen. Myddle 186. 1734. Elizabeth d. of Adam and Elizabeth Breithin. 235. 1764. Elizabeth Breethen. Great Ness 185. 1788. John s. of Thomas Brethen. Wem 712. 1756. Roger Breathen, p. Preston Gubbalds. (Index gives: Breathen, Brathen, Breathing, Brethin.)

PRESENT-DAY REGISTERS

Knutsford, Church Lawton, Breathen; Congleton-Smallwood, ditto. These various forms represent the name of the Breiddin hills, inside the Welsh border, no great distance from Shrewsbury. The locations of the examples make *Breiddin* an obvious explanation.

Brethen *v.* Breiddin

Bretherick *v.* Rhydderch

Brethyn *v.* Breiddin

Brice *v.* Rhys

Brobin, Brobyn *v.* Robert

Brochfael

In OW orthography it is written Brocmayl (in the pedigrees in Harley, 3859, XXII), Brochmail (in LL 272): these forms represent Brochfael, as in Taliesin's poem to Kynan, CT I.; line 15 calls Kynan, Mab brochfael brolet, son of B. (ruler of) large kingdom. Ifor Williams in CT XV-XVIII deals with

Brochfael, with the form of the name, and with the personage. It passed through the stage of Brochfel to give Brochwel, and for comparison, Llandderwfael giving Llandderfel; Cil-mael giving Cilmel (= Kinmel), Dinmael, Dinmel. The land ruled by Brochfael Ysgithrog was in the seventh century the Powys not only of Montgomeryshire but a far bigger kingdom stretching east and it is not an unreasonable assumption that before Wales and the old Northern kingdom were separated, the kingdom of Brochfael reached beyond Cheshire to include parts of Lancashire.

The name occurs occasionally in the medieval period: RecCa 65, 66, Brogwell ap Griffri; 54, Ph' ap Roghwell. B10. 158, AnglCrown Rental, text editor's introduction refers to 'gwely Vrochwel ap Gryffri'. Bartrum, 300-985, Brochwel, eight examples.

In the Shropshire registers we find the following: Oswestry 308. 1610, Robert filius Brochwell Lloyd de Llay, bap. Kinnerley 224, 1783, My Brochall. The following from the Oswestry register look like versions of Brochwel/Brochall: 86. 1582. Alyn the base sonne of Fraunces Broche'. 89. 1582. Elizabeth vz Thomas Brocher. 117. 1587. John Brochawe corrisr [sic].

Brochwel v. Brochfael
Brodrick v. Rhydderch
Brotherhood v. Rhydderch
Brotheroe v. Rhydderch
Brotherwood v. Rhydderch
Broughton v. Introd. Place-names
Brute
Name not in Reaney, but cf. B2.248, Charters of Brecon, amongst the witnesses of (1) Charter of Henry V, *Johanne le Brut*; OG 109-10 Walter Brut, a Lollard supporter of Owain Glyndŵr, a landowner at Lyde near Hereford, but who claimed (in 1393) both his parents were Welsh. The name is found in the following places: S. Hereford TD Whitchurch; Brecon-Rads, Llanfihangel Ystradyw; Llangenny, Llanddety Dyffryn Crawnon; Newport Malpas 3; Monmouth-Abergavenny, Cantref and Grofield; and there is a 'Brutes Row' in Torfaen, Blaenavon.

Finding a satisfactory origin is difficult, but it may in origin have meant 'rough' or 'gross' rather than 'brutish'. The consonant -t- is evidence against a Welsh origin. The surname seems to have a contInuous existence in Breconshire from an early period onwards.
Bryce v. Rhys
Brych
Brych, fem. *brech*, adj. 'speckled, freckled', the examples occurring in *brech, bregh* are not necessarily the fem. but just the use of *e* for *y*. CA 977 (p.39), dyuynwal vrych. (= Dyfnwal Frych) B13. 221. SR 1292. Madoc ab Bregh .. David ab Bregh. (One does not expect to find the adj. after *ab* unless the adj. has def. art.; and this may be an abbr. of Brychan.) 229. Taxed in Cilgerran : Kediuor ap David Brech. Mer LSR 53. Kenuric map Brek. Caern CR 50. Madog Frych [MS Vregh]. ALMA 231. Edward Hughes signs p.s. to letter, 'Iorwerth Frych'. Bartrum 1215-1350. 314. Ieuan ap y Brych Cadarn.
Examples of *brych* in a two adj. compound: B23. 166. Arundel Charters, Chirk 14c. Einion ap y Moelfrych ('bald-speckled', possibly in origin the name of a cow or bull).

L'Estrange Ewen 124-5 includes *voylvrych* in list of W surnames found in documents in PRO.

SHROPSHIRE REGISTERS
Selattyn 40. 1594. John ap David Vrych. (Footnote, i.e. freckled.) Oswestry 40. 1564. David Vrych. 189, 1657. John David Vrygh a beggar.

We have found no recent example of a name which could be regarded as a version of *brych*.
Brychan,   Brecon,   Brecknock, Brecknockshire
The names of the town and of the former county come from the name of the fifth century saint and ruler *Brychan*; -*iog* was one of the suffixes used when a territory was named after its ruler; as in Tudwal, Tudweiliog; Rhufawn, Rhufoniog; the suffix caused vowel affection to the vowel -*a*, hence Brycheiniog: the English version Brecknock is a corrupt form of Brycheiniog: Brecknockshire and Breconshire have both been in use for the former county.

Early instance of *Braghan*, probably representing Brecon town:
B13. 225. SR 1292. At Sweynssaye, jurors ... Nicholas Braghan. Cf. InvECP 151.

Monts 1551 ... late of William Brekenock. PRShipton 12. 1577. Jacobi Brecknocke. Hughley 15. 1667. Robert Breaknot, of Didlebury. Clunbury 41. 1644. Elianor Brecknocke of Clunton. Neenton 33, 34, 37, 38, 39. Breakneck on p.39; the others, Brecknock. Stanton Lacy 3. 1561, Thomas Brecknock.

PRESENT DAY REGISTERS

Shropshire 1959. Shrewsbury, Albrighton, Breckon. Wirral, Whitby Ward; Irby and Thursteston, Breckon. CT Tewkesbury 1. Brokenshire (several; not a misprint). Monmouth. Wyesham, ditto.

Brumor v. Brynmore

Brunker v. Introd. Place-names

Brymor v. Brynmor

Brynker v. Introd. Place-names

Brynmor, Brymor

PRConway 1706. Joannes Williams de Brymor Armiger; cf. p.362, Inscription – John Williams of Brymor, Esq. 4th son of Sr Griff Williams of Penrhyn, Baronet. This seems to be the explanation of Brumor, Brumore, 1557, 1559, Brymore, 1589. JEG 186. Cochwillan and Llandegai. The Williams family: John Williams = Gaynor, 'had Brynmor, ob. July 25, 1706, aged 63, s.p.'

The origin, quite obviously, is the residential name *Brynmawr*: with the accent on the penult. this becomes *Brẏnmor*. The *nm* in natural speech cannot be kept distinct, and the name which became fairly common as a boy's christian name during the present century, is generally pronounced 'Brymor', v. p.31.

Buach v. Bach

Bugail

This is the usual W word for *shepherd* or *neatherd*; an early example as epithet is BBStD 23, Ieuan Bugeil. L'Estrange Ewen 125 includes *Bugel* in the list of Welsh surnames found in documents in PRO.

Bumffrey, Bumphrey v. Humphrey

Bunner v. Ynyr

Bunnion, Bunyan, Bunyon v. Einion

Burian v. Urien

Bychan, fem. Bechan (Vaughan etc.)

Because of its meaning or function, of distinguishing between the father and the son who had the same name, this epithet occurs very frequently, so that in the vast number of instances one is bound to find a variety of spellings in the documents written by scribes not within the Welsh tradition. The standard form, mutated after a personal name, should be *Fychan* (i.e. *Vychan*); the 'unclear' vowel *y* may become *a*, sometimes *o*, sometimes *i*, and oftenest of all, it is represented as *au* in the anglicised version *Vaughan*. In early texts one must be prepared to find *w* for the initial *f* or *u*. There may also be examples of using the radical (i.e. unmutated) form *Bychan*, probably arising from a self-conscious act and the knowledge that the original or 'correct' version of the adj. had *b*, and this sort of restoration probably accounts for *Baughan* (v. pp.59, 60 below). The *ch* sound is expressed in ways that appear odd to us who have become inured to the standard form.

The variations described above are largely matters of orthography, but there are others which come about through sound changes in natural speech. The examples of *-am* (instead of *-an*) are not errors; this change of final *n* into *m* was fairly common in the med period, e.g. *Mawdlam* in Glam for *Mawdlan/Magdalen*. The particle *ab*, *ap* is an obvious example of the loss of initial *f* (*u*), in a word that is unaccented and treated as a proclitic, just like the possessive pron. *fy* (from *my* originally) becoming '*y* in ordinary speech. In the same way, *Fychan* may lose the initial *f* (or *v*) and become '*Ychan*. In the writers' SW dialect *bachan* is used instead of the noun *bachgen*, 'boy', and this, in the vocative, is generally '*achan*. These two changes can produce *Ychan, Ichan, Icham, Igham, Eghan*, as will be seen below.

The other change arises from the English orthography and allowing the spelling to decide the pronunciation. The *gh* in the first place is meant to express the sound of *ch*; but the *gh* of English words had become 'silent' (if not changed to *ff*): if one makes the *gh* of disyllabic *Vaughan* silent, it will be difficult to keep *Vau-an* disyllabic and the word naturally contracts into a monosyllable with a long vowel to make up for the two half-length vowels, just as *Lacharn*, (from Talacharn), spelt Laugharne, came to be pronounced 'Larne' with long vowel.

Examples showing son and father bearing the same name:
B4. 159. Ardudwy Court 1325. Guyn Vaghan ap Guyn. B10. 145. West W. 1352.

Iorwerth Vaghaun ap Iorwerth ap Gurgan = ibid 261. I. Vichan ap I. ap G. B23. 342. Mawddwy Court 1415, Res Vaughan ap Res Vonge. (early ex. of Vaughan). HBr 439. David Ychan ap David y Rhingyll. PWLMA, Index, under 'Ieuan-ab-Ieuan', eight examples requiring *Fychan* after the son's name, to distinguish between him and his father.

In the genealogies one sees examples of father, son and grandson with the same name, and in some, epithets other than *Fychan* being used, for instance, *Leiaf* 'smallest' for the grandson, where the father has 'Fychan', *hen* for the father. Bartrum 1215-1350, 211. Cadwgon Leia ap Cadwgon Fychan ab Cadwgon. 220. Dafydd Fychan ab Dafydd Deg ap Dafydd Fras. 220. Dafydd Leia ap Dafydd Fychan ap Dafydd Ddu. 390. Maredudd Fychan ab yr Hen Faredudd ap Hywel. 1350-1415, 812. Roger Vaughan ap Roger Hen ap Gwallter Sais. Dwnn 1. 16, Kiliau Aeron . . . ap Kydwgan o Garog ap Kydwgan vychan ap Kydwgan vawr . . . .

Selected examples to illustrate various forms of spelling: B13. 216, SR 1292. Phillip ap Adam Waghan; Gorgeneu Vaghan. 226. Iuan vochan ap Donewal. 228. Iuan Vachan; Iuan ap Iuor Vochan. B15. 140. NW Edw. I. Yereward Vahham. AnglPleas 34. T. Wyn ap Gruffith Vichan. InvECP 149, Monts 1551, David John Ychan = 150. 1551. David ap John Vaughan. ibid. 151. Monts, David ap Meredith Vauzan . . . of the demise of John ap Howell Vawzan. ibid. 186. Rads. Walter Vahan. ibid. 229. Monm 1538, Howell John Veghan son of John Veghan. ibid. 254. Marches. Richard Voghan, Knight; Thomas Voghan, Esquire.

Examples of final n as m:
Cf. the following, in addition to those in the quotations above:
B10. 139. West W. 1352, Griffith ap Res Boughan . . . Bougham; ibid. 141. Boughan . . . Boughaum; 142. Boughaum. InvECP 28. Merioneth, 1533 John ap Hoell Vagham. 54. Carms 1547 Owen ap Thomas ap Gwallter Icham . . . Lleyke Igham (cf. 54. gwenlliam). ibid. 257. Marches, Hugh ap John Vaughen (Igham). HM i, 296. Llanvapley '. . . late of John Richard John

Egham. 440. Llanover. A Bill of Complaint 1616 mentions William Rosser David Egham. Surveys GK 104. 1583. Johes Tho Jo(n) Ychom senior et Thomas Jo(n) Ychom. Examples in addition to those occurring above of omission of initial *f*:
B10. 87. Kemes Pembs Phe Dd ap Ieuan Ychan. B25. 202. Lands Earl of Worcester 1530. Rogeri William ap Ieuane David Egane. ibid. 329. Lands Earl of Worcester 1530. Morgan Thomas Llewelyn Eghan. CatAncDeeds III. D.980. Carms temp. Henry VII. Philip ap David Ychan. MLSW 132. Llywelyn Hechan ap Morgan. InvECP 55. Carms 1551. Rice Yghaun ap Morgan. 73. Pembs 1556. Even yghan, David ap Ieuan llwyd yghan. HM i, 378-9. Llanover. 'Court' records 1544 mentions Phe' Ieuan Ychan. Footnote 'Eghan is one of the forms in which Fychan, the younger or junior appears. It is often written Ychan'. PRCaerwent and Ll. Disc., Caerwent 1569. Thomas Oughan.

Examples of restoring the radical Bychan:
When the adj. is used instead of the proper name itself, it requires the def. art. for it means 'the younger one'; and as it stands for a masc. noun, it retains the radical consonant. The examples of this paragraph are of using *Bychan* unmutated, contrary to general usage, when it follows the personal name. In addition to the example above, from B10. 139, cf. the following:
B25. Lands Earl of Worcester, Index of persons 334. John Boghan, Bohane. DLancaster 231 (Kidwelly) Thomas Willim David Bivan Bichan. PWLMA 480. Ieuan Du Bychan. 455. Y Moeth ap Ieuan Bychan. After fem names the form 'fechan' is to be expected:
Bartrum 1350-1415. 757. Angharad Fechan f. Hywel . . . 773. Dyddgu Fechan f. Ieuan.

SHROPSHIRE REGISTERS
The registers reproduce the variety and confusion of the analysis above. In the St Asaph parishes one is not surprised to find examples of the original usage, of distinguishing son from father:
Whittington 105. 1618. Edward ap Edward alias Edward Vaughan, of Ebnall and one expects to see the fem. form used correctly: ibid. 124. 1631. Lowry verch John, widow, alias Lowry Vechan, of Fernhill. bur.

Oswestry 490. 1632. Elin Vechen vid. (fem. form with touch of dialect).

In conveying the variety of spelling, it would be unreasonable to give more than one specimen of each kind:

Shipton 10. 1573. Vahan. Hopton Castle. Index. Vaughan, several, with Voane as one variant. Neenton 3. Vahane. Billingsley Voughan (several). Alberbury 86. 1623, Vahanne. Cleobury Mortimer 60. 1651. Vahon; 134. 1708. Voughon; 143. 1702. Vauhon. Pontesbury 20. 1561. Vauchan. Burford 198. 1784. Vaughn. Smethcote 24. 1702. Vohan. Myddle 4. 1544. Vachan. 24. 1570. Vaugham. Wroxeter 129. 1773. Vaghen, Vaughen. St Mary's Shrewsbury, Index, Under *Goures*, there is an 'alias Vawn'. Examples of retaining the radical: Ludlow 2. 1561. Johan Baugham; 585. 1697. Anne Baugham. Edgmond 3. 1671. Baughan; 4. 1672. ditto. The example above from Ludlow 2. 1561 has final *m* for *n*; cf. Whittington 81. 1637 ... Bangham = 85. 1640. Baughan.

Collecting examples of *Vaughan* from modern registers was unnecessary; the following examples of the unmutated version perpetuate the form quoted above:

Baughn, in CT Cirencester 3; Baughan, in City of Hereford, St Nicholas; Stroud, Minchinhampton-Brimscombe.

Byddar

Adj. 'deaf'; pl. byddair.

B15. 57. AS 1406. Je(uan) Saer byddar. PRSelattyn 156. 1660. Margaret verch Hugh, w. of Ellis fyddar. PRLlCrossenny & Penrhos 2. 1611. Anna, filia Joh'n ap John vyddar.

Bynner *v.* Ynyr

Byollin *v.* Iorwerth

Byrgam *v.* Bergam

Byr

The usual adj. for 'short'; fem. ber; the vowel is short.

B5. 61. Lleyn Subs. late 13th century : Kenric vyr. B15. 290. Aberystwyth-Cardigan, 14th century : David Vir. MerLSR 83. Ieuan Byr. BYale 140. Eden Bir. PWLMA 466. Gruffydd ab Ieuan ap Llywelyn Fyr. (1462, Reeves, Cardigan). ibid. Huw Llwyd Fyr (poem of). Dwnn 1. 17 ... ap Gruffydd Sais ap Llewelyn vyrr ap Howel ...

The compound *byrgyff*, not in GPC, appears to be simply *byr* and *cyff* (from L *cippus*), the main meaning of which is 'tree trunk, stump'; applied to a person, it must have meant 'short-legged'; the usual order is noun + adj., but there are examples of the order adj. + noun, e.g. hirgoes, hirben.

MerLSR 71. *Birgif*. (with no personal name preceding). B10. 165. AnglRental 16th century : dros dir dd ap dd ap *y byrgryff* (? correct to *byrgyff*).

The other compound, *byrgoch*, seems to mean 'short (bodied) and red (haired)':

B2. 64. West W. 1401. Griffith Birgogh ... Gruffith Birgogh = the same person as PWLMA 484, 544. G. Byrgoch; JEG 223. Madog ap Gruffydd Virgôch.

C

Cadarn (Cadhaearn, Cateyrn)
There are a few examples of the adj. *cadarn*
'strong' after the personal name:
B15. 47. AS 1406. Ken' ap Je(uan) gadarn.
InvECP 8. 1551 – Anglesey, Tythyn Eygon
Gadarn. Bartrum 985-1250. 98. Cynddelw
Gadarn; 158. Môr ap Cynddelw Gadarn.
1215-1350. 314. Ieuan ap y Brych Cadarn;
315. Ieuan Gadarn ap ...; 1215-1350. 474.
Hawis Gadarn. HM iv, 136. Caerwent 1337,
license granted. ... witnesses ... John
Kadarne. B3. 32 (GPJ) Efrog Gadarn, ...
Hawys G. temp. Ed. II.
In spite of the unusual spelling, the following
seems to be for 'Gadarn':
MLSW 1415-1536, p.89, Johannis ap Ieuan
ap Llywelyn Gedorne. In the following the
editor may have standardized the original
version, ibid 211, Ieuan Vachan ap Ieuan
Gadarn.

It is fairly certain that the above are the adj.
cadarn; in spite of the early Caerwent instance,
it was normal to mutate. Present-day
examples are rare, Islwyn, Tŷ-isaf, Risca
South, *Gaddarn*; and one may include *James
Gaddarn* who is a well-known orchestral
conductor, cf. D. Tel 13.7.84, Deaths, Allen
Gaddarn Bowling, Llanreath, Pembroke
Dock. There are doubts concerning the
following for they may not be forms of the
adj.: BBStD 23. *Walt(er)us Cader(n)*; 26.
Joh(ann)es Cader(n).

G has no example of *Cadhaearn* in early
poetry, and the texts that provide examples of
Trahaearn have none which are indisputable.
Bartrum 985-1215, 95 has, *Cathaearn ab Blaidd
ap Elfarch*, [in the Bennett Pedigree Book,
Ped. no. 79, this is *Cathaiarn Vlaidh*] and
Cathaearn ap Gweirydd ap Rhys Goch, and the
following look to be examples:
RecCa 68. *Catharn ap Ken'*; 60. *Hoell ap
Cathayran*.

The only area which has examples that appear
to be forms of *Cadhaearn* is Prendergast –
Haverfordwest, S. Pembs. The *d* + *h* should
result in *-t-*, but it is significant that the *h*
survives in the spelling of so many examples,
for the *-th-* is probably not the spirant but *t* +
h. All the examples collected refer to the same
family in S. Pembs.
BBStD 328, the report or survey is signed,
as examined, by H. Cadarne. B13. 93,
reference to Henry Catharne of Prendergast.
WPortBooks 315. Thomas Catharne
(Pembs). Public Records Pembs 56. 1511.
Henry Cadherne (Footnote, Catharne of
Prendergast.) InvECP 48. Carms 1530-
Henry Cadarne. 63. Pembs. 1529- Henry
Katern. 67. Pembs 1533 Henry Katharn (?)
68. Pembs 1540 Thomas Kathren son and
heir of Henry Cathren, esquire. L & P 1. 149.
71. Henry Katerne (context, Bishopric St
David's). CRHaverford 191. Jane Gatharne;
196, Jane Catharne; 228. Jane Cathan.
WG 182 deals with *catéyrn* as an example
illustrating *d* + *d* giving -*t*-; the composition is
straightforward *cad* + *teyrn* (*teyrn*, 'ruler,
king', being disyllabic, the accent falls on the
syllable which was the penult before
contraction). LHEB has a variety of primitive
forms, *Categirn* etc., *Catihernus* (*v.* Index for the
several forms and the matters of discussion).
Categirn etc. is obviously a form of *catéyrn*
before the disappearance of *g*, that is, the loss
of *g* in this position; *Catihernus* holds out a
promise of being a primitive version of *cadhaearn*, but this Jackson is not willing to
accept. To go back to the Welsh names:
Catarn, Catharne etc. are probably from
Cadhaearn, but the possibility of a connexion
with *catéyrn* should not be dismissed entirely.
Caddick, Caddock *v.* Cadog
Cadell
Cadell is a name borne by kings and chieftains

in the early period, *v.* HW Index. Examples from texts:

B13. 219. SR 1292. Barony of Rupa (Dyfed), Cadel Gely. RecCa Index, six, as forename. Bartrum 300-985, eight as forename. L'Estrange Ewen 125 includes Caddell (warlike) in the list of W surnames found in documents in PRO.

The following examples in spite of spelling are of Cadell:

Mer LSR 21, 46, Ieuan ap Cathel; 45, Win ap Cathel.

It is given in MacLysaght, *Guide to Irish Ss.* 36: 'Cadell, Cadal (W). In co. Galway since the thirteenth century'. The meaning of (W) is that the Gaelic form so marked is that given in Woulfe and that no other authority has been found to confirm it.

The name fell into disuse in Wales and it would be difficult to show that the occasional examples found in the border counties could be traced back directly to an origin in Wales, for the name might have moved indirectly through Ireland. Examples were collected from:

Caddel South Hereford FA Aston Ingham; *Caddell* Barrow-in-Furness, Ramsden Central; D. Tel 25.5.78, Deaths, Beckford, Worcs. East Flint, Hawarden Mancot and Moor; *Cadell* Preseli Houghton-Burton. *Cadel* D. Tel 23.4.79, Latest wills.

Caddno

Morris-Jones in *Cerdd Dafod* 41 mentions *Cadno* and *Madyn* (Madog) – and *Reynard* in English – as examples of personification occurring in natural speech, names of persons in origin being given to an animal, 'the fox', and remaining in the language as common nouns: *cadno* (or 'canddo') is the usual word in use in SW; *madyn* is NW. *Cadno* has the element seen in *Tudno, Machno, Gwyddno*, derived from *-gno*, the *g* lenited, disappearing in the compound. GPC offers the same explanation that it is originally a personal name, transferred to the fox, but with a question mark of doubt. It does strengthen the assumption a little, that *Madyn*, through personification, is also used for 'fox'. G 90 has two references, but only as a common noun, that is, there is no example of *cadno* as a personal name.

In SW dialects *-dn-* quite often becomes *-ddn-*, e.g. *gwydn* 'tough', *gwddyn*; the word *gwadn* 'sole of foot' illustrates the development

in a monosyll. and in a disyll., the sg. becomes *gwaddan*, the pl. *gwadnau* becomes *gwandde*, through a metathesis of *-ddn-*. Therefore the form *Caddno* must have preceded the form in general use in SW for 'fox'. The form *caddno* does occur as a surname: BBStD 60. Thom' Cathno, Dd Cathno, 78. Isabella Cathno, Griff Cathno.

Cadhaearn, Cateyrn, *v.* Trahaearn, Cadarn.

Cadifor, Cedifor

The composition is straightforward, and although examples of Cadifor occur, the other is more regular because the vowel *a* is affected by the vowel *i* in the syllable which follows. B13. 217. SR 1292. Madauc ap Kediuor; ib. Meuric ap Kedyuor. 218. Kedyvor ab Meiller; 219. Cadivor Cadigan. B2. 65. West W. 1301-2. Kedivor ab Lewelin. B15. 288. Aberystwyth-Cardigan 14th century. Kedyuor Sutor. Glam Cartae, 964. 1189. Cadivor; BYale 88. Kydyvor et Madoc ap Edenewyn; 110. Eigon ap Kydivor; Lp Oswestry 40. Rental 1607. Gavell Cadenor (correct to Cadeuor). Surveys GK (. . 1326). Gwele Je(uan) ap Kedinor (misreading).

The name *Caduor, Catuor* is also found; G quotes a small number of examples, and refers to LL 279.10 catmor filius mor; Cy IX. 180 Catmor map Merguid; cf. also, Mer LSR 86 Cadvaur.

Cadog, Cadock

The name of a famous saint, contemporary with St David: two versions of the name (mutated) are seen in the place-names, Llangadog, Llangatwg; cf. also Cadoxton. The saint's proper name was *Cadfael*, (HW 158), *Cadog* being a hypocoristic version on a pattern commonly found in the names of Welsh saints.

Glam Cartae 2238 Francis Cadock. Ex Pro James I. 211. Cadock Deere (Llanmaes Glam.).

There is no example of the name in Clark, Genealogies.

PRClaverley, Index, Caddick (Caddock, Cadwick, Chadwick, Kaddick, put together); 281. 1750, Edward, s. of William and Mary Caddock; 344. 1775, Mary Cadwick, wid. bur.; 326. 1780, Caddick, 344. 1775, Cadwick. Pontesbury 259. 1714, Ann Caddock.

Occasional examples were collected from contemporary registers:

Caddock, Conway, Bangor, South 2 (B). Caddick, Ludlow, Worfield; Wrekin, Albrighton; Islwyn, Newbridge – Part, Abercarn – Llanfach, Abercarn West.

The vowel in the final syllable should be compared with Maddick and Maddix, *infra*.

Cadwaladr

Compound of *cad* and *gwaladr* and therefore meaning 'battle-leader', this name, naturally, was given to the sons of kings and princes, for instance, Cadwaladr the son of Gruffydd ap Cynan.

When in daily colloquial usage one can expect to see two possible changes or developments; the most obvious would be the appearance of a vowel sound between *d* and *r*, to give *Cadwalader* or *Cadwaladar*: the appearance and growth of the epenthetic vowel in *dr, br, gr*, etc. or *-dl, -bl, -gl* is very common in Welsh speech. The other possibility is the dropping of the final *r* because of its distance from the accent: this happens in the dialect pronunciations of *aradr* 'plough', *taradr* 'auger', (tarad y coed, 'woodpecker'); this results in *Cadwalad*.

There is a third possible change, Cadwalader (with the accent on *-wal-*) becoming *Cadwalder*. This is not a hypothesis, the examples below show this change quite clearly. A fourth change is the conversion of *d* to *t*. This is not due to the 'hardening' of consonants *g, b, d*, characteristic of the dialects of Brecknock, Glamorgan and Gwent, for the *d* in this case is unaccented; and in any case, this change occurred some distance from these particular areas. One sees evidence of it in official papers and over the Border in the English counties, and it would be fair to infer that English ears heard the *d* sounded as if it were *-t*. This produces the form *Cadwalater, Cadwaliter*. The fifth change is the elision of *Cad-* in colloquial speech in the English border, to give *Walliter* etc. Still further changes will be shown in the examples below. (There will be no purpose in quoting examples of the abbreviations used by scribes, e.g. B15. 50. AS 1406. Kadr; 52, Kaddr; Caddr.)

B13. 222. SR 1292. Cadewalader ab Meurich. B7. 306. N. Pembs 1599. Kedwalader ap Robert of Ludchurch. Sannan 1584. Cadwallade Wms: 1685. Cadwallad Evans. B10. 181. Vermin Payments, Llanuwchllyn, 18th century.: I Rowland Cadwalad; [cf. the colloquial W form 'Dwalad' especially common in NW] 183. i John Cadwalad Shone. InvECP 39. Cards 1547. Kydwalter Robert Aprothydie . . . the said Kydwaller. 137. Monts 1515. Kydwelleder ap Thomas of Mochnant. 140. Monts, 1538. Richard ap Kydwallatur. 145. Monts, 1544. Cadwaladwr ap Rice. 148. Monts, 1547. Kydwallader ap Thomas. 253. ? Marches 1533. Kydwaliter Gryffith of London, tailor.

SHROPSHIRE REGISTERS

The registers have a great range of variants and one specimen of each, with its location, is quoted here:

Shipton 21. 1614. Jane Cadwallader. Ford 27. 1729. Kadwalleter (this family in earlier entries is Cadwallader). Hanwood 3. 1563. David ap John Cadwaliter. More, Index has six variants including Cadvallator, Cadwalleten. Clunbury 59. 1668. Hugh Chadwallader = 70. 1685. Hugh Cad. 93. 1720. Hugh Cadwalad = 95. 1723. Hugh Cadwalader. Bromfield 23, Cadwadr – ? abbreviation; 164, Walleter (index has Cadwalleder for this). Cardeston, Index. Walliter, Waliter, Walitter. Alberbury 616. Wallader. Chirbury 170. 1741. Cudwalliter = 186. 1749. Cadwalliter. Worthen. Index includes Cudwalader. Burford 1. 1588. Kydwaletur; 3. 1563. Cadwaletur. Badger, 1. Cadwallender. Shipton 10. 1572. Johannes ap Thomas Cadwalder; Shipton 12. 1580. Cadwallade. Wrockwardine 298. 1802. Mary Cadwalder. Alberbury 6. 1568. Anna Cadwallads. Claverley 246. 1729. Cutwallot. Westbury 317. 1798. Whalleter. Diddlesbury 182. 1753. Wallet. Neen Savage 11. 1591. John Cuttwallet. Wistanstow 107. 1752. Richard Cadwalliter = 108. 1753. Cadwallider = 114. 1759. Cadwallader. 154. 1792. Sarah Welliter. 155. 1793. William s. of Richard and Sarah Welliter. 176. 1806. Elizabeth Wallider. 163. 1799. Mary Chadwallader. Eaton-under-Heywood, Index includes Wallardor. Stoke S. Milborough 18. 1683. Susanna Walltor. Moreton Corbet 18. 1669. Cattwoalliter Hughes. Sheinton 29. 1804. Ann d. of William and Sarrah Cadwaleter bap. 30. 1806. Jane d. of William and Sarah Walliter. 30. 1809. Sarah d. of William and Sarah

Cadwalliter. Tong 3. 1633. Widdow Cutwalleder. Wroxeter 154. 1791. Mary Wallet; St Chad's, Index, twenty permutations of Cadwaladder, including Cadwaldier, forms with Cut-, including Cutwaller; also Waller, Wallet, Wallatt. Edgmond 52. 1697. Elizabeth Catwallit. Waters Upton 69. 1801. Martha Walleten. Bitterley has no example of Cadwallader and the easily identifiable variants, but it has 204. 1802, John Cadwall, which is classified in the index as a variant of Caldwall.

The examples quoted are self-explanatory. One comment may be offered, that forms such as Walliter etc. could easily merge with Walter.

PRESENT-DAY REGISTERS
The correct or original W version is still found, not only in Wales (Cerrigydrudion, Newport St. Julians 4, Risca North, Caernarfon-Abererch), but also the E Border counties, Ludlow, Little Wenlock; Stanton Long; Wrekin, Ketley-Wellington Rural. The version Cadwallader is plentiful throughout the Shrewsbury constituency, and Ludlow, Wrekin, City of Hereford, Leominster; Ludlow town has many families; the spelling Cadwallider is also found, e.g. Hereford, Burtonsham. Some of the curious forms of the Shropshire parish registers have survived:
Wallador, Wrekin, High Ercall. Walder, Shrewsbury, Meole Brace; CT Cirencester 9. Wallder, Westmorland, Kendal-Strickland. Walders, Barrow-in-Furness, Hawcoat; Dalton-in-Furness. Cadwaller, South Pembs. St Issell's, South Ward.
Cadwallinder v. Cadwaladr
Cadwgan, Cadogan.
The OW version in Harl MS 3859, Genealogy 2, Catguocaun shows the composition quite clearly, the second element being Gwogawn. This final syllable changes to -on, with variant -an which is the version occurring oftenest. It is worth noting the Gwo- of the original version; words which have gwo- and gwor- in their original form normally become go- and gor- (for instance, gochel, variant gwachel), but the consonantal w of Gwogawn persisted into the medieval period; the Anglo-Normans generally changed initial gw- into w- (e.g. Wenllian, Weirful etc.), and this explains the S. Pembs Wogan.

In the compound form, the initial consonant of the second element undergoes mutation and this means the loss of g-, to give Cadogan, but the persistence of the cons. w obviously produced another version, Cadwgan, which on the whole is the standard version: the version Cadugan below stands for Cadwgan; cf. also the form Caduugaun quoted by Jackson LHEB 298, occurring in the Anglo-Saxon Chronicle.
B13. 143. Bonds keeping peace 1295. Cadugan thu; Cadugan yloyd. B13. 217. SR 1292. Cadugan ap Roser; 220. Phelipp ap Kadugannus Wyneu; 223. Cadogan Ringild; B14. 241. temp. Edw. I. Ririd ap Caducan. Mer LSR 6 Cadugan ap Ospers.
There are various odd spellings in early texts and in some instances it is obvious that Cardigan became confused with Cadwgan.
B13. 219. SR 1292. Cadivor Cadigan. B14. 240. de Ririd ap Cradugan; 241. R. ap Caducan; 303. R. ap Cradigan; 303. R. ab Cadugan; 312. R. ab Categan. BBStD 168. Cadogy Goch; 178. Cadogy Gouth. Lp Oswestry 34-35, Names of 'gwelyau': Cadugan gwthieth (1393); Kadegan chwith (1586), Kydogan Ystwyth (1602). Rads Soc XLI. 56, Cadocan ap Yeuaf. XL. 61, Cadogn ap Gwilym ap Rs. (Painscastle). XLV. 66, Roger Kydwgan, Incumbent of Heyope 1575. InvECP 140. Monts 1538, M. ap B. Acodokan. 164. Breckn 1533. Owen Codoken. 186. Rads 1556. Lands . . . late of Goddogan Ab bedow goghe. 195. lands called 'Codogan Landes'. 241. Monm 1556 . . . lewis Codogan.
There is little doubt that many families named Duggan, Dougan, living in England and Wales, are of Irish extraction; but there is evidence that Cadogan became Dogan, Dwgan within Wales and in the Border counties, and these versions are found so far back, one cannot accept that they are Irish immigrants and their descendants.
ADClun 41. Adam Dygan; 42. ditto (1328-29, Roll of the 'Hundredum de Clone', Clone Borough); Adam or David Dygan occurring in 44, 45, 47, 49, 50; cf. 47. A. digan; 53. D. digan; 98. A. Degon, . . . John Degon. RadsSoc XXX. 43, (Wills), 1566. Rs Dogan; XXXI. 23, 1577. John Dogan, Old Radnor. XXXIX. 71, Aberedw, Hoell ap Rs Dogan. XLV. 53, 1554. Walter Duggan of

New Radnor. PRConway 1585. Alis ver. John doogane.

SHROPSHIRE REGISTERS

Ludlow 193. 1635. Evan Coduggan; 198. 1673. do. 204. 1640. Evan Cadugan; 501. 1677. Evan Codoogan. 225. 1572. Lucrece Codwogan. 252. 1587. Maud Carduggan. Diddlesbury 11. 1588. Willelmus filius Morgani Douggan. Burford 50. 1637. Moses Duggan.

There appears to be a similar name of Irish origin. MacLysaght, *Irish Families* 131-2 gives O'Duggan, O'Dugan; and states that Duggan, (in Irish O Dubhagain) is in some places given in English speech approximately the Irish pronunciation, namely Doogan. The *Guide* 36 has (O) Cadogan, O'Ceadagain. 'A co. Cork sept, to be distinguished from the Welsh family of Cadogan who were prominent in Dublin and Meath in the seventeenth century'; p.72. '(O) Dug(g)an ... The two principal septs are in Munster and Connacht.' As so many other Welsh names found their way into Ireland in the wake of the Anglo-Norman invasion and occupation, one naturally thinks that the Irish name is possibly a version of the Welsh name; but it must be left to Irish scholarship and research. The introduction of Cadogan into Ireland in the seventeenth century is easily documented; for example, HBr 301, Pedigree of the family of Llwyncadwgan (Llangamarch), leading to William Cadwgan of Dublin; 'Henry Cadwgan or Cadogan of Dublin, ... his son William was created baron Cadogan of Oakley, in the county of Bucks. in 1718'.

There has been so much movement between Ireland and Wales it is impossible to say (without detailed knowledge of the persons or families concerned) whether a person named *Dogan* in Pembrokeshire, for instance, represents a name that has remained and continued there, or whether it represents an Irish immigrant bringing the name back, e.g. CRHaverford 39 *Thomas Dogan*. This difficulty also applies to the constituencies on the Border. One is aware that there has been a movement of Irish families and yet one asks why should there be so many Irish named Duggan in the constituency of Leominster, so why not believe that they are of Welsh extraction?

There are examples of Cadwgan, South Worcs, Bildon and Cadogan [*Cadogan* and *Cadwgan* are not prominent in Wales itself; South Pembs, Cosheston has ten; and Cosheston-Nash five]. Cf. City of Hereford St Martin's, Gadogan (misprint ?) Cadagan, Oswestry, West Felton. R. xi Towns; Runcorn, Moore; Cadigan, Wirral, Westminster Ward 2. *Duggan* is widespread, Shrewsbury, Monkmoor; Ludlow, Madeley, Clun; Clungunford, Diddlesbury, Craven Arms; Wrekin, Dawley, Wellington – Regent Portion. One need not quote any more, but it is of importance that BrRad has a good number, e.g. Builth, Knighton, Bleddfa, Michaelchurch, Evenjobb Newcastle, Llandegley, Llanfihangel.

Dogan. Shrewsbury, Belle Vue; Anglesey, Llangoed; Wrexham, Wrexham Boro, Brynffynnon; Conway, Bangor South 2 (B). *Doogan*. Shrewsbury, Condover; Church Pulverbatch; Oswestry, Whittington. *Dougan*. West Gloucs, S. Briavel's 1.; CT, Bourton-on-the-water; Kidderminster, No. 5. Park; Northwich Rural, Cuddington. *Douggan*. Macclesfield Disley 2. *Deegan*. Shrewsbury, Abbey Foregate, Abbey ward, Atcham; City of Gloucester, Longlevens Ward, p.4.

Caerleon

The Roman town of *Caerllion (Caerleon)* in Gwent is never known by an abbreviated form; but Chester which originally is *Caerllion* (Fawr) is generally referred to as 'Caer'. One may surmise, from the location of the examples, that both have become surnames. Those found in Monm, Glam, and Gloucestershire probably have their origin in the Gwent Caerleon; those found in Cheshire, Shropshire etc. could possibly go back to the Welsh name for Chester.

Glam Cartae, Index – Cairlion, Carlyon, Karelion, Karlyon. HM iv, 74. Fourteenth century document mentioning – infra dominium de Karlyon; ... in curia de Karlyon; 87. document of 1469, dominium de Kairelyon; 82. record of 1667, James Jones of Carlion; iii. part ii. 113. Morgan of Kerlyn; 189, Inquisitio post mortem 1248-9, mentions Morgan de Karlyon.

PRESENT-DAY REGISTERS

Carlyon, South Worcs, Upton Snodsbury – Spetchley; West Gloucs, Longlevens Div. 1;

CT Tewkesbury 2; Stroud, Chalford Div. 3; Newport St Julian's 3. *Corlyon*, Runcorn, Walton. *Carlon*, Northwich, Northwich No. 1. (Castle 2); Winnington, Northwich 3, Witton Part 2; Northwich Rural, Cuddington – Sandiway, Rudheath. *Carline*, Wrekin Priorslee – St George's, Oakengates – Wombridge Ward; Oakengates Trench, Lilleshall – Donnington Ward; City of Chester, Trinity Ward 4. *Carlin*, Northwich, Witton 1, Weaverham – Owley Wood. City of Chester, Newton Ward. Wirral, Neston – Willaston Ward. Newport, Alway 3, Victoria 1.

Cain

G distinguishes between *Cain* and *Kein*: the diphthong *ai* of mod. W is almost invariably written *ei* in med. W (regardless of its position in the word) so that a word written as 'Cain' must be 'Caïn'; and the fact that this name rhymes with *diwerin* and *cyffredin* confirms; this is the biblical *Cain*. *Cain(Kein)* is a female saint's name, as in *Llan-gain*; it is found also in compounds such as *Ceinfryd, Ceinwen* etc.

The Cain which developed into a surname is a place-name element found in the names of streams, e.g. *Cain* and *Cilcain* (*Kilken*) in Flint; *Cain* near Trawsfynydd, and the form *Mechain, v.* examples in WATU 154. Cf. *Flints Place-names* 29 '*Cain* river in Cilcain parish ...', quoting Paroch. 1. 81 'Kain springs at Moel Vamma'. The art. in DWB on the poet Rhys Cain (ob. 1614) states that the name comes from the river Cain in Mechain Iscoed. The poet spent most of his life in Oswestry: the PR between 65. 1579 and 356. 1616 has many entries referring to Rees Kain (or Kaine) or to his wife or daughter. There is one entry of the name Cain in PRClunbury 175. Also Lp Oswestry 51, Survey of 1602, Rice Kayn; InvECP 251. Marches, Oswestry 1529. Johan Kayns.

The forms *Cain, Caine, Cains* are fairly common in the E border counties adjacent to Flints; no doubt men from the area of the R. Cain were given the epithet as a label of their place of origin. The following figures illustrate the frequency: TD of Wirral and Chester, Cain 53, Caine 16, Cains 2; the TD of West Midlands-North, Cain, Caine, Caines, half column; West Midlands-South, Cain 7, Caine 3, Caines 1.

Cam, Gam, Games

Adj. meaning 'bent, not straight' used frequently in its uncompounded form, and found also in compounds, with *pen, bôn, ber, gwar*, etc. It normally mutates after the personal name, but there are many examples in early texts which retain the radical consonant (or fail to indicate the mutation); certain texts have examples both of mutation and of the radical consonant. B13. 217. SR 1292. Dauid Gam; 220. Adam Cam. 226. Phillip Cam.

In certain texts in the Glam charters the form *Cham* is used, 533, 535, 562, Leysan fil Morgan Cham. It is quite likely that *ch* is meant for *g*, cf. the use of *choch* where one expects 'goch'; 474, *Knaytho Choch*.

HM i, 32 has a reference to *John Cam* of Lystone in Herefordshire. In a purely Welsh context one expects -*Gam*, even in an *ad hoc* example, e.g. ALMA 924 (John Hughes to Edw H.) *Gwilym Gam* (probably referring to William Morris), but one must be prepared to find -*Cam* outside the W context.

There is no doubt that *Gam* produced the surname *Games*; one first finds the form *Game*, L & P 7. 1607 *John Game*, the father being Gam, Appendix 27. Star CP 21. Brec. *Jno Games*, J.P.; 22, ditto. Cf. the following spelling: MLSW 137, Llywelyn ap Morgan ap David Gamme.

It is strange that in spite of the many instances showing the use of *Gam* as an epithet after personal names, the family of the famous Dafydd Gam of Breconshire seems to be the only one that has a surname derived from *Gam*. In this particular instance it is usually thought that the epithet means 'squinting': HBr 80, 'David Llewelyn or Dafydd ap Llewelyn, generally called David Gam, or squinting David ...' A footnote on p.82 corrects Carte and Pennant for confusing two men with the epithet 'Gam': 'Cam is crooked, but when applied to the person means any defect in the eyes or limbs'. HM ii, 337 has the same explanation that in the case of Dafydd Gam it meant 'squint in one eye', and it is the origin of Games, and that the descendants bearing the name are still found in Breconshire. Theophilus Jones on p.246 shows that the source of his explanation is Powel in his *History of Wales*, who 'has taken care not only to record this deformity, but he

wishes his readers to believe that nature has perpetuated it, and that all his family continue to squint to this day. It is unnecessary to deny so absurd an assertion'. There is a footnote attached to this paragraph, 'From hence (as I conceive) the vulgar English phrase of Gameleg, meaning a crooked or bandy leg'. It should be noted that Lloyd, HW referring to Dafydd Gam, gives the meaning of squint; GPC also gives it. On p.485 Theophilus translates *Ysgwd Einon Gam* as 'Einon the lame's waterfall'; a footnote states that *Cam* has a variety of meanings, but it does not mean 'lame', which would be *cloff*.
Ludlow 188. 1633 Thomas Cam, = 193. 1635 Camme; 199.1637 Thomas Cham. 336. 1625 Richard Cam, gent. 971. 1772 Elizth d. of Henry Games & Catherine. St Chad's Index, Cam. (one entry).
PRESENT-DAY REGISTERS:
Cam, S. Worcs, Bredon and Ecklington, Birlingham; Malvern East – Link, South Gloucs, Brookethorpe with Whaddon. *Camm*, S. Worcs, Evesham East/West; Westmorland, Kendal – Castle AJ, Sedgwick. *Game*, Caernarfon, Llanfairfechan North; Ll. South. *Games*, BrRad Crickhowell (several), Llanfihangel Cwmdu; Llanf. Tretower, Torfaen; Cwm-ffrwd-oer-Abersychan.
A simple word such as *Cam* could of course come from more than one source. Finally, the quality of the vowel, needless to say, will be different in *Games*, due to the English spelling.
Candeland, Candelan, Candland, Canland *v.* Cynddylan
Candell *v.* Cynddelw
Canvin *v.* Cynfyn
Caradog
Its derivation is British *Caratacus*, giving *Caradawg*, later *Caradog*. G 111 gives examples of *Caradawc* in early poetry texts; it is worth noting that he gives no example of *Cradog*; instruction in the poetic craft no doubt insisted on the three syllables. Jackson in LHEB 688-9 discusses the date of the accent-shift which would make possible the form Cradog (Cradoc, Cradock) in early Welsh and its dating, the shift would have occurred before the earliest dateable example of *Cradog*.
Whatever the rules of poetry *Cradoc* is very common in official documents:
B13. 226. SR 1292. Craddoc Bentan; 228. Knayth ap Cradok, Craddoc Patty;

Craddock ap Gorgeny; Craddoc Bedar; 229. Yewan ap Cradoc oythel.
The following versions are difficult to explain: B13. 216. SR 1292. Creddac ap hwetheleu (? = Wyddelen) voil. 217. Creidoc ap Seysil. BYale 116. Hona (= Hofa) ap Criadog.
The Index of Glam Cartae classifies Caradocus etc. separately from Cradocus, Cradoc etc.; it has very many examples of *Cradoc* etc.
CRHaverford 177, David Cardocke is likely to be a clerical error, cf. 30, 174, 190, David Cradok.
The Shropshire registers have the following: Albrighton 11. 1587. Alice Credocke, William Credocke. Donington 30. 1646. ... Credock.
Present-day registers have (1) occasional examples of Caradog, e.g. Torfaen, Cwmbran – Oakfield; (2) fairly widespread examples of Craddock; (3) and a few examples of Cradduck, e.g. Leominster, Bircher; Wirral, Hoylake, Caldy and Frankly ward 2.
Carew *v.* Introd. Place-names
Carlin, Carline, Carlyon *v.* Caerleon
Carn, Carne
Carne is well-known as the name of very influential families in the Vale of Glamorgan, Nash and Ewenni: their pedigrees given in Clark 374-8. They are said to be the descendants of 'Ynir Vachan', Prince of Gwent; the prince's grandson is called Thomas *o'r Carne* of Pencarn; the move from Gwent to Glamorgan seems to have come about in the time of Howel Carne of Cowbridge. If the surname is to be properly attributed to a place-name, it should be read as 'Carn', monosyllabic. The charters of Glamorgan have frequent references to the family, and the name occurs often in the official papers of the Tudor period, e.g. Star CP 6. Henry VII: Roger Carne; 76, Elizabeth, William Garne; 77, Elizabeth, Thomas Carne. In the PRLlantrithyd it is attached to the names of members of the Bassett family as a place-name of origin: 2. 1600 John Basset the son of Tho. Basset de Garne; similar entries 4. 1607; 6. 1620. Cf. R.T. Gunther (ed.) *Early Science at Oxford, XIV. The Life and Letters of Edward Lhwyd*, Oxford 1948; p.542, correspondence of Lhwyd with Philip Williams of Dyffryn Bryn

Coch, Neath, for the sake of answering the queries of the antiquary Thomas Tonkin of Lambrigan as to the origins of the surname *Carne*. Agreement is expressed that it comes from Pen carn or Pen y garn in Monmouthshire though the family is settled in the sixteenth century in Glam. The place-name is probably *Pen-y-garn, carn* = 'cairn', being feminine, in the lenited form after the def. art.; the example of *William Garne* above probably represents the correct lenited form, but for use as a surname it was no doubt thought right to use the radical form *Carn*. *Garn* occurs as a surname in CT, Coberley, Severhampton; City of Hereford, Central.

Carreg (*v.* also Introd. Place-names)
The early use of the residence name *Carreg* (of Aberdaron) as a permanent surname was mentioned above p.17. Examples are found in various papers:
CaernQSR 154. Robert Carrek; 229. John Carreg nuper de Aberdaron. Robert Carreg of the same, gent. B7. 343. Caern 1597. Jevano Karreg.
The surname survives in the following places: City of Hereford, St Martin's; St Nicholas, Carreck. Western Mail 1.12.80, news item p.1, Charmayne Carreg, Trethomas, Gwent.

Catharne *v.* Cadarn

Cecil *v.* Seisyll

Cefnog
This adj. is derived from the noun *cefn* 'back'; GPC puts the meanings 'valiant, strong' first; and 'wealthy, well-to-do' second. The second meaning is the only one in contemporary Welsh. Its use as an epithet after a personal name was infrequent and only two early examples were found:
B15. 53 AS 1406. Je(uan) Kefnog. Mer LSR 37. Kefnauc (with no pers. name).
The following in the PR of Pontesbury seems to be the same word:
473. 1805. John Kevenoak (not mentioned in Index). 486. 1810. Willm Cevenock. 488. 1810. John Cevenoch.

Cemais
In spite of the uncertainty as to the spelling, *Cemais, Cemaes, (Kemeys)*, one may be certain these forms represent the same name or place-name. The Gazetteer has Cemais in Monts, Cemais (Cemaes Bay) in Anglesey, Cemais (Kemeys) in Monm and Cemais Comawndwr (Kemeys Commander) in

Monm. To these can be added the lordship etc. of Cemaes in north Pembs. Any of these place-names might be attached to a person's name, denoting place of origin or residence, but we shall probably find that the landowning family of *Kemeys*, identified with the 'Cemais' east of Newport, or the one north of Usk, in Gwent is the main source of the surname.
AnglCourt 1346. 38. Einion Kemeys. BBStD 228. Ieuan Kemys. Glam Cartae, Index, variety of examples of Kemeys, Kemys, Kemmis. L & P VII. 1169. David Morgan Kemyes (Cardyf – Rummeney). Star CP 7. Henry VIII. Glam, Dd Kemys; p.8 Wm Morgan Kemes, p.8 Rosser Kemeys, Cardiff. InvECP has a number of examples of Kemmes, Kemys of Monmouthshire; also: 219. Monm, 1518. Arthur and Harry Kemys of Bristol/Arthur Camewys of Bristol. PRLlantrithyd 66. 1644. Sʳ Nicholas Chemish Knight and Barronett. 69. 1701. Sʳ Charles Kemmyes. HM naturally has several references: i. Skenfrith, p.13. Surname Kemeys (of Bertholey) occurs more than once, Pt II Abergavenny, 159, ref. to ... Kemeys-Tynte of Cefn Mabli. Vol. iii (Part 2) 173, deals with 'Kemeys Inferior. The seat of the senior line of the Welsh branch of the family of Kemeys or, as it was originally, Camoys or Cemeis'. p.176. Pedigree of the Family of Kemeys (Cameis) of Kemeys, starts with John de Cameyes, at the Battle of Hastings 1066, who took the surname from Kemeys in Gwent, the pedigree includes the forms Cameis, de Chemeis, Camoys.

PRESENT-DAY REGISTERS
Kemeys, West Gloucs, Longlevens; City of Glouc, Westgate Ward, p.3, p.27; Kingsholm Ward p.31, Longlevens Ward p.23. *Kemys*, BlGwent, Ebbw Vale Central, Tallistown – Cwm. *Cemmais*, Monts, Llanwrin; Is-y-garreg (probably adopted, of late, to replace another name). *Kemish*, BrRad, Knighton.

Ceri, Kerry
Ceri was a commote of S.E.Monts and N.E.Rads to the west of Clun; the name occurs in the name of a breed of sheep. It is found occasionally attached to personal names:
Mer LSR 46. Ieuan Keri ... Teguared Keri; 70. Iockin Keri. ADClun 124. Griffith Kery.

Star CP 11. Henry VIII. Monts, Thos Kery. Glam Hearth Tax, St Fagans, Rowland Kery (this no doubt is to be associated with Porthceri, near Barry, in South Glam).

Cethin (Gethin)

The surname derived from *cethin* is very frequently confused with variant forms of *Gutyn* so that it is first of all necessary to state with emphasis that *cethin* is an adj., which means (1) ruddy, dark, swarthy; (2) fierce, ugly, hideous. As an epithet placed after a personal name, it probably meant 'swarthy'. It is often spelt *cethyn/gethyn* by scribes and in areas that did not hear any difference between *-in* and *-yn*; the quotations will show other spelling versions.

It was normal to use the mutated form but there are many examples of retaining the radical. Of course, if *cethin* is used, after the def. art., to represent noun + adj., it will be correct to keep the radical consonant if a masc. noun is understood; (and to use a mutated form if a fem. noun is understood). Bartrum 1350-1415, 523. Y Cethin, three examples. ibid 881. Y Cethin ap Gruffudd Sais. B15. 45. AS 1406. Ednyvet ap Meilir ap y Kethin.

There are occasional examples of *ap Kethin*, as if it were a personal name, but the probable explanation is that the def. art. has been lost through elision:

B15. 47. AS 1406. Deia ap Kethin; 57. ditto. Mer LSR 24. Ieuan ap Kethin.

A few examples to represent the normal usage of the mutation:

B4. 162. Ardudwy Court 1325. Iorwerth Gethyn; 163. Madoc Gethin B6. 357. NW 1326. Iorwerth gethyn; B15. 43. AS 1406. Je(uan) Gethin. B10. 162. AnglRent, 16th century, ffrith gronogethin.

Examples of the radical consonant:

B13. 217. SR 1292. Res Kethin. BBStD 204. Ieuan ap Dd Kethin. B13. 97. Pembs 16th century. Richard Kethine; 98, Harry Kethen; 100, James Kethine; 102. Willm Keathen; 104. Richard Keathen. CRHaverford 193, 241-2, Walter Kethin (Keathen, Kethen).

SHROPSHIRE REGISTERS

In the Shropshire registers one expects such variations as *-ing*; the final vowel becoming neutral as shown by *-en*; spellings which are based on English values and some that are to be explained (if at all) in terms of analogy. The index of the More register is an example of classifying *Gethin* etc. with *Gittins* etc.

Shipton 27. 1648. Thomas Geathen; 39. 1713. Geathing. Ford 3. 1598. Gethen. Sibdon Carwood 6. 1673. Geathing. More 1. 1572, 2. 1573. Gethine. Stanton Lacy 231. 1791. Geethin. Ludlow 895. 1754. Jno Getthin (? an attempt to explain as Get-thin ?) 928. 1760. Jno Jethin (the same person). Norbury 2. 1563. Gethyne (with many later entries). Eaton-under-Heywood 46. 1714. Guethin; 49. 1717. Gwethwyn = 81. 1752. Gethin = 85. 1755, Gethen; 81. 1752. Ann Gwethyn. Battlefield 19. 1742. Gwethin. Albrighton 148. 1775. Githin (the only entry, but there are also examples of Gething and Geathing).

The above are representative specimens. It is hardly necessary to quote examples from present-day registers, but the following are worth recording: Kidderminster, No.2. Baxter, *Gethins*; Blaenau Gwent (BrRad) Llanelly – Gilwern, *Gethings*.

Cedweli, Kidwelly

v. p.29 above for examples of Kidwelley, Kydwale. Also *v.* Introd. Place-names.

Chwith, Whith

Chwith is very often used as an epithet after a pers. name. It means 'left, left-handed', and has the other meanings which follow from that, 'awkward, bungling, uncouth, sinister, sorry-feeling' etc. Reaney has an example of *Gauche*, 'left-handed, awkward'. Initial *chw-* becomes *wh-* in South Wales speech, *whech*, 'six', *whare*, 'play', etc. That is one reason for having examples of *Whith*. In addition, Anglo-Norman scribes found it difficult to convey the *chw-* sound, and used the nearest means they could find. There is a possibility of confusion in early texts between *whith*, (often written *whyth*) and the word *gwehydd*, lenited to *wehydd*: with the accent on the first syllable the *h* becomes ineffective, to give *gwëydd* which contracts to *gweydd* and *gwŷdd* (cf. Llëyn becoming Llŷn); it remains *gweydd* (monosyllable) in SW speech. The following examples are doubtful:

AnglPleas 18. Hugh ap Jevan ap Hoell Wyth. AnglCourt 1346. 41. Ithel Chwith (edited; MS = Wethe). B13. 225. SR 1292. Howel Hwyth; 229. Guyaun Huiz; Eynon huiz. B15. 42. AS 1406. Adda Chwith; 44. dye ap

Dikws chwith – this page has several examples, sometimes written Chwith; the whole list has examples throughout; 59. Deikws ap Je(uan) Chwith. B26. 86. ScottCampaign 1326. Maddok Whiz. B3. 68, 69. (Criccieth) Edenus Whith; 70. Edenus Whyth. B6. 359. NW 1326. Madoc Whyth ap tegwaret; Mer LSR 31. Griffid Whith. (These texts with NW context have been chosen to show *Wh* being used though local speech would have *chw-*.)

Used after *vap*, with no pers. name: B2. 157. Criccieth 1320. Eyno vap hwyth.

RecCa has Chewith, Chywith, as well as Chwith; and the following seem to be versions:
99. Mad. Cheche; Mad. Chethe. CalACW 227. Dafydd Qwhyth. BYale 52. Ienna Whieth.

In the Welsh-speaking period, PROswestry has *Chwith*:
102. 1584. Margret the base daughter of Thoms ap Wm Chwith. 140. 1590. John ap William Chwith ap Kyrynion. 147. 1591. Ros vz Ed'd ap Holl' ap Rees chwith.

Cloff (Clough)

Early examples of the adj. *cloff* 'lame' occur, placed after personal names, normally with mutation, although there is one example of the radical:
B 5. 56, Lleyn SR jevan glof; B15, 47, A S 1406 Ho(we)ll glof person Rhosgolyn; B 23, 341, Mawddwy 1415, David ap Moel Gloff; ADClun, 76, John Clof, HM i, 229, Ped. of family of Gilbert of Hen Gastell, mention in second generation of Richard Herbert, gloff; ib. 415, Goitre, 15 century, Thomas Herbert Gloff (cf. iv, 250, Clough); PRLlanbadoc 1629 Jeoneta John alias Gloffe.

SHROPSHIRE REGISTERS:
Selattyn 26, 1573, Richard ap Meredith alias gloff; ib. 26, 1574, Jonett verch John, late w. to Richard gloff (probably same person); ib. 178, 1670, Robert Jones, gloff; Oswestry 660, 1667, Mary the base daughter of Gwen ach Hugh als Gloffe.

In some of the examples the adj. *Gloff* is on the point, it appears, of becoming a surname, displacing the original 'correct' name.

An English family named *Clough* lived in Denbigh in the 16th and 17th centuries, becoming patrons of bards, and references to them in bardic verse are as *Clwch*, rhyming with *tristwch*, and harmonising in *cynghanedd* with *cloch* and *clychiaid*. The ped. in JEG 329 shows how Clough and Williams-Ellis were joined, leading eventually to the name of the architect Clough Williams-Ellis.

Most of the references to Clough are connected with Denbigh:
Star CP Denbs. Humffrey Clough; Ex Pro James I, Wm Clough (Denbighs), WPortBooks 260, Hugh Cloughe of Denbigh.

Cilan (Keelan)

WATU has three examples of *Cilan* as township, in Merioneth, Caernarvon and Denbs; the following examples as surname probably have their origin in the Cilan of Llanfair Dyffryn Clwyd, Denbs.
PRWhittington 5. 1591. Thomas Kilan. Oswestry 34. 1563. Richard Keelan; 35. 1563. Beniamin Keelan. 232. 1602. Richard Kilane; 234. 1602. Richard Kellan. PRSelattyn has Kilyn, Kylan. PRAlberbury 122. 1633, Joanna Keelen, p. de Pattesoll in com. Stafford.

Cissill *v.* Seisyll

Clewet, Clewitt *v.* Clwyd

Clwyd

This in origin is the name of the river in N.E. Wales; it has of late become the name of the county. The following entry in PR of Church Preen 15. 1724 . . . p. *Clanver Daffry Cluet* co. Denby (for Llanfair Dyffryn Clwyd) is proof that the following forms represent an origin in Clwyd; the location also, in Shropshire, is further confirmation:
Chelmarsh 66, 73, Cluet; Uffington, 25. 1697. ditto. Claverley 340. 1773. John and Mary Clewett. Meole Brace, 285. Clewitt. Donington 45. 1740. Beniamen Clewet. Wrockwardine 1. 1591. Thomas Cludd; 4. 1598 . . . Thomas Cludd, gent. 5. 1601. Edward Cludd, esq. St Chad, Index, Cludde, Cllud, Cludd, Clued. 256. 1655. Mrs Dorothy Cllud [Cludd] [sic]; 1469. 1786. Cludde, Harriett; 1902. 1809. Mary Cludde; 1655. 1803. Clued, Sarah. Eaton Constantine 9. 1725. John and William, sons of Roger and Ann Cluett.

PRESENT-DAY REGISTERS
Cluett, CT, Uckington: Denbigh, Llandrillo-yn Rhos, Rhos Ward 1.

Cnaith, Cneitho, Cneithwr

G 243 quotes examples of *Cynaethwy*, e.g. BT 68, cu kynaethwy; CBS 66, Cynaethuy, LD ii, Kynaithwy hir; cf. Bradney, HM iii, 218, Caerlleon and Llangattock, ped. showing descendants of Adam Gwent in the male line; second generation includes *Cynaethwy*, 1270. LL 292 has J ... Knaytho in a list of witnesses; this is mistakenly made into *Knaithus* in the Index, in the belief, presumably, that the *-o* is ablative. The forms *Kannaytho, Cnaitho, Cneitho* appear to be a version of *Cynaethwy*, and it is a pers. name in spite of the *de* found occasionally preceding it: B13. 215. SR 1292. Whitecastle, David ap Cnaytho, ... Maddoc ap Kneytho. 215. Caldecote, Henry de Kneitho; 216. 'Bergauenny', Yuan ap Adam ap Kneytho. 218. free tenants of Cade Well (= Cydweli) Griffith ab Kneytho. 220. Kilgarran, Dyfed. Lewelin ab Kennaytho. 227, 228, further examples of Knaytho; 230, examples of Kenaytho. Dwnn 1. 12. Kneytho vab Kornelys – Fredrik vab Kneytho. RadsSoc XLI. 57. Min. Accts 13-15cc, Ioruerd ap Knaytho.

The form *Knayth* occurs alongside examples of Cnaitho:

B13. 226. SR 1292. David ap Knayth; 228. Knayth ap Wasmer. B22. 376. Gower 1590. Owen Knayth; B23. 95-8 Index, Owen Knaith = Surveys GK 14; ibid 110. Eliz. 1583. Owen Kneath.

The form *Cnaithwr* is obviously connected: Glam Cartae 2296, Cnaithurus Broch; 2347, Knaithure Cogh; index includes Cnaithur, Cnaithurus, Kenithur, Keneithur; cf. also 2318, Kanaithen Coch. B24. 193. Fasti Cist. Camb. Names of monks, Cnaithur; 225, Names of Conversi, Cnaithur Broch.

The *Cnaithur* versions are almost certainly due to false analogy. The change of Cynaethwy, Cnaethw (spelt Cnaithw) is a natural development, final *-wy* becoming *-w*, as in Goronwy > Gronw. The final *-w* was then thought to be a form of *gŵr/ŵr* 'man', occurring in many compounds, thus producing *Cnaithwr*, written *Cnaithur* – especially if it is to take Latin case endings.

The form *Kneath* is still found in the Swansea area; read as if it were English, the spelling has influenced the pronunciation, i.e. silent *K*: v. B.G. Charles, *Non-Celtic Place-names in Wales*, pp.27-8, s.n. Knaveston, for a place-name based on the name *Canaethwr*, found in 1287 as *Canatherystoune*, in 1632 as

Trecanoythwoy, and still called in Welsh *Treganeithw*.

Coch

Coch when used of a person means 'red-haired'; the compound *pengoch* 'red-head(ed)' conveys the same meaning. These two forms are used extensively and are the source of several surnames, mainly due to the several ways of spelling *coch/goch* in documents written by non-Welsh scribes. There is a noun derived from *coch*, namely *cochyn*; this is much used in colloquial speech, with a slight nickname connotation; an occasional example will be found below. The normal usage is to use the mutated form *goch* after the personal name; examples occur of retaining the radical consonant where one expects the lenited form. The radical consonant can sometimes be explained. The text editor has rightly filled in the name of Cynwrig in the following, B4. 351, AnglCourt 1346, *Ken(ewric)* Cogh; in natural speech the join of the *-g* + *g-* would produce the *k* sound, and it is more than likely that in this man's name the *Cogh (Coch)* was the natural pronunciation; cf. Mer LSR 27 Itak Coch. But there are other instances which cannot be defended or explained by means of phonetic laws, and *Coch* is written self-consciously (and contrary to usage) because *Coch* is the 'proper' version of the word:

AnglPleas 18 John ap Guttyn Coch; 22 ... Tanno verch Jevan Gogh; 34, John Guttyn Cogh; 49, Llewelin ap Tudur Cogh.

Needless to say, if *Coch* follows the def. art., meaning 'the red-head', it will retain the radical cons. as a masc. noun would.

B15. 57 AS 1406. Je(uan) ap y Koz mawr. AnglPleas 47. Y Coch Pendraws. CaernHS 26. Bolde Rental, 35. Mally vz y Coz ab Atha; 45. Y Coz Moel.

If it follows what grammatically is a common noun (masc.) the radical will of course be retained: BBStD 40. Gwas Coch.

When *coch* follows *ap*, the def. art. (one feels) has gone through elision: B15. 44. AS 1406. Gruffith ap Coch. BBStD 52. Lewel(in) ap Coch.

When *cochyn* is used for the person, it ought to have the def. art. B15. 57. AS 1406. Heilin ap y Kozyn; ... dd ap y Kochyn. cf. examples of omitting the def. art.: ibid 60, dd ap cochyn; AnglCourt 43. Dafydd ap Iorwerth ap Cochyn.

To illustrate the various ways of spelling or writing -*goch*:
Gogh: B4. 160. Ardudwy 1325. Edenoweyn Gogh. Gouch: B13. 216. SR 1292. David Gouch ap Iereward. Gooch: B13. 143. Bonds Peace 1295. Eyner gooch. Gough, Goughe, Glam Cartae, Index; together with Go', Gouz, Gouh, Gozhe. Choch (with *ch* for G), Cartae 474. Knaytho Choch (*v.* ex. of *cham* for *gam* above). Gouth: BBStD 168. Cadogy Gogh; 178. Cadogy Gouth. Goz: B15. 43. AS 1406. Gruff ap Jollyn goz. Gotch: ADClun 71. David gotch. Goygh: ibid 146. Ieuan ap Gruff Goygh. Gok: B7. 315. NPemFairs William gok. Gohc: RadsSoc XLIII. 83. Assessment 1293, Lewelin Gohc (ibid. . . . ap Mapgohc).
Examples of cochyn; fem. cochen:
B13. 228. SR 1292. Ieuan gouchyn. B15. 57. AS 1406. Heilin ap y Kozyn. RecCa 285. Cochyn ap Talboeth; 34. Annon Cokkyn; 38. Annon Cokyn; 289. Goch y Cossyn; 280. Ll' Goche ap y cossyn. Lp Oswestry 161. Coghin Llanymynegh. CaernCR 57, 64. Cochen

The official papers of the sixteenth and seventeenth centuries have the same variety: InvECP 3. Richard Couche; 6. Ieuan ap Gwilym Goughe. 10. Hugh ap Robert alias Gough . . . the said Gouch. 15. I. ap Gronowe Gogh; 29. . . . Ivan Gowyth; 30. John ap David Goz. 38. Examples of Goz and coz; 125. . . . David Guoghe. 139. Edmund ap Gytton, Coogth. 258. David Gouz. Ex Proc James I. 67. Barnabie Gouche, Master of Magdalen College, Cambridge. ibid 284. David Llewys ap Griffith Gowch. 98. Ievan Cough Weydd.

Goch in an English context (i.e. heard, written and read by English scribes, or taken over into England and pronounced by the English), could undergo two sorts of changes: it could possibly change by a natural process in English speech on the pattern of *tough, enough*, but it is much more likely that the changes which took place arose from the spelling, i.e. versions such as -*gogh, gough* were read and pronounced as if they corresponded to *tough, enough*, and versions such as *gooch, gouch*, were read and pronounced as if they corresponded to *mooch* and *couch*; (it should

have been explained that the vowel in *coch* is long and the -*oo*- is probably meant to convey the length and that it was not the vowel sound of *rock*). A further change comes about, in the reverse order, the pronunciation producing a new spelling; the form *Gough* having acquired the 'off' sound produces a new phonetic spelling, *Goff, Goffe*.

The records of Haverfordwest have the usual variants, Gouge, Gouth; p.107, William Gough . . . Goff . . . 108. Gooffe; p.122 Colonel William Gooffe. [Editor's note: William Goffe (Gough) the Regicide, was probably the son of Stephen Goffe, the Puritanical rector of Stanmer, Sussex, who has been identified with Stephen Goffe, 'lecteur' in the Church of St. Mary's Haverfordwest, in 1620.]

SHROPSHIRE REGISTERS
The Shropshire records have examples which show the processes mentioned above: the obvious forms will not be quoted except to illustrate equivalence with less obvious versions:
Sidbury 30. 1766. Goff; Hopton Castle 58. Gouf (index has Gough, Goughe, Gouf). Chelmarsh 14. 1588; 43. 1649. Gowghe. Stanton Lacy 30. 1605. Thomas Gohe, = 31. 1607. Thomas Gough (Index has Ghoff). Bromfield, Index includes Goghf, Goff, Goffe. Middleton Scriven 15. Cooching. Hopton Wafers 33. 1732. Goof = 34. 1733. Goff; cf. 60. 1783. Gofe. Pontesbury 75. 1598. Gohe (Index puts this with Gower, not with Gough etc. cf. 117. 1627. Maria Goahe, Iona Goahe, Elnora Goahe, and refer to Bengoahe in Neen Savage 7. 1583). Ludlow 217. 1564. Thomas Goze, infans. 877. 1747. Richd. Gouch; 886. 1749. Alexander s of Alexander Gouch and Elizth; 893. 1753. ditto = 896. 1754. Alexander Goudge; 912. 1756. Neen Savage 14. 1595, 15. 1596, etc. Goah. (Index puts with Gower). Stokesay 2. 1561. Johannis Coch. High Ercall 35. 1604. Gozgh. Acton Burnell 57. 1659. Gohfgh. Wrockwardine 200. 1765. Goff = 200. 1766. Gough.

In the registers of the parishes within the St Asaph diocese, one finds, in the early Welsh-speaking period, that *Goch* is added as an *alias* e.g. Whittington 95. 1609 George Brytaine als George goch of Whittington; there are similar examples in Selattyn and St Martin's.

In the Shrewsbury Burgess Roll, Goze 1570, is listed separately from Gough, Goch; the editor obviously being unaware that the *z* stood for *ch*.

The present-day registers include the permutations set out above; only specimens of the less usual versions are given here:
Goff, Wrekin, Rodington; Bromsgrove, Redditch No.5; Westmorland, Kendal Nether. Gooch, Ludlow Ch. Stretton; Chester, Hoole Ward 1; Knutsford, Bucklow Rural – Pickmere, West Gloucs, Newent (abundant); Westmorland Lakes, Ambleside, Troutbeck. Goodge, Stalybridge-Hyde, Staly No. 1; Lancashire Ward Pt 2; Conway Llandudno North (A); City of Glouc, Matson Ward p.31. Gotch, Wirral, Oldfield; Ellesmere Port, Grange Ward 2. Goache, Cardigan, Cardigan North H2. Cooch, South Worcs. Fladbury – Cropthorne, Malvern South No.3. Couch, West Gloucs, Lydney 3, South Hereford, Kings Caple, Penrith, Brampton, Brampton Portion.

The word for 'smith' is *gof* (-*v* sound) and it is right to inquire whether *gof* as an epithet became involved with *goch, gough*. There is some evidence, not much. In the papers of the Duchy of Lancaster, pp.74, 78, 81, 87 there are instances such as *Morgan Phillip y Gove,* and amongst them, on p.81 *Phillipe Powell y Gough*, cf. 87 *Phillippe Hoell y gove*.

For the celebrated Matthew or Mathau Goch *v*. DWB s.n. His fighting in France made him famous – 'For years after his death the name 'Matago' was fondly remembered by the inhabitants of Bellême'. *v*. article by Major Ynyr Probert, TrC 1961 (Part ii), 34-44, esp. 34-5: 'Sir John Fastolf in his will dated 1459 leaves money for masses for the soul of Matthew Gouge Squier. To the French he was known as "Matago" ... to them it was synonymous with valour and his reputation there was even greater than in England. Only a few years ago, I saw this "Matago" used as a shop sign in Boulogne'.

Coedmor, Coetmor, etc.

As this is an improper compound of *coed-mawr*, 'great wood' or 'forest', it is the sort of place-name that could occur in more than one area. It is found in the name of the parish and church of *Llangoedmor*, near Cardigan. There is a tendency for *-dm-* accented to become *-tm-*.

CAP 394, 1390. Howel Coytmore (Coytmaure). CaernQSR 32, 193. Will'm Cotmore. Glam Hearth Tax, Margam. Rees Coydmore. PRLudlow 215. 1562. Robert Coytmore, infans.

The form *Cadmore* may be connected; found in BrRad, Brecon St John's West, St David's Within.

Occasional examples of *Coed* as surname are found, e.g. Glam Hearth Tax, St Athan, John Coyd. In the articles in DNB on Tomos Prys and William Myddleton it is said that these sea captains were the first to be seen smoking tobacco in the streets of London: there was a third sea captain with them named *Thomas Koet*.

Coedwr, Goyder

Two early references to versions of *Coedwr* 'woodman' were found in sixteenth century papers: InvECP 70 under Pembs, although Laugharne is strictly in S.W. Carms, John *Coydowre*, 1538-44. The other occurs in R. Flenley, ed. *Register of the Council of the Marches of Wales* (1916) 185, David *Coyder*, date 1569-91, parish of Llansadyrnin, which is quite close to Laugharne. Mr J. Barry Davies of Lisvane, Cardiff, came across the next example from the MSS of David Jones of Wallington in the Cardiff Library. David Jones took it from the Plea Rolls, Glamorgan, '27 Eliz. July 1585, Ann Giles, widow, by Alexander Seys, attorney, Statute of Rhuddlan against William Goyder'. The Glam Hearth Tax returns in the Public Record Office confirm that there were Goyders in Glamorgan around 1672. PRO E 179/221/294 (circa 1669) has John Goydoore in Pendoylan, John Goyder in Flemingston, and John Goydoore in St Athan's, and James, William and Christopher Goyder in St Bride's super Ely. E 179/221/297 (*c*. 1672) also contains most of these references, and E 179/375-6 (Hundred of Dinas Powis) (1672) has James Goyder in St Georges super Ely. Mr. J. Barry Davies was to find other examples of the name. In the MS copy at the Cardiff Library of the diary of William Thomas of Michaelston he produced nine examples of Goyder from 1769 to 1779 taken from parishes around Cardiff, and one of them is 'Joan Goidwr buried Leckwith 1777'. The PR of Llandough, Glam has a record of the marriage of James and Mary

Goider in 1734, and record of Goider children born there between 1732 and 1737. The largest number of the name Goyder are taken from the PR of Pendoylan, from 1728 to 1764, fourteen in all and two that are doubtful. Pendoylan had had one John Goydoore around 1669.

Coetmor *v.* Introd. Place-names

Cogan (Coggan) *v.* also Introd. Place-names
This is mentioned above with names taken to Ireland, as a territorial name of a person living in *Cogan*, which is between Cardiff and Penarth. Cf. a local example, InvECP 201, Glam, 1538. John Cogan; Star CP 8 . . . late of John Cogan of Cardiff. (Clark has a number of examples of . . . de Cogan.)

In the following, CAP 158. Tudor ap Cogan, . . . 'lands which Cogan ap Togwaret (Tegwared) formerly held', it is fairly certain that this is a form of 'Cadogan, Cadwgan', either as a scribe's abbreviation or as a contraction in natural speech.

Connah, Cunnah (Conws)
The form *Conws*, is hypocoristic, the standard form being *Conna(h), Cwnna(h)*.
Bartrum 1215-1350. 214. Cwna, two examples; Cwnws, four; 1350-1415. 522. Cwna, five; 523-4. Cwnws, eighteen. B15. 43. AS1406. Cona ddu. B10. AnglCrown Rental 162, dros dir lly(we)lyn ap Kwnna. Cf. examples in the pedigrees of the hypocoristic version, Dwnn 2. 77. Angharad verch Howel ap Cwnws; 2. 83. . . . ab Cwnwsddu; 2. 88. . . . ap Conws . . . ap Jockws.

It is the name found in *Connah's Quay*, cf. *Flintshire Placenames* 40, Connah's He, Hawarden (formerly), not in maps, or known locally; 1699, Paroch i. 94; Pennant, Tours i. 118 also mentions it.

In present-day registers *Cunnah* or *Connah* is found scattered in the N.E. counties and the English counties best situated to receive a spread:
Wrexham – Brymbo, Esclusham Below, Broughton – Cefn Ward. Wirral – Ellesmere Port, Poole Ward 1. Wrekin – Oakengates – Wrockwardine, Shifnal. City of Chester – St Oswald's, 2; Trinity 2; Ch. Rural – Dodleston. Cheadle – Ch Hulme, East Ward; Hazelgrove and Bramhall, North. Chester & N.W. – Cunnah, distributed right across the area.

Conway
The origin of the form is the name of the river *Conwy*; this was made into Conway, which also became the name of the town and the castle. It would be natural for a person from the place, or associated with the castle, to be called Conway.

JEG 290. Bryneuryn, Llandrillo; Footnote, 'Hugh Conwy Hên was the first who borrowed from the river which bounded his territory the permanent family surname of "Conwy" '. B15. 59. AS 1406. William Conoway fr minor de llanvaes. CaernQSR 55. David Lloyd Conwye. InvECP 15. Caern 1501. David Conway prior of Bethkelert. Star CP 34. Caern, Eliz. Edwd Conway. PRSelattyn 14. 1565, John David ap William Conwey; 114. 1637. Elizabeth verch Roger Conweye.

The name Conias (Coniers, Conyers) seems to have merged with Conway.
HBr 411. ' . . . the family of Conyers, Coniers or Conway . . . This John Conyers was of Richmond in Yorkshire, and came to Conway in North Wales, from which time they bore the name of Conway'.
Cf. JEG 260, Bodrhyddan, Conias (or Coniers), becomes Conwy, the form Conwy is kept throughout.

MacLysaght, *Families* 305-7. Appendix A, is a list of 'Surnames indigenous and common in Britain which are used as the Anglicized forms of Gaelic Irish Surnames'. The list includes *Conway* with the Irish names of which it is an approximation, *MacConowe, O'Conowe, Convey* etc.

Coyse, Coysh
HM iv. 133-4, Caerwent, 'Great Llanmelyn was in the sixteenth century the seat of a family with the surname of Coys, more properly Coes, meaning a leg'; footnote refers reader to vol. i. 49 which gives the pedigree of Coysh, 'probably the same race, spelt in this way it represents the Gwentian pronunciation'. It may be the local pronunciation of the surname, but it certainly would not be the local pronunciation of *coes* 'leg', for that would be *côs*: p.134. Thomas ap Gwilym Coes . . . end of sixteenth century; footnote quotes from PR of Portskewet, 20 May 1596, 'bap. William, s. of John Coyse'; 27. Feb 1600/1 bur. wife of John Coyse. Also

p.r. Caerwent 1578, Feb. 6 bur. Bryget dau. of Robert Coyse.

In his edition of the Caerwent PR, in connexion with these entries, Bradney says in a footnote, 'Coyse would be more correctly spelt *coes* ('leg')'. In the visitation of Essex, Harl. Soc. xiij. 184. 1612. . . . is the pedigree of a family of Coys descended from Roger Coys of Shirenewton, a parish adjoining Caerwent.

The name is found in MLSW 1415-1536: p.26, Ralph Coys the king's bailiff of Nether-went; 99, Radulfum Coys; 108, Thome ap Howell ap Llywelyn Coes. Also, RCA 455 . . . lands of Roger Coys (context, Chepstow – Usk).

The name is still found, e.g. A.W. Coysh, Sunday Times/Magazine, June 1, 1980, p.36; and there is one entry in the TD of Cardiff and S.E. Also D. Tel 29.8.80 Marriage, Low-Coysh, Stanmore, Middlesex, ibid 4.6.84, news item p.19, Coysh, Paignton, Devon.

Coytmore *v.* Introd. Place-names

Crach

Crach is a collective plural meaning 'scabs, disfiguring the skin'; it occurs quite often as an epithet immediately after the personal name, generally showing lenition, but at times with the radical consonant retained. It is sometimes used after the def. art. instead of the personal name. It is sometimes *Crath*, either through miscopying or misreading of text.

B13. 143. Bonds Peace, Maredud grach. B13. 228. SR 1292. Griffyd Crach. 229. Roppert Crach. BBStD 232. . . . viz Oyron Kenewr' Crath. (The editor having no idea of the meaning of Oyron makes a quite wrong translation; *Oyron* is for *Wyrion*, 'grandchildren of Cynwrig Crach'.) 234. . . . ap Ieuan Grath; 310. Cadogan Grach.

After the def. art.

B11. 57-8, Broniarth Court, 15c. Ieuan Dduy ap y Krach. JEG 181. Evan ap y Crach ap Jenkin.

This solitary example was found in the Shropshire registers:

Oswestry 91. 1583. . . . Anne vz John als Grach.

Craddock *v.* Caradog

Cras

B15. 287. Aberyst-Cardn 14c. Steph'n *Cras*.

BBStD 176. Johnes *Cras*.

There is a range of meanings to *cras*, 'dry, parched, coarse, grating (voice)', and the word retains most of these meanings. If one had to choose for the above examples, one would prefer 'harsh-voiced' first.

Crichard, Crichett *v.* Richard

Crych

The meaning when used as an epithet attached to a pers. name is 'curly-haired'. The examples are few because the meaning is usually expressed by means of the compound *pengrych*, 'curly-headed'.

CaernCR 21. Madog Grych [MS Gregh]. B15. 44. AS 1406. Dykws goch crech (variant source, greith; probably *crych*). RecDenb Lp. 59. Jevan ap Mad' Creche (qy. Crydd or Crach; does not appear to be either, and is more likely to be *Crych*).

Cryg

The only meaning in modern W is 'hoarse', but it had other meanings, 'defective of speech, especially stammering'. There is a feminine form, *creg*, very rarely used; Bartrum 1215-1350, 460, *Gwenhwyfar Greg f. Gruffudd ab Iorwerth*. The examples below which appear to have the vowel *e*, arise from the scribe's orthography. It normally mutated after the pers. name, e.g. the two famous examples, *Rhys Gryg*, (the 'Resi Grek' below), and *Gruffydd Gryg*, Dafydd ap Gwilym's contemporary. Because of the oddities of medieval writing one should guard against confusion with *Crych*, 'curly-haired'.

B13. 143. Bonds Peace, 1295. pethil Cryck (= Pill gryg). B13. 227. SR 1292. Iuan ap David Crek. B5. 69. Lleyn, 13c. david cryg. B10. 78. West W. 1352. per cartam Resi Grek. ADClun 16. Ieuan ap Lewelin grek. BBStD 304. Dauid Greccke.

Examples of mis-spelling:

CalACW, 21. Einion Grug, of Kerry. ALMA 181. Gruffydd grug (David Lewis to Lewis Morris).

Cudwalliter, Cudwallot, *v.* Cadwaladr

Cudwaler *v.* Cadwaladr

Cuhelyn

G 185 has a small number of examples, some of which are spelt *Kuelyn*; *v.* also Brynley F Roberts, B25. 274-290, art. dealing with forms of personal names in the various versions of *Historia Regum Britanniae*; which include the Latinized Cuelinus.

B10. 172. dros dir Kyhelyn y nant. B13. 93. 'Some records of a 16th century Estate', ref. to 'Cyhylyn Fardd'. B15. 54. dd ap Mad. ap Kyhelyn. B24. 193. FastiCistCamb 1231-4. Cueline. Mer LSR 17. Ithel ap Cuhelin; 72. Kuelin Goch; 80. Iarword ab Cuhelyn. RecCa Index: Cuelin, Cuelyn, Cuhelin, several entries; 106. Knelyn; 111. Mad ap Knelyn; 91. Eign ap Kukelyn ap Cad. (misreadings). CaernCR 32. Ieuan ap Ieuan ap Cuhelyn (MS Kuhelyn). 46. Madyn ap Cuhelyn (MS Cuheli). JEG 219. Plas Einion DC, Long pedigree back to ... Jefah ap Cuhelyn. ALMA 775. Cadwgan Cyhelyn (John Jones, Jesus Coll. to RM; refers to musical compositions by C.C.). PRSt Chad's 882. 1716. Margaret Kyellin; examples also in Index of Keiling, Kellen. 862. 1709. Jas Kewelling (possibly *Quellyn*, but probably *Cuelyn*).

Cul

Cul means 'narrow, thin, small'. The following seem to be examples of it as an epithet fixed after pers. name; (it does not occur often because *main* 'narrow' seems to have been preferred): *v.* 'Ieuan pengul' *infra* article on compounds of 'Pen'.
CaernHS 26. Bolde Rental 46. Gavell Ieva Gule; 49. Table of 'Gafaelion' – Ieuan Gul (1352 Extent, Ieuaph Cuyl; Bolde, Ieva Gule). CaernCR 124. Gwenllian ferch Ieuan Kule. 144. Gwenllian ferch Ieuan Gule. Lp Oswestry 158. Ieuan Culle.
The surname *Cule* (with pronunciation following this E spelling) is still found in South Wales. An example was collected from Monmouth, Shirenewton.

Cule *v.* Cul

Cundell *v.* Cynddelw

Cundle *v.* Cynddelw

Cunnah *v.* Connah, Cwna

Cunvin *v.* Cynfyn

Cwta *(fem.* **Cota***)*

Borrowing from ME *cutte*, giving the meaning 'clipped'; other meanings, 'meagre, stingy, curt, bob-tailed'.
B5. 66. Lleyn 13c. philip y cwta. B10. 162. AnglRent 16th century. Je(uan) gwtta. 174. jeuan ap da(vi)d ap jev(an) gwtta. B13. 229. SR 1292. Dauid Cotta (read as Cwta). CaernCR 76. Meilir Cotte. Cwtta Cyf. intro p.11. Quot. from sale catalogue, 'Allan o lyfr Llelo Gwtta 1563'. ML ii. 185, 191. Llelo

Gwtta (= Llewelyn ap Maredydd). Cotta, Gutta as if it were a forename: ADClun 166. Cotta Herour accused Ieuan ap Kethyn; (the para then has Cotta' only). 193. Gutta Harper. CatAncDeeds III. *c.*3461. Merion, temp H.VI. Jevan ap Cotte. PROswestry 557. 1654. Jane ... als Gutta.

Cybi

B15. 43. AS 1406. Madog ap Je(uan) Kybi. RecCa 55. Ieuan Kuby.
These two references (which may refer to the same person) probably have a name derived from Caergybi (i.e. Holyhead).
Cf. PWLMA 422, 424. John Gyby, 1376, Reeves, Cardigan; 419, 421. Philip Gyby, 1376, Reeves, Cardigan. There is a Llangybi in Ceredigion; is it possible that the *Gyby* is taken from the mutated form of *Cybi* in the place-name? Cf. also the name *Kibbey* found in Monmouth – Rogiet; there is a *Llangybi*, variously spelt, in Monmouthshire.

Cyfeiliog *(v.* also Introd. Place-names).

The commote of Cyfeiliog was in the river Dovey region. It was attached to the name of its lord, Owain Cyfeiliog. Earlier in the tenth century there was a Cyfeiliog, Bishop of Llandaff. The name has not been found in the usual sources but the following rare example was picked up: Leyester and Mainwaring, *Tracts ... respecting the legitimacy of Amicia, daughter of Hugh Cyveliok*, 1673-79, ed. by W. Beaumont, Manchester, Chetham Society, 1869.

Cyfnerth

This name has not become a surname; recording examples here from early texts may help someone who has to deal with early materials. The *-fn-*, especially when written *-un-* causes great difficulty to copyists and editors, and the intrusive or epenthetic vowel sound put between *f* and *n* makes matters worse.

AnglCourt 1346 (translated and edited text) 39. Dafydd ap Cyfnerth, 40. Cyfnerth ap Ieuan (MS = Kefn'). B1. 263. NW 1304 De Keffnerth ap David. B5. 60. Lleyn, late 13th century. Keynerch ap y palla (leg. Keunerth ?). B5. 145. CaernLSR 1292. Kyfner. B14. 237. NW temp. Edw 1. David AbKenenard; (= ap Keuenarth). 241. de Kenenard ap Leulyn; 241. David ap Keneward. B15. 46. AS 1406 (partly edited) Mad ap Kyfnerth ... 50. Kynfnerth. B26. 81. Fragment of Welsh

Roll: Keneuardum ab David (= Keuenard mab). Lp Oswestry 32/33. Kyneverth (1393) = Kyvnerth (1586) = Kyfnerth (1602).

Cyffin (Kyffin)

Cyffin as a common noun means 'border, limit, boundary, neighbourhood'; it could become a place-name or residential name in more than one place. The context of the following examples implies three (at least) quite different places named *Cyffin* becoming a surname:

B23. 166. Arundel Charters, Lp of Chirk, 14th century. Madog Kyffin. PWLMA 248. 1399- Rhys Kyffin. Star CP 222. James I, Miscellaneous: Ric'd Kyffin als Lloyd, of Twyford. DLancaster (Kidwelly) 260. Roger Kyffin. JEG 196. Maenan, near Llanrwst: 'Madog Kyffin', 'He took the surname Kyffin (or Cyffin), being nursed in a place of that name in Llangedwyn [= Chirk, Denbs] to distinguish himself from his father Madog Gôch'; pp.196-7, and p.198, large number of descendants named Kyffin.

SHROPSHIRE REGISTERS

Alberbury 357, 1720. .... d. of Edward and Elizabeth Kyffin; p.301, Kyffin occurs as a christian name. Pontesbury 90. 1608. Johis Kiffin. Ludlow 46. 1638. John Keffin; 177. 1628. John Kephin. Myddle 159. 1723. Simon Cuffin (this conveys the proper pronunciation). Condover 149. 1692. Mary Keffin. Wrockwardine 44. 1671. John ... s. of Henry Kiffen and Jane; 46. 1673. .... d. of Henry Kiffin and Jane; 77. 1695. John Cuffin; 170. 1745. Samuel Kyffin, of p. of St Chads. Whittington 99. 1614. Elin Kyffin, wife of Tyrston ap David, of Francton.

The name survives in the Border counties: *Kyffin*, City of Chester, Trinity Ward 3; Cheadle Bredbury Ward South; Wirral, Hoglake, Hoose Ward, Greasby Ward 2; Wrexham, Esclusham Below, Rhosllannerchrugog, Ponciau North. *Cuffin*, Llangollen Rural, Trevor Isa; Wrexham, Cefn-mawr; Rhosymedre and Cefn bychan, Cefn 2 - Acrefair and Penybryn, Ruabon South.

Cymro

It is understandable that a man from Wales can earn for himself the epithet *Welsh, Welch, Walsh*, but why should a man be called *Cymro* in Wales? One possible answer is that the epithet might be earned within an English community or a bilingual society.

RecCa 105 Ieuan Gymro. InvECP 166 Brecs 1538 John ap Rice Gymrowe. Reg Council Marches - Llanidloes 176 David ap Lewis Comro. BBStD 69 Dauid Kymro (cf. 26 Ieuan Welch; 30 Clemens Wlach - surely Welch).

SHROPSHIRE REGISTERS:

Ruyton 33. 1749 John Richards, Cumro. 34. 1750 Mary Richards, vid. Cumro. Whittington 74. 1634. John *s* of John Vaughan alias Kimro [?] of Daywall. Oswestry 71. 1580. Robert ap Ieuan als Gymro. 77. 1581. David ap John Wyn Gymro.

Following *ap*, as if it were a pers. name:

B4. 156. Ardudwy 1325. Iorwerth Loit ap Kymero.

Cynddelw

LHEB 677 gives the derivation Brit. **Cunodeluos*. This name is best known in the med. period as the name of the great twelfth century poet Cynddelw Brydydd Mawr ('Cynddelw the Great Poet'). It should be made clear that -*w* is consonantal and does not amount to a syllable; in other words, the name is disyllabic, with the accent falling on the *cyn-*. Because of its distance from the accent there is a strong tendency for the -*w* to disappear in normal pronunciation of comparable words, arddelw/arddel; syberw/syber; cefnderw/ cefnder.

B6. 359. NW 1326. Iorwerth ap Kendalo ap Eignon. B13. 142. Bonds Peace 1283. Yorward fil Kyndelv. BBStD 286. Cradoc ap Kendelou. Mer LSR 9. Ithel ap Candalo; 15. Candalou; 18. Candalo; 31. Kendalo Croum; 62. Madoco Kenthlu; 71. Candalo 'An(er)in. Glam Cartae 544. Candelo ab Walter. RecCa 95. David ap Kindelw; 70. Kendal ap Dauid; 100. Dd ap Kendell; 108. Kyndol Goch. (Index: Kendal, Kendall, Kendell, Kyndel, Kyndell', Kyndelw, Kyndol, Kindelw, Kynthell). B10. 163. AnglCrownRental, 16th century ... ap Kynddel, 172. ditto; 172. ... ap Kynddell; 174. Kynddel ap madoc; Kyndel voyl. B15. 46. AS 1406. Kynddel dew; 48. ... ap Je(uan) gynddel; 53. ... ap Kynthell. [A few examples were collected of *Knethell, Knythull*: B7. 285. N. Pembs 1599. Baultozar Knethell of Haverfordwest; 314. Baulthaser Knether; B13. 93. N. Pembs 16th century estate, ref. to John Knethell; B.22. 36. Acct. Swansea 1449, Philip Knythull. Is it possible that these are versions, through metathesis, of Cynddel/ Kynthell?] CaernHS 26. Bolde Rental, 44. Eva vz Nest vz Kenthel. CaernCR 62. Gwilym ap Cynddelw (MS Willi ap Kendal). RCA 190. ... hamlet of botkendalo. JEG 85. ... of Gardd Gynddel, in the parish of Bodedern. 135. a long line, including ... Howel Chwith ap Cynddal ap H. ap S. 185. a long line, including Dafydd ab Ednyfed Chwith ap Cynddel ap Howel. HBr (2 edition) Append VI. vol. 2. Survey of Manor of Brecknock taken 13 Henry 8th, Honor of Hereford Breknok, Robert Kendall holdeth a knight's fee in Avenbury. PRLlantrithyd 42. 1671. ffrancis Kendell of the p'sh of Welsh St Donatts.

There are forms in the Shropshire registers, and in present-day registers which are quite certainly versions of Cynddelw:
Ludlow 71. Isabel Candell. 68. 1572. Thomas Cundell (Index includes with it, 64. 1568. Richard Cuttdell). TD Shrewsbury – Hereford, Cundale, Bosbury; Cundall, Hereford; Cundle, Shrewsbury. D. Tel 3.5.78. Deaths, Herbert Fletcher Cundall (no address given). D. Tel 17.10.78 Deaths, Cundell (no address). D. Tel 30.8.79. Letters to editor, Cundall; ibid 13.11.79, Deaths, ditto (Chichester). D. Tel 14.2.79. Deaths, Cundelu, Percy Lionel, 1 Hill Road, Swanage, aged 83.

Before proceeding it is interesting to observe that Förster regarded the English name Condell as a loan from Cynddelw; v. LHEB 677, 670. A name found quite often in the Shropshire registers is Kendal, Kendall. The name of the town in Cumbria comes to mind at once as the origin of the surname, but the versions above of Kendal, Kendell etc. which are obviously for Cynddel(w), and the location of the examples found on the Welsh border justify the suggestion that in some cases the name Kendal, Kendell is derived from an attempt to spell Cynddel(w).

A few references in the Shropshire registers: Kendal, Hughley 52, Badger, 26; Kendall, Ludlow 666, 756, 649; Oldbury 17, Milson 5. There is a fairly high incidence of Kendel/ Kendell on the Border, for instance the TD for Chester and NW has 21 entries, and one significant entry is spelt Kendell, a form also collected from D. Tel 4.1.78.

Cynddylan
This is the name in the famous verses *Ystafell Gynddylan*. The name is not found often in the medieval period, e.g. Bartrum 300-985, 65, Cynddylan ap Cyndrwyn – the prince, being the only example; 985-1215, no example. A few random instances were collected:
B14. 240. NW temp Edw I. de Maddoco filio Candelan. B16. 131. NW temp Edw I. Tuderi ap Kandalon. BBStD 114. Lleukeu filia Kendelau (trans. Kendelau; correct to Kendelan). RecCa 96. Elidir ap Pendelon (surely Kendelon). Glam Cartae 246. Kandalanus, presb. Surveys GK (Clase and Landewy in Gower 1326) 192. Cradocus ap Kendelan. RCA 11, Anglesey, place-name, Careg Cynthylan.

There are forms in the Shropshire registers which bear some resemblance:
Tasley 4, 8, 9, 13, 14, 15, 16, 20. Canland, Candland, Candlan. Bromfield 23. Ann Candland (the only entry: cf. 20. Ankret. Jn. Caudland, looks as if it is a misreading of Candland). Ludlow, Index, Candland, Canland, Clanland, a dozen entries.

The form *Candeland* is still found and it is quite remarkable that it is found oftenest in the area more or less identified with the seventh century Cynddylan. *Candeland*, TD (1978) Chester and NW (address in Chester); Wirral, Ellesmere Port, Grange Ward 2, Romeley Rd; Hoylake, Grange and Newton Ward; Neston, Leighton and Parkgate; Wirral, Haswell Ward; Irby and Thurstaston. *Candlin*, TD Chester and NW (address Tyn-y-gongl); Shrewsbury – Hereford, ten entries.

MacLysaght, *Irish Families* 250 puts three surnames together, O'Quinlan, Quinlevan, Kindellan: 'Quinlan is the Munster form of the Gaelic O'Caoindealbhin which in Leinster, where the sept originated, was usually anglicized as Kindellan, and in modern times as Conlan and Connellan ... At that time (i.e. defeat of James II) the form of the name in use in co. Meath was Kindellan and this has been retained in Spain, the country in which they settled as exiles. The Kindellans have been prominent in Spain since then', v. also MacLysaght *Guide* 124, '(O)Kendillon, A co. Louth variant of Kindellan'.
Kindellan, in spite of the O'Caoindealbhin, is

suspiciously like Cynddylan, but any connexion must be left to Irish scholarship. Examples of *Kindellan* found in Wales, and in Britain generally, must be the names of families of Irish origin. *Kindelan*, TD Chester and NW (1978) Deeside; Holyhead (= Elect. Reg. Holyhead Southern Ward) Elect. Reg. East Flint, Bagillt West. *Quindelin*, Preseli, H'west, Haroldston St Issel.

Cynffig (Kenfig)
The original Cynffig in mid-Glamorgan is best known as 'the buried city of Kenfig'; the name remains in Abercynffig and Mynydd Cynffig (Kenfig Hill). Glam Cartae 517 has David fil Wasmeri de Kenefec, but there is no example in Clark of Kenfig as a personal name, but Swansea TD has 3 examples of *Kenifick* in Port Talbot.
Kennifeck is given in C L'Estrange Ewen p.242 as a surname found in Ireland; MacLysaght, *Guide* 125 has 'Kenefick – It is taken from a Welsh placename'. One may surmise that a Norman or Welshman from the area, included in the forces which invaded Ireland, adopted it as a territorial name.

Cynfyn
This pers. name occurs in the place-name Ysbyty Cynfyn, in Cwmrheidol, Dyfed. There is no lack of examples; the chief variations are *Cen-* in the first syllable and *-wyn* in the final syllable. Its special habitat is Gwent.
B13. 223 SR 1292. 'Talgar-Ystrad-ew' Kenuyn Vaghan. Mer LSR 48. Cad(ugan) ap Kenwain. RecCa 272. M'edd Voel ap Conovane. DLancaster, 'Grossemont', 71. Johannes William Kynvin; cf. 127. J.W. Kenvin. Albo Castro 124. . . . nuper Howelli Kynven, 129. Howellus Kenvin nuper Willelmi Hoell Kenwyn. B25. 229. re. lands of Earl of Worcester in 1530s . . . De Thoma Kenwyn (Crickhowell, Tretŵr). Star CP 96. Monm Eliz. Howell Kenwyn (Llantilio), 110. Howell Kynwyn. 197. Monm Hywel Kynvyn. PRLlanfair Discoed 1683. Henry Kunvin, 1702. Bowles Kunvin. BYale 88. Wyon ap Ior Kengwyn.
In present-day electoral regs. *Kenvyn* (*Kenvin*) is found in several places, but the biggest concentration is in the southern portion of Brecon-Radnor; (cf. an address in Llanfighangel Cwmdu-Tretower: *Tycynfin*) and in the several constituencies of Gwent.

Examples at a distance from Gwent:
S. Gloucs, Siston, Sodbury – Yate, Mangotsfield Rural 1; Bromsgrove, Redditch NW; Runcorn, Halton. *Cunvin*, Brecon Rad. Llanelly – Darrenfelin; Brynmawr Western. *Canvin*, City of Hereford, Bartonsham RC; Crewe North 3; BrRad, Old Radnor. *Kenevin*, Copeland, St John's Backermet.

Kenyon
Mer LSR 52. Cunnian (Trawsfynydd); 71. Ririd Cannian. BYale 102. Madoc ap Kynnyon, Grono ap Kennyon.
These forms are obviously separate from *Cynan* etc.

Cynan
Cynan is a distinguished name in the royal line of Gwynedd and it is strange, in view of this, that it is not a popularly adopted name. Bartrum 300-985 has fourteen examples. LHEB 666 has Britt. *Cunagnos > OW Cinan, MW Cynan, OB Conan; *v.* also B26. 2, Old Breton Genealogies, Conan/Kenan. BBStD 250. Kenan ap Kenewric . . . Ieuan ap Kediuor Canan. Kanan ap Kenewric . . . Ieuan ap Kenan. PWLMA 16. Cynan ap Hywel, lord of Emlyn Vwch Cuch. BYale 82. Kenon ap Iagowe (trans. Cynan; cf. 96 Conyn Vergan, tr. Cynan Fychan). Lp Oswestry 34-35. Kinan (1393) = Konan (1586) = Kynan (1602). PRConway 1625. Wm ap Conan. Star CP 133. Pembs, Eliz. Jas ap Kynon. PRWhittington 17. 1598. Margret verch Tho Kynon.
PRESENT-DAY REGISTERS
The names set out below are generally regarded as Irish but as shown above, names very much like some of them were formerly in use in Wales:
Kinnon, Stalybridge & Hyde, Hyde – Godley; Westmorland Kendal, Fell. Kennon, Penrith and Border, Wetheral – Wetheral Ward; Carlisle, Petteril, Morton Workington, Cockermouth (several), Broughton, Lorton. Kennan, Workington, Cockermouth. Keenan, Workington, Cockermouth. Connon, Carlisle, Belle Vue.

Cynwrig, Cynfrig
One may judge how popular the name used to be by a count from the Genealogies: Bartrum 1215-1350, 215-218 has 95 examples as first name. The origin given in Reaney cannot possibly be right, i.e. the letters *-wr-* cannot be

for (g)ŵr, 'man', with a suffix added, because *Cynwrig* is disyllabic, with the accent on *Cyn-*, i.e. the *w* is consonantal; the variant *Cynfrig* is itself sufficient evidence. The combination of *-nwr-* is not going to remain stable in colloquial speech: one of the changes that can be expected is *-nfr-*, but more likely still the simple change to *-nr-*, to give *Cynrig*. The two sonants together, *-nr-*, will either produce an epenthetic vowel or change to *-ndr-*, for instance, *Hennery*, *Hendry*. Some of the examples quoted below will show the epenthetic vowel, others will show the *-ndr-*. Certain words in Welsh dialect have *-nthr-* instead of *-ndr-*: the best known example is *Y Felenrhyd* becoming *Lenthryd*, v. PKM 263; the note quotes *Penthryn, cynthron* for *Penrhyn, cynron*; in all three cases, they are sometimes found as *Pendryn, cyndron, Lendryd (Lentryd)*.

The following represent the variety of forms and spellings:
B1. 263. 1304. De Kenewrico Seys; B15. 131. de Cunewrico Seys. B2. 54. 1304. Eynon ab Kenewreik. B4. 227. Keneric ap Eignon. B5. 60, 61, 65, 67. Kenric. B10. 260. 1352. Iorwerth ap Kenwric. B13. 143. 1295. Kenewreck. B13. 221. Kenewrich, 226. Kenewryg. B15. 43. Kynrick, Kynrik. B26. 85. 1322. (Welsh troops on Scott. Campaign) Kenewerk. BBStD 216. Knewrik. CaernQSR 182. Kynerik. Mer LSR 44. Kenuric; 86. Kenneric; 87. Kennewric (cf. 36. kenuig; could be for Kenffig, but more likely to be miscopy of Kenurig). Star CP 145, Miscell. Kenverick; cf. PRConway 1573. Joes Kenverickes. Ex Pro James I. 17 Kynrige. InvECP 6. Kynneryke; 106. Kenerek; 119. Kenrigge; 123. Kynuryche; 123. Kenrike; 126. Conrycke.

There is an early example of *-ndr-* in B5. 59, late 13th century : Ade ap Kendric; cf. Shrops R. Myddle 93. 1636. Sep Kendrici, f. Willielmi Jones; 156. 1723. Martha Kynderick.

The following specimen examples were taken from the Shropshire registers:
Highley 15. Kenricke, cf. 4. Kenwicke.

Hopesay, Index, Kendright, included with Kenrick, Kendricke. (Reaney classifies *Kenwright* as a variant; 'Kenwright [from Kenwrig]' is given in L'Estrange Ewen p.125 amongst the Welsh surnames found in documents in the PRO.) Condover 2. 1571. Kenrigg. Selattyn 203. 1685. (place-name) ... of Pentre cynthrig. 217. 1695. Richard Centhrick; 263. 1735. Cynthric Wynn, of Chirk = 278. 1744. Kynfrig Wynn. Whittington 168. 1647. Kingricke. Kinnerley, Index, Centrick, Centhrig.

Cf. Sannan 1729, 1730. Jarrett filius spurius Jarretti *Kynthric* et ... Glam Hearth Tax, 'Penthery', Thomas Gunrick (a scribal error, the difference between *-sk-* and *-sg-* being hard to distinguish).

In the present-day registers there is a widespread distribution of *Kendrick* all along the Border; there is an address, Pentrekendrick, in the p. of Whittington, Gobowen Ward. One is surprised to find so many instances of *Kenwrick* surviving, Bromsgrove S.E.; N.E.; Redditch N.W.; South Worcs, Malvern West.

There are occasional examples of *Kenrick*, Kidderminster, Wolverley No.1; Abertillery, Blaina South (v), Nantyglo. Cf. also Preseli, Milford – Hakin Ward, *Kenderick*.

There is an Irish *Mackendrick*; this is given in MacLysaght, *Guide*, 125, '(Mac) Kendrick, MacEanraic. In north-west Ulster the prefix is usually retained; elsewhere the name has become Kenrick'.

Cynyr

G has examples, not many, of this name; there is no historical person of this name in the index of Lloyd, HW. TYP 307 has a fairly full note on *Kenyr/Cynyr*. Structurally the form *Cynyr* is derived from the nominative form in Brythonic; the oblique cases giving *Cynri*, which occurs in the Gododdin poem, CA 127, (cf. Tudyr, Tudri).
Star CP 208. Pem James I. Francis, son of Jno and Eliz. Kynner, 209. Francis Kinner, gent. This is the only example discovered.

D

Dafydd, David, Dewi

Dewi and *Dafydd* represent two stages of borrowing *David* (through Latin) into Welsh. The form *Dewi* (v. LHEB 427) shows the loss of the final -*dd* which the name would have in its earliest Welsh form; the loss of final -*dd* is not an invariable characteristic of Welsh, but it does occur in a number of instances, and in the speech of Pembrokeshire it is a regular feature. The other change in the process of borrowing is the affection of -*a* into *e* before -*i*. (The early instances of the name in the form *Degui*, as in LL 275, have the orthographic device or mannerism of using *gu* for *w*.) The saint's name is seen in the many churches and parishes of *Llanddewi* which generally have some additional distinguishing element; and in English versions such as *Dewchurch*.

Dafydd was borrowed at a later stage, and the later date probably explains why the -*a*- is not affected. This form of name was very widely adopted in the medieval period, whereas the use of *Dewi* is rare. (*Dewi* has become a popular christian name in the twentieth century). *Dafydd* remained as standard version, i.e. with no loss of final -*dd*, but this did happen colloquially, to produce *Dafy'* (*Davy*). There was always an awareness that *Dafydd* was the Welsh for *David*, and scribes generally use *Dauid* or *David* in the med. period. Later, in the early modern period, it became regular practice to register boys as David, and the use of *Dafydd* went out of fashion.

Official documents, on the whole, use the abbreviation *Dd* or *dd* which textual editors generally fill out; or they have the standard form *David*, but one can safely assume that these represent *Dafydd*: e.g. B6. 256, Lleyn, Ministers' Accounts, 1350, *Davith ap hona*

(leg. *houa*); there are four other instances on the same page, all *David*; in the Conway PR 1586, ap David and Davies are seen together, but one must assume that 'ap David' was in fact 'ap Dafydd'. One naturally finds examples of *Dafydd* in texts which are the result of editing, such as the pedigrees of Bartrum, but in texts which reproduce the original, examples which show 'Dafydd' clearly are rare. But in the transition which turned the father's name into a fixed surname for son (and descendants) *Dafydd* survived as surname in a few instances, e.g. WPortBooks 95 *Yevan Davethe* of Pembroke, and one can refer to the hymn writers of the 18th century, John Dafydd and Morgan Dafydd, both of Caeo, and Owen Dafydd, the local poet of Cwmaman.

No amount of research will determine where and when the first example of *Dafy'* (*Davy*) came about, but the tendency in Dyfed to drop final *dd* provides an obvious explanation.

BBStD 18. Wills Davy (= William Davy); 26. Davy Ibell; 154. Margeria Davy, Isabell Dauy; (cf. 18. Dauid Coyg; 24. Dauid le Proute 28. Dauid Benedic). CAP 228-9. Davy Adain (1330-1. Pembroke, text French). 207-8. Davy ap Madok (1305-7. Gower). DLancaster (Fforrenry Dominii de Kedwelly) 198. Thomas Davye; 227, three examples of Davy. Star CP 6. Glam, Owen Davye. PWLMA. Index, entries of John Davy; 423. Philip Davy; 1418. Reeve, Cardigan. InvECP 49. Carms 1533-6. David ap David alias Davy Davy.

The addition of the E genitive *'s* produces *Davys, Davis, Davies*:

BX 69 Crown Lands, W. Wales 1352. Oliver

Daveys nuper constablarium Castri de Kermerdyn.

Bartrum has no example of *Davy*, but there is one entry which combines 'Davies' and the patronymic system, 1350-1415, 533. Dafydd Davies ap Gwilym ap Dafydd.

English administration brought about a spread of *Davies* in the sixteenth century and the following examples illustrate:
Star CP 141. Jno Davys of London, poor, true and faithful. 200. Jno ap Dd als Davyes. InvECP 63. Pembs 1518. William Davys. 102. Denbs. 1556. John Davys. 102. 1556. John and Edward Davys of the City of London.

There was always a possibility that certain families would have the surname *David*, the father's name at the time of acquiring the fixed surname being the 'standard' form of David, and in those cases 'David' continued (i.e. without the addition of *'s*) just as *John* remained in other families without becoming 'Jones'. The records of Haverfordwest show the addition of *-s* to *David*; the index has twelve entries of David as surname: cf. 243. Alban Davids; several more entries of Davids, Davides. These forms would eventually succumb to *Davies*. One finds many instances of wavering between *David* and *Davis/Davies* as surname. HM iii, pt. ii, p.159 gives the reading on flat stones in the church of Llantrisant, Evan Davis 1773, Thomas the son of Evan Davis 1753, aged 13; a footnote points out that the PR in each case has David, and when Anne wife of Evan died, she is called David. Later still, Thomas Essile Davies (1820-91), of Dinas Powys, South Glam. was christened 'David'; his parents were 'David', and he is Thomas David in the certificate of marriage, but he chose to use the form Davies generally; his gravestone has 'David', his son used David.

The Shropshire registers have the following:
Stanton Lacy 10. 1576. William s. of Hugh ap Davith; 25. 1599. Mathew ap Davith. Alberbury 4. 1565. Franciscus ap David's. Bromfield, p.11. Owen ap Yevan Davids; p.2. Edm. Davids ap Morice. Donington 13. 1583. Yeavan Davye; 14. 1584. Davye Bedward.

The following single instance of *Dewie* was collected, which may have had its origin in the parish name of Llanddewi:
Diddlesbury 29. 1688. Abraham Dewie.

A few examples of *Dewey* were picked up from present-day registers:
S. Gloucs Sodbury – Wickwar; CT Leckhampton S., Woodmancote. Ludlow, Bridgnorth St Leonard; Oswestry, Whitchurch Urban; City of Hereford.

HYPOCORISTIC AND COLLOQUIAL FORMS OF DAI, DEI, DEIO, DEIA, DEIAN, DEITO, DEICYN, DEIWYN, DEICWS.

Examples of Dai, Dei (Dye, Day)
Dai is much in use as a familiar form of David, especially in the colloquial speech of boys and young men; this colloquial usage has brought about a feeling that it is not 'good form' to use it in a context requiring respect. As medieval writing usually uses *ei* (for modern *ei* and *ai* regardless of position in the word) one cannot be quite sure whether the text should be understood as Dai or Dei, and in many cases modern editing may have altered the original text. (In case of misunderstanding it should be made clear that although the evidence of the examples to be quoted prove that Dai/Dei is the probable origin of Day, Dayes as surname in the E. Border counties, it does not exclude the possibility that *Day* as an E. surname may come from an English source as well, for example, ELS Cumberland [Armathwaite], p.29, John Day.)

Examples of *Dai/Dei* abound, occasionally with the def. art. but generally without.
B5. 58. Lleyn, 13c. y dei duy (D. black). B15. 145. Caern 1293. y dai du; 146. dai bach; 147. dai ap arthur. B23. 343. Mawddwy Court 1415. Day Moel. CaernQSR 11. Retherch ap Day; 232. Rhydderch ap Thomas ap Day. ADClun 93. Lewelin ap Day; 183. Deye Powys; 189. Thomas Dye; 208. Gutto ap Howel ap Dye. Bartrum 1215-1350. 241, Dai Moel ap Einion; 241, Dai ap Ieuan ap Dafydd Goch; 1350-1415. 552. four examples. 585. Gutun ap y Dai ap Madog Llwyd; 599. Hywel ap y Dai ap Madog Llwyd. p.570 has the five variants, Gruffudd ap Dafydd . . . ap Dai; ap Dakin, ap Deicws, ap Deio.

The Shropshire registers have many examples, with a variety of spelling, together with examples of adding the genitive *s*.
Bromfield. Index. Day (Dey). Alberbury 16. 1573. Hugo Deyes; 17. Johannes Deyes. Claverley. Index puts the following together,

Dee, Day, Dayes, Dey, Deye (*Dee* should be kept separate). Ludlow. Index. Day, Daye, Dey, Deyes. Oswestry 462. 1628. Elizabeth the wife of thomas ap Evan Daie. 640. 1665. Simon the sonne of Samuell sherman. The said Simon sonne of the said Samuell Dai. 671. 1668. Richard the sonne of Samuell Day sherman. 659. 1667. Elizabeth Davies als Daye the wief of Henry the weaver. Shrewsbury BR 1519. Lewis Day . . . s. Madoc ap Day of Welshpool (i.e. *Day* becoming surname, instead of 'ap Madoc'). In the case of some entries it is difficult to keep the genitive *s* form of Day and Deio apart: Alberbury 18. 1575. Rogerus Deyos, ib. 6. Johanna fil. Rogeri Deyes; 43. 1611. Willimus Dyos de Rowton; 44. 1611. Catherina Deyes de Rowton; 44. 1611, Margareta f. Willimi Deyes de Rowton; 264. 1689. Roger Dioss.

Examples of Day, Daye, Dey, Dye, are scattered throughout the border counties, and in Wales more especially in South Pembroke-shire. A few locations are noted here:
Day: Ludlow, Hopton Wafers; Leominster, Linton, Whitbourne; W. Gloucs, Newent; South Pembs, Penally, L. Velfrey, Narberth. *Daye*: S. Pembs, Begelley; Preseli, Wiston. *Dey*: Oswestry, Llanymynech; City of Glouc, Longlevens p.29; Islwyn, Pengam. *Deyes*: Hereford, Shipton. *Dye*: Conway, Bangor North 1.

Examples of Deio, with various spellings
The first examples show an awareness that *Deio* is a synonym of David (Dafydd):
B11. 58. Broniarth i429-, David et Goleuddith . . . Gwenhoyvar fil' dict' Deio et Goleuddith. InvECP 165, Brecknocke 1553-, John David alias John Dyow Ronowe; 226. Usk Monm. 1538. Thomas Dio alias Davy. Bartrum 1215-1350. 542. Dafydd/Deio ap Iorwerth ap Hwfa. 543. Dafydd/Deio ap John ap Hywel. Phillimore, 588. Montgomery, ref. to one of the Welsh archers at Agincourt, 'Deyow ap Llewellyn Guynva', which occurs in a roll of the Earl of Arundel (Arch. Camb III. XII. 398-9). B11. 61. Broniarth 1429- Deio ap ll' ap Ieu(a)n. 60. Deio ap Egyn' duy . . . Deio baz ap Deio . . . 67. Dio ap Eignus duy . . . Deio ap Eignus Duy. BBStD 68. Ieuan ap Deyo. Glam Cartae, Index, Dio, Dyo – abundance. Bartrum 1350-1415. 553-4. Deio, forty-six examples. Star CP 50.

Ievan Harry Deyo; 77. Wm Dyo; 180. Wm Lewis Dio. InvECP 31. . . . ap Dio; 126. . . . ap Dyogh; 150. . . . ap Dyo Baugh . . . ap Dio Baugh. 212. Hoell(ap) Ieuan Dyoo of St George, co Glam . . . John Ieuan Dyo of Wells, co. Somerset.

In the Shropshire registers *Deio* and *Deios*, variously spelt, are found in abundance; the following selection illustrates the range of variants:
More 6. Eliz. Deyos. Clunbury 92. Dyas. Lydham 8. 1617. . . . Owen Dio; 52. 1792. Benjamin Dyos. Bromfield, Index, Dayhouse, Deyus, Deyas. Middleton Scriven 7. Dyos. Alberbury 18. 1575. Rogerus Deyos, *v*. above. Ch. Stretton 100. 1731. Thomas Dayhouse p. of Tuckford. 114. 1766. Martha Dayhouse; 18. 1768. Anna Dayhouse. Worthen, Index, Dyas, Deios, Deyos, Dias, Diass, Dios, Dioss, Dyass, Dyos, Dyoss, Dyus. Pontesbury 203. 1681. . . . Dyoes; 204. 1682. . . . Dious; Westbury 13. 1644. . . . Dioce, of Minsterley. Ludlow 20. 1596. John Dyous; 339. 1627. Henry Deyose. 1169. 1812; 1239. 1811. . . . Dayus; 1231. 1804. . . . Dayos. Index: Dayus; Dayars, Dayas, Dayos, Deios, Dejos etc. Diddlesbury 51. 1746. Richard Dyhouse. 101. 1700. Edward Dayas. 202. 1773. Mary d. of Samuel Dyhouse and Mary. 204. 1773. Anne d. of William Dyhorse and Mary. 213. 1783. Esther d. of William Dyhorse and Mary. Kinlet 105. 1747. Daniel s. of Wm Dayhouse and Ann; 107. 1749. ditto. 101. 1741. Sarah d. of William Dayus and Ann. 111. 1754. William Dayus (Churchwarden). 122. 1763. William Dayhouse, buried. 128. 1770. Ann Dayhouse, buried. High Ercall 198. 1676. Johannes Dioz. Eaton under Heywood 73. 1743. Dayus; Daus (variants of same person) = 79. 1750. Dayace. Sheinton 34. 1805. John Dayhus.

Examples of Dyhouse, Dayhouse, Dayhus have been included on the assumption that they are versions of Deios. The register of Diddlesbury has Gitthouse which is an attempt to explain, or give a meaning to, Gittoes, Gittus; and the register of Ch. Stretton has 148. 1764, Joseph Dackhouse, 159. 1773, Joseph Dacus, which is obviously Deicws. On the other hand a surname derived from Dyehouse/Dayhouse, is far from impossible for it occurs in these registers as the

name of a residence; e.g. High Ercall 214.
1681, ... Be it remembered that I, Thomas
Lawrenson, of the Day-house, in the
township of Crudgington and parish of High
Ercall ... for ye said Dayhouse tenement;
217. 1682, Elizabetha Lawranson, de
Mansione vocata Day-house; Leebotwood
50. 1734, ... of John Langford of the
Dayhouse; 76. 1800, Richard Everalt,
Dayhouse; 80. 1809, born ... at the
dayhouse, Cardington; Tibberton; 11.1734,
... of the Dayhouse; 51. 1791, Mrs Elizabeth
Taylor, Dayhouse; 54. 1803, Mr John
Taylor, Dayhouse.

EXAMPLES FROM PRESENT-DAY REGISTERS

Dayas, BrRad, Presteigne. *Dayos*, Ludlow,
Broad St. *Dayus*, Ludlow, Burford; Cleobury
Mortimer; Wrekin, Wellington, Hadley.
Leominster, Bishops Frome; Macclesfield,
Congleton North 2. *Dyas*, Shrewsbury,
Westbury; Ludlow, Benthall; Wrekin,
Woodcote. Wrexham, Ponciau North;
Monmouth, Buckholt. *Dyoss*, Kidderminster,
Dodenham. *Dyus*, Cirencester 1. *Dyehouse*,
S. Worcs, Evesham West, Hampton.
Dyhouse, Bromsgrove No. 6. N.E.; Denbigh,
Ll-yn-Rhos – Eirias Ward. *Dayhhouse* as a
place-name and as the name of a house
survives in Cardington, Dayhouse Cottage
and Lower Dayhouse. The pers. name *Dayus*
is also found in the village.

Examples of Deicyn, Dackyn, etc:

B7. 144. Caern 1303. Daykyn grach. B14.
312. temp. Edw I, Daykyn Cran. B15. 44, AS
1406. Dykan ap Atha. B11. 57. Broniarth
1429 – Dackyn ap Dack' ap Ior'; 65. Ieuan
ap Dackyn ap Dackus ap Io'. Mer LSR 70.
Deykin. CaernQSR 173. Robert ap Ieuan
Dackyn. BBStD 38. Daykyn Aylmer.
ADClun 48. Johanne Dykonns; 86. John
Decon. PWLMA 461, 466, 467. Deicyn
Powys. Bartrum 1350-1415. 552, Dakin;
thirteen examples. InvECP 141. Monts 1538.
Gattyn ap Dickon alias Griffyn ap Dacken.
257. Marches, 1547. Hoell Dackyn son ... of
Dackyn ap Dyo. 260. Marches, 1553 ...
heirs of Dackyn ap Gittyn ap Madwyn, of
Camberwell, co. Surrey.

SHROPSHIRE REGISTERS

Ford 18. Deacon; 48. Dickin. Hanwood 50,
53, 54, 69. Dackin, Dackine; 10. Deakon.
Hopton Castle 28, 31. Dekin, Dekyn.
Lydham 49, 50. Dicken. Cardeston, Index,

Dackin, Dacken, Dacking, Dicken. Burford
11. 1587. Richard Deykynes = 14. 1594.
Richard Deykines. 11. 1588. Johane Deykyns

PRESENT-DAY REGISTERS

Dakin, Wrekin, Shifnal, Sheriffhales; S.
Hereford, Linton. *Dakeyne*, Cheadle, Gatley
No.3. *Daking*, Newport, Dyffryn. *Daykin*,
City of Glouc, Westgate p.21; Cheadle, Ch.
Hulme No.2; Newport, Shaftesbury 1. St
Julian's 3, Caerleon. *Deakin*, Ludlow,
Bishops Castle, Colebatch; City of Hereford,
Holmer; S. Hereford, Bridstow. Leominster,
Staunton; Kidderminster, Alberley; S.
Pembs, St Issells, S. Ward. *Deakins*, City of
Glouc, Westgate p.21; Ludlow, Bishops
Castle, Mainstone; Leominster, Staunton.
Dekin, Torfaen, Griffithstown and
Sebastopol; Conway, Conway Marl 1.
Dekins, S. Hereford, Ross; Stroud, Upton St
Leonards, C. of Glouc, Longlevens p.7.
Deykin, S. Worcs, Malvern South, No.1 or
Priory; Preseli, Dale. *Dykins*, S. Gloucs,
Cinderford 3; West Flints, Mold West; East
Flints, Connahs Quay, Wepre. *Dickin,*
Dicken, Ludlow, Bishops Castle.

Examples of Deicws:

B15. 43. AS 1406. Deikws ap Tegau; 44.
Dykws goch crech; Dykws ap dd ap Ithel
Kneivio; 45. Matto ap Dikws chwith. (Many
others in this text.) B23. 338. Mawddwy
1415. Daicws ap y Bady. AnglPleas 6. Res ap
Hoell ap Gruffith ap Dicus. PWLMA 423.
Hywel Deicws (1420 ... Cardigan.) 422.
Walter Deicus (1413 ... Cardigan.) Bartrum
1215-1350. 218. Dacws, two examples, cf.
315. Ieuan ap Dacws. 241. Deicws, eleven.
539. Dafydd ap Ieuan ap Heilin = 554.
Deicws ap Ieuan ap Heilin. 546. Dafydd/
Deicws ap Madog Mwyn ap Madog.
1350-1415. 553-4. Deicws, thirty eight.
InvECP 20. Caern 1553 Howell ap David
Dicus ... D. ap I. ap Dicus. H Asaph 1. 528.
Edward Dacus, AB, Vicar of Cedewain 1525.
Cf. Caernarfon Electoral Register,
Llanbedrog, place-name, Caedeicws.

SHROPSHIRE REGISTERS:

Oswestry 2. 1558. Elen Dicus. 255. 1604.
John Thomas Dacus. 306. 1610. Moris fil
Georgij Dickws. Ch. Stretton 148. 1764.
Joseph Dackhouse, 159. 1773. Joseph Dacus.

Examples of Deia:

In med writing the letter *n* is often, for the sake

of economy, indicated by means of a stroke over the vowel preceding; because of this one suspects that examples of *Deia* are really *Deian*, due to a failure in the copying or in the editing. But the variant -*a* for -*o* occurs in other names and there is no reason for rejecting *Deia*.

B15. 42. AS 1406. Deia ap Tuddr; 43. Deia Tew ... deia ap Je(uan); 44. dya ap dd whith ... Deia Mawr; 45. dd ap Deia Moel; 50. Deio ap Jockyn ... Deia ap Je(uan) ffrom. RecCa 253. Deya ap Roukyn.

Examples of Deian:

B6. 268. Lleyn 1350. jorwerth ap y dyan. B15. 45. AS 1406. Eign ap deian; 51. Dd ap Ior deian ... Gron ap deian; 52. Je(uan) ap Deian ap Pwt. B10. 173. AnglRent morvydd verch jevan ap dyan; 174. dros dir grono ap dian.

Examples of Deito/Deita:

B15. 48. AS 1406. Deito ap Ithell. Star CP 5. Flints, Henry VII. Robt Dytowe. 173. Flints, Jas I. Ellis Jno Deita. PROswestry 34. 1563. Thomas Dyto.

Examples of Deiwyn, Deicwyn:

B11. 64. Broniarth 1429-, yollin ap Daywyn; William ap yollyn ap daywin. B23. 337. Mawddwy 1415- Madog ap Daiwin; 338. Mathe ap Daiwyn; 344. Llywelyn ap Daiwyn ap Llywelyn ap Meilir. RCA 431. welle daywyn (Maentwrog; = 'gwely'). B15. 45. AS 1406. Dykwyn goz.

It may be that examples of *Dai Wyn* should be regarded as Daiwyn/Deiwyn:

Bartrum 1215-1350. 241. Dai Wyn ap Dafydd ap Cynwrig. 353. John ap Dai Wyn ap Dafydd. 1350-1415. 618. Ieuan Llwyd ap Dai Wyn.

Dackyn *v.* Dafydd
Dakin *v.* Dafydd
Daniel(s) *v.* Deiniol
Davies, Davis *v.* Dafydd
Day, Daye *v.* Dafydd
Deag *v.* Teg
Decka *v.* Teg
Dedwydd

The adj. *dedwydd* now means 'happy', but it has had a wide range of meanings, 'lucky, wise' etc. GPC 911 gives examples of personal names in Old Breton, *Detuuidhael, Haeldetuuid, Gurdetgued*, and refers to the surname *Dedwydd, Didwydd* occurring in Pembrokeshire. G.P. Jones has no example of it as an

epithet in his collection, B3. 31-48. BBStD 108. Henr' Dedewyth; 110. Henr' Dedewith. B7. 304. NPem Fairs 1599. Lewis griffith Dedwith of Hariesmote, co. Pembs; 313. ditto.

Do the following represent the same epithet? B5. 57. AS 1406. Je(uan) Hedwydd. B10. 162. AnglRent 16th century : dros dir mad(oc) dutyth.

PRESENT-DAY REGISTERS

Caernarvon, Ynyscynhaiarn, Gest Ward, Dedwith. Cf. W. Mail 16.2.84, Deaths, Howard Didwith Lewis, Fishguard.

Dee *v.* Du
Degge *v.* Teg
Degon *v.* Cadwgan
Deicyn, Deicws *v.* Dafydd
Deheueint, Deheuwynt

G 309 has two examples of Deheuwynt as a personal name: the first, occurring in LL 127 is in the pedigree of St Beuno, ten generations back; the other is in IGE, cviii (cii in second edition), a poem setting out a pedigree; these examples lack historical value. The word as a common noun means 'south wind', unless -*wynt* is a variant termination of -*eint*. The examples of *Deheueint* come from reliable sources, BBC 68 and LL 245 although the orthography of the examples varies and causes difficulty; but whatever the composition, the first element seems to be *deheu*, which together with the meaning of 'south', means 'right-handed, skilful'; the -*eint* is the abstract noun suffix.

The other examples collected are of *Deheuwynt*:

Bartrum 985-1215, 103. Deheuwynt ab Ithel ap Dolffyn. Mer LSR 24. Yago ap Dehewint, Dechewint ap Iago. 25. Heylin ap Dehewint, Tudgoch uxore Dehewint. 30. Kediuor ap Dehewint.

The word *dehau* (for 'south' and for 'right-hand') is generally contracted to *de* in normal speech; but it remains disyllabic in the variants used in dialect with the meaning 'skilful', *dechau, dethau*.

Deiniol

The early borrowing of *Daniel* should properly give *Deinioel, Deiniol*, and with suffix -*en*, this gives *Deiniolen*; there is a Llanddeiniol in Ceredigion, and Llanddeiniolen and Deiniolen in Arfon; there is a Llanddinol (originally Llandeiniol) in St Arvan's,

Gwent. It was not much used in the early period; the following may be a version of Deiniol, RadsSoc XLIII. 84, Assessment 1293, *Griffin ap Denaul*. *Daniel* was borrowed at a later stage (in the medieval period), and remained unchanged as in *Llanddaniel-fab*, Anglesey.

The following single example was collected from the Shropshire registers:

Abdon 1. (? 1561) Edward (?) Deinole. bap. Is it possible that this surname came from the name of the parish which was the place of origin?

Derfel

We need not concern ourselves with *Derfel Gadarn*, the warrior who turned to religion and after his death came to be numbered among the Welsh Saints; the saint's name remains in the name of the church of Llandderfel, Merioneth. The name became the 'surname' of Robert Jones (1824-1905), a native of Llandderfel who spent most of his life in Manchester. He was a noted poet, hymnwriter and socialist, and was one of the founders of the Manchester and District Fabian Society.

Derwas

G 313 states 'placename or personal name', and after a list of references, adds that in addition to the possible source being *derw* 'oak' as a place-name it could possibly be a form of Defras, i.e. Devereux. Although there is no example in GPC one would expect 'derwos, derwas', for a place noted for oak trees, for words of this kind occur, *grugos, gwernos, helygos*, and in the place-name *Bedwas* the vowel is *a*. The element *derw* also occurs in nouns denoting kinship e.g. *cefnderw, cyfnithdderw, cyfyrderw*.

There is one example of the name (as a forename) showing it as a compound of *dewr* and *gwas*, B23. 340. Mawddwy Court 1415, *Dewrwas ap Ieuan ap Eignon*; *dewr* now means 'brave', but it formerly meant 'handsome, in prime of life', (CA 254) and with *gwas* in the sense of 'youth', *Dewrwas* would be an appropriate name. One is naturally suspicious of this form or maybe spelling, since it could be an attempt to provide an etymology. On the other hand, if *Derwas* were used only as a 'surname' (i.e. a name added to the forename) one would be persuaded that it was in origin a residential name; [T.E.

Morris 137 states, 'Derwas is presumably a Montgomeryshire place name' and quotes examples from the county occurring in the 16th and 18th centuries] but it is used as a forename, and as 'surname', and *Dewrwas* (as an origin) suits this well.

PRConway 1726. Derwas filius Jacobi Williams. HM iv (part 3), Index Nominum. Derwas. Mont Coll 49. Select Mont Deeds, 28, the house of Richd Derwas.

SHROPSHIRE REGISTERS

Non. Con. Oswestry Old Chapel, 103. 1786. Richard s. of Derwas and Alice Ellis, skinner, p. Llanymynech, co. Denbigh. Alberbury, Index, several entries of Derwas as surname. Pontesbury p.507. Jane Derwas. Great Ness 62. 1685. David Derwas of Lloynymapsis, p. of Oswestry. St Mary's Shrewsbury, Index – Derwas. Hanwood 56, 61, 64, 65, 71. Durwas. *Derwas* survives, e.g. in Shrewsbury, Harlescott, Meole Brace, Monts, Llandrinio, Buttington.

Deuddwr, Deythur

WATU 57. In Cwmwd-Deuddwr the juncture of *d-d* produces *t*, and the contraction makes the place-name into 'Cwmteuddwr'. ADClun 107. Griffit Teuthor. PRAlberbury. 230. 1679. John s. of Sarah Deythur . . . fil. pop.

Devonald *v.* Dyfnwal

Dew *v.* Tew

Dewey, Dewie *v.* Dafydd

Dey, Deyes *v.* Dafydd

Deyos *v.* Dafydd

Didwyth *v.* Dedwydd

Distain

This is used in the Welsh law texts for the principal court steward; it is a borrowing from English *discthegn*, 'dish-servant', which was pronounced as *dishthein* in the eleventh century. It was put to use in the translation of the Bible, but only rarely used and is now obsolete. G.P. Jones picked up one example of it as an epithet, B3. 44. Einion ddistain, *c*.1230; Bartrum includes this person, together with other examples: 985-1215, Carwed ap Gwyn Ddistain ab Ednywain; 108. Einion Ddistain ap Iorwerth; 125. Gwyn Ddistain ab Ednywain; in volume 300-985, Bartrum has an example of it as a forename: 67. Distain ap Rhun; cf. also BYale 58. Madoc ap Disteyn, 116. ditto.

It is assumed in this discussion that the

word lasted longer in Welsh than in English and that it became a personal name in Welsh, and it is tentatively suggested that the following represent the same name:
D. Tel 18.7.77, Deaths: Distin, Falcombe, Devon. 30.10.78, Deaths: Distin-Maddick, Southsea. Cheadle, Cheadle Hulme South, Distin. South Gloucs, Yate 1. Distin; Filton, Conygree Ward; Chipping Sodbury.
Dogan, Doogane v. Cadwgan
Dovenallt v. Dyfnwal
Du, Dee
Du 'black' was much used as an epithet and no doubt referred to black hair. It was normal to use the lenited form *Ddu* after the personal name but the contact of *s* and *dd* gave -*sd*-, and of *n* and *dd* gave -*nd*-, so that *Ieuan Du* could be expected especially in the language of medieval poetry, and *Rhys Du* and even *Gwladus Du, v.* TC 116. It will be remembered that quite often the system of writing used *d* for *d* and for *dd*, so that what appears to be the radical form after a pers. name, is due to an inadequate system of writing. The special quality of the vowel *u* caused difficulty to medieval scribes and it was the usual practice to use *duy*. In South Wales this vowel lost its peculiar quality and came to be pronounced as *i*, so that English *ee* conveys exactly the SW sound. Every text has examples and only a few specimens are quoted here:
B13. 143. Bonds Peace 1295. Yerward thu ab Eygnon; Cadugan thu. B13. 218. SR 1292. Meiler du; 226. Wasmeyr du; 228. Iuan dyu. B2. 56. West W. 1301. Griffith Duy; 57. De Lewelino Duy. CAP 527. 1402. text French: Lowys Duy. ADClun 200. Atha Duy; 207. R ap Bedo Due. Lp Oswestry 30/31. Grono Dduy (1393), Grono Ddy (1586), Grono Ddye (1602).
The adj., with no pers. name, following the article: B15. 48. Jor ap Mad ap y Du; Je(uan) ap gr ap y du; PWLMA 435, 436. Dafydd ap y Du.
The adj. after common noun:
AnglCourt 1346. 41. Dafydd ab Ithel ap y Mab Du.
   Official documents such as Chancery and Star Chamber proceedings have *Dee*, with *Dye* occasionally.
InvECP 163. Breckn, 1529. John Dee ap Traheron. CatAncDeeds V. 11474. Hereford, 19 Henry VII: Lewis Dee. Star CP

10. Monm, Php Dee; 76. Glam, Wm Howell Dye, 81. Glam, Jno Dd ap Evan Dee; 85. Glam, Ievan Dye ap Powell.
   The celebrated astrologer of the Elizabethan period Dr John Dee was the son of Rowland Dee, who served in Henry VII's Court; the pedigree shows up 'Du'. In H Rads 209 he is referred to as 'the learned John Du, *Anglice* Black Jack'.
   The Shropshire registers have a number of examples. In the early Welsh-speaking period in Oswestry one finds *Du*.
118. 1587. Katherine vz Will'm Relict Jeu(a)n *Du*. 119. 1587. Ellenor vz Owen ap Jeu(a)n *Du*. [The Oswestry register, 112. 1586, has: David ap Jenkin *Bardu, obijt*. This is the compound *parddu* = 'soot', used, it seems, as an epithet.]
Examples of Dee:
Hopton Castle 1684. Anthony Jones als Dee. Condover 85. 1633. Thos s. of George and Elizabeth Dee: 88. 1633. Thomas Dee, bur.
   In the present-day electoral registers one finds a sprinkling of *Dee* throughout all constituencies:
Oswestry, M. Drayton; South Worcs, Bredon-Norton, Bushley, South Gl., Pucklechurch – Westerleigh.
   The only example of *Dees* picked up was in City of Hereford, Tupsley.
Duggan v. Cadwgan
Dye v. Dafydd
Dyfnwal, Dyfnawal
The trisyllabic form through syncope has the variant form *Dyfnwal, v.* LHEB 648, OW Dumnagual and Dumngual, going back to *Dumno-uales in Brythonic; see also Brynley F. Roberts, B25. 274-290 dealing with the personal names in the various versions of *Historia Regum Britanniae*, Dunvalle Molmutius for the Welsh Dyfnwal Moelmud. G 412 has examples of Dyfnwal, often spelt Dyfynwal 'because of the epenthetic "vowel" heard between *f* and *n*;' there are also examples, though fewer, of Dyfnawal; this is sometimes spelt Dinawal, and it is inevitable that at times this becomes Dynawel, as if it contained *awel* 'breeze', e.g. B10. 158. AnglRent 16th century, text editor's introduction, *gwely Denawel ap Gryffri*. There can be no doubt that the form *Devonald* below is derived from the disyllabic *Dyfnwal*, because there is only one syllable after the *n*;

the *Devon-* (as if it were two syllables) corresponds to the *Dyf(y)nwal*, with its epenthetic sound developed into a vowel.

It is apparent that *Dyfnwal* was not merely the name of a mythical character, it was in use in the med period; here are some examples showing various spellings: B13. 223. SR 1292. Yeuan ab Dounwal; 226. Kediuor ap Donewal; Mer LSR 57. Adaf filio Denowalt. BBStD 154. Elena Donynwald; 268. Relict' Johis Donynwale. 272. Devynwas ap Gorgy (three misreadings). RecCa 65, 66. Doynyowell ap Griffri (this may be for *Deinyoel*). 257. Place-name, Llwyndynwal. HM i. 378. Llanover, Manor of Dyfnwal = Downwall. iii. 189. Caerlleon and Llangattock; Inquisitio post mortem 1248 mentions Grifin filius Donewal. Clark, 92. Donnell ap Robert. HBr 56. 'Dugdale says, he was killed by Senel the son of Donwald ... and perhaps Senel the son of Donwald is an anglicism for Sitsyllt ap Dyfnwal, a man of considerable weight at that time in the neighbourhood of Abergavenny'. ... 'Maddox ... speaks of Donewalde's lands within the town of Abergavenny'. Reaney 111, under Ewan etc. quotes *Dovenaldus Ewain* = 1165 Black (= *Surnames of Scotland*, New York 1965). B10. 92. Thomas

Devenald (Kemes, Pem. 16th century; text editor's note: Thomas Devonald was the son of James Devonald, died 1584-5. PRSt Mary's Shrewsbury, Index, Devonell, Davonell, Davnor, Davenhall. *Devonald* is very common in South Pembrokeshire, and especially in the Wards of Preseli, and if one plotted the examples on the map in detail, it would be seen that they are found mainly in the English-speaking parts of Pembrokeshire.

It would be absurd to make a list of the places in which *Devonald* occurs in South Pembrokeshire. Examples away from Dyfed were found in the following places: Anglesey, Llanynghenedl; Denbigh, Llandrillo-yn-Rhos, Glyn Ward; BrRad, Vaynor, Trefechan; Shrewsbury, Belle Vue; Hereford, Bartonsham; West Gloucs, Longlevens 1; City of Glouc, Longlevens Ward p.27; Morecambe – Lonsdale, Urswick.

The form *Davnall* occurring in Copeland, Seascale, is a continuation of the forms found in St Mary's Shrewsbury; and *De Vonald* (husband and wife) occurring in Penrith and Border, Brampton (Brampton Portion) seems to be an attempt to find a French origin.

Dyas, Dyos *v.* Dafydd

Dylowe *v.* Teilo

E

Ednowain *v.* Owain

Ednyfed

The standard form is *Ednyfed*. Final *d* is very often written *t* in medieval script. The epenthetic sound which is heard between *d* and *n* is very often written in:
B13. 142. Bonds for peace 1283. Ednuyed fil Anyan; 143, Second bond 1295. Edeneuet ab yerward. B13. 222. SR 1292. Edeneuet ab Meurich; B6. 355. NW 1326. Edenevet Saer.

One of the common errors of copying or of reading and publishing texts occurs in this name, the confusion of *u* (representing the *v* sound) and *n*: e.g. B9. 68. ville de Trefedenenet. It was common practice to use *Eden* as an abbreviation; for instance there is not a single instance of the full form in the text of BYale but there is an abundance of Eden, e.g. 54, Eden ap Tudur, and on p.58 there are eight examples. Sometimes this abbreviated form is latinized, B3. 68 ... terrarum ... que Edenus whith tenet. The name occurs again on p.69 and p.70, and p.71, with genitive and accusative forms, Edeni, Edenum. The following appears to be another sort of abbreviation, RecCa 115, Cad' ap Idnaf'. A name of this sort which was very common in North Wales would inevitably have variations and natural, colloquial contractions, and these are represented by the following:
B26. 86. Welsh Troops Scott. campaign 1322. Griffini ap Adinet. CaernHS 8. Early Hist.Conway, p.17. Adynet Patyn. RecCa 164. Will'us Adynet. CaernQSR 180. D'd ap Donowed. CaernCR 36. Eninet Ddu (? correct to Eniued). Star CP 4. Denbs, Jno Denyfed. ... 14. Jno ap Denevet. (183. Humphrey Ednevell, clerk, ? misreading) RadsSoc XXIX. 46. Will, Presteigne, John

Denevett. Ex Pro James I. 237. Griffeth ap Ednevett = 270. ap Ednevet (cf. 6. Tre Ednyfed, Tredefnett, Tredenwett, Trefdenevett, – township Llanfaethlu, Anglesey). InvECP has a variety of examples, especially the abbreviation *Eden*, and the following: 119. Flints 1538. Rees and Donevet Deyo. 250. Marches, Oswestry 1518. Richard ap Hoell ap Deneved.

The commonest colloquial form was Nevet, Nevett:
CAP 302, 1295. Bardsey [Ed]nevet ap Ig[none]

Cwtta Cyf. XIV, editor remarks upon use of old Welsh names and, amongst others, quotes *Ednyved (Nevett)*. H Asaph 110, mid 17th century, Committee of Approvers, Rowland Nevett (ap Ednyfed), episcopally ordained, turned congregationalist; cf. Shrop Parish registers: Non-con. Bridgnorth Stoneway p.iii, Names of ministers, 1705, John Nevet, s. of Rev. Rowland Nevet, M.A. Oswestry.

In the following the equivalence of Knyvett/Knevet and Nevett (Ednyfed) is quite certain from the context:
L & P, 20, p.679 of part 1, 1545. Pensions ... and leases for that year. Maurice ap Knyvett. Augmentation Book 216. f. 54b ... Maurice ap Knyvett of the household; 8 tenements in Conway, co. Montgomery [sic] Llanlligan Abbey. Cf. RCA 150 Morys Knyvet (Llanllugan parsonage); 465 (Late Abbey of Llanlligan) ... late demised to Maurice Knevet, 29 Henry VIII.

SHROPSHIRE REGISTERS

The Shropshire registers show as much variety as the examples above. Welsh-speaking Oswestry has the following:
48. 1566. Douse vz Holl' ap Ednyvet; 66.

1579 ... vz Ieuan Edenevett; 66. 1579. ...
Jeuan ap Ednevett.
The following we presume to be a written abbreviation:
Whittington 99. 1614. Jonet verch Edny.
There are examples of the corruptions of the kind quoted already:
Worthen 49. Denovet; cf. 70 Dav. ap Edinoved. Shrewsbury BR 240. David's. Rice ap Denevett, of Ruabon, 1575.
But the form found most frequently is Nevet, with variations, including *'s* added:
Cardeston, Index, Nevett, Nevet. Alberbury, Index, Nevett, Nevet, fifty entries. Hodnet, variations include 10. 1662, Neavett; 92. 1715. Nevitt. Tasley 32. 1783. John Nevettes. St Chad's, Index, includes Nevetes. Cf. also Claverley 30. 1594. Evets (surname), 37. 1559. Evet; 75. 1633. Evette.

The surnames *Nevett, Nevitt* are found widely distributed through N.E. Wales and throughout Cheshire and Salop; but they are not to be found towards the South, in Herefordshire and Gloucestershire. *Nevatt*, found in Shrewsbury – Kingsland Portion is an obvious variant, and *Newitt*, Conway, Llandudno North (A) seems to be, unless it is from *newydd*. And bearing in mind the corruptions of earlier periods quoted above, one is justified in asking whether the following examples are from the same source:
Evennet, CT Bishops Cleeve; Evennett, Morecambe and Lonsdale, Grange. Dennett, Anglesey, Ll. Mathafarn-eithaf. Adnitt, East Flints, Hawarden, Bannel-Pentrobin.

There is a very curious variant back in the thirteenth century, mentioned in H Asaph, VIII. 185, Welshpool, Vicars, 1289, Griffin fitz Edenwerth (Griffith ap Ednyfed) – the addition in brackets is the editor's.

The name *Ednywain, Ednowain* which seems to be a name made up of Owain and the first syllable of *Ednyfed*, will be dealt with under *Owain*.

NOTE, BENED, BENNETT
This is not a question as to the origin of *Bennet(t)* for that is well-known, but whether a colloquial form of *Ednyfed* (after *ab*) has merged with Bennet in certain families. It appears reasonable to suggest that *Ednyfed* could become 'Ened' colloquially.

It is curious that *ap Benet* remains without provection, for instance, Cwtta Cyf. has

examples of ... Rees ap Bennett, 47. 1613; ... Rob't ap Benet, 46. 1614, ... Rees ap Benet, 146. 1632. It may be that *Benet*, not being native Welsh, was treated differently. That is seen in the following in which Benett is the form as forename:
InvECP 85. Da ... ap Benett of Llanfair, co. Merioneth, tanner, son and heir of Benett Owne (alias Smyth); i.e. Benett Owen.
Provection is shown in the second example:
ibid 92. Griffith ap Bened of Temple Brewer, co. Lincoln (Denbs. 1547. 96. Robert ap Rice ap Penet (Denbs 1551.)

Edward

One may judge from the following how the use of this name spread in the middle ages: Bartrum 1215-1350, three instances; 1350-1415, thirty-two. It eventually came to be regarded as a form of Iorwerth, or an English 'translation', and displaced the Welsh name in very many instances. In the records of CaernQSR there are not many examples of Iorwerth: there is one of a grandfather (202) and one of a great-grandfather (200); there are eight of Edward as forename. The increased use of Edward by the time the patronymic system was discontinued, explains why *Edwards* became a common surname, especially in North Wales.

There are very many instances of the interchangeability of Edward and Iorwerth: the name of the English kings being regarded as Iorwerth in a Welsh context; poets named Edward, adopting Iorwerth as a bardic name, (*v.* four examples from the nineteenth century named in DWB, such as Edward Roberts = Iorwerth Glan Aled;) and in some cases, Edward adopting the hypocoristic Iolo, as in the case of Iolo Morganwg and Iolo Trefaldwyn.
Cf. Dwnn 2. 307-8, Mostyn Pedigree, Table: Ierwerth surnamed Edwart – Footnote 'Ierwerth is the Welsh for Edward; 2. 327, Y Plas Newydd yn y Wayn, – John Edwards sonne and heire to John Edwards ... ap John Edwards a elwyd yn iawn John ap Ierwerth ap Ievan (= 'whose proper name was').

The use of Edo, Nedw, Nedws, as hypocoristic forms, and Edo as the source of the surname Eddowes etc. *v.* p. 34.

Although *Edward* was borrowed and came into use in the middle ages, it did not result in many instances of the surname *Bedward*, the preference being for *Edwards*.

InvECP 28. Merioneth 1538. Hoell ap Bedward. H Rads 189. John Bedward (1688, benefactor).

SHROPSHIRE REGISTERS

Hanwood, 55. 1703. Edward ap Bedwart. Wolstaston 3. 1617. Hugh ap Bedward, cf. 3. 1618. Hugonis ap Edward. Alberbury 3. 1565. Robertus ap Edward's; 345. 1716 ... John and Mary Abeddart. 349. 1717. Elizabeth Abeddart; 449. Beddard. 429, 431, 458, 541. Bedward. Albrighton 31. 1613. Bedward = 35. 1618. Beddard = 38. 1622. Bedward (same person). 71. 1671. Bedard. Further examples of *Bedward*: Clunbury 161. 1789; Edgton 7; Bromfield, 125. Chirbury 267, 276: Bederd, Chirbury 127. 1715. Albrighton 117. 1737 Bedart, Ludlow 878. 1748 Bettard. For comparison, Cleobury Mortimer 50. 1634 *Woddard*, which is almost certainly *Woodward*. Also: Albrighton 188. 1807. ... Edward and Martha Bedwood = 192. 1811, ... Edward and Martha Bedward.

Egham, Eghane *v.* Bychan

Eines *v.* Einion (note)

Einion, Ennion

The name *Einion (Einyawn)* was one of the commonest names in Wales; today it is less so. It demands special attention because of the sound changes that have produced variations, and, as a result, a host of surnames. It is difficult to keep separate from it the names *Enion, Ennion*, (and *Inion, Innion*), and whatever their relation may be philologically, these will be treated in this article as variants.

The relation of another variant is less difficult to explain, namely the form *Anian*. Bishops of Bangor and of St Asaph in the 13th and 14th centuries were named Anian, or altered their name in the episcopal office: Lloyd, HW 744, footnote states: 'The name Anianus was in use in the early Gallican Church and became popular in Wales at this time, no doubt as an ecclesiastical rendering of Einion'. Somehow or other this ecclesiastical version became a surname as the examples below will show.

The other changes were phonetic changes to the form *Einion* itself in ordinary speech. When used in South Wales, as in the place-name *Gorseinon*, the consonantal *i* is not sounded, and this is consistent with the habits

of SW speech, e.g. the plural termination *-ion* is generally *-on*, *sane gwynnon*, 'white stockings'. It remains *Einon* (in SW) in an official place-name or as christian name, but the same word, *einion* 'anvil', is *eingon* or *ingon* in SW dialects, and *engan* in NW; as in the name of Llanengan (= B6. 273. 1350, de Laneynon).

Another change is the tendency in the medieval period in certain places for final *-n* to become *-m*, as in *cotwm*, 'cotton', *botwm*, 'button'; examples below will show this change to the name *Einion*.

One must also be prepared to see in medieval MSS a variety of spelling due to the deficiencies of the writing systems, and to orthographical mannerisms or fashions, for example, the us of *gn* as in *Boulogne, lorgnette, peigner*. In the examples below, no attempt is made to make separate categories of *Einion, Eignon, Egnon* etc. for to a great extent, these merely represent different schools of writing. B2. 60. 1304. De Eynono ab Traharn. B2. 159. 1320. Egnon Loyt, Egnon Abbot. B4. 154. 1325. Eignon ap Iorwerth. B5. 56. late 13c. Eynion bo'ly; 62. Eynion penwras. B6. 274. 1350. Eigion Voil. B10. 69. 1352. Wenthlean Vergheygnon. B10. 166. Anglesey 16c. eingion ap elidach. B26. 80. Fragment W. Roll 1294. Lewelinum Voyl ap Yginon ap ...

As they were written at different times over a long period, certain texts when published as if they were a single piece, quite naturally have various methods of writing *Einion*. The Broniarth Court records in B11 represent the period 1429-64, so that one sees Eynō 57; Eygn' 58; Egyn 60; Eigoñ 72. One does not really need such an explanation to account for the variation: the second bond of peace 1295 in B13 uses Anian (*v.* below) and Eygnon, Eynnon, Eynion, all on p.143. The text of the Anglesey Submission of 1406 has Enion, 43, 44, alongside Eingian 43, Eigian 44, and no doubt *Eingian* in this instance is evidence of the phonetic change already mentioned, the tendency of *n* pronounced with the quality of the vowel *i* to become *ng*. The RecCa generally uses abbreviations, but the index has five instances of *Eigan*, probably representing the sound of *Eingan, Engan*.

Before quoting variant versions, it should be said that the habits of medieval scribes continue in the official government papers of later periods such as the Chancery proceedings:

InvECP 8. Angl, 1551. Tythyn Eygan Gadarn. 18. Caerns 1539. . . . ap Eignon; 28. Mer. 1533. ap Eignon. 131. Flints 1556. ap Eigyon. RadsSoc XXX. 43. early 17th century. Hugh Beyghnon (several times).

Examples of Anian:

B10. 155. . . . heres Aniani ap Gwylym. B13. 142. Bonds peace 1283. Owen fil Anyan, Anyan fil Grenoc. 143. 2nd Bond. Anian ab Kenewreck, Anian ab Richard. B16. 125. per mortem Aniani Dudu(r) Episcopi Bangoriensis. B24. p.181 – Names of 'White monks' in Wales: several examples, espec. the Bishops of Bangor and St Asaph, and p. 192, several monks. BBStD 290. Anianus (Capellanus). Mer LSR uses Eynon mostly, except 44 Aniano ap Loward, 54. uxore Aniani. RecCa has examples of Anianus other than the Bp of Bangor; cf. also 210 Amanus ap Ieuan (misreading).

In the following it is a surname:

CatAncDeeds iii. C 3571. City of Chester, Henry VIII. Richard Anyon. CalACW 224, 225, 1489, 1393. William Annion of Chester. Star CP 105. Monm, Marshfield, Lewis Anian.

Examples of Enion, Ennion:

B15. 43. AS 1406. Je(uan) Saer ap Enion; 44. Hwlkyn ap gronw ap Enion. 45. Enion ove ap dd coly, Gr ap Enion ap y Trwin; 48. Tudr ap Eden ap Enian. Lp Oswestry 30-31. Names of 'Gwelyau' . . . Enion Bengoch. Glam Cartae – Index, Enniaun, Enyon (a number of entries, as well as instances of Einon, Anianus). InvECP 30. Merion. Lewis ap Ennyon; 87. Denbs. 1538. David ap Enyon.

Examples of Inion, Innion:

One cannot be too sure whether the initial *I* in some instances has the sound of *Ei*, *I* being given its E value: the following probably stand for *Einon*:

HM iv, p.54. Mathern. Roll of 1711 mentions . . . 'formerly of Richard Inon'; iv. (part 3), 29, 238. John Inon; 54, 237, 240, Richard Inon; 28. Wm Inon. InvECP 43. Cards, 1556. Inon ap David. 57. Carms, 1556. Inon ap Rice of London.

The following are certainly *Inion/Innion*:

InvECP 17. Caerns 1533. G. ap D. ap Innyon. 97. Denbs 1553. Morgan ap Inion.

138. Monts 1518. son of Meryk ap Ineon.

One expects therefore to find Beinion, Beinon (spelt Beynon, and Bynon, possibly), Bennion, and Binion (Binnion):

DLancaster (Man. de Grossemont) 82. Johannis Bynon. WPortBooks 62. Philip abenon = 63. Philip Bynan; 67. Philip ap Eynon. InvECP 96. Denbs 1551. (context 'Herathog') Howell ap Bynyan. 117. Flints 1538. Ralph Benyon. CRHaverford 174. Thomas Baynon. Ex Pro James I. 189, 191. Denbs John Bennion.

Examples of *-n* changed to *-ng*:

In the following it is fairly certain that the *-ng-* is not due to a spelling mannerism, but that it does stand for *-ng*.

InvECP 3. Angl, 1529. Morice ap Inghan. 7. Angl, 1547. David ap Llewelin Ingham; ditto 278, Appendix C. 18. Caern, 1539. I. ap R. ap Yngham. 19. Caern, 1542. J ap D ap Powell ap Byn(g)yon (we take this to mean that Bynyon and Byngyon are both used in the same case) = 19. . . . ap Powel apyngham.) 89. Denbs, 1539. Griffith ap Yngham. 169. Breck. 1547. . . . grandson and heir of Thomas Ongham . . . (?) PRCaerwent 1570. David Beynge (?) Cwtta Cyf. 206. 1642. Jo'n Gr' ap Engion. ML 1. 189. W to R. Iemwnt Bengham = 2. 82. Iemwnd ap Engan. Sannan 1748. Hugh Benghan . . . of this Parish.

Final n changed to m:

There are examples immediately above of this change, and there is no need to have doubts because the same person is involved in the two versions; the following is unmistakable:

WPortBooks 62. Griffin abenon of Carmarthen = 103. Griffith ap Beynam of Carmarthen. Cf. InvECP 89. Denbs, 1539. Griffith ap Yngham; 15. Caern, 1395. John Banham. HM i, 212. Upper Bettws . . . property of a family named Baynham: Footnote: 'Baynham is from ap Einon'. Bradney gives no proof based on the pedigree of this family, but this derivation is theoretically possible. Reaney, under Beynon etc. agrees with this.

SHROPSHIRE REGISTERS

The registers have a very large and varied collection of names derived from the above and an attempt must be made to summarize. The St Asaph parishes have instances of the earlier orthography surviving:

Selattyn 5. 1559. 35. 1589. ... ap Eignon.
Whittington 23. 1604. ... John Roger
Beignion, 54. 1624. ... ap Roger Benion.
There are examples which virtually retain
good semblance of the original Einion, Einon,
Enion, Inion:
Shipton 3. Benion; 11; benyan. Ford 3. 1595.
Sara Beinion; 4. 1605. Benion = 1609.
Bennyon (19. 1673. Sara Bainom; editor puts
Benion, Beinion, Bennyon, Bainom
together). Chirbury, Index, Benyan, Benian,
Binnion, Bennion, Bennian, Bennyon.
Worthen, Index, Bunnian (Bunnion),
Inions, Ineon, Inion. Kinlet, 135. Benion =
137. Binion (and 139). High Ercall 202. 1678.
... f. Beneon Davyes. Acton Burnell 7. 1584.
... of Thomas Beynion. Ludlow 883, 1173.
Bunyan. (Index, Baynon, Benyon, Benyons).
The addition of genitive 's:
Chelmarsh 39. 1643. Margery Inyons.
Pontesbury 49. 1580. ... Inians; 402. 1778.
Inions. Ludlow, Benyons, Inyons, Inons.
Diddlesbury, Benions, Benians [Beinons, =
Bennions, = Benyon]. High Ercall, 68. 1618.
Innians.
Final n changed to m:
This change can be seen in the versions of the
name of the same persons:
Chelmarsh 53. 1661. Cornelius Benion, =
55. 1662. Beniam; 59. 1665. Beinons, 66.
1674. Bennions and the change of -*om*, -*um*,
-*am* to appear as -*ham* is shown in the
Alberbury register, 203. 1670, James and
Sarah Baynum become Bynam, Bymum,
Bynam, Baynom, and in 277. 1693 and 290.
1698 they are Baynham. The Thomas
Benions of Bitterley 165. 1786 is the same as
138. 1788 Thos Bennioms.
Cf. some specimen examples:
Tasley 21. 1725. Baynum; 23. Bainaum.
Stanton Lacy 138. 1736. ... Beniams.
Bitterley 126. 131. Benniums. Index,
Bennion ... Bennioms, Benniams ...
Greete 5. 1686. Jane Banyham. Cleobury
Mortimer 220. 1756. Banum. Ludlow 221.
1568. John Abeynam. Diddlesbury 4. 1585.
... Beniames; 8. 1587. ... Beiniams; 120.
1714. Beniam; Index, Beinames. Munslow
17. 1568. Beyniams. Kinlet 190. 1801.
Bayname.
There is good evidence in the Shropshire
registers that the surname Onion, Onian etc.
is a version of Enion, or that forms of Enion,

Inyon have merged with Onion. There are
very many examples of *Onion* etc. and the
numbers and the location add a little to the
value of this suggestion. Here are some
examples:
Onians, Sibdon Carwood, Hopton Castle,
Edgton, Bitterley. *Onion*, Ludlow. *Onyon*,
Chelmarsh 30. 1624. Margareta Baugh, alias
Onyon. *Onions*, Claverley (Index, Oniens.
Onnyons, Onyanes, Onyans, Onyons,
Onyones). *Oynion*, Myddle. *Oynions*, Tong.
Oinyans, Wrockwardine.
The register of High Ercall provides fairly
reliable proof: Robert Inians and Jane Smyth
were married, p.28. 1599, Sept 30; when the
children are christened the name is Onions or
Onians, and when Robert is buried he is
Onion. A William from the same village as
Robert is entered as Unnion, p.100. 1632,
and 107. 1634, but as Onians in p.110. 1635.
The versions which have the diphthong,
Oynion, are very valuable evidence when
compared with examples quoted earlier, and
with instances such as the following:
InvECP 187. Rads 1556. Thomas ap Hoell ap
Aynyon.

PRESENT-DAY REGISTERS
Einon/Eynon and *Beynon* abound and there is
no need to give references; the spelling *Bynon*
occurs in BrRad, Llangattock; Newport,
Alway 1; *Ennion* is found, e. g. Kidderminster,
Clifton-on-Teme; Nantwich, Alpraham –
Wardle; occasionally spelt *Enion*, e. g.
Stalybridge, Stayley Wood Pt. 2. The
surname *Bennion, Benyon* is widespread,
especially in Shrewsbury, Nantwich and
Northwich constituencies: occasionally
Bennions, Wrexham Boro. Acton Ward.
Inions, Shrewsb., Castle and Stone; Frankwell
and the Mount; Oswestry, Clive –
Shawbury; the corresponding *B-* forms occur
here and there. *Binnian*, S. Hereford, Whit-
church; Kidderminster, Bewdley No. 3,
Wolverley No. 1; S. Worcs, Malvern South
No. 3. *Binnion*, Wrexham, Brymbo Ward;
Kidderminster, Oldington; cf. *Binnions*,
Newport, Dyffryn, *Binions*, Newport,
Rogerstone; *Binyon*, Leominster, Bromyard;
Stroud, Upton St Leonard. *Bynyon*, Conway,
Llandudno – Penrhyn Ward.
Anyan: it is difficult to believe that the version
of ecclesiastical origin ever had ordinary
colloquial usage and it may be that *Anyan*

comes from a dialect pronunciation in the Shropshire and Cheshire areas. Anyhow the name does occur: Wrekin, Wellington, Part Portion; City of Hereford, City; Wirral, Ellesmere Port, Central Ward 1, Hoylake – Hoose Ward, Neston – Little Neston, Little Neston 2, Neston East, N. West. etc.; Wrexham, Llay; Conway, Penrhyn Ward.

Onion, Onions: as in the Shropshire registers this name in various forms abounds throughout Salop and Cheshire and other border counties and naming locations is superfluous. The form becomes *O'Nions* occasionally, e.g. Shrewsbury, Abbey Ward, Monkmoor Ward; Wirral, Stanlow Ward 2; and *O'Neans*, Anglesey, Llechylched. The form *Onione* is found in CT Presbury.

The name *Bunyon* has its own derivation but in view of the occurrence of *Anyan, Onion, Unnion*, it is difficult to suppress the suggestion that the examples of *Bunnion, Bunyan* in the same locality are *ab* forms.

Bunyan occurs in City of Hereford; South Hereford, Fownhope; South Worcs, Broadway, – Wickhamford; Kidderminster, Churchill, Cookley; Cirencester – Tewkesbury and Pembroke. The form *Bunion* occurs in Torfaen, Griffithstown – Sebastopol.

Beniams, Ludlow, Ludlow Broad St, Corve St, East Hamlet, Ludlow-town; Torfaen, Cwmbran – Oakfield.

Beniums, City of Hereford, Holmer.

Baynham: if this name is derived, after several sound changes, from *Einon*, there is no lack of examples: Shrewsbury, Abbey Foregate, St Michael's; Pontesbury, Longdon; Ludlow, Broseley.

HYPOCORISTIC FORMS OF EINWS, ETC.

The hypocoristic forms of Einion (Enion, Inion) were relatively infrequent compared with the corresponding forms of David, Gruffydd, Ieuan, Iorwerth. The form seen in BBStD 84 *Oweyn fil Enote* appears to be *Enod, Ennod*, the stem possibly of Ennion with the -*od* termination seen in *Lysod, Maesod*. Cf. also CaernCR 141, Dafydd ap Griff' ab *Ennynow*: this may be a version with the -*o* termination. Only one example was picked up of *Einyn*, in B5. 58, late 13th century; is this a version of Einion, with the termination used in Gutyn etc.? The number of examples prove that the usual pet form of Einion was *Einws*:

B11. 61. Broniarth 1429-, Guttyn ap Eygnus goz; 67. Dio ap Eignus Duy. CaernHS 26. Bolde Rental 35. Eygns ap Grono. CaernQSR 46. Lewis ap E. ap M. ap Inus; 117. G. ap H. ap I. ap Inus. Lp Oswestry 157. Einus ap plleu' (sic). CatAncDeeds VI. C4456, Salop Eliz: John ap Madoc ap Eignus. C7071, Monts 35 Eliz: J ap D ap J ap Llywelyn ap Eynus. CaernCR 148, Einws (MS Eynus). InvECP 131. Marches 1553. Lloid ap David ap Eynof ap Meredith (misreading at some stage of Eynos = Einws). PRSelattyn 9. 1562. Margaret verch Guttyn Einws; PROswestry 107. 1585. Edward ap Gitten Eynws. 184. 1596. Moris a child of Richard ap Thomas Bynws.

Phillimore 210, starting with the use of Roderick for Rhodri, Edward for Iorwerth, and earlier Gervasius for Iorwerth, mentions also the use of Eneas for Einion, with the reference, Geraldus, Rolls Ed. VI. 14, 17. Although this is 'falsely equating', to use Phillimore's words, the form Einws would help to create this false identification.

NOTE

T.E. Morris 109-10 has the following: ' "The Haines Arms" a small book by A.M. Haines, of Illinois, U.S.A., published early this century, states that the Haines families had their origin in Shropshire and Montgomeryshire. "The name spelt in many ways as Eines, Eynes, Eynns, with the initial H prefixed, became Heines, Heynes, Haynes and Haines". He refers to a Welsh custom that if a father named Einion had a son bearing the same name, he would be familiarly called Einws, "the Welsh diminutive of Einion", hence the transition from Einws to Eines. The pedigree of Heynes or Eynes of Church Stretton, given in the "Heraldic Visitation of Shropshire" made in 1613, and printed by the Harleian Society in 1889 is as follows:

Eignion — Einnes ap Einion — Johannes Einnes, m. Gwenhwyfer ... — Thomas Einnes, *alias* Haynes.'

This does not explain the linguistic origin of the surname Haynes, Heines, etc. Reaney has *Hain, Haine, Hayne, Heyne*, derived from a place-name: ME Heyne, Hain, Hayn, 'a mean wretch' is also added. *Hain(e)s* and several variant forms are given under *Hagan*, — *Hain, Haine* etc. being included here as well.

It is not difficult to believe that the Haines families had their origin in Shropshire and Montgomeryshire for the name is found in fairly large numbers in these counties and down along the border. Even the pedigree quoted is not linguistic proof that the origin is hypocoristic *Einws, Eines*, for names (or words) do not acquire initial *h* by any natural process. The pedigree may be genuine and shows the name Einws/Einnes being altered to Haines, the E name being substituted for the W version, because of the resemblance. One may add that the possibility of a connexion with the W epithet *hen* 'old' came to mind when the names Hain, Haynes etc. were observed.

Elias *v.* Elis

Elidir

G 469 has a number of examples including the twelfth century poet, *Elidir Sais*. A few examples, showing varied spellings, will suffice:

B13. 143. Bonds peace 1283, Kyn' fil Elidir; Bond 1295, Kenewreck ab Elydyr (same person). B15. 46. AS 1406. Elidir ap Symon; 51. Dd ap Hwfa ap Elidr. [This makes it appear a word of two syllables as if the vowel between *d* and *r* in the other examples was epenthetic, but it is three syllables, and the probable explanation is that the scribe has confused this name with *lleidr* 'thief'; and oddly enough, he has inserted the epenthetic vowel into the epithet, p.45 dd ab Eing Lidir. Cf. another instance of the epithet 'thief' after a man's name. B13. 227: SR1292 Dauid ap Wronu Leyder. Cf. also MLSW 23. Morgan ap Richard Lydur, vagabond; footnote, 'His name is significant, *lleidr* means thief or robber'; 108, Morgan ap Richard Lyder; 230, David Lydur.] RecCa 91. Clyder ap Doywyk. (leg. Elyder). Mer LSR 47. Eynon ap Eloder. BYale 50. Uthar ap Elider.

The full name of an electoral ward in S. Pembs is Stackpole Elidor, spelt correctly and given as *Stackpole Elidir/Cheriton* in WATU 198. It becomes a surname in the following: Star CP 43. Francis Elidir et al. all Welshmen (Llanelli).

This single instance in the Shropshire registers looks as if it is a mis-spelling: Myddle 77. 1620. Thomas Eildir.

The above form might have come about by transferring the accent on to the first syllable.

Elis, (Ellis, Bellis)

Appearance suggests a connexion with, or derivation from the biblical names, *Elias* and *Eliseus*, but this is very doubtful because there is in early Welsh a separate name, *Elisedd*; assuming that this is the original form, (in Welsh), it can quite easily lose the *dd* and become *Elise*, and there are plenty of examples in early texts of this version. A medieval scribe might be misled into thinking that the final *-e* sound was a colloquial version of other vocalic sounds which change to *-e* in dialect, such as *-ai, -au*, and this accounts for the examples of *Elisau*. The various texts of the chronicles show all this:

B Tyw Pen 20 (Trans.) 3. Elise ap Cyngen; 7, Cyngen ab Elisedd; 82, Elise. B Tyw RBH. 6. Elisse (trans. Elise), 12. A Chyngen vab Elised (trans. C. ab Elisedd), 184, Elisy (twice, variant, Elisse, trans. Elise). BrSaeson, 32. Ellissed (var. text Elisev, trans. Elisedd); 198. Elisav ap Madoc (trans. Elise ap Madog).

Another sound change would be final *-e* giving *-a* in many dialects, especially in Gwynedd, one of the areas in which *Elis, Elissa* is found in fairly high numbers. In the earliest records, the *-s-* of the name is represented by *-z-* in some cases, and by *-t-* in one case; and it is extremely difficult to understand why these letters should be used, unless the actual sound was different from the ordinary *-s-* sound of Welsh; the matter is discussed by Jackson, LHEB 708-9. It probably has no relevance but it is remarkable that so many examples collected from later periods have *-z-*; this may be just the influence of *Elizabeth*. And it is strange that the name *Ellison* should have *z* in the following: CRHaverford 74, William ap Elizon. The further change is the dropping of the final *-e* or *-n*, e.g. JEG 181. *Ellis Lloyd* alias *Eliza*. But it is surprising to find versions with the final vowel surviving in the eighteenth century.

RecCa 150, 151. Mad' ap Glisse (*recte* Elisse). CaernQSR 31. Morys ap Elyssa = 38. Moris ap Eliza. 96. Elis ap John ap Richard; ditto 98. BBStD 28. Ph'us Elys. InvECP 70. Denbs 1529. ... ap Elysse (three instances). Star CP 35. Caern. ... ap Eliza; 42. Cards. Andrew Eliza. 88. Merion. Rowland ap Eliza of Rhiwaedog, = 185. R. ap Elissa. 184. Elissey ap Lewis ap Meredith. B7. 286. (N. Pembs

Fairs 1599) Elys ap Lewis of Llanelltyd, co. Merion. ALMA 378. Elisa Gowper (= Elis Roberts). PRConway 1589. Johnes Willims fils Willimi Belio (recte Belis); cf. 1593. jana filius Willimi Belis. Ex Pro James I, see note, Eliza, Elliza; Index provides several examples of *Ellice*. A good example of adopting the version of *Ellice* is seen in the entry of Robert Ellice (Ellis) fl. 1640, in DWB. He was the son of Gruffydd Ellis ap Risiart. Robert was not the only 'Ellice': his brother Thomas Ellice became governor of Barbados. Cf. PRLlantrithyd 32. 1571 Evan Elice; 35. 1597. Wenllian Elice . . . John Elic; 62. 1594. Edward Elis: these are all entered under *Ellis* in the index.

SHROPSHIRE REGISTERS

Whittington 48. 1618. Edward s. of Edward ap Ellisey. Chirbury 117. 1708. Abelis (= Christian name). High Ercall 452. 1758. William Belas, of St Julian's p. in Shrewsbury. Longdon-upon-Tern 7. 1783, examples showing Bellis becoming Belless, and 8. 1789, becoming Bellas. Astley 25. 1762. Martha Bellhouse. 28. 1773. Elizabeth Bellas; 29. 1777. Elizabeth Bellus. 33. 1797. Richard Bellis. Uffington 31. 1715. John Bellis and Dorothy; 31. 1716. John Belles; 31. 1718. ditto, 32. 1721. 34. 1724. 35. 1726. Bellies; 43. 1750. Thomas and Elizabeth Bellas. 35.

Ellis and *Bellis* are well-known names in N. Wales; *Ellis* is abundant in Denbigh, Cerrig-y-drudion; Wrexham, Allington has many named *Bellis*; a name found in the Border counties also: Hereford, Madley; S. Gloucs, Bitton, Winterbourne; City of Chester, St Mary's. The spelling *Bellyse* also occurs, e.g. Nantwich, Audlem, West Ward. The name *Ellison* is fairly common in Cheshire, cf. Bellison, occurring in Kidderminster, No. 6 St John's.

The biblical *Elias* was no doubt adopted mainly during the Puritan period, which was early enough for it to become a surname. If they can be relied on, the following are especially early: B15. 59. AS 1406. Deicws ap Elias; CalACW 96-97. 1286. *Elias* son of Alianus . . . *Elias* son of Guer.; these may be due to the scribe; cf. JEG 253, The Eliases of Plas y Glyn: Elias ap Richard, *nat.* 1674, a Smith; his son William Elias, *nat.* 1708, with

half a page of descendants. Reaney, under *Ellis* etc., states that *Elias* is not common as a surname. It is fairly common in Wales, e.g. in the Swansea area TD there are thirty-nine entries; the fondness for Old Testament names amongst Welsh nonconformists is the obvious reason. The name *Lias* is found here and there and it seems to be a form of *Elias*; as a forename, *Elias* is generally pronounced 'Lias' colloquially in Wales. Here are a few locations:
BrRad Llanelly – Gilwern; Islwyn, Newbridge – Pant.

Ellice *v.* Elis

Elvet

WPortBooks 165. Patrick Elvett (Ireland). Elfed, spelt *Elvet* in official documents, was a *cantref*, in Dyfed, north of Carmarthen; the name is kept in the place-name Cynwyl Elfed. It appears from the example above that the name was taken to Ireland.

Emlyn

Emlyn was one of the seven *cantrefi* of the ancient Dyfed; the name remains in Newcastle Emlyn. It is found occasionally in the medieval period obviously indicating the place of origin.
PWLMA 523, Gruffydd ap Rhys Emlyn; (1357, Beadles, Iscoed-is-Hirwern), 527, Gwilym Emlyn (1485, Beadles, Iscoed), 525, Ieuan ap Gwilym Emlyn; B7. 293. N. Pembs Fairs, Gytto Emlyn; Glam Hearth Tax, Port Eynon, Margaret Emlyn. There is hardly any evidence that it became a surname in Wales during the formative period.

The following interesting example is located in England and without detailed research, any possible connexion with the *cantref* of Emlyn will remain unknown:
'Thomas Emlyn. b. Stamford, Lincs of substantial and respectable family, 1663. Educated by dissenters, becomes an early Unitarian divine in Ireland, died 1743. His son is legal writer, Solomon Emlyn, died 1756, and grandson is lawyer Thomas Emlyn, FRS', M. Noble, *Biographical History of England*, iii, London 1806, 161-2.

A few examples of the surname were found in present-day registers:
Wrekin, Hadley (husband and wife); Monmouth, Chepstow – Larkfield; Islwyn, Risca, North; D. Tel, Deaths, 17.12.77, loc. Bournemouth.

The above examples may have their origin outside Wales.

Enharad *v.* Angharad

Enion, Ennion *v.* Einion

Erwood

This village in Breconshire is the source of the following:

Ludlow PR. 265. 1593. Thomas Erwod. BrRad, Vaynor – North, Erwood. Cf. also D. Tel, 16.8.80, Deaths: Erwood, Peacehaven, Brighton.

Ethall, Ethell *v.* Ithel

Evance, Evans *v.* Ieuan

Evanson *v.* Ieuan

Evennet(t) *v.* Ednyfed

Ewen(s) *v.* Ieuan

Eynes, Eynns, Eynon *v.* Einion

Eyrthig, Eyrthick *v.* Introd. Place-names

Eyton, Eytun *v.* Introd. Place-names

F

Fachnalt *v.* Introd. Place-names

Ffagan, Fagan

The surname *Fagan*, found in S. Gloucs, Filton – Northville Ward; Stroud, Miserden, looks as if it were the same as the saint's name of St Fagan's, near Cardiff: in Welsh, Sain Ffagan.

MacLysaght, *Irish Families* 137, says of Fagan, 'in spite of its very Irish appearance (it) must be regarded . . . as a family name of Norman origin . . . It is derived from the Latin word *paganus*'. The Latin *paganus* would most certainly not give *Ffagan* in Welsh according to the known rules of philology, but whatever the origin of the saint's name may be it is not unreasonable to suggest that the name was brought to Ireland by a Norman, possibly a Cambro-Norman. In Appendix E MacLysaght has a list of 'The best known of the Norse, Norman and English names which have become ''naturalized'' by long association with Ireland', and *Fagan* is included. *Paganus* might have become *Fagan* through some intermediate form such as *MacFagan*.

Ffili, Filly

Examples:

BBStD 118. Filly Witt. ADClun 195. John Filly. Surveys GK (Oxwich area 1632) 129 John Philly . . . Owen Philly . . . Margaret Filly. PR Hopton Castle 1. 1542. Hugo Filly; 1543. Elizth Ffilly. 2. 1545. John Ffilly; William Ffilly.

Even the examples occurring in Wales are found in an Anglo-Welsh context, and it may be that the name is not Welsh in origin; but it is included in case it is connected with Caerffili/Caerphilly.

Flello, Flellow *v.* Llywelyn

Flewelin, Flewelling *v.* Llywelyn

Flewett, Flewitt *v.* Llwyd

Flood *v.* Llwyd

Floyd *v.* Llwyd

Fludde, Flude *v.* Llwyd

Fluelling *v.* Llywellyn

Foulkes, Ffowc

This surname is obviously a borrowing of *Fulk*. In the form *Ffowc*, it is common in North Wales:

B10. 271. Recusancy in Caerns. 1641. Thomas Ffoulke. Cwtta Cyf. 48. . . . John Ffoulke of Vaynol; 131. 1630. John Ffoulkes . . . 132 Grace Ffoulkes. InvECP 70. Pembs 1538. Fowlke Raynold.

During scrutiny of modern registers the name was found in fairly large numbers in certain places, e.g. Denbigh, Llandyrnog; West Flints, Ysceifiog, Lixwm.

Fuelling *v.* Llywelyn

G

Gadarn, Gaddern *v.* Cadarn
Gam, Games *v.* Cam
Gatharn, Gatharne *v.* Cadarn
Garnon(s)
Reaney also has the variants *Gernan, Garnham, Grennan,* and traces the name back to OFr *grenon, gernon,* 'moustache'; its use as a nickname made it eventually, in the form *Algernon,* into a christian name. Dauzat puts *Garnon,* with other names, as 'hypocoristic and derivative', under *Garnaud.* In any case, it is not a surname of Welsh origin, but it is of interest in Wales for the name is fairly well-known, especially in Pembs. The evidence is against the assumption that it was brought to Pembrokeshire by the Normans, for the examples do not date from the medieval period; and one may suggest that the name came to Pembs through a French sailor, or a French family trading with a port in Pembs and at some stage settling there. But the name also came into Breconshire from Gloucestershire and Hereford, and the example below 'of Garnons' should not lead us into believing the surname came from the place-name; the other way around is more likely. Indeed the evidence of the examples in the Welsh Port Books suggests that the name might have come from Gloucester.
B13. 103. Pembs 16th century. Jhon Garnons. Star CP 17. Miscell. Philip and Mary: Jno Garnons (context Hereford). 22. Eliz. Brecs Wm Garnons, dep-sheriff. 131. Eliz. Pem. Jno Garnons of London. 138. Eliz. Rads Thos Lewis, of Garnons, Gloucestershire, gent... Jas Garnons, of Glasbury, gent. WPortBooks, 101. Lucas Garnance of Gloucester; 107. Lucas Garnaunce; 111. Lucas Garnons. HM iv, 278. Llanddewi Scyrrid, Pedigree ... Morgan (Herbert) of Ll. Scyrrid ... mention of William Garnons of Blackmore, and grandson Garnons Morgan. CRHaverford 31, 184. John Garnons. JEG 157. Pant Du, Llanllyfni. The marriage of one of the daughters to Richard Garnons of Garnons Hall in Pembrokeshire, brought the name to Arfon.
PRESENT-DAY REGISTERS
BrRad, Garnons-Williams, Llanhamlach; Pen-pont; Hay Rural. Bl.Gwent, Abertillery BG (2), Cwmtillery, Garnon; Blaina Coedcae (Q), Nantyglo. S. Pembs St Mary D. Llanion 1. Garnon. Preseli, Many in and around Fishguard and Haverfordwest.

Gatharn, Gatharne *v.* Cadarn

Gayner, Gaynor *v.* Gwenhwyfar

Gealy
The name is found as *Gelhi filius Arihtiud* in the Marginalia of the Book of Saint Chad, printed in LL, xliii. The discussion in Melville Richards's article 'The "Lichfield" Gospels (the Book of "Saint Chad")' in NLWJ, xviii, 135-144, states that this entry cannot be later than the end of the eighth century, and is probably much earlier, and one may conclude that this Gelhi belongs to S.W. Wales. An occasional example is found in the medieval period, B, 13, 219, SR 1292, Jurors of the Barony of Rupa: Cadel Gely. Note also the place-name Gellyswick in Pembrokeshire and the name Gelly in Sir Gelly Meyrick, follower of the Elizabethan Earl of Essex. For examples of the surname Gelly, Gely in the neighbourhood of Gellyswick in the fifteenth century, *v.* B.G. Charles, *Non-Celtic Placenames in Wales,* pp 63-4. The surname, now spelt Gealy, is fairly well known in Carmarthenshire, the Swansea and S.W. Wales TD has a number of examples.

Genever *v.* Gwenhwyfar

Gennah, Genner, Genno, Gennoe, Gennowe v. Ieuan

Gervase v. Iorwerth

Gethin, Gething, Gethings v. Cethin

Ginifer, Ginnever v. Gwenhwyfar

Gittas, Gitthouse, Gittins, Gittings, Gittoes, Gittowes, Gittus v. Gruffudd

Givens, Givons v. Ieuan

Gladis v. Gwladus

Glandeg, Landeg

The adj. *glân* has a wide range of meanings, 'pure, sacred, clean, handsome'; it is the word normally used in SW for 'good-looking'. The compound of *glân* and *teg*, namely *glandeg*, has the same meaning, and this was used as an epithet after a personal name in the lenited form and became eventually a surname in certain parts of Wales. A similar formation, used as an epithet, and even as a first name, is *mwyndeg* (*mwyn*, now meaning 'gentle', used to mean 'well-bred' as well). There seems to be an instance in RecCa 253 of using *(g)lan* as an epithet, *Conruŭ(?) lan*; and the following, from the same text, 110, is almost certainly a misreading of *Landeg*: *Jeuan Vandeck* ... *Vondek* (or ? from *mwyndeg*).

In some of the examples below, *ll* is used instead of the correct single *l*. Surveys GK. 80. John Landecke; 98, 1583. David Landegg gent; 305. 1583. Jurors ... John Landeye (misreading); 325. 1650. John Landecke; 334. 1687. John Landeike. B22. 372. re. Gower 1590. John Llandegg; 374. ditto. B23. re. Gower 1590. Index of persons 95-8, David Landigg. Glam Hearth Tax, Clase, Rosser Landecke and John Landecke, Bishopston, Owen Landeck. B3. 142. Glam, Loyalists 1696. John Llandegg, William Llandegg.

PRESENT-DAY REGISTERS

Landeg, BrRad, Crickhowell; Cardigan, Llanarth; Monm, Chepstow, St Christopher's.

Glas, Las

This adj. covers a range of colours: it is mainly 'blue', but it may include 'green', (e.g. glas-wellt, gwelltglas, 'green pasture') and 'silver grey' (e.g. arian gleision, 'silver coins' in SW). It was used, in its lenited form, after personal names:

B2. 254. Charters Brecon, Llandovery, David Gryffyth lase; BBStD 316. Dauid Las, 326. ... Willi Las. RadsSoc. XXVII. 27-32.

Notes on Powells ... David ap Powell and David Laise, ... a brother Hugh ap Holl David Lace; XXXIV. 39, Will, 1590, Richard Glace, John Glace. HM i, 264. Llan-vetherine, Ped. of Fam. of Powell of Pant-glas. Ievan Lace alias Vaughan. Bartrum 985-1215, 116. Gruffudd Las ap Adda Fras; 117. ... ap Ieuan Las. Cf. Star CP 193. Monm, Dd Greene als Blewe (? trans of *Las*) 202. 205. Monts, Matthew Glace. Cf. PRLlCrossenny p.4. 1615. Catherin vz Merick al's Blewe.

The following from the Shropshire registers may be forms of *Glas*:

Stokesay 23. 1616. Christopher Glaze; 82. 1757. William Glaze. Wistanstow 49. 1699. Abraham Glace, a pauper; 162. 1792. Fely Glaze.

A few examples of *Glas* were found in present-day registers: CT Tewkesbury 3; City of Glouc, Brocklethorpe-with-Whaddon; Stroud, Central. This spelling suggests they are the Welsh adj.

Glynn(e) v. Introd. Place-names

Goider v. Coedwr

Gooch, Goodge v. Coch

Goronwy, Gronow, Grono

Goronwy is regarded as the standard form; with the accent on the penult, the name easily changes into *Gronwy, Gronow* etc. The practice of the medieval Anglo-Norman scribe of changing *gw-* into *w-* brings about *Woronou, Wronu* etc. in some of the examples below:

B13. 216. SR 1292. David ap Wronu uelyn; Yuor ap Wronou; 217. Yuan ap Gronnou ap Predith; 217. Gronu ab Hener'; 220. Gronow ab Miler; 221. Mailler ab Worenou; 222. Oweyn ab Wronou; 223. Gronou ab Ceicil; 225. Woronou de Cutehille; B2. 61. NW 1303. Gwyon ap Grono. CAP. 386. David ap Wronow, 1320- Gwent, French text. Mer LSR 7. Gronou ap Wion; 10. Grono Alchlwy.

In the text of B13. 142-, Bonds for keeping peace 1283, there are several examples of *Grenoc*; e.g. 142, Anyan fil Grenoc; 143, grnoc fil Kyn'; this version has come about in order to have a name which can take Latin declensions, and is possibly based on *Madoc*; cf. B26. 80 (Fragment of Roll, Edw 1. 1294-), Gronocum ap Moyleweys; 82, Madocum ab Euyas (misread. = Enyas). Cf. further examples:

Dwnn 2. 26. Y Dre-Newydd (= Newton,

Llandeilo, Dynevor Fam) ... ab Rs ab Gronwey. Star CP 7. David Gronno. RCA 415. Edward Gronewey. InvECP 4, Anglesey 1533. ... ap Growno ... ap Grono. 11, Anglesey 1536. ... ap Groney; 15. Caerns 1395. ... ap Gronowe Gogh. 72. Pembs 1547, context Tenby: William Grenowe of Cowbridge. 165. Brecs 1533 John David alias John Dyow Ronowe. Glam Hearth Tax St Andrew's, Wm Grinnow.

There are examples above of *Grenow*; cf. also, although the context is Cornwall: CatAncDeeds III. D 958. John Grenowe. Note also example of adding -s, H Rads, p.97. List of High Sheriffs, 1733, Thomas Gronous, London; cf. RadsSoc XXV. 43, High Sheriffs, 1733, John Gronous, Norton.

SHROPSHIRE REGISTERS

In the Shropshire registers the name is a surname only. Examples are found not far removed from the Welsh original (quite apart from instances in Welsh speaking parishes), Pontesbury 19. 1559. Josia Gronnow; 42. 1575. Matilda Gronnowe. Diddlesbury 9. 1587. Rycharde Grenower. St. Mary's Shrewsbury, Index, no example of Grono, but one of Grunna; St Chad's, Index, Gronna, Gronnor, Gronnow.

With -s added:

Clunbury 18. 1618. Ricardus Gronowes (Index refers to this entry as Gronoulls); cf. 20. 1620. Margeria Gromwaies.

Examples of *Gren-* and *Gron-* are probably variants, although there is always the possibility that names derived from Green- can become *gren-* and be confused; Green- house could become Grennoes, but the probability is that Grennoes, which made no sense and provided no explanation, was altered to Greenhouse:

Edgton 1. 1722. John Grennoes; 2. 1762. John Greenhouse. 7. 1747. Hannah Green- house, buried – (probably the Hannah, d. of John Grennoes of the 1722 entry). 8. 1753. Charles Greenhouse; 10. 1757, Ann Green- house, buried, (prob. the Anne Grennoes of 1. 1722). Claverley 28. 1589. Grenhow; 38. 1598, John Grenhowse, ib. ib. Greenhouse; 41. 1601, 46. 1605, 66. 1626. Greenhouse. Pontesbury 16. 1554. Elizabeth Grennoh. Ludlow 30. 1618. William Grinouse; 44. 1636, John Greenhouse. 690. 1715. John Grinnees. Burford 192. 1777. Eliz Greenow

(omitted from Index). 234. 1777. ditto (marriage cert.). Fitz 25. 1662. ... Elizabeth Grannos. 25. 1663. John s of John Grannos. 31. 1681. Anne d. of Richard Greenehouse. St Chad's, Index, Greenous (Greenhouse). One is tempted to ask whether examples such as the following are 'corruptions': Diddlesbury 5. 1585. ... filius Francisci Grenways. Ludlow 12. 1582. ... Greeneway.

An assembly of examples collected in the border counties shows a great spread of most of the forms quoted above: Gronow, CT Presbury; Grenow, S. Hereford, St Margaret's Vowchurch; Greenow, City of Hereford, Bartonsham; cf. Greeno, Cardigan, Aberaeron.

But the English names Greenhouse, Greenhough, Greenhow cannot be separated from Grennoes which may be derived from Grono. One interesting point is the spelling Greenhous which is fairly common in the Shrewsbury area and Ludlow, Bishops Castle.

Gouge, Gough *v.* Coch

Gower

Reaney has Gower, Gowar, Gowers, with early examples, and explanations, which are not associated with Gower of West Glamorgan; but an example is also given of 'Walter de Guher ... (Carmarthen). From Gower (Glamorgan)'. As there are origins far removed from South Wales, one finds the name in many places – and the name should be pronounced, so it is said, as 'Gore'. On the other hand it is plain that the surname in many cases is derived from the West Glam Gower, which is not pronounced 'Gore': e.g. Badminton Manorial Papers, No. 2628, Gower Survey of 1594-5, includes the name David Gower. The TD of Swansea and S.W. Wales has forty-five entries of the surname Gower and one Gowers (not counting the names of business concerns, hotels etc.), and these, or most of them, probably have an origin in West Glam.

Goyder *v.* Coedwr

Grach *v.* Crach

Greeneway, Greenhouse *v.* Goronwy

Grege, Grek *v.* Cryg

Grenow *v.* Goronwy

Griffey, Griffies, Griffis, Griffin, Griffyn, Griffith, Griffiths *v.* Gruffudd

Griffri v. Gruffudd
Grono, Gronow v. Goronwy
Gruffudd, Gruffydd, Griffith(s), Guto, Gitto, Gutyn, Gittins, Gittings etc., Griffri, Griffyn

The OW form was *Grippiud (Gripiud)*; this would change in the first place to Griffudd, and then to Gruffudd, for when *i* was followed in the next syllable by *u*, the *i* changed to *u*. (In the name *Griffri*, the *i* of Gripp – or Griff – remained unchanged). When *u* came to have the same quality as the 'clear y' (the *y* of monosyllables and final syllables) the name generally became Gruffydd, and this is now regarded as the standard form. But forms such as Gruffith, Gryffydd are not uncommon in early documents. In South Wales the peculiar vowel sound of *u/y* was lost entirely and 'Griffidd' would be the normal pronunciation. The medieval scribes who were not Welsh generally wrote *Griffith*, even when they heard the original Welsh vowel, for *Griffith* would be the nearest they could get within their writing system. And this form, *Griffith* and *Griffiths* came to be used almost universally, as forename and surname, throughout Wales – *Griff* is used colloquially as an abbreviated form, especially amongst boys and young men; it is also found in documents, and one assumes it is an abbreviation for the sake of economy, but there may be examples of the colloquial abbreviation having become the proper name. In medieval writing *Gr.* is very often used as an abbreviation. A few examples will illustrate the variation of spelling:
B1. 264. (1304) De Griff' grach = B2. 59. Griffith Crach. B2. 68. De Willelmo et Gruffith filius ... Aniani ... B2. 254 (13 cent.) David Gryffyth lase. B13. 143 (1295). Blethin ab Gryffyd. B13. 219. SR 1292. Gruffuth ab Caurda ... Ihewan ab Gruffut Wyth. 220. Grufud hirsays; 222. Griffuth ab Hodelou. 226. Griffyth ap Knaytho; Griffyt Keneu Iolyn. Lp Oswestry 50. Survey 1602: Jeuany Graffitt. ADClun 68. Griffit ap Howel. Athaf ap Griffit. Ex Pro James I. 237. Griffeth ap Ednevett; Griffith ap ... InvECP 156. Alice Griffeth, late the wife of Griffith Lloit and Ellen verch Griffeth his daughter, of Southwark, co. Surrey. (context, Monts 1556). ibid 158. Greffeth app Davyd app Vaughan.

Example of *ap* becoming *up*:
InvECP 260. Marches 1553, Thomas Upgriffith Gogh.
One cannot tell whether the following are written abbreviations or the actual surnames:
InvECP 72. Pembs 1553. John Griff, parson of Burton. 151. Monts 1552. Richard Gruff. 238. Monm 1551. John Griff of Newport, son and heir of John Griff.
These may have been the economy versions of a Chancery clerk during 1551-3. Cf. also CatAncDeeds 111. C3373, Merioneth, Henry VII. Richard Gruff alias Richard ap Guttyn.
The form Griffin was used extensively in the medieval period as an anglicized and latinized version of Gruffydd, and one of the advantages of this form was that it was better suited to take the case endings of the Latin declension; v. example of Griffin in Feilitzen: Pre-Conq Domesday: he calls it 'hypocoristic'; in some texts both the original Welsh and the *Griffin* version are used:
B6. 362. Griffith episcopi Bangorensis (1309-10); 363. Griffini episcopi B. CalChancProc 292. Griffin ap Yerward, bishop of Bangor. B9. 54. (1295-1301) Lewelinus filius Griffini. ADClun 137. Gruffin Unpeys. InvECP 58. Griffin Donne = 53. Griffith D. 58. Griffin Hygon = 53. Griffith Hyggons.
The addition of *-s* to Griffith, which came about when the name became a surname, might not cause any alteration in appearance, i.e. in the spelling, but the pronunciations of *-iths* cannot be expected to stay unaltered and *Griffiths* is inevitably simplified to *Griffis* (which is the way the surname is usually pronounced) or *Griffies*. Versions of this kind are found in the Shropshire registers, and it is possible that other versions such as *Griffits* represent a simplification of *-iths*. There is very little point in trying to classify the many versions and provide an explanation because in most cases the various versions merely represent attempts to spell in English a name of Welsh origin with an unusual combination of sounds. The following specimens are a summary:
Shipton 14. 1587 ... ap Griffiths; ibid 14. 1587. Ricardus Griffitte. Ford 2. 1592. Greffeth Foxe; 2. 1592. Henry Greeffes; 3. 1595. William Greffes. Hughley 4. 1598.

Isabell Greeffethes. Hanwood, Index, Griffiths, Gruffyths, Griffice, Gruffes, Griffes, Gruffitt, Grifiths, Griffis, Griffies. Hopton Castle 11. 1614. Griffehes; 38. 1731. Griffits. More 10. 1610. Griffices; 18. 1630. Griffice. Bitterley, Index, Griffits, Griffitts, Griffies. Munslow 5. 1544. Greffet Pownd. Oldbury 16. 1687. Thomas Gripthis. Burford 13. 1592. Edward Griffite. Great Ness 50. 1663. Thomas Gripphes. Myddle 36. 1581. Nup. Griffiths ap Rees; 37. 1583. Bap. Thomae f. Griffiths ap Reese. 39. 1585 . . . f. Griffithi . . . 46. 1590 . . f. Griffithi . . . (the same person throughout, the clerk of 1585 finding a way of showing the genitive).

The name *Griffri* is probably the result of reshuffling the elements found in names, by taking the element *-ri* from *Tudri* etc. and adding it to *Griff.*
B13. 222. SR 1292. Wyn ap Griffri . . . Griffri Voel. Mer LSR 4. Iorword ap Griffri. PWLMA 439. Reginald ap Griffry (1391. Genau'r Glyn). Bartrum 1215-1350, 254-5. Griffri, thirty-one examples, three being Griffri ap Gruffudd. CaernHS 28. Bolde Rental 38, 39. Teyre Gruffre (= Tir).
The only examples in the Shropshire registers are the following:
Great Ness 113. 1724. Andrew Griffrie = 120. 163. Andrew Griffie. Myddle 25. 1571. Nup. Griffrini Jones, p. de Llangunnon (analogy of Griffini).

PRESENT-DAY REGISTERS
No examples are being plotted of *Griffith(s)* or *Griffin* for they abound. The tendency of the vowel of the final syllable to lose its distinctness in the speech of the border counties produces *Griffen*, e.g. Ludlow, Bridgnorth St Leonard's; Oswestry, Ellesmere; S. Gloucs, Berkeley, Hawkesbury, Badminton; CT Cirencester, Fairford.

Many of the versions quoted above from the Shropshire registers survive in modern registers:
Griffis, Bromsgrove, Alvechurch – Hopwood Ward, Rowney Green; Kidderminster, Kidd. Foreign, Stoke Bliss. *Griffies*, Shrewsbury, Belle Vue; Oswestry, Whitchurch Urban; Nantwich. *Griffey*, S. Gloucs, Cromhall; Berkeley, Hinton-Berkeley, (several); *Griffee*, S. Gloucs, Bitton, Winterbourne No. 3, Hanham Abbots 2. *Griffett*, S. Gloucs, Churchdown 1; City of

Glouc., Kingsholm Ward p 9; Barton p 13, Matson p 19, Linden p 3. *Griffets*, CT Twyning. *Griffice*, Crewe, Crewe North 3.
No examples of *Griffri* were picked up; one example of Griff, as *Griff-Preston*, in Cemaes, Montgomeryshire.

HYPOCORISTIC FORMS OF GRUFFYDD, GUTO, GUTYN (GITTOES, GITTINS ETC) GRIFFYN(?).

It is fairly certain that the original pet forms of Gruffydd were Guto and Gutyn; this *-yn* form does not appear to have been much used in South Wales. There are plenty of examples showing both forms were much used in their respective spheres. The first examples show the connexion between the proper version and the colloquial version as operative, i.e. an awareness of the connexion.

CaernQSR 58. Gruffydd ap Robert otherwise called Gutyn Elen; 73. Gruffydd ap Rhys ap Hywel alias Gutyn Felyn. CatAncDeeds 111. C3373. Merioneth Henry VII. Richard Gruff alias Richard ap Guttyn. PWLMA 428. Gruffydd (or Guto) ap Hywel ap Dafydd (1500. Reeves, Cardigan.) 399, 400. Gruffydd (or Guto) ap Hywel ap Philip (1479, Foresters, Glyncothi). Bartrum 1350-1415. 571. Gruffudd/Gutun Glinie ab Einion ap Dafydd. 575. Gruffudd/Gutun ap Ieuan Ddu. InvECP 141. Gattyn ap Dickon alias Griffyn ap Dacken (Monts 1538). ibid., 202. Glam 1538. Griffith (Gytto) Thomas.

The specimen examples quoted below will show the form Guto becoming Gitto in South Wales, there will also be an example of the final *-o* becoming *-a, v.* p.34. When one comes upon examples spelt *Getyn*, these represent a failure on the part of the copyist, but forms such as *Gitton*, especially if they are located in areas on the Border or over it, are probably due to the English tendency to give to the vowels of final syllables a neutral quality. In some instances, Guto/Gutyn is virtually a surname.

B11. 58. Broniarth 1429-64. Guttyn ap Eygn' duy. 58. Guttyn Gwyn; Guttyn gweth; Guttyn ap Iolyn. 61. Guttyn ap Eygnus goz. B10. 86. 1352-3. gytto ap john; ibid. Phillip Gitto ap Ieuan David Penry; ibid 90. Phe John gitto ap Ieuan. ADClun 150. Gutto Madoc. 36, 37. Guttyn Mantach. 39. Guttyn Pengam. 193. Gutta Harper. B7. 288. 1599-1603. Pembs, William Gitto penry of

Whitchurch. 293. 'Gytto Emlyn'; 310. Thomas John Gytto of Llangyndeirn, co. Carms. B7. 339. Caern 1597. Rob'to ap Richard Gyttyn. StarCP 4. Jno ap Gytin ap Rees. 76. Griffith Gitto (Glam). 116. Ricd ap Gittin (Monts). AnglPleas 5. Guttyn ap Llewelin ap Gruffydd ap Ieuan. InvECP 30. Merioneth 1547. Robert ap Getyn and Robert ap Yevyn ap Getyn. 39. Cards 1547. Jenkyn ap Gutto ap Gwallter. 139. Monts 1533. Edmund ap Gytton, Coogth [comma not needed]. 144. Monts 1544. Edmund ap Gytten Gough. 151. Monts 1551. Ieuan ap Richard ap Gitton sinke. 248. (Marches 1501-) . . Gitton ap Baty.

NOTE

Examples of *Griffyn, Griffin* are found in a variety of documents throughout the early period and one is persuaded at times to believe it was a natural hypocoristic version of Gruffydd/Griffith; but we prefer to think it was a form used by Anglo-Norman and English clerks, (as a sort of translation); they were familiar with a word like it, namely the mythical bird *Griffin*; and there is evidence that Griffin was an English surname in the thirteenth century, e.g. ELS Cumberland, p.7, Blencow, Thomas Griffin, Adam Griffin; p.18, Rouclef, Adam Griffin.

This form persisted in the English courts, InvECP 58 . . . Elizabeth . . . daughter and heir of Griffin Donne; John Donne father of the said Edward and Griffin; (Carms 1544) 53. Griffith Donne; ibid Griffin Hygon of New Carmarthen = Griffith Hyggons (1544. we do not therefore think it proper to treat it as a hypocoristic name.

There is another name which appears to be related to *Gruffydd* and to be a mixture of *Gruffydd* and *Gutyn*:
CaernQSR 45. Morgan ap Ieuan ap Gruttan. 54. Ionet ferch Llywelyn ap Gryttan (cf. 209. Ionet ferch Llywelyn Gruttan). 117, 190. John ap Madog ap Gruttyn; 175. John ap Madog ap Gryttyn.

These are the only examples collected and because there is only one source one is urged to explain these examples away, that they are meant to be 'Guttyn'. The examples of *Gruttan* are against this. The ending in *-an* suggests an Irish origin or influence, and one thinks of the name *Grattan*. MacLysaght, *Irish Families* 293 mentions the name *Grattan* but it

so happens he is unable to trace any kind of origin.

SHROPSHIRE REGISTERS

These contain an extraordinary variety of versions derived from *Guto* and *Gutyn*, but before attempting to summarize these, it is worth drawing attention to the following late example of the connexion *Gruffydd/Guto*, especially since the versions are *Griffiths/Gittoes*:

Non-con. M. Drayton Ind. 282-1821, Edward Gittoes and William, sons of Isaac and Elizabeth Griffiths, Drayton in Hales, Salop.

Derived from Guto:

Most forms have genitive '*s*, *Gittoes* etc. but occasional examples without '*s* are found, Barford 18. 1601 Willm Gittoe; 23. 1608, 25. 1609. Roger Gitto, cf. 27. 1611, Roger Gyttes; 29. 1613, Rog'i Gyttos.

The version found most often is *Gittoes*: Hanwood Index; Clunbury Index; cf. 93. 1720, Edward Gittos = 95 1723, Edward Gittoes; Stanton Lacy Index; Chirbury 109; Worthen Index; Hopesay; Shrewsbury St Mary's; Shrewsbury St Chad's.

Examples of *Gittowes*, Bromfield, Index; Onibury 18. 1604, Humfrey Gittowes, 26, 1619, Elizabeth Gittowes. *Gittos*: Sibdon Carwood 12. 1721, John Gittos; Clunbury 6. 1596. William Gittos; Ludlow 31. 1619; *Gittose*: Ludlow 45. 1636. *Gittoss*: Clunbury Index. *Gittas*: Clunbury 71. 1689. John Gittas; Diddlesbury 33. 1696; 34. 1697; 42. 1719. Munslow 203. 1742; Ludlow 630. 1705, Onibury 75. 1710 = 76. 1712. Gittoes. *Gyttes*: Burford 27. 1711; cf. Habberley Index, *Gitts*, *Gytts*. *Gittus*: Chirbury 95; Burford 150. 1735; Hopesay Index. *Githouse*: Diddlesbury 1666. 1742, Elizabeth Githouse = probably 130. Eliz. Gittoes.

Sundry exceptional versions:

Stanton Lacy 81. 1680. Anne Gyttors; Index, Geters, Gitters; Bromfield, Gettoes; Pontesbury 123. 1631. Gittoes = 124. 1632. Gittonce (same family). Hopesay, Index, Gitters.

Bearing in mind the local pronunciation of the border dialects it is not impossible to understand how the name *Gitto* could become *Gittal*:

Condover 2. 1571 John Gittall; 2. 1572 Francis Gyttall . . . Jone Gittall: cf. *Bristol* and

Bristow; the pronunciation of *football* in many parts strikes many of us as 'footbaw'.

Derived from Gutyn:

The index in more than one volume confuses *Gethin* and its versions and the variants of *Gittin*: More, Lydham, Burford, Hopesay. The form found oftenest is *Gittins*; Hanwood Index; Hopton Castle 33. 1711 Margery Gettins, Martha Gettins = probably 25. 1718 Martha Gittins; Clunbury, Habberley, Alberbury, Hopesay, Shrewsbury St Chad's. *Gittines*: Hanwood; Habberley. *Gyttyns or Gyttins*: Hanwood, Habberley (Gyttyne); Condover. *Gytteens*: Frodesley 4. 1558.

Versions with the vowel of the final syllable showing unclear neutral quality:
More 11. 1602 Getten; Stanton Lacy 129. Gitton; Bitterley 100. 1781, ditto, 108. 1760, 109. 1761; Habberley, Gyttyons; Westbury 19. 1648 Gittans = 23. 1651, Gittins; Ludlow 816. 1735, Gitten; Shrewsbury St Mary's, Gittens, Gittons.

Examples of *-ing, ings*:
Hanwood; Clunbury, Gittinges; Lydham, Gettinge; Frodesley 5. 1577. Gyttynges.

It is hard to explain the following variants unless they are misreadings:
Alberbury 8. 1569. Anna ver. John Gitlin; 9, 1569. Rogerus Gitlins. (cf. 11. 1570. Rogerus Gittins); 12. 1571. Alicia Gitlin; Ludlow 580. 1696. John Geitlin.

PRESENT-DAY REGISTERS

The various versions exemplified above are found in greater abundance in today's electoral registers. It would be absurd to give reference for *Gittoes, Gittos, Gittus* in the border constituencies; they are found much further afield – *Gittos* in Windermere/Bowness; *Gittus* in Bromsgrove No. 2. S.W. and Cofton Common, to give just two instances. One naturally picked up examples of the name *Gatehouse*, e.g. in Ludlow: Ludlow, Ludford, Bitterley, Stanton Lacy; Leominster: Eye, Leominster town; S. Gloucester: Filton, W. Gloucester: Newent. There is a house in Church Street, Leominster called *The Gatehouse*: and a farm in Bircher called *Gatehouse Farm*, and such a place-name might well be the source of the surname. It would be rash to say that *Gatehouse* came from *Gittoes*, but a researcher tracing the history of a family from generation to generation might possibly find evidence at a certain point, of changing to

Gatehouse from *Gittoes*, or from *Gitthouse* as shown above in the register of Diddlesbury.

Similarly, surnames derived from *Gutyn* abound in modern electoral registers, *Gittins, Gittens, Gittings*; there are instances of *Gettings*: Market Drayton; City of Gloucester, Kingsholm p.11, Longlevens p.14; Runcorn, Stockton Heath, Latchford; and in Wales, South Pembrokeshire, St Mary's 'A', Pennar Pembroke; Preseli, Llangwm; Wrexham, Rhosllannerchrugog, Pant Ward.

One could mention several places in Welsh constituencies which have examples of *Gittoes, Gittus* etc. (Brecon-Radnor mainly), and of *Gittins* etc. (Montgomeryshire mainly), with only occasional examples in other constituencies.

Grwca *v.* Crwca
Gryg(e) *v.* Cryg
Guilt *v.* Gwyllt
Guyan *v.* Gwion
Gwalchmai, Gwalhafed

LHEB 449 suggests that *-mai* is from the gen. sing. of *ma* 'field', (which is the termination *-fa* in so many words denoting places or sites, and in another form in *Myddfai*, and in the word *maes*) so that the meaning is 'Hawk of the Plain, and not 'of May'. Dr Rachel Bromwich TYP 369 expresses agreement with this, but notes that there is no lenition to the *m* in *Gwalchmai*, which would be the case if it were a 'close' or a proper compound in Welsh. Whatever the meaning it is not a proper compound, but an improper compound of noun and genitive, (the proper compound would be 'Meiwalch'). [The name *Kytemay* occurs in BBStD 42; is it a 'translation' of Gwalchmai?]

The most famous *Gwalchmai* is the Gwalchmai fab Gwyar of the Arthurian stories; it was also the name of one of the outstanding poets of the 12th century, Gwalchmai ap Meilyr. Its use as a name was not widespread but there are occasional instances in the med period:
B15. 56. AS 1406. Dd ap Eign Gwalchmay. RecCa 48. David ap Gwalghmay. CaernQSR 65. Gwalchmai ap Ieuan ap David Velenyth.

The example above in B15. 56 has no 'ap'; there is a place in Anglesey called Gwalchmai, originally Trewalchmai (WATU 81) and maybe in this instance Gwalchmai stands for

the place; cf. also B15. 292, Aberystwyth –
Cardigan, 140. Philip Walkemey. A number
of examples are found in the PR of Conway:
1557, Hugh ap gr fil Gwalmay gr., 1558,
Hugh gwalchmaie; 1559, Katherin fil
Gwalchmay, 1626, Jane gwalchmaij, 1627,
Harry gwalchmay filia Gwalchmay moyses
[sic] the 'Harry' must have been misread by
the editor), 1629, Richard gwalchma filius
gwalchmay moyses.

Gwalchmai is still found as surname:
Oswestry, West Felton; East Flints, Buckley
Argoed, Holywell West, Marford and
Hoseley; Monts, Berriew, Darowen, Kerry,
Machynlleth, Meifod, Buttington,
Welshpool-Castle, Guilsfield Ward.

In the tale of *Culhwch ac Olwen*, the name of
Gwalchmei mab Gwyar is followed by his
brother's, *Gwalhauet mab Gwyar*, WM 469. 3.
Arguing from the form *Gwalchmai* one would
naturally assume that the brother's name
contained *gwalch-*, and that the WM text was
defective; but the instances that occur do not
seem to show *gwalch-*. The examples in G 610
in the early poetry are *gwalhafed, Gwal(l)haued*;
and the instances collected from various texts
show no sign of the form *gwalch-*. [Rhŷs,
Arthurian Legend deals with Gwalchmai and
'Gwalhauet' in several places in the book; and
takes for granted that the name should be
Gwalchafed. It is a perfectly reasonable
assumption to make, especially since in
Rhŷs's time, the only known example of the
name was the one occurring in the Culhwch
tale, so that other examples of the name not
showing *gwalch-*, were not available in print to
raise doubts about the assumption: *v*. in
particular chap. VIII Galahad and
Gwalchaved 166-183. Rhŷs, p.168 assumes
that Gwalchmai means 'the hawk of the
month of May', and that *Gwalchaved* contains
haf 'summer', and has a similar meaning. The
name is regarded as the larva which turned
into Galahad, but this theory or surmise does
not receive support from recent scholarship;
TYP 353.]

Glam Cartae, Index, Walaueht, Walaveth,
Walawet; 480. Gillemich' Walaueth. Clark
29 pedigree, Gwlhaved → Gwlhaued →
Gwilin ap Gwlhauen Vachan (? misprint);
Dwnn 1. 26, *Gwlhafed*, occurring twice in
'Karnwillon' pedigree. B13. 218. SR 218.
Yuan ab Gwoluet. Mer LSR 8. Yer(word) ap

Gwahalet, Eynon ap Whahalet.

Gwallter

This is borrowed from Walter, with two
changes. The change of *lt* into *llt* is not just a
'literary' change to make the name more
Welsh: the writer is familiar with the
pronunciation 'Wallter' of an older generation, in the surname of a family officially
named 'Walters'. The other change, initial *w*
becoming *gw-*, is very common and easily
understood. The lenition of words with initial
gw- is *w*, e.g. *gwaun* 'moorland', becomes *y*
waun, (fem. noun following def. art.); this sort
of lenition occurs in hundreds of words and in
hundreds of cases; as a result, if the language
becomes possessed of a word with initial *w*,
there is a very strong tendency to make it *gw-*;
e.g. *ewin* 'finger nail' has *ewinedd* as plural: the
e unaccented, is dropped in colloquial speech,
giving *'winedd* and then *gwinedd*.

G 612 gives a number of examples of
Gwallter in early texts, and of *Gwalter/Gwallter*
occurring in place-names, Tir Gwalter,
Trewalter, Trewallter. There are also
examples of *Gwater*, and the pl. *Gwatteryeid*.
Some of the examples show a 'silent' *l*, and
this produces 'Water':

B10. 72. West W. 1352. Walter ap
Tomy . . . Wauter ap Res; 75. Llewelyn ap
Ieuan ap Wauter. PWLMA 434 (date 1437).
Dafydd ap Water; 434 (1472) Maurice ap
Dafydd ap Water. (Index has a number of
examples of Walter too.) PRLlanbadoc,
1599. Howell Walter, son of Watter Jo(n)
Morice. 1600. John Watter, son of Watkin
Edward. (This shows Watter and Watkin as if
interchangeable, cf. InvECP 166, Brecs 1538,
Hugh Walker alias Hugh Thomas Walter.)
B5. 147. CaernLS 1293. philip ap guallter.
Bartrum 1215-1350, 283. a pageful of
Gwallter; it includes one example in which
Watkin is a variant or alias; the same example
is given under *Watkin* on p.430. ibid
1350-1415, 586-7. Gwallter, twenty-eight
examples. InvECP 39. Cards 1547. Jenkyn
ap Gutto ap Gwallter. HBr 196. David
Gwalter of Dan y fedw, gent. StarCP 119.
Monts, Eliz. Dd Gwalter of Staunton Hare-
croft, Oxon.

SHROPSHIRE REGISTERS
Ludlow 123. 1601. Gwalter s. William Aston.
RC regs. 84. 1834. (Plowden) Maria Gualter.
It was suggested above that *Walder,* derived

from *Cadwaladr*, may have merged with *Walter*.

Gwas

Gwas means 'boy, young man, servant': pl. *gweision*; medieval Welsh has a shortened pl. *gweis*, used after numerals. It was used extensively in the sense of 'servant' in a great variety of functions such as *gwas y meirch* ('stable-boy', groom'), *gwas ystafell* ('room boy, i.e. page boy'), and from an early date it came to be used with the names of holy persons, like *gille* in Ireland and Scotland (Gilchrist, Gilmour), to make 'christian names'. The names that can be clearly identified are Gwas-Duw, Mair, Dewi, Teilo, Mihangel, Deiniol, Sanffraid (Brigid), Padrig, Dunwd (Dinot, Donatus), Cain. The usage or context of these names originally may have been religious and possibly monastic but usage was not confined to this context, e.g. the 'Gwas-San-ffraid' whose death is lamented in one of Cynddelw's verses, died fighting in the service of Owain Gwynedd. It will be noticed that the *s* of *Gwas-* may affect the way the name following is spelt: the sound of *-sDewi* might strike the ear as *st*; and because of this *Deiniol* is not easily identified (and the *-st-* of *Gwastewy* and *Gwasteilo* probably explains the spelling of (G)Wastmeir etc). There is an example below of *Gwas Badric* although there should not be any lenition after *gwas*; this arises from the combination of *s-p* which changes into *sb* in Welsh, e.g. when E 'spite' is borrowed, it is written *sbeit*, and in Welsh prosody, *s + p* counts as *sb*. Examples occur of 'Gwas duy': because of the usual context one naturally asks whether this stands for 'Gwas Duw', which is not an unreasonable assumption bearing in mind also that *Duw* 'God' could be 'Dwyw' in OW, and an example does actually occur in LL 279, guasduiu (i.e. 'Gwas-dwyw'), which corresponds to Old Breton Guasdoe, but on the other hand, *duy* was the usual version of *du* 'black' in the writing of the Anglo-Norman scribe, and since examples of 'Gwas coch' occur it might be safer to believe that 'Gwas duy' meant 'the black-haired boy or servant'. Some examples show *moren* = morwyn 'maid' as a girl's name.

Dewi:
B5. 147, 1293. guas dewi. B13. 215. SR 1292.

David ap Wastewy, Dauid ap Wastwy; 237. Phillip ap Wastewy ap Seysyl; 228. Iuan ap Wastewy. Mer LSR 5. Tuder Goch filio Wasdewy; 6. Madoco ap Wasdewy; 15. Generys uxore Wasdewy, Ieuan ap Wasdewy; also 24, 27, 65. Surveys GK. Manor de Priorston 1642. 200. Gwayne gwase dewy ... neere the Three Crosses in Lanridian. ADClun 134. Wenllian daughter of Was Tewe (this may be *tew* 'fat').
Cf. example of *Non*, St David's mother: RadsSoc XLIV. 65, Assessment 1293, Wassenon.

Teilo:
B13. 215. 1292. Yuan ap Wasteylou (Monm); 226. Uxor William ap Wasteylou; 228. Wasteyloa Gouch. B24. p.181. Fasti Cist.Camb. 227. List of Conversi, Wastelius, Llantarnam, 1203, or somewhat later. BBStD 268. Angarad fil. Gwasteyllan (misreading, – teyllau = teilaw). Glam Cartae 590. Wastelius conv. of Karleon.
In the following *gwas* and *glas* have been confused: MLSW 92. Llywelyn ap Glastilo.

Deiniol:
Mer LSR 60. Yer(word) ap Wasteyuol (= – Deynol). RecCa 47. Wele Gwasteynell ap Grono (= Gwas-deynell).

Duw, Dwyw:
LL 279. guasduiu. RecCa 268. Dd ap Grono ap Gwas Duy; 68. Ph' was duy; 268. Gauell Gwas Duy.

Dunawd:
Mer LSR 21. uxore Wasdinot.

Padrig:
B13. 225. SR 1292. Dauid ap Waspateric; MerLSR 26. Was Patrik; 34. Wir ap Was Patric; RecCa 17. Wele de Gwas Padryk. Phillimore 376. Ieuan Gwâs Badrig, the patron saint with St Mary Magdalen of Cerrig y Drudion. (*v.* Reports WMSS 11. 476 and Thomas, St Asaph, ed. 1874, p.533) Cf. the following paragraph of G.P. Jones's lecture, *Brittonic Traces in the Lake Counties*, p.12: 'An instance [of Brittonic names] is Gospatric father of the Dolphin whom William Rufus drove from Cumberland in 1092; the same name had been borne earlier in the 11th century by Gospatric son of Uhtred and was to be borne about the middle of the 12th century by Gospatric son of Orme. It survived in two place-names: Cospatricseye (1169), in Walton and Waspatricwath (1300,

1381) in Thursby'. Also, Feilitzen 274, who has several references to Gospatric, located in Yorks: 'From OW Guaspatric ... *Gos* is a variant of *Guas*, see Watson 178. In Sim(on) of Durham we find the form Cospatric which is borne by several 11th c. Northumbrian magnates of Scand-Celtic parentage'.

Mair:

B13. 216. SR 1292. Wastmer ap Kneukyn; 218. Geoffrey Wasmer; 221. Westmer ab Yuan; 226. Wasmeyr du; B10. 151. Morwyn Veir; B13. 226. SR 1292. Morenueyr ver' Willim, Morenueyr ver' Adam. 227. Wasmeyr ap Seysil. CaernCR 46. Gwasmair (several examples); RecCa 71. Wasmeir Vaghan. Glam Cartae 517. Dauid fil' Wasmeri; 982. Ryvan Wasmeir; 531. Wasmeir, 527, 528, 690. 437, 2293. Wasmerus; 398. 2211. Wasmerus fil Iago; 2357. Wastmer fil Zowan. BBStD 320. Meur[c] ap Gwasmeyr. [ADClun 90. Madoc ap Lewelin gives 20s for the office of Wasmair in Isporlog and Ugwporlog(= uwch): this appears to be 'gwas y maer', i.e. the steward's assistant; G quotes examples of *gwas y maer*.]

Mihangel:

B5. 68. late 13th century gwas myagel. B13. 227. Iuan ap wasmyhangel; 228. Wasmyhangel; 229. Yewan ap Gwasmihangel. BBStD 28. Wasmyhangel, (ditto 204, 222); 58. Gwasmyhangel, ditto 200. CatAncDeeds IV. A6573. Hereford, 15 Edw 1. Zevan son of David ab Wasinyhangel (misreading). Ex Pro James I. 8. Anglesey. Gronw ap Gwas Mihangel. Cf. RadsSoc XLI. 68. Miscell. Ministers' Accts 13-15cc. Sothegh vz Gwesungell (prob. misreading of Dothegh, a way of writing Dyddgu; and a contraction of Gwasmihangel).

Sainffraid:

H176. gwas safreyd (= sanfreyd, *v.* note p.347). B13. 229. Wasamfreyd. RecCa 58, 59. David ap Gwelsanfrait (?); 105. Dd ap Gwassanfrait; 251. filii Goussanfrayd: 46. Welsonfraide ap Tauarn (?). Glam Cartae 544. Candelo ap Walter ab Wassamfret; 544. Wronu de Wassamfret; 123. Wassefrei fil Ruelen.

Cain:

Mer LSR 82. *Waskeyn.* (*Cain*, saint's name; *v.* Cain).

In addition to the above types, *gwas* was used in other nomenclature formations. It could be used as a common noun with an identifying adjective to make it function as a pers. name:

(a) With the def. art. Mer LSR 100. Y guas trusgul (trwsgl = 'leprous' or 'clumsy'). B15. 45, AS 1406. Gr ap Je(uan) ap y gwas chwith ('left-handed'); (b) With no def. art. BBStD 40, Gwas Coch; AnglCourt 1346. 39. Einion ap Gwasmoel; Mer LSR 5. Wasmel (? moel); 29, Yer(word) ap Wasmoel; 53. Yerword ap Was With – Was with (= chwith); 54. Win ap Was Crek (? Cryg, 'stammering'); ADClun 70. Gwas Pyr (cf. 72. Ieuan Pyr, 73. Ieuan Byr); 124. William ap Wasburr; 131. Willim ap Gwasbyr (? adj. *byr* 'short', with uncertainty of the sound of -sb-, giving -sp.); CaernCR 97. Ieuan ap Einion ap was da.

It could also be used as an epithet fixed after a personal name:

CaernCR 34. Tudur was; 57. Tang' wife of Ieuan was; 64. ditto; B15. 55. Edd ap dd was.

L'Estrange Ewen 125 includes *was* (with nothing attached) in the list of surnames found in PRO papers. Cf. MLSW 212 Ieuan ap Madoc ap Gwase. The following paragraph from T.E. Morris's article deserves to be quoted, p.129: 'Wace and Wase come from *gwas* or *was* "a servant". It is a descriptive term found in old Welsh records, e.g. Richard was and Adaf ap Wastew, "fat servant", in the Black Book of St David's, and *Gwasmawr* "head servant" in George Owen's "Pembrokeshire" etc. The name survives in the form Wass in Flintshire, and, if lists of Parliamentary voters in the Marches were examined Wass would very likely be discovered'.

[The use of Irish *gille* in the following examples is worth noting: BBStD 84. Agnes Gille; CaernCR 26. Mab y gille; 35. mab Gylle; RecCa 222. David ap Gillaythel; PRConway 1663, 1664. William Gilsanon; 1669. Gilsonan.]

Gwatkin

G 634 has Gwatgyn (-tc-), with a cross-ref. to the name Gwallter, and examples p.612 of Gwatcyn, Watcyn. The change of initial *w* into initial gw- (*v.* Gwallter) gave *Gwatgyn*, *Gwatkin*. The form usually found in Wales is *Watkin(s)*, the form *Gwatkin* being found far more frequently in the English border counties; plotting examples in South Hereford and Leominster constituencies is unnecessary as they are so common; rare examples were found in BrRad, Llanelly – Gilwern; Torfaen, Cwmbran, Two Locks. The form *Gwatkins* was found in West Gloucs, Ruardean.

Gweir

G 649 has a number of examples of the name occurring in ancient tales: *v.* also PKM 248-9, the note concerning *Mabinogi Mynweir a Mynord*. The following show it was used occasionally:
Glam Cartae 624, 625. Jewan ap Gweyr; 2292. Urien filio Weir (Margam Charter, early 13c.).

Gweirful

This woman's name was much used in the med period: the second element is seen also in Tudful (Tydfil), Gwenful, Unful. There are several versions of *Gweirful*: the final vowel is sometimes *y* or *i*; the diphthong is occasionally vowel, *Gwerfyl*, *Gwirfil*, and the initial *gw* may be initial *w*. There are examples of all these variations in G, 650.
B2. 150. Criccieth 1320. Gueyervil uxor Ierueriod. B4. 155. Ardudwy 1325. Eignon ap Ririd . . . et Weirvil soror sua. B5. 71. Lleyn Subs. gwerwyl filia Kwel'. B6. 354. NW 1326. gweirvyl uxor madoci vawr. B10. 169. AnglRent dros dir jer(werth) ap gwervil. B15. 287. Aberystwyth – Cardn 14th century Hugyn ap Weyrvil. CaernHS 26. Bolde Rental 44. Wirvill vz Ievan ap Gwenhover. Mer LSR 33. Weruel uxore Gof; ADClun 27. Wernel quondam uxor dauid Coly; 74. Weyrnil filia Cad'; (misreadings). CatAncDeeds VI. *c.* 6266. Chester. to Weryl his daughter. MLSW 94. Gwirwilla verch David ap Griffith. RadsSoc XXII. 41. Court Rolls, Presteigne and Norton: Meredith ap Griffith and Weiril his wife, . . . Weril daughter of David. L & P 8. 291. (51). parcels of land . . . Rythyn, Glam . . . late of Quyrill, son of Jevan ap Glam. (? correct to 'daughter'). PRLlantrithyd 44. 1686. Gwirrill David. InvECP 24. Caern 1508. Gwyrevell verch Rees. 29. Merion. 1544. Quevrull verghe Madocke. PRAlberbury 154. 1643. Guernill Jones de Ballsley, vidua (misreading).

The BBStD has examples of the name as christian name, and one example as surname:
28. Weyruyl fil David (trans. 29, the *son* of D). 216. Weyruyll Vammayth. 224. Veyruylt Gogh; 226. Weyruyll Gogh. 186, 188. Thomas Gueyruyll.

The name and its variants do not seem to have produced surnames as often as Gaynor or Ankaret, but the following is an example: Preseli, Llanychaer, Worvell: cf. W. Mail 14.11.79, Deaths, a member of the Worvell family of Llanychaer. TD/London Postal Area, Wyrill; TD/N.W. Kent, Wyrill (Orpington).

Gwelt *v.* Gwyllt

Gwenhwyfar

G 660-1 discusses *Gwenhwyfar*, King Arthur's wife; has references in early poetry to other women named Gwenhwyfar; the use of Gwenhwyfar in love poetry, in a figurative sense for the loved one; and then states under G[5] that the name possibly was not popular in the med. period although a few historical examples are quoted. Rhŷs, *Arthurian Legend* naturally has very many references; what is stated on p.49 is of interest to the present work: '. . . in the Anglo-Norman romances becomes Guenièvre, and the English metrical romances have the still shorter forms Wannour or Wannore, also Gwenore and even Gonore, Ganor, or Gaynore. This last has been introduced to North Wales, where it is by no means an uncommon name for a woman, but it is not associated with the name of Arthur's queen, which is rarely to be met with in Welsh history, for, in some parts of the Principality, to call a girl a Gwenhwyvar is as much as to suggest that she is no better than she should be'. A popular rhyme is quoted implying the infidelity of Arthur's Gwenhwyfar, and this is taken as evidence that the rarity of the name in Welsh history is due to the queen's infidelity. This cannot bear a moment's examination. An examination will show that the name of Arthur is only rarely met with in Welsh history, but that Gwenhwyfar occurs as often as any other female name. A few examples were collected from JEG Pedigrees, which has the form Gwenhwyfer throughout, pp.5, 25, 40, 111, 256, and here are a few more random examples:
B7. 342. CaernQSR 1597. gwenhwyvar vz Jevin. B10. 168. AnglRent, dros dir gwenhwyvar verch Tangwystyl. B11. 58. Broniarth 1429. David & Goleuddith . . . Gwenhoyvar fil' dict' Deio & Goleuddith.

B23. 340. Mawddwy 1415. Wenhouer verch Eignon. AnglPleas 5. Gwenhoyver verch . . . 30. Gwenhover verch Gwillim. 18. Gwenhwyfar verch Lewis. 48. Gwenhowvar verch . . . CaernHS 26. Bolde Rental 44. wirvill vz Ievan ap Gwenhover. RadsSoc VII. 12, Will 1559 . . . Gwenthowe wife to Gwenhowr wife . . . to Gwenhovar wife; XLVII. 87, Will 1576 . . . Gwenhoyvar verch John ap Rees. InvECP 11. Angl 1556. Gwenhover late wife of . . . 87. Denbigh 1538 Gwenover ap Ethel. 254. Marches 1538. Guinevere ap Res. PRConway 1544. Gwenhoyn ver Res. PRCaerwent. 1590. Gwenhoyvar Howell. Ex Pro James I. 155. Gwenhivar. CatAncDeeds 111. *c.* 3676. Merion. Gwenhour vergh Hoell. Lp Oswestry 77 (1602) Gwever Williams widow. What Rhŷs says about Gaynore is also wide of the mark if he means by the words 'has been introduced to North Wales' that the name was brought back to NW from outside Wales or outside sources. The evidence seems to prove that Gwenhwyfar underwent changes in colloquial speech and *Gaynor(e)* is one of the versions that came about through these changes in Wales and in Welsh speech. An example of *Gwenhour* is quoted above and one of *Gwenhowr*; this is a stage further than the forms Gwenhover, Gwenover. If it can be relied upon, there is a much earlier example of *Ginawr* in B5. 143. CaernSubs 1293. Bartrum 985-1215, 186 has *Gwenhwyfar [Wennour] f. Dafydd ab Owain Gwynedd*, and this means two versions of the same pedigree. The parishes in Shropshire which were still Welsh-speaking in the 16th century and early 17th provide useful evidence: one noted that the registers of Selattyn, Whittington and Oswestry had a fair number of instances of *Gwenhoivar* (or some other spelling) in the first few generations, e.g. Oswestry 125. 1588, Gwenhoivar vz John. Then one noted that it fell into disuse and was replaced by *Gainor* etc. Whittington 33. 1610. Gaynore, d. of William ap David Tanner. Selattyn 117. 1639. Gainer d. of William ap Davidd. 125. 1643. Gainor and Jane, daus of Griffith ap Evan. 146. 1656. Gainor verch Elisa. 146. 1656. Mary d. of John ap Hugh, by Gainor his w. The parish of Alberbury had a good deal of Welsh left in it at this period:
9. 1569. Gwennor Gough; 11. 1570. Gwenna

Hill, Gwenna Foulke; 13. 1572, Gwenna Weaver; 87. 1624. Gwena verch Roger als Vayne; 76. 1621. Gaynar f. Thomei et Margeriae Davies = 85. 1623. Gayner = 142. 1638. Gainer, Gainner; 205. 1671. Gaineor, w. of Will Chamber. Cf. also Chirbury 37. 1651. Gaynorae Evans; Cleobury Mortimer 47. 1632. Gayner (woman's christian name). Pontesbury 157. 1653. Gaynor (woman's christian name); Ludlow, 30. 1618. Gayner Evans.
To return to Welsh sources: the pedigrees of JEG show Gaynor, which first appears in the middle of the 16th century, replacing Gwenhwyfer; e.g. 40. Gwenhwyfer, mid 16th century – Gaynor, two generations later; 256. Gwenhwyfer (early 16th century) – Gaynor, twice, two and three generations later; similar evidence on p.111. The Conway PR has examples in the middle of the 16th century: 1561. Gaynor ver. William; 1568. Gaynor Hookes; 1571. Gaynor Bared. (The name is much used up to *circa* 1700, but seems to disappear in the 18th century: 1786. Buried, Gaynor Jones, a pauper – this is a rare survival). The Cwtta Cyf. diary has examples of *Gaynor* in 1625 and 1626, the Llansannan register has *Gainor* more than once between 1731 and 1739, and has the spelling *Gaenor* in 1720; but note Lewis Morris's spelling, ALMA p.45, Modryb *Gaunor* o'r Newry (to Wm Bulkeley).
The Shropshire registers show the name as a surname:
Alberbury 456, 539. Gainer; Chirbury 90. 1690, Pontesbury 153. 1651, . . . f. Gulielmi Gainor; . . . f. Rogeri Gainor; Ludlow 430. 1622, Walter Gaynor; Munslow 12. 1559. Ryc. Ganner = 55. 1559 (another copy) Richard Gannie.
Gaynor still survives as a surname, e.g. Shrewsbury, Withington; Ludlow, St Leonard.
MacLysaght 308, Appendix B includes *Gaynor* amongst the 'surnames commonly and correctly regarded as Gaelic Irish which are nevertheless found indigenous outside Ireland'. Cf. also the following versions used as surnames:
Genever, West Gloucs, Dymock; Kidderminster, Grimley; Hallow; Kidderm. Foreign, Martley; South Worcs, Croome – Kempsey; Torfaen, Pontypool, Park Ter-

race; South Pembs, Carew. Ginifer,
Bromsgrove, Bromsgrove No. 1. South;
South Worcs, Powick, Welland, Croome –
Kempsey. Ginnifer, South Worcs, Upton-
upon-Severn. Ginnever, Westmorland,
Lakes, Ambleside; Cardigan, Aberystwyth
(student).

Gwenllïan

The early form was *Gwenllïant*; changing to
Gwenllian, cf. Morcant/Morgan, ariant/
arian, L *argentum*. The *i* is a full vowel, i.e. not
consonantal *i*, therefore the name has three
syllables with the accent falling on the *i*. The
abbreviation *Gwen* is used colloquially and the
use of *Gwen* as the registered name is not
uncommon. The hypocoristic form *Llio* is
obviously taken from the accented syllable; it
is not much used, and the form *Gwenno* is
probably much oftener used today. In the
examples collected one finds some with initial
W instead of initial *Gw*, and the *-nll-*
inevitably causes difficulties of pronunciation
and spelling. When the name *Gwenllian* gets
into an English context, (i.e. not controlled by
Welsh usage) it will be subjected to the
English tendency to place main stress on the
first syllable and this pronunciation will tend
to reduce the three syllables to two.

B5. 147. Caern Subs 1293. Gwenllian wedes:
B2. 254. BrecLlandov 13th century.
Wanthliane filiae Houelli. B10. 69. W.Wales
1352. Wenthlean Vergheynon; 72. et
Wentllian filie Traharn ap Meuric. Mer LSR
44. Wentliana filia Kerwiot; 48. Wentliana
filia Hanalt. [DNB s.n. John Maltravers
1290-1365, Lord Maltravers, – son John
Maltravers d. 1350 or 1360, leaving by his
wife *Wensliana* a son Henry and two
daughters.] ADClun 27. Wenlliana; 49.
Wenlliane dot; 168. Wellian, daughter of
Lewelin Drom; 226. Gwenlian verch Howel
Rayston. CatAncDeeds VI. *c*. 7359. Monm
37 Henry VIII. Wenleana William; *c*. 6307.
1 Henry IV. Wenthliana. iii c.3486. ...
Gwenllean vergh Angharat vergh Mally. L &
P VII. 923(3). Welthyan Richard.
DLancaster 159. Caldicot 1613. Gwenlian
vergh David. InvECP 37. Cards 1538.
Wenthlian. 39. Cards 1547. Guenllean vergh
Rice. 49. Carms 1544. Gwenllyen verch
David alias Margaret Harreys. 54. Carms
1551. Gwenlliam vergh John. 99. Denbs
1551. John ap David Floyd Guellian

(Guenthan his wife). 206. Glam 1547.
Gwenllyan (Gewllyan = Julian, as an
approximation). MLSW 31. Gwenllian
Flouen, 1098. Guellian ap (sic) Flouen. HM
i. 428. Stone in Mamhilad Church 1718/9.
'the body of Wenlian Lewis'. PRCaerwent.
1570. Gwenliana Alon.

Oldbury 27. 1725-6. Gwenthian Edwards;
54. 1725. Gwenthian Jones of Kinlet;
Wistanstow 24. 1681. Gwynllion. cf. Hopton
Castle, 15. 1625. Gwentlionilla Jones.

The PR of Llanddewi Rhydderch shows the
name in the forms *Wenlan, Gwenlan* as
surname in the seventeenth century:
14. 1697. Lewis ye son of Thomas Wenlan;
17. 1704. Nov 3. bap. Gulielmus fil Thomae
Gwenlan.

The will of Eustance Whitney of Clifford,
Probate Hereford 1599, names 'Thomas
Wenland and his children', RadsSoc XIX. 37;
this is probably a form of *(G)wenlan*.

The name *Gwenllian*, generally in altered form
is still found as a christian name in English
border counties:
Leominster, Whitney, Dora Gwenthllian
Bent; Hope-in-Dinmore, Gwenllyn Woolley;
Leominster town, Gwenlion Gwladys
Kybett. cf. New Radnor, Gwenthlin Stead.
Gwenlan as surname is found in:
City of Gloucs, Hucclecote Ward p.22;
BrRad, Vaynor South; Crickhowell;
Newport, Allt-yr-yn 3.

Gwent

Occasional examples of *Gwent* and *Went* are
found in early records:
B24. 186. Fasti Cist. Camb. John Went.
L & P VII. Index, several refs. to Ric.
Gwent, Dean of Arches. PRStokesay 133.
1809. Henry, s. of John and Sarah Went.
In contemporary registers the form *Whent* also
occurs: it is probably a variant spelling:
Went, Ludlow, East Hamlet; Old St; Kidder-
minster, Tenbury; S. Gloucs, Patchway 1;
Bl. Gwent. E. Vale Central, Hilltop, Rassau
North, Beaufort Ward; Abertillery North J.
Whent, Cheadle, Heald Green Ward 1; South
Worcs, Bredon and Eckerton/Comberton
Great.
The name *Whant* occurring in Newport is not
a misprint for it occurs several times, it is
probably a corruption; Beechwood 5;
Newport Central 2; Liswerry 1.

Gwgawn, Gwogawn, Gwogon, Gwogan

The first element is *gwo-* originally: OW *Guoccaun* in Ann Camb under the year 871. *Gwo-* as a rule changes to *go-*, the word *gobaith* 'hope' is an example, and *gobenydd* 'pillow, bolster'; but *gwo-* occasionally changes to *gŵ-*, e.g. GPC quotes an example of *gwbennydd*. Final *-aw* changed to *-o*, e.g. *trindawd/trindod*; therefore *Gogawn, Gwgawn* will become Gogon, Gwgon, with variant Gwgan. The initial *gw-* of the original form *Gwog-* will lose the *g* in Anglo-Norman usage, to give eventually *Wogan*, in the usage of South Pembrokeshire. Examples of all these variant forms are given in G 675-6, as personal names or as part of place-names.

B9. 54. Lewelinus filius Griffini filii Gogan; cf. CalChanc Proc 63, Lewelin son of Griffin ap Gougon. B26. 79 (Fragment Roll 1294) Edmundi fil' Galfridi Agogan. Mer LSR 54. Cogan; 55. Tuder ap Gogan, Gron(ou) ap Gogan. BBStD 12. Petrus Gogaun; 28. Petr ap Gogaun; 38. Ph'us Cogaun; 44. Dauid ap Gogaun; 130. Io'hes Wogan. 256. Gogaun ap Lowarth; 284. Gogaun ap Ieuan. Glam Cartae 317. Wgan Droyn; 2320. Gnaitha fil. Wgan. Fenton 176 Wiston, Pembs. Gwgan ap Bleddyn > next generation, Wogan etc. Glam Hearth Tax, Llancarfan. Richd Gugan. B6. 161. Further Eliz. Doc. John Ougan esquier. B7. 285. Rice Wogan of llanstinan, gent. (N. Pembs Fairs 1599). PWLMA, Wogan, several entries in index as surname: note 129. reference to the 'Irish property' going to Thomas. Star CP 135, 210. Wogan; = 210, 212. Woogan. WPortBooks 179. Richard Woogan of Haverfordwest. RCA 164. Pembs, Sir John Ogan; 163. Thomas Owgan, clerk, parson of Lawreny. CRHaverford Wogan, Woogan, several entries of both forms; Wougan, two entries. RadsSoc V. 54. Will 1635 Location, Knighton. To late servant Mary Vogan (unless meant for Vaughan). Cf. an example with 's: Dwnn 2. 206. Wm Woogans (in a pedigree).

Care must be taken not to confuse Gwgan and Gwrgan which is *Gwrgant*: an example of the confusion is seen in HBr 46, footnote, 'Bleddin (ap Maenarch) ... left two sons, Gwrgan, from whom are descended the Wogans of Pembrokeshire and several families in Brecknockshire ...'; cf. 50. Sir

Walter Gwrgan or Wogan.

Only a few examples were found in the Shropshire registers:

Ludlow 15. 1587. William Wogan, 27 (1613) Marie Wogan.

Wogan is found in English border counties; e.g. S. Gloucs. Filton, Conygre Ward 1; Knutsford, Wilmslow, Dunham Massey; these may very well be from Ireland. *Wogan* is included in Appendix E of MacLysaght, *Families*, 'The best known of the Norse, Norman and English names which have become "naturalized" by long association with Ireland'; for 'Norman', read 'Welsh'. The *Guide* 204 has 'Welsh Gwgan. An important family since they first came to Ireland in 1295 ...'

Finally, *Gwgon* did not survive in Welsh-speaking Wales, to become a surname, and *Wogan* may be rightly regarded as a typical S. Pembs name, a Welsh name, like Meyler, Gwyther, Gwion, surviving among the English-speaking settlers.

Gwilliam, Gwillim *v.* Gwilym

Gwilt *v.* Gwyllt

Gwilym

One would expect to find examples in Welsh sources in a few generations after the Norman conquest. Lloyd Jones provides a 'count' of the variant forms in certain important texts of the 13th-14th centuries, G 679: *Gwilim*, once in WM, 2 in RM, 36 in RB, 6 in BT; *Gwilym*, 17 in RB, 8 in BT; *Gwiliam* (or W), 12 in BT; *Gwilyam* (or W), 9 in BT. In medieval poetry the system of rhyming generally shows *-ym*, as compared with *-im*, which is unusual; in the *cywydd* poetry *Wiliam* occurs frequently (i.e. with no initial *g* and rhyming as *-am*). One may add that Bartrum 1350-1415 has seven pages of *Gwilym*, pp.687-92. It is more than an academic point to observe that the name was borrowed with initial *gw-*; it was also borrowed at a later stage from the form *William*, and this generally remained *Wiliam*, but was liable to become *Gwiliam* since initial *w* in Welsh was usually the lenited form of *gw-*. There is no need to quote examples of the standard forms: the following represent the departures from the standard forms in some way or other:

BYale 42. Willimus filius Eigon; B13. 222. SR 1292. 'At La Pole' (i.e. Welshpool) Griffith ab Wilemyn (*-yn* suffix). ibid 222.

paid at 'Bergauenny': Nicholas ap Wylmiot (prob. = Wylimot, -od suffix). ibid 229. taxed in Cilgerran, Eynon ab Wilmot. ADClun 81. Willim ap Meiler; DLancaster (Monm 1610) 7. William Gwillin; Moore Gwillin, cf. 11. Moore Gwillim. ibid (Kidwelly) 215. John William Gwillon. InvECP 164. Brecs 1533. Guyllam ap Thomas Lloyd. ibid 178. Rads 1533. Rice ap Guillan, Guillam ap Jenkyn (cf. 187, Gwenlliam Payne; 208. Glam 1553. Land in Seintatham – examples of the interchange of n and m). ibid 235. Monm 1547. David ap Guellin; 249. Marches 1515. John ap Gwelym. CatAncDeeds V. 12510. Hereford. John Agwyllym, of Treries. L & P VII. 802. John Guilliams/John a G'lm, variants of same name. InvECP 208. Glam 1553. Roger ApWilliamz, son of Robert ApWilliam. PRConway 1655. Margrett Willoms, 1656. John Willoms . . . Richard Willoms. PRLudlow 449. 1676. Rose Quillam (cf. 443. 1671. Dorothee Qwynn = 571. 1694. Dorothy Gwinne).

The following appear to be the E hypocoristic or dimin. 'Billy':
BBStD 142. Ph(ilip)us Billy. CaernHS 26. Bolde Rental 38. llel ap y bille. Bartrum, 1350-1415. 521. Bili ap Cynwrig Moel ap Einion.

It is quite unnecessary to plot examples of *Gwilym*, *Gwillim* in present-day registers. *Gwilliam* is also plentiful right down the whole length of the border. The *s* form, *Gwilliams* occurs also, e.g. Shrewsbury Belle Vue; Kingsland Coleham, Monkmoor, Welsh Ward; Ludlow, Lydham; S. Glouc, Thornbury. The spelling *Gwilliames* is found in Kidderminster, Oldington.

Examples of *Gwillam*, Shrewsbury, Wollaston (as christian name); Stroud, Dursley; Bromsgrove, Redditch S. Central; Torfaen, Upper Cwmbran; Conway, Llandudno East 1. *Cwillem* in Newport, Newport Central; *Gwelliam* in Monts, Churchstoke. *Gwillian* might be a misprint but it occurs in two places, Stroud, Tetbury Upton; S. Worcs, Fladbury.

Gwinneth, Gwinnett, Gwinnutt *v.*
Gwynedd

Gwion

This is classified in G 676 under *Gwiawn* (-an, -on); examples are quoted of persons named *Gwion* and of place-names and plant names

containing the name; but the most celebrated character to bear the name was *Gwion Bach* of the folk tale, *Hanes Taliesin*, who swallowed the magic drops taken from Ceridwen's cauldron, and while pursued by Ceridwen went through several animal transformations, in the end becoming Taliesin.

B13. 217. SR 1292. Ihewan ab Gwion; Howel ab Gwyann. 229. Guyaun Huiz. B5. 68. Lleyn, late 13th century madoc ap gwyon; B4. 159. Ardudwy 1325. Guyon ap Gwyn; 160. Wyon ap D; B15. 50. AnglSubm 1406. Jos ap Teg ap Wyon. Mer LSR 7, 35, 37, 41, 46, 55, 61. Wion; 68. Gwion Pellipario. Lp Oswestry 40. Gavell Weeon; 154. Ieuan ap Gweon; 169. Ieuan ap gweion; Ieuan ap gwion. Glam Hearth Tax, Llancarfan, Gayon or Guyon (occurring twice). PRLlantrithyd 61. 1576. Elizabeth Giyon (name omitted from index).

The name fell into disuse and virtually disappeared. There is no person named Gwion in the DWB except that a Rev C. Gwion is mentioned on p.851 in the art. on David Richards. He is named in Hanes Eg. Anni, III, 71 and 138, Caleb Guion, IV. 342. Caleb Gwion. He was a native of the Pembs-Carms boundary area. The few examples collected from present-day registers are from Dyfed: *Gwyon:* Preseli, Rudbaxton; St Dogmaels; Cardigan, Cardigan N. H2, Cardigan S. H4; Llangoedmor. *Guyan:* Preseli, Llangwm.

Gwladus

The correct form of med texts quite often changed to *Gwladys*; this colloquially became *Gladys*, as in Benett Pedigrees. Ped. 7: *Gladys vz Lln*. Glam Hearth Tax, St Donatt's, four people with surname *Gladis*. One cannot expect to find many examples of the mother's name becoming a surname; the following examples are to be found in the TDs of London and surrounding districts: London Postal Area (1); N.E. Surrey (1, Byfleet); West Middx (1, Sunbury-on-Thames); South Herts and Mx (1, St Albans).

Gwrgan(t)

The final -*nt* changed to -*n*, as in *Morgan* (OW *Morcant*) and *arian(t)*; it is worth noting that the name retained -*nt* at times in the med period, e.g. it rhymes with *blant* in IGE[2] 316, 2, so that examples both of *Gwrgant* and of *Gwrgan* occur in med. records. G 708 has examples as pers. name and as part of place-names; there was a Cornish *Gurcant*, and an early Breton *Uuorcantoe*. G 708 also gives one example of the name *Gwrgein/Gwrgain*, occurring in IGE² 308, 14 and rhyming with *Cain*. There is always a possibility of confusing *Gwrgan* with *Gwrgeneu/Gwrgenau*, especially if the abbreviation *Gwrgen', Gorgen'* is used. The versions of the surveys of the Lordship of Oswestry show how the copyists were misled:

32/33. Howell Gouch ap Gorgen (1393) = Hoell Gough ap Gwrgan. ibid Rise ap David ap Gorgen (1393) = Rhirid ap Gwrgan (1586). 120. Howel Gough ap Gorgon, Rhyrid ap gurgan. 170. Meredith ap David ap Gorgen.

To add to the difficulty, in the edition of BYale, whenever *Gourgene* occurs in the text, which obviously stands for *Gwrgenau*, the translation uses *Gwrgen*, e.g. 76: *v.* under *Gwgawn/Wogan* example of confusing *G(w)ogan* and *Gwrgan*.

Examples of Gwrgan:

B10. 145. W. Wales 145, 261. Iorwerth Vaghaun ap Iorwerth ap Gurgan. ALMA 246. pyrth Bôd-Wrgan . . . Côd Gwrgan.

One finds in present-day registers and directories the following forms, *Worgan, Wargen, Worgen*, and there are also examples of *Wargent* which looks like a survival of the *-nt* of *Gwrgant*.

Worgan: Ludlow; S. Hereford, Ross, St Margaret's Vowchurch; S. Gloucs, Patchway, Lydney – Ashleworth, Awre, Aylburton, Cinderford (abundant), Coleford. The examples in West Gloucs were not collected for there were so many, e.g. 28 in West Dean; and the examples of Stroud were left for the same reason, but a note was made of the address, Worgan's Farm in the Slad Ward of Painswick; scattered examples were picked up in Kidderminster, Nantwich, Runcorn, the Wirral; Gwent has too many to plot but note the address in Llandenny – Raglan, Treworgan Court, Treworgan Common. *Worgen:* City of Hereford; S. Hereford, Weston-under-Penyard, Leominster, Ledbury Rural; Monmouth, St Christopher's. *Wargen:* City of Hereford (throughout constituency); S. Hereford, Fownhope; Leominster, Canon Pyon; Bl. Gwent, Bryn Ithel, Aberbeeg, Llanhilleth. *Wargent:* Ludlow, Wistanstow; City of

Hereford, St Martin's, St Nicholas; S. Hereford, Stoke Edith; Leominster, Kington Rural, Weobley.

Gwrgenau, Gwrgi

The components of this compound name are *gŵr*, 'man' ('fighter' in martial context) and *cenau*, 'whelp, young dog', often used in heroic poetry for a soldier ferocious in attack; cf. *Gwrgi* 'man-hound'; *v.* TYP 391 and G 709 and of BBStD 272. Devynwas ap Gorgy; example in place-name, MLSW 199 apud Croesworgy. There are occasional examples which have *gwor-*, (*v.* G 708 and below) and this might suggest that the first element is *gwor-, gor-*, used as intensive prefix; that would be a false inference for this prefix in early composition would cause aspirate mutation to *c, p, t*. Other names using *cenau* are *Rhigenau* (BBC 68. 12 *rigenev*), *Morgenau* ('great whelp'). As already mentioned there is a possibility in reading early records of confusing *Gwrgan(t)* and *Gwrgeneu*, especially in documents which make use of abbreviations: e.g. B4. 162. Court Ardudwy 1325, *Ieuan ap Gorgen'*; 164. *Gorgen' Crethe*, these have a mark of abbreviation; B6. 258. Lleyn, 1350. *Madoci ap Gurgen*, has no such sign. The following specimens represent the various spellings:

Glam Cartae, Index, Gurceneu, Gurcenou. B13. 143. Bonds for peace 1283. Kyn' fil gwrgenau (edited). B13. 216. SR 1292. Gorgenau vaghan; 217. Meydoc ap Gorgeneu; 218. Madoc ab Worgeneu; 221. Gorgeyn ab David; 222. ditto; 222. Tuder ab Gurgenneu; 228. Craddock ap Gorgeny; 229. Gurgeney ab Kediuor. B2. 62. West W. 1301. Howel ab Gorgenou. Mer LSR 28. Gurgenu Coyt Maur. CalACW 21. Gruffydd ap Grogeneu; (index has Gwrgeneu); date 1259. ADClun has a number of examples of gurgenon, 11, 13, 14, 15, 16, 19; prob. misreadings; 68, 91, 95, has Gurgene; 85 has Gurge. BBStD has Gurgene, 30, 46; Gurgen', 60, 84 (i.e. with a sign of abbrev.), and Gurgen 64, 218 (with no such sign).

It has already been noted that in the text/ translation of BYale, whenever *Gourgene* occurs in the text, (obviously = *Gwrgeneu*) the translation has *Gwrgen*, e.g. 76.

Gwri

In the first of the Four Branches of the Mabinogi, Pryderi, Rhiannon's son, is given

his name when he is restored to his parents after his disappearance; the name he was first given was *Gwri Wallt Euryn*. The examples in G 710 are allusions to *Gwri Wallt Euryn*; attention is also drawn to examples of *Gwrhy*, and to *Gurhi* in LL 251, 279. There is little evidence that the name was in common use, the following are rare examples:
InvECP 194. Glam 1528. Context, 'St Kewg in Gowersland': Thomas and Miles Urye, alias de la Hay. 209. context, messuage in 'Llangewg' in the lordship of Gower, Thomas and Myles Woorye, sons of Woorye ap Evan.

Gwriad

G 710 has a number of examples (*Gwryat*) from early texts, e.g. from Aneirin, and there are a number of historical references; but in spite of the statement that it was not a rare name, there are no examples quoted from the *cywydd* poetry, and very few from the poetry of the preceding period. TYP 396 has a note on the name (< *Viriatus*) and quotes a number of examples:
Bartrum 1215-1350. 450. Efa f. Gwrgan ap Gwiort (leg. Gwiriot, Gwriot). B10. 63. W. Wales 1352 Ricardi Wyriot. Star CP 11. Pembs Henry Wyryat. PRCaerwent 1573. Neast, dau. of William Wiriet. *Gentry of S. W. Wales*, Index, spelling is Wyrriott – family, of Orielton; Henry, George, Thomas.

Gwrwared

G 271 has a number of examples from early poetry and prose texts; also the form Lewelinus filius Gwrwareth, Ann Camb *s.a.* 1252; there was a Cornish *Guruaret*, and a Breton *Uuoruuoret*.
B13. 220. SR 1292. jurors Kemmeys (N. Pembs) Iewan ab Growared. BBStD 108. Gour Wared (as if there were two words); 168. in manu M'educi ap Gourwared; CalACW 48. William ap Gurwareth. CaernQSR 241. Ho'll ap D'd ap Lli' ap Grwert. PWLMA 368. Gwilym ap Ieuan ap Gwrwared (1412, Beadles, Caeo).

The name fell into disuse and the only example of its survival is the solitary example of *Orwarod* found in Monts, Llangynog. The *-wared* component is used also in *Cadwared*: the index of LL has examples of *Catguaret, Catguoret, Cathgwareth*.

Gwyddelan

G 733 has the form with *-an* for the saint's name, and in Dolwyddelan and Llan-

wyddelan; WATU also has Dolwyddelan; Llanwyddelan. The pers. name must be a derivative of *gwyddel*, 'Irishman', f. gwyddeles. G 733 has examples of Gwyddel as an epithet (lenited) following a pers. name, *Ifan Wyddel*. Examples of *Gwyddel, Gwyddeles* (still a common noun) used in names:
AnglCourt 1346, 34. Iorwerth Wyddel; 40. Merch yr Wyddeles (MS mergh yr Wedeles). B15. 42. AS 1406. Ior ap Je(uan) ap Gwythell; 43. llen ap y Gwythel; RadsSoc XLI. 57. Misc. Minister's Accts. 1355, Wethel ap Eynon. BBStD 250. Ieuan ap Oythlen; ibid Oythel; 268. Ieuan ap Madoc Oythel. PRLlantilio Cross. 1626. Morice David al's Gwijddel.
The following are derivative forms making pers. names:
B13. 216. SR 1292. At Brekenok: Creddoc ap hwetheleu voil; 218. Maynaur Kein, Lewelyn ab Wetheleu (? suffix *-en*). RecCa 61. Joz ap Goythelyn. HBr 424. Llanfihangel Cwm-du, List of Incumbents, Hugh or George Whethelen or Whethley, date 1234.

Gwyllt, Wyllt, Gwilt

The adj. *gwyllt* 'wild' when used after a personal name retains the radical form in some places even today, *v.* TC 115; in other places it lenites, like most adjectives; it is not easy to see why the two usages exist. It is not possible to say with regard to examples of *-wyllt* in early records whether the initial *w* was meant to be for the lenited form. The relative similarity of W *(g)wyllt* and E *wild* will tend to influence the spelling in certain examples:
Mer LSR 5. Howello Wild. ADClun 21, 27. lewelin welt; 24. Ieuan vachan ab Ieuan welt; 71. Ieuan ap Ieuan weld; PRLlantrithyd 34. 1593. Howell Willt, (missing in index). HM i. 306. Howel wyllt of Henrhiw. MLSW 93. Trahayrn Willte; Bartrum 1350-1415, 627. Ieuan Wyllt ap Hywel ap Ieuan.
The Shropshire registers have *Gwilt* in several places:
Clunbury 14. 1607, 157. 1786; Stanton Lacy 15. 1584; Chirbury 95. 1694; Ludlow 1047. 1788.
There are several examples also of *Quilt*:
Chirbury 194. 1753. Maurice and Elizabeth Quilt (= 198. 1757 Maurice and Elizabeth Gwilt;) 52. 1664. Richardus Quilt; More 65. 1750. Clunbury 141. 1769; Pontesbury 398; Stokesay 137. 1756.

There are occasional examples of *Guilt*:
Stanton Lacy 190. 1785; 218. 1788;
Bromfield, Index, Guilt, Quilt; Westbury
300. 1791. The register of Stokesay has Gwillt
(148. 1805); St Chad's, Index, has Gwilt,
Gwillet, Gwillt: and the Non-con register of
Wem 300. 1833 has Gwilty.

Gwilt is widely distributed throughout Shropshire, Herefordshire, Gloucs, Worcs. The
only part of Wales which has a fair number is
the anglicized part of Monts. and BrRad; rare
examples were found in Wrexham/ Chirk;
Islwyn, Cardigan (Cwmrheidol). This
suggests the epithet did not become a surname
in Welsh-speaking Wales, and that the
surname has returned to Wales from over the
border or from beyond the Welsh-speaking
area. The form *Gwelt* was found in Chepstow
– Larkfield; there is a word *gwellt* 'straw', but
the surname is probably a variant spelling or a
mis-spelling.

**Gwyn, Gwynn, Gwynne : Wyn, Wynn,
Wynne**

Gwyn, fem. *gwen* is the adj. meaning 'white'; it
could also, in the proper context, have the
meaning 'blessed, sacred', e.g. *Duw gwyn*
(or *wyn*), and have the meaning 'white-headed,
favourite' in the appropriate context. As in the
case of *Glyn, Glynn, Glynne*, it was common
practice at times to use *nn* to ensure that the
preceding vowel was short; the forms Gwynne
and Glynne must have come from an English
pattern; they cannot be Welsh for Welsh writing is 'phonetic' and the *-e* would therefore
produce a misleading pronunciation.

The modern surnames Gwyn/Wyn etc.
come from the use of the adj., placed after a
name, as a distinguishing epithet, with the
meaning, 'fair complexioned' or possibly
'white-headed' of endearment, but it is
important to remember that *Gwyn* existed
(and still exists) as a man or boy's name, like
the cognate *Finn* in Irish. The first list of
examples will be of *Gwyn* as a christian name;
Gwyn as a noun or christian name would lenite
for syntactical reasons like any other noun,
but there will be examples below of having
Wyn with no syntactical reason to account for
it; this is almost certainly due to the orthographic habits of Anglo-Norman writing
which failed to differentiate. The instances of
leniting *Gwyn* for syntactic reasons will be
pointed out:

B1. 263. NW 1304. De ririt ap Wyn; 264. De
Wyn ap Mereduc. B2. 150. Court Criccieth
1320. Lewelyni ap gwyn. B4. 152. Court
Ardudwy 1325. Gwyn ap Adaf Ringildus.
158. Tud' ap Gwyn. B5. 65. Lleyn 13th
century gwyn goch . . . gwyn croch; 69. gwyn
ap y brawt; 71. gwyn ap howa. B5. 144.
Caern 1293. Gwyn ap yanto. B13. 222. SR
1292. Wyn ap Griffri. B6. 357. NW 1326.
gwyn ap gwyn ap gronou. B11. 72. Broniarth
1429 Ieuan ap gwyn duy. Mer LSR 24.
Moridic ap Gwin; 33. Win ap Idenerth; 56.
Win Duy; 59. Win Goch. ADClun 13. Dauid
ap Wyn; 34. Dauid ap Gwyn; 14. Wyn Seys.

In the following examples the proper name
Gwyn is in the genitive case following a fem.
sing. noun, *ferch*, and should therefore have a
soft mut. in med. W; in the second example
the actual text in the MS is correct, but the
editing has missed this point:
CaernHS 26. Bolde Rental 36. Mabot vz
Wyn. CaernCR 151. Lleucu ferch Gwyngoch
[MS Leuq v'gh wyn coz; this means 'ferch
Wyn goch'] RadsSoc XLI. 66. Miscell. 13-15
centuries, Jeuan ap D'd Achewyn, ? vch/
verch Wyn.

It is reasonably certain that it was the rule in
med W for the adj. *gwyn* to lenite when, for
the purpose of making distinction of identity,
it followed a personal name. It may not
appear to have been the case for so many of the
examples keep the radical consonant. This is
due mainly to the habit of official scribes of
treating *gw* and *w* as if there were no
difference; but there may also have been
another force at work even in the med. period
namely the deliberate restoration of *Gwyn*
when the word had come to function as a
name, and not as an epithet: this motive for
restoring *Gwyn* is fairly obvious in the early
modern period.

The following illustrates how unreliable the
med text can be:
AnglPleas 34. Tudur Wyn ap Gruffith Vechan
. . . Tudur Gwyn ap Gruffith Vichan.

The following seems to show that *Gwyn* was
being treated as a surname for if it were an
epithet, it would most definitely lenite after a
fem. noun, and be in the fem. form *Wen*: B2.
254, Brec. Lland. Charters, *Alicie Gwyn*.

In the 15th, 16th and 17th seventeenth
centuries, when the patronymic system was
being abandoned, in many cases the epithet

attached to the father's name (and not the father's christian name) became the son's surname: in some families it resulted in *Wyn, (Wynn, Wynne)*, in others, *Gwyn, (Gwynn, Gwynne)*, and this difference occurs within the same family. The following pedigrees illustrate the confusion:
JEG 111. John Owen alias Wynn → Hugh Gwyn, alias Hugh ap John Owen → John Wyn ap Hugh Gwyn→ William Wynne (17th century). HM iii. 162. Llangwm Ucha, ped. of fam. of Gwyn of Tŷ-fry; First gen., Hugh Wynn of the family of Wynn of Tower, co. Flint; his son becomes Hugh Gwyn, and from then on Gwyn remains, or Gwynne. Bradney has a footnote, that Wyn is generally used in NW and Gwyn in SW; the word 'generally' should be kept in mind to allow for exceptions both ways. The following show the dangers of generalizing:
Star CP 19. Anglesey, Ricd Gwyn, muster master for Anglesey and Caerns. 20. Anglesey, Rowland Wyn ap Dd Wm of Penheskyn. InvECP 21. Caerns, John Wyn/ David ap Hugh Gwynne (1553-7, the same case).

The epithet after a woman's name would naturally be *Wen*:
PRCaerwent & Ll. Discoed, Caerwent 1580. John son of Johan wenne (footnote, 'Johan Wen, Johan the White or Fair': Her burial is on p.7).
Even after *Wyn* had become a family surname, there must have been a period when it would have offended one's sense of correct speech to use *Wyn* after the daughter's or grand-daughter's name; it was instinctive to use the fem. *Wen*:
Cwtta Cyf. Introd. XXX. Ped. of Lloyd of Wickwer, Names Alice Wen, d. of Robt ap John Wyn. d. 1625. (= Text 110). Catherine Wen, (d. of Cadwaladr Wynn of Havodymaidd = Text 113). ibid 13. Will'm Holland ... Jane Wen his wief; 129. 1629, and one Anne Wen his first wieff (being one of the daughters of Robert Wynne). 132. begotten upon the body of Katherin Wen of Voylas ... Grace Ffoulkes and Ellen Wen (her mother's sisters) ... being goships. JEG 59. Margaret Wen (heiress of Rûg).
The registers of Selattyn, Whittington and Oswestry have examples:
Selattyn 4. 1588. Ales Wenne widow was

buried. Whittington 176. 1644. Elner Wenn, of Daywell ... bur. Oswestry 120. 1587. Margret Wen Rel. 125. 1588. Jane Wenn.
Examples in Star Chamber records:
Star CP 130. Monts Catherine Wenn als Griffiths, of Maesbroke, Salop; 169. Margaret Wenn (Botffari).
Sooner or later the instinct to keep this distinction would be dulled:
Cwtta Cyf. 132. 1630. John Owen now Lord Bishop ... was married to one Ellen Wynne. 138. 1631. Dorothie Wynne ... sole daughter and heire of Harrie Wynne Esq're, begotten upon the body of Ellen Wynne ... 208. 1643. Grace Wyn the wief of John Parry gent.

A short note on other forms of spelling Gwyn, Wyn may be found useful. The vowel of *Gwyn* is the 'clear' sound of *y*, this sound has gone entirely from the speech of SW, where it is pronounced 'gwin', rhyming with *pin*; and one can expect examples of the name in the form *Gwin* in areas where there would be no knowledge of Welsh to protect the original spelling; examples occur in Kidderminster, Hallow, Wichenford. The Index of CRHaverford has the following versions: Gwin, Gwine, Gwyn, Gwynne, Gwyne, Gwynn. The following unusual form stands for *Gwyn*, RadsSoc XVIII. 54, Medieval Clergy, Master Maurice Gweyn. Occasionally in early records, the vowel is *e*, e.g. ADClun 165. Ieuan ap Gurgene Wene; 175. Dac' Gwene; these are probably meant to be *Wyn, Gwyn*, and are not the adj. *gwinau*, 'chestnut coloured'.
Examples of translating the name *Gwyn* into 'white' *v.* above p.17.
Examples of using -*wyn* apparently as a suffix, *v.* p.85.
MacLysaght, *Irish Families*, 305-7, has Appendix A, of surnames 'indigenous and common in Britain ... used as the Anglicized forms of Gaelic Irish surnames'; the name *Wynne* is the approximation of *Geehan, Mulgechy*. The name *Gwynn* was taken to Ireland by Welsh families, MacLysaght *Irish Families* 294, *Guide* 104.
The following shows that *Quinn* can be in odd instances an incorrect version of *Gwyn*:
PRLudlow 443. 1671. Dorothie Qwynn = 571. 1694 Dorothy Gwinne, Widow, bur.; cf. 449. 1676. Rose Quillam = Gwillam; 449.

1676, Quene Morris (= ? Gwen), and *v.* under *Gwyllt* examples of it being spelt as 'Quilt'.

Gwynedd

Gwynedd was the name of the ancient principality of N.W. Wales: it was attached to the name of its prince or overlord in the twelfth century, Owain Gwynedd. The name Gwynedd never fell into disuse as the name of the area and it has now become the name of the administrative area of a County Council. The stem for making derivative words was *gwyndod*, e.g. the language was 'Gwyndodeg', the people 'Gwyndyd'. But it was the name of the area which became a surname, as the name of the place of origin given to natives when they went elsewhere.

Star CP 2, 3. Jno Gwyneth, provost of Clynnog Fawr. InvECP 5. Angl 1533 John Gwenethe; 21. Caern 1553, John Guyneth, parson or provost of Clenokvaure, and vicar resident of Luton; 22. 1556 John Guynett. ibid 140. Monts 1538. Griffith Gonneth. CaernCR 153. Dafydd Gowyneth. RadsSoc XXXII. 59. Will, 1584, Morice Gwynnethe. PRLlCrossenny et Penrhos; 5. 1616. Nestia, ux' Joh'is Hughe Gwynedd. p.39. 1614. Thomas David als Gwyneth; 41. 1624. Lowry Howell, uxor Thome Gwyneth; 42. 1627. Anna Thomas Gwyneth.

There are several examples in the Shropshire registers. Some have initial *W*; other variations affect the final syllable; the vowel may become neutral; the *dd* sound may become *-s*, but more often *-ett*, as in the case of Gruffydd/Griffett. The following represent the various forms of the registers:

Gwinneth, Clunbury 30. 1634. *Gwinnett*, Pontesbury 15. 1552. *Gwyneth*, Ludlow 10. 1578. *Gwynneis*, Ludlow 229. 1574. (cf. Worthen 32. Quennis ap John). *Gwynnit*, *Gwynit*, St Chad's, Index. *Winnett* (as christian name), Non-con. Shrewsbury High St, 29. 1793. Susanna Winnett, dau. of James and Mary Meaton.

Before quoting from present-day registers it is necessary to inquire whether the very popular girl's name *Gwyneth* has its origin in the name *Gwynedd*. *Gwyneth* is not known as a christian name in the early period, G has no example and it does not occur in the pedigrees. The earliest examples collected are in the records of Conwy:

PRConway: 1577, Gwineth ver' Robert. 1629, Dorothe Willms the daughter of Wm ap Edward and Gwenett the mother; [cf. also 1581. Elena ver' Thomas gwynethe als gwrach y gwenniath. 1630. Gwinne hookes gentlewoman].

It is difficult to explain why *Gwynedd/ Gwyneth* came to be used as a girl's name in the first place. There are more recent examples of *Gwynedd* (i.e. not Gwyneth) as christian name, e.g. JEG 187, a girl called 'Gwynedd', born 1879, in the Douglas-Pennant family: Shrewsbury, Greenfields, Gwynedd Evans, = wife's name; Harlescott, Gwynedd Jones, = wife's name; Oswestry, Wem Urban, Gwynedd Moss, wife's name. Cf. S. Worcs Croome-Ripple, Gwynett E. Thomas = rector's wife.

There are variants of the name, probably variants of Gwyneth, such as Gweneth (e.g. D. Tel 9.5.84, Lady Gweneth Cavendish, age 95, obituary) and Gwenydd, and it is faintly possible that the word *gwenith* 'wheat' is connected with the use of 'Gwyneth' as a girl's name (i.e. that 'Gwenith' was first intended) for the word was used in poetry for 'the favourite' or 'the pick of the bunch'. The great popularity of the name *Gwyneth* in the present century is probably due to some famous woman who had or used this name; and the spread of Gwyneth was probably due to the influence of Annie Harriet Hughes (1852-1910) who adopted the name 'Gwyneth Vaughan' as a writer; she was a vigorous temperance worker, took a very active part in politics, wrote a series of novels, and contributed to all sorts of papers and journals, published in Welsh and in English.

In present-day registers, *Gwinnett, Winnett, Gwinnut* are found in fairly large numbers in the border counties, far too many to plot. *Gwinnutt* is found in Monmouth, Llanhennock; and *Quinnette*, probably another variant, in Wirral, Whitby Ward. These surnames have come, not from Gwyneth as a mother's name, but from Gwynedd (Gwyneth), used originally as place-name.

Gwynne *v.* Gwyn

Gwynlliw (-yw)

G 742 has both spellings of this name and a good number of examples. It is best known as the name of the 'saint' whose church in Newport is now the cathedral church of the diocese of Monmouth, St Woollos. *Gwynllyw* was the son of Gliwys, a prince of S.E. Wales; he was the father of St Cadog. The suffix *-wg* added to the name (with a contraction of the second and third syllables) gave *Gwynllŵg*, the name of the *cantref* from the Rhymney to the Usk; in other words, the area between Newport and Cardiff called 'Wentloog': the *Went-* obviously comes from a wrong inference that it stood for 'Gwent'; *v.* Lloyd, HW 273, 278, 442.

There does not seem to be evidence that *Gwynllyw* was much used as a name; there are no examples shown in the index of the Glam charters or by the index of Clark's genealogies, although the latter volume has several refs. to St Woollos as a place. It is possible that names like *Woolhouse* may conceal the name *Woolos*, the Bristol TD has one example of *Woollow*.

Gwyon *v.* Gwion

Gwyther *v.* Gwythyr

Gwythyr

G 754 classifies under *Gwythur*, which would strictly be the form derived from Latin *victor* (oblique case); the character bearing this name in the story of *Kulhwch ac Olwen* is *Gwythyr uab greidawl*, in WM 460.23, 470, 8-9; RM 132. 17 etc. Note that *Eglwys Wythwr* (or *Eglois Withir . . . E. woythwir* NLWJ v. 268) is the native name of 'Monington' in N. Pembs and G assumes this is the church of Gwythyr. One striking thing to note is that G has not a single example of the name occurring in med

poetry. The second striking thing is that the name seems to have survived outside Welsh-speaking Wales, i.e. S. Pembs, Gower peninsula, and the English border area, and a third thing is that it retained initial *G*, although there may be examples of initial *W*. Glam Cartae 544. Heylin ab Goythur. RecCa 46. Gwethir ab Caderod; 61. Gwedir ap Caderod; ibid Gwidir ap Catherod; 58. Mad' ap Gwithir. DLancaster (Forrenry-Kidwelly) 292. Morgan Harry David Weither. WPortBooks 87. Roger Gwyther of Tenby; 314. Roger Gwithur (Tenbie-Manerbeire). Ex Pro James I. 287, 307. John Gwyther (Manorbier); CRHaverford 68. George Gwyther; 152. George Gwither. Surveys GK (Oxwich *c.* 1632) 132. Anne Gwithir; Millwood 1584, 170. Rees Gwither. In present-day registers the name abounds in S. Pembs and it is likely that the instances found elsewhere in South Wales have their origin in S. Pembs. But it is found, in small numbers, in all the counties of the Border; e.g. Ludlow, Bishops Castle, Little Stretton; Oswestry, Oswestry Urban; C. of Hereford, St Nicholas, Tupsley; S. Hereford, Mordiford; Leominster, Cradley – to name only a few places: and one has to conclude that the name surviving in the border counties came from sources in Powys.

Gyby *v.* Cybi

Gymro, Gymrow *v.* Cymro

Gyttes *v.* Gruffudd

H

Hagr

Hagr 'ugly' is quite often found attached to a pers. name in the med. period. It is hardly possible to pronounce the word without some sort of vowel escaping between the *g* and *r*: this epenthetic sound is generally represented by *y* in med. writing; in South Wales, this 'unavoidable' vocalic sound has developed into a full vowel, to give *hagar*.

B15. 50. AS 1406. Hwfa ap Je(uan) hagr. B5. 146. CaernsLS. 1293. Madyn hagyr. B13. 222. SR 1292. Gween ap Griffith Hager. MerLSR 53. Blethint Hagor. CaernCR 26. Goronwy ap Iorwerth Hagr (MS Hagyr). CalInqu Edw III. 320. Hager (surname, context Salop).

The following may be further examples:
PRMunslow 27. 1582 . . . f. Thomas Hagar. PRActon Burnell 5. 1575. Harry Haggar.

Hargest *v*. Introd. Place-names

Harries, Harris, Harry *v*. Henry

Hayling, Haylins *v*. Heilyn

Hangharot, Hegnareth *v*. Angharad

Heilyn

A very common name in the med period: Heilyn fab Gwyn Hen was one of the survivors of the great massacre in the story of Branwen. PKM 214*n* and reference to *Hail*, implies it is a derivative of the stem meaning 'minister, serving at table'. The examples in med texts are numerous; the following are representative specimens:

B13. 142. Bonds peace 1283, Yorwerth fil Heilyn. B13. 217. SR 1292. Reynaud Haulyn; 222. Uuaf ab Heylyn. B5. 144. Caern 1293. helin ap llywelyn; 148. helin. B15. 44. AS 1406. William ap Heilyn ddu. Mer LSR 14. Heylin ap Glackoun;

There is a name *Helling(s)* and with that in mind one cannot be definite that all the following stand for Heilin/Heilyn:

BBStD 132. Henr' Helyn. CalChancProc 529. Helyn Du. CatAncDeeds VI. C.6408, 12 Elz. Monts, Owen ap John ap Jevan ap Dio ap Helin. 1C. A.6403, Hereford, Henry VIII. Nicholas Helyn.

In the following there is a form which could be called 'hypocoristic' or the complement form of the suffix -*yn* in Heilyn, corresponding to Gutyn and Guto: B15. 56. AS 1406. heilo ap Meredyth.

SHROPSHIRE REGISTERS

One expects to find examples of -*in* turning to -*ing*; *ab* + *h* to give *p*; and a variety of spellings of the diphthong:

Selattyn 7. 1561. Edward ap William Heilin. Myddle 112. 1692. Habbackuk Heylin. St Chad's, Index, Healing, Hailing, Halin, Haylin, Healling, Heelin, Heeling, Heelinge, Heling, Helinge, Heylin. Alberbury 228. 1678. . . . Heiling. Pontesbury 81. 1602. Heilinge. Ludlow 1034. 1786. Thomas Heylings. ChStretton 90. 1725. James s of James and Ann Paylin; 97. 1743. James Palin of C.S. 110. 1743. Mary Pelin. Ruyton 92. 1782. James Paling, p. of Whitchurch; 94. 1787. Elizabeth Paling. Wrockwardine 2. 1594. Lucey d. of John Palyn; 5. 1600. John Palin. Moreton Say 102. 1768. Samuel Payling (signs Paling). Wem 547. 1753. Thomas Payling (several variants, including 648. 1752. Paylen; 704. 1748. Thomas Palinge). Condover 169. 1709. Sarah, d. of Thos and Eliz. Palin; 172. 1712. Tho. s. of Tho. and Eliz. Pealing.

The various versions seen in the Shropshire registers are to be found today: in Ludlow, Brompton-Chirbury, there are the following addresses, Pentreheilin Cottage and Pentreheyling House. Hayling, West Gloucs, Longlevens, Staunton, Twigworth; Stroud, Dursley; City of Gloucester, Eastgate p26;

Kingsholm p13; Torfaen, Cwmbrân Central and Llantarnam. Haylings, City of Hereford, SA Central; City of Gloucs, Matson Ward, p. 24; Newport, Malpas 2. Heylings, City of Gloucs. Tuffley Ward 4. Pailing, City of Hereford, VB St Nicholas; South Hereford, Mordiford. Payling, CT, Tewkesbury 4; Nantwich, Wistaston. Palin, Shrewsbury, Abbey Foregate. Pailin, Cheadle, Hazelgrove and Bramhall, South Ward.

Heir *v.* Hir

Hen, Hynaf

Hen 'old', and the superlative *hynaf* were used as epithets for the purpose of distinguishing father from son bearing the same name, or grandfather from son and grandson; the text does not at all times include sufficient to demonstrate the purpose of the epithet: B13. 228. SR 1292. Ieuan ap Wronu Heen; Ieuan Heen. B10. 72. West W. 1352. Eynon ap Ieuan ap Eynon Hene. Mer LSR 33. D(aui)d Hene; 62. Iockin Hen. ADClun 13. Ada hen; 40. Griff' ab Ada hen; 107. Griffit ap Atha Heen; BBStD 30. Joh'es Hene. Rec Denb Lp 40. Eignon Heen. MLSW 92. . . . ap Hoell Hene; 112. . . . ap Howell Heyn.

The attributive adj. in Welsh usually follows the noun; *hen*, with a few others, are exceptions and precede the noun. In the examples quoted above, *hen*, departing from its own idiomatic position, follows the noun like any other adj. In Bartrum's Genealogies there are a few examples of *hen* (with the def. art.) preceding the personal name, just as it would precede a common noun: Bartrum 1215-1350. 390. Maredudd Fychan ab yr Hen Faredudd ap Hywel; 446. . . . Iorwerth Fychan ab yr Hen Iorwerth ab Owain.

The following show *hen* and *hynaf* together, *hen* following the pers. name; in the case of the superlative it is normal for *hynaf* to follow: Bartrum 1215-1350. 354. John Haliwel Hen ap John H. Hyna ap Dafydd; John Haliwel ap John H. Hen ap John H. Hyna.

BBStD 100. Ieuan Henaf. PWLMA 520. Dafydd Hyna ap Llywelyn ap Hywel. PRSelattyn 41. 1594. Katherine, d. of John ap Richard ap Ieuan, Hynaf ('John' and 'Ieuan' obviously regarded as the same name; the editor of the text is prone to insert commas and the comma after 'Ieuan' should be disregarded).

Example of compound *henwr* ('old man', elder). MLSW218 Grono ap Ieuan Henour. L'Estrange Ewen 125 includes *Henn* (sic) and *Henwas* ('old-manservant') in the list of surnames occurring in PRO papers.

See above, the note at the end of *Einion*, the argument of A.M. Haines (quoted by T.E. Morris, art. cit.) that Haines is derived from Einion, on rather doubtful evidence. If a Welsh origin must be sought for Haines, then 'Hen' would be less unlikely.

Henry, Harry, Penry, Parry

The numbers in Bartrum show the general spread of Henry: 1215-1350, p.293, Henry, twenty, Harry, two; 1350-1415, pp.593-5, Henry/Harry thirty nine.

B13. 218. SR 1292. 'jury of the land of Care Warlan': Henry ab Helidir; 229. taxed in Cilgerran David ab Henry . . . Yewan ab Henry . . . Henry ab Ener. CaernQSR 138. Morgan ap Harry, son of Henry ap William ap David ab Siencyn. PRConway 1577. Salomone ap harry, f. henrici Taylor; 1580. Willmus ap Harry filius Henrici gr. tayler; 1582. Blanch ap Harry fil. henrici gr. tayler. InvECP 150, Monts 1551. Adam ap Harry.

The following represent the changed versions: B10. 86. Roll of Wards, L.M. Kemes 16th century. Phillip Gitto ap Ieuan David Penry. Star CP 9. Monm. Henry VII. Wm Aparry, Adam Aparry. PRWrockwardine 18. 1628. Morres ap Henry, alias Parry.

The combination of *nr* may develop an epenthetic vowel in colloquial E Henery; but the tendency in W would be to develop an intrusive *d*, to give Hendry.

CRHaverford 129. John Hendrie. InvECP 184. Rads 1553. Lewis Appendrye. PRLlantrithyd 71. 1735. Margaret Hendry.

It is difficult to account for the following spellings, except to suggest the influence of the *ff* and *th* in *Griffith*: L & P i. 368. Gryffith. Appenryth; 884. Griffith Appenriff.

The form *Henry* did not take the genitive *-s*, but *Harry/Harri* did become *Harries* or *Harris*, as if an alternative surname to 'ap Harry'. InvECP 49. Carms 1544. Margaret Harreys. CRHaverford, Index, has the following variant spellings: Haries, Harriez, Harys, Harris, Hares, Harryes.

It sounds 'unidiomatic' to Welsh speakers to add 's to the *ap/P* form:
PRWroxeter 53. 1681. Humphrey ap Harris; PRHanwood 48. 1682. Maria Parries.

No examples of the normal forms, *Henry*, *Harry* etc. were picked up from present-day registers; cf. the following: Wrekin, Kebley – Wellington Rural, Hendrie; West Gloucs, West Dean 1, Hendrey (– Pendrey, in West Dean 2).

Pen(y)dref is in common use, meaning the 'top-end of the town', and this should not be excluded completely from being a possible source of some of the following, although the probability is that they represent 'ap-Henry': *Pendry*, Oswestry, Osw. Urban, Castle Ward, North W., East W.; Leominster, Colwall. *Pendree*, S. Worcs, Malvern S, Priory; ditto Wells; Newport, Allt-yr-yn 2; Newport Central. *Pendre*, Monm, Monmouth Overmonnow; Monmouth town; Islwyn, Newbridge – Greenfield, Abercarn, Chapel of Ease; Cwmfelinfach, Abercarn – Llanfach. *Pendrey*, S. Gloucs, Coleford; West Gloucs, Lydbrook; Monmouth town; Torfaen, Cwmbran, Fairwater and Henllys.

Herbert

This name, though of foreign origin, has been long established in Wales, as the surname of a group of great landowners, but also as the surname of many more obscure lines, quite unconnected with families such as the Herberts of Raglan. Sir William ap Thomas of Raglan adopted Herbert as his family's surname, and the eminence of the family probably accounts for the frequency of the surname in South Wales. The PR of Kinnerley has the following versions of Herbert and of names derived from 'ab-Herbert':

Index: Herbert, Harbett, Harbutt; Parbut, Parboth, Porbut.
Further examples of 'ab-Herbert' formations: Eaton Constantine 14. 1744. Richard s. of Richard and Mary Perbert, (three other similar entries on p.15). 18. 1763; 28. 1793. Francis Parbutt. 26. 1772. William Parbutt; 29. 1793. Mary Parbutt. (Index puts Perbert and Parbutt together). Great Ness 83. 1702. Mary Parbot; 224. 1786. Mary Parbut. St Mary's Shrewsbury, Index, Parbutt. St Chad's, Index, Parbott. L'Estrange Ewen 125 includes *Parbert* in the list of W surnames found in PRO papers.

Shrewsbury, Frankwell Mount, Parbutt.
Hier, Hire *v.* Hir
Hir
Hir 'long' originally included the sense of 'tall': the E adj. has been borrowed and is the adj. usually used in modern Welsh for the height of persons, the W adj., although in general use for all other meanings or contexts, being hardly ever used; it might still be appropriate in a bardic name, such as 'Pedr Hir'. The vowel is long: the examples quoted below are chosen to represent the various spellings:
B13. 220. SR 1292. Grufud hirseys (= hir seys). B2. 154. Criccieth 1320. Mad' Hir; BBStD 216. Ieuan Sayrhir (leg. Saer Hir). B15. 44. AS 1406. Je(uan) Hir. B26. 87. Welsh Troops, Scot Campaign 1326. Willelmi Hire. ADClun 123. Philip ap Lewelin hyr. B2. 253. Brec. Llandov. Charters. Johanni Hyre Webbe. ADClun 35. Dauid heyr. 165. Meredith ap Hoell Heir. InvECP 152. Monts 1553. Katherine Gryffyth, alias Heyre. ibid 225. Monm 1542. Howell Heere, of Holy Trinity Mon = 226 Howell Hyre. L & P vii. 1225 (111) John ap Thomas ap Griffith alias John Here; in (iv) and (vi) he is referred to only as John Here.

Some of these spellings are still found in electoral registers:
Hire: Newport, Malpas 3; Preseli, Milford Central, Milford North, M. West; S. Pembs, St Mary 'D' Llanion. *Hier*: S. Gloucs, Filton Conygre Ward 1, Churchdown 1; Stroud, Upton St Leonards; S. Pembs, St Mary – Pembs West; Preseli, Neyland, Llanstadwell. *Heir*: City of Hereford, Holmer, St Martin's.
There are occasional examples of *hir* compounded with *coes* 'leg', B24. 227. Fasti Cist. Camb. Richard Hyrgois.

Hiscog
There would be no reason to include this name, obviously a borrowing of E Hiscock, except that there is an example of ap-Hiscog or Piscog in Bartrum:
1215-1350, 288. Gwilym ap Piscog; 350. Jenkin ap Gwilym ap Piscog.
Hodilow *v.* Hoeddlyw
Hoeddlyw
The presence of *-dl-* in med script raises doubt in the mind whether it stands for -dl- or for -ddl-, not only because *d* may stand for *dd*

but more so because -dl- and -ddl- are so liable to change in either direction, v. WG 185; *bodlon* for '*boddlon*'; *chwedl* becoming *wheddel* in SW dialect; *hoedl* (read *hoeddl*) making 'cynghanedd' with *heddwch*, RP 1248. The examples which use -*thl*- prove that the name is 'Hoeddlyw' but Hoedlyw was probably an early variant.

LL 277. hodliu. B13. 222. SR 1292. Griffuth ab Hodelou; 225. Mereduth fil Hwiteloue. B24. 226. Fasti Cist. Cambr. Hodelew. Mer LSR 30. Gronou ap Hodelov; 78. D(aui)d ab Hudolou. RecCa 59. Hoydelew ap Gorndur. BBStD 262. Dauid ap Hoythlowe; 264. Dauid ap Hoythlou; 294. Hothlowe Medwe (trans. takes 'medwe' to be 'meadow'; it must be 'meudwy' or 'meddw'). RadsSoc XI. 41, quoting pedigree from Harl. 1566, the generations from 'Res Greige' (= Rhys Gryg); the sixth is *Hoodlow*; RCA 297, gavel of Holdelowe Gilberte.

The name was never widely used and fell into disuse, but there is at least one surviving example in the seventeenth century: H Asaph iv. 29. 1633. Hodilow, Arthur, Clare Hall, Cambridge (in sinecure rectors of Denbigh).

Hopcyn

Hopkin, according to Reaney, is Hobbekin, a diminutive of Hob, a pet form of Robert. The name has been in use in Wales since the thirteenth century, and is common in Glam and certain parts of N. Cards. The E spelling is still regarded as the proper one but the W spelling is also used.

Examples of ab-Hopkin:

DLancaster 17 (Monm. 1610) William Popkyn, Johannis ap Popkin. HM i. 7. Skenfrith, List of landowners in 1606 includes John Popkin and Wiliam Popkin. ibid vol. 3. Llandegveth 274. amongst witnesses, Jenkin ap Popkin. Surveys GK, Millwood 1641. 287. Thomas Popkin Morgan; 289. Thomas Popkin. Manor of Kilvey, temp James I. 344. Thomas Popkins, Gent, John Popkins, Gent. B3. 140. Glam. Loyalists 1696. John Popkins ... Tho Popkins.

Clark, Genealogies, has a large number of Hopkins and a good number of Popkin.

Hope v. Introd. Place-names

Hopkin, Hopkins v. Hopcyn

Hoskin(s)

Hoskin may be a form of Hodgkin, which is a diminutive of Hodge; cf. BBStD 296 Adam Hochekyn. It may have been altered in English, i.e. before being borrowed: anyhow Hodgkin would certainly be changed to Hoskin in Welsh, for Welsh speakers were incapable of producing the -*dj*- sound and would change it to -*s* + *k*. Reaney proposes a separate origin for Hoskin, as a diminutive of *Os*-, a short form of such names as Osgod, etc.

Glam Cartae 1697. Thomas Hoisgekyn. AnglPleas 5. Robert ap Huskyn, late of Tremaylgoch; 6. William ap Huskyn. 19. Llewelin ap Huskyn. MLSW 53. Jenkin ap Hosshkyn. DLancaster (Kidwelly) 198. John Arnold Hoskyn; JEG 81. Richard ap Hugh ap Hoesgyn (16c); 110. Roger, alias Hoeskin, Holland (15c). Bartrum 1215-1350. 293. Hoesgyn ap Rhys ap Richard; 444. Robin ap Hoesgyn Holland. HM i. 374. Philip Hoyskin; 4.10, Caldicot, ll'n ap Jeyne ap Hoiskin; 11. Court Roll 1716. Llewelyn Jeyne ap Hoyskin.

AP-FORMATIONS

H Asaph 1. 319. List of Deans, Richard Puskyn (Ap Hoeskyn – editor's addition); in iv. 6, the date is given, Richard Puskin 1543. L'Estrange Ewen 255. Puskin (ap Hoesgyn). HM i. 416. A will of 1729 "my messuage in Raglan, Thomas Poiskin" (editorial footnote: 'Poiskin is ap Hoiskin or Hoskyn, a form of Hopkin'). Ibid vol. iii. (part ii). Llangwm Ucha, Pedigree mentions a marriage in 1727-8 to Herbert Poyskin of Raglan. PRLlanbadoc 1588. Watter, supposed son of Charles Poyskin; 1593. Charles ap Poskin. PRLlCrossenny 1623, p.38. Georgius Poyskins.

The following conceals the name *Poyskyn*: InvECP 72. Pembs 1553 (Manordeifi) Thomas ap Price ap Weskyn.

In the dialect of Pembs. the diphthong *oe* becomes *we*, oen → ẅen; oedd → wedd or we. Castell Gorfod 8. f. 149 is a copy found by the anonymous 'I.H.' at Killay, Swansea *c*. 1677, of a deed dated second year of Richard III (*c*. 1485), which has to do with a dispute between David Howell and Hoyskyn ap David. The surname Hoskin survives in the Killay area. The TD of Swansea and SWW has a good number of Hoskin, Hoskins, Hosking, Hoskings, and one entry of Hosken.

Hova, Hovey v. Hwfa

Howell(s) v. Hywel
Howelet, Howelot v. Hywel
Howls v. Hywel
Huffa, Huffer v. Hwfa
Hughes v. Hywel
Hugyn, Huwcyn v. Hywel
Hullah, Hullin, Hullyn v. Hywel

Humphrey

This name is not found often in the early periods, and its use amongst the Welsh must have started rather late, and yet early enough to have *ab* formations; it is more typical of North Wales than of the South. There must have been a version of the name that had no aspirate, for there is a colloquial 'Wmffra' in North Wales, and NW speech does not fail to sound the aspirate; and there is evidence that there was an unaspirated version in NW England, e.g. PRWhicham, 60. 1686. Mrs Annes Umphra. Cf. Clark, Genealogies 463-4, 'The Umfrevilles, Umfravilles, Humphravilles, or Humphrevilles, were undoubtedly among the earliest settlers in Glamorgan'. They came to Glamorgan from Devon; the pedigree starts in the twelfth century; Reaney gives Umfreville, derived from Umfreville (La Manche). In the art. on Humphrey, (and its variant versions) in Reaney, there is no suggestion that the *h* is (or was) silent, but one example of *Umfrey* 1293 is quoted. Note especially that in spite of Humffrey or Humphrey as official versions, the use of the more colloquial version *Wmffre* in these two entries in DWB: Davies, Humffrey, 'Wmffre Dafydd ab Ifan', fl. 1600-1664, Davies, Humphrey or Wmffre Dafis, died 1635, Vicar of Darowen. The letters of ML and ALMA were written by the same people, cf. ML Index, Wmffras, included in refs. of Humphreys; ALMA 192 (Morris Prichard to Lewis Morris) Hoffre Robeds (index gives it as Howffre). The form 'Umffrey', or in other words, the silent *h*, explains the examples of Bummfrey, e.g. PRConway 1542 Hugh ap Bumffre; 1718. Thomas ap Wm Bymphrey; cf. 1708 Griffinus ap Hu : ap Humphrey.

SHROPSHIRE REGISTERS

Ford 4. Ap Humffre. Pontesbury 468. Bumfrey. Westbury 38. 1659. David a Bumfrey. Munslow 206. 1745. Elizabeth Bumfrey; 224. 1767. Thos Bumfry (alias Humfries).

There must have been an aspirate version to give Pumphrey: both versions *P* and *B* from present-day registers are shown below, and it should be borne in mind that there is a spelling *Homfray*.

Bumfrey or *Bumphrey*: City of Hereford, Central, Holmer, St Martin's; Leominster, Eastnor; S. Worcs, Malvern West No. 5; Malvern South No. 3. *Bomfrey*: S. Worcs Malvern South No. 1. *Boumphrey*: Northwich, Northwich Rural – Oakmere; Cheadle, Hazelgrove & Bramhall, East 1; Wirral, Hoylake, Greasby 2, Park Ward, Neston – Willaston Ward; Westmorland, Kirkby Lonsdale. *Buffrey*: West Gloucs, Little Dean; Newland, Ruspidge. *Buffery*: CT, Stow-in-the Wold. *Pumphrey* or *Pumfrey*: Leominster, Marden, Sutton; CT, Southam, Winchcombe; Bromsgrove, Bromsgrove 3; South Worcs, Croome-Ripple; Wirral, Hoylake South Ward. *Pomphrey*: Macclesfield, Poynton-with-Worth (central).

Huwcyn v. Hywel

Hwfa

Hwfa is regarded as the standard form, but *Hofa* or *Hova* is found quite as often, if not oftener, in med records. Because of the use of *u* in med script it is often misread as *Hona*, and the misreading may be by a medieval copyist so that it is not always the fault of a modern textual editor: v. p.6 above. Very rarely is it found in South Wales.

B13. 221. SR 1292. Houa ap David, (Powys); ibid. Ythel ab Houa ('Hwitinton'). B5. 147. CaernLSR 1293. huwa ap adgyn. B5. 58. Lleyn, late 13th century jorwerth ap howa; 71. gwyn ap howa. B9. 66. NW 1295. de progenie houa. (Footnote, Clan of Hwfa ap Cynddelw). B6. 256. Lleyn 1350. ada ap hona, Davith ap hona [sic]. B26. 79. Fragment Roll 1294. Hova ap Yerwart. RecCa 246. 247. Bledrys ap Hova; 95. Hwna ap Cad' [sic], 246. Hona ap Plethyn [sic]. LpOswestry 170. Ieuan ap Madoc ap Houar [sic]. BYale 54. Llewelyn ap Hona (trans. ap Hwfa; editor uses *Hwfa* in translation throughout).

The Oswestry register has the place-name which is given as *Carreghwfa* in the Gazetteer, but shows the phonetic change of the juncture of *g* + *h*: 73. 1580. *Thom's ap D'd ap John Carreckova*; 586. 1657 . . . *of Kaercova in the parish of Llanymynech*; the editor has put

Carreghova in brackets.

SHROPSHIRE REGISTERS

The examples collected from the registers include *ap-* formations and the changes taking place in the final vowel which eventually give *Hovey* and *Povey:*

Whittington 312. 1739. William Povah, of Hinford. 445. 1754. Elizabeth d. of John Povah (?) [sic] and Mary his wife, of Ebnal; 462. 1762. E. d. of William Povah and Margaret ... of Ebnal; 468. 1766. John s. of William Poval and Margaret his wife, of Ebnal. 502. 1776. W. s. William Poval and Mary ... of Ebnal: 579. 1761. William Povah; 580. 1763. Dorothy Povah. (Editor puts Povah and Povall together in index.) St Martin's 179. 1759. ... of Jonathan Haffa and Elinor his wife. 194. 1759. Mary d. of Jonathan Hoffa and Elinor. 272. 1798. William s. of John and Ann Pevah, [sic] Whittington p. 321. 1792. (Marriage) John Povey, b. and Ann Jones, sp. Chirbury, Index, Huffa, Huffer, Hofart. Ludlow 17, 22. Huffa. Burford 32. Apofer. Acton Burnell 4. 1575. Ellenor d. of Mathew Pivah (?). Great Ness 76. 1698. Margaret Pova; 83. 1702. William Pova. 97. 1714. Margaret, w. of W. Povah (other examples occur: editor puts Pova(h) and Povey together in the index). Non-con., Shrewsbury, Claremont Bapt. 22. Eliz Hovay (Index gives Hovah).

The spelling *Poval(l)*, however odd it appears on paper, is not so difficult to understand if one bears in mind that the quality of the *l* in the speech of these parishes has no dental sound, and 'football' sounds like 'footbaw'. As to the change which produced *Hovey*, the intermediate stage is seen in the form *Hovay*.

PRESENT-DAY REGISTERS

Povah: Oswestry, Weston Rhyn. Runcorn, Heath 1; Northwich, Tarporley South. Examples in Wales are found mainly in the Flint constituencies and Wrexham; there is an address in Radnor – Llanbister, Hova Cottage. *Pover:* Shrewsbury, Westbury; Ludlow, Wenlock-Much Wenlock; Stal. and Hyde, Stalybridge No. 1 (Lancashire Ward Pt. 2); Nantwich, Hankelow. *Hovey:* Denbigh, Llandrillo-yn-Rhos. *Povey:* Wrexham, Chirk 1; Caernarfon, Dolbenmaen, Garn Ward, Criccieth, Llanystumdwy, Llanystumdwy – Llanarmon, Ynyscynhaearn.

The name Povey spread down to S.E. Wales; there are twenty-three entries in the TD of Cardiff and S.E. Wales, and three entries of Povall, the form seen above in the PR of Whittington. The Swansea TD has only three entries of Povey, and no entry of Povall.

Hywel

The standard pronunciation of the first syllable is exactly like the E interrogative 'how'. In Welsh this diphthong, in such words as *bywyd, cywydd, tywydd, cywir,* has been, at times, inclined to change to have the sound of E *tow, flow,* and before spelling became standardized these words were often written – as they were sounded – *bowyd, cowydd, towydd, cowir,* and the word *tywyn,* 'strand, beach' in place-names was pronounced and written as 'Towyn'; this *-ow* sound is still heard, in colloquial speech, e.g. 'yn gowir'. Therefore the change of *Hywel* to *Howel* could take place in Welsh, and need not be regarded as maltreatment of Welsh. But the use of *-ell* must be regarded as an 'English' spelling, for the *ll* would be misleading in Welsh writing. In med records it is very often written *Hoel,* or *Hoell,* or *Holl,* B11. 61. Broniarth Court Rolls 1429, Hoel ap Ienc' ap Ieuan; AnglPleas 4. Gwillim ap Hoell; InvECP 3, Anglesey 1504, Ithell ap Hoell; 169. Brecs. 1547. Hoel Domosse ap Hoel Prynnayt, William ap Hoell (Apoll), and note in particular 129, Flints 1556-8, *Richard Hall (Howell),* which implies that during the proceedings these two forms are used for the same person. In certain Welsh dialects, however, *Hywel* is pronounced *Hiwel,* and this may have given rise to the interchangeability of *Huw* and *Hywel,* and thus the interchangeability of *Hughes* and *Howells.*

There are variant spellings in the Shropshire registers which may be clues to certain surnames:

Shipton 31. 1667. John Hawwells (the form Howells occurs on same page). 34. 1685. Thomas Hawwells. Donington 71. 1690. Thomas Howell, als Howle, of Albrighton.

The formation *ab-Howel > Powel, Powell* is obvious and hardly needs historical references to illustrate: Glam Cartae, Index, has *Apowel, Appowel, Aphoel.* It is interesting to observe the vowel *a* surviving in certain entries. CRHaverford 191. Lewis Apo(we)ll; 211. Thomas a Powell; 209. Thomas apowell; 211.

Thomas a powell, tucker; 175, 179. Meredith a Powell.

As with so many other names, in some families the fixed surname became *Howell* or *Howells*, in others *Powell*. Both forms are very common in S. Wales; Breconshire has a concentration of Powell. Mention has already been made of the substitution of *Hugh (Huw)* for Hywel, but although rare examples of this can be found in SW, this change took place mainly in Gwynedd. Examination of the names of Cwtta Cyf., which brings in parts of Flints and Denbs in the seventeenth century, provides evidence that Howell and Powell occur with reasonable regularity and it is clear that Hugh did not displace Hywel in the north east to any great extent. Even today one finds fair numbers of Howell(s) in the N.E., e.g. eighteen in Llanrhaeadr-ym-Mochnant, compared with a typical Arfon parish, Llan-llyfni/Talysarn Ward which has a whole column of Hughes and not a single instance of Hywel/Howells or Powell.

There are examples of *Howls*, e.g. South Hereford, Walford; and *Powles*, e.g. S. Her. Walford; Leominster, Bromyard; and the example above of 'Howell, *als Howle'* from PRDonington 71. 1690 provides some ground for thinking these are from *Howel*. The form *Hole* is also found, e.g. S. Herefords, St Devereux; S. Gloucs, Patchway; Reaney has E examples and offers the meaning, 'dweller in the hollow', but it would not be unreasonable to believe that an example on the W border might represent *Hoel, Hoell, v.* above.

The use of *Hugh* instead of *Hywel* is dealt with on p.20. *Hugh* as christian name would inevitably result in it becoming a surname. Examples without addition of *s* are found occasionally, but generally it is *Hughes*, or *Pugh, Pughe*. The forms *Pugh, Pughe* are typical of Monts, e.g. they abound in Darowen. With the movements of population especially to the industrial south, these forms, *Hughes* and *Pugh*, are now found scattered throughout Wales.

The idea that Welsh spelling should be 'phonetic' converts *Hugh* to *Huw* and *Huw* as christian name occurs as often as *Hugh*. This has also changed the surname to *Huws*, there are three named *Huws* in the DWB, of the second half of the nineteenth century: in the

case of two, the articles provide no evidence whether the name was a change from registered 'Hughes', but in the case of W. Pari Huws, his brothers are named, G. Parry Hughes and Rowland Hughes. The writers know a number of people who have chosen the form Huws.

The use of the 'phonetic' form goes back a good deal earlier, and one possible reason for this is that it may be the colloquial abbreviation of Hywel. The early documents of ADClun have *Howel*, and *Hugo*: the later, e.g. 211, have Huw ap Muric Bach, 225, Huw Lluccas. Cf. also: PWLMA 392 John 'Hewe' (1472, Constables, Caeo-Mallaen). Bartrum 1350-1415, 596, prints *Huw*, in twenty-three examples; this may be due to the need for a standardised form; (for comparison of numbers of *Huw/Hugh* with *Hywel*, there are over four hundred Hywel, pp. 597-613).
Star CP3. Robert Apewe (Conwy, Talcafn). InvECP 51. Carms 1544 John ap Hew. 81. Denbs 1533 John Hewes. 157. Monts John Hewes alias Lloied of Burford, Co, Oxford.
Reaney has *Hugget, Huget;'* (1) A variant of Hewet, from *Hug-et*, a diminutive of *Hugh*. (2) Robert de Hugat ... From Huggate (East Riding Yorks)'. Cf. Star CP 176, Glamorgan, *Dd Hugh als Huggatt.*

DERIVATIVE AND HYPOCORISTIC FORMS OF HYWEL

The forms *Hwlyn* (= Hullin) and *Hwlcyn* have occasionally been used as hypocoristic forms of Hywel. The basic form of which Hwlyn and Hwlcyn are derivatives, namely *Hull*, is not a version of Hywel; it is a borrowing from English, and it looks as if the resemblance of the two names brought them into a kind of association.

Reaney deals with *Hullin* and *Hullah* separately, but there is a good reason for regarding them as variants, forming a 'pair' as one finds so often in the case of hypocoristic names. The name Hullah is not found in a Welsh context, but there are examples of Hulta (Pulta) which seems to have the *-to* (*-ta*) ending of W Guto; and examples of Hulka which looks as if it were the counterpart of Hwlcyn. The change of the final vowel, varying from *-o* to *-a* is not exceptional, it is seen in Deia, Gutta, Llela, *v.* p.34. [The forms *Hull* and *Hulk* where they occur in Welsh texts or contexts are prob.

abbreviations, e.g. AnglPleas 5, William ap David ap Hoell ap Hulk, late of Clyneoke; 8. David ap John ap Howell ap Hull; cf. also, InvECP 151. Monts 1553. David ap Ieuan ap Hull Tome; 263. Marches 1556, Howell ap Gwyllym Hully.]

The form *Hullyn* (with English double *l*) is found quite early in a variety of documents, and note that in one of the examples below, from the Bolde Rental, Hullyn is an alias of Hoell:

CaernQSR 103. Robert ap Gruffydd ap Llywelyn ap Hullyn; 106. ditto. RecCa 25. Teg' ap Hollyn. CaernHS 26, Bolde Rental 36. Res ap Hullyn ap Dikyn. 37. Marvret vz Hullyn ap Eden. 37. Margaret vz hoell ap Tangwistil vz grono; otherwise Margaret vz hullyn ap y purse. Glam Cartae 1938. Leodovicus Will. Hullyn. Surveys GK, Reynoldston 1665, 268. John Hullin; 268. Nicholas Hullins. MLSW 94. Willelmi Hullyn (Bedwellty). Llantrisant and District L.H.S. Newsletter 5, 1976, p.l. Farm, Perth Andro, owned 1506 by Llywelyn ap Hullyn Crother and Gwladys his wife, ' "Hullyn" was a common name amongst 16 century copyholders in Pentyrch and Clun, but does not occur in Clark's Genealogies' – information received from Mr Barry Davies of the local history society.

PR Llantrithyd has a number of entries of Hullin in the early seventeenth century. Obviously ab-Hullin would give *Pullin*; the only such entry is 1: 1598 *David Pullim*. Assuming that this is a correct reading, it represents the unstable *n/m* of words such as *reason/rheswm*; *cotton/cotwm*. The form *Pullen* is probably another variant form, e.g. RCA 22. John ap Ryce Pullen, Brecon.

The form with the suffix *-cyn* is found as early as the fourteenth century, and when it occurs in the name of the great-great-grand-father, the dating can be fixed a century earlier. Morris Jones thought possibly that Hwlcyn was actually composed of the diminutive ending *-cyn* added to a contracted form of Hywel; WG 230; cf. also Dwnn 2. 142. Footnote '. . . *Hwlcyn* . . . contraction of *Hywelcyn*, the diminutive of *Hywel*'.

RadsSoc XLIII. 82. Assessment 1293. Howel Hulkin. CaernQSR 13. John ap Harry ap Res ap Gruff' ap Hulkyn; three other examples on p.106 . . . ap Hwlcyn. B15.

43. AS 1406. Hwlkyn ap ho ap Eingian. 47, 61. Hwlkyn . . . ; 49. Hulkyn . . . It is found in the genealogies, e.g. Bartrum 1215-1350. 295. five examples; JEG 1 . . . ap Hwlkin Lloyd of Glynllifon; 2. Family name Kerver, . . . includes ap Hwlkin; 35. Hwlkin, father's name, Howel. JEG also has examples of Pwlkin: 71. Henry Pwlkin, Robert Pwlkin, cross-reference to 123, early 17th century shows both to be great grandsons of Dafydd ap Hwlkyn. Cf. also the name of the poet, 'Lln or Llyw-ap-Hwlcyn', to quote the versions of the name appended to his verses; at the end of one poem, 'llywelyn ap Hywel ap Jeuan ap Gronwy ai Kant'. In this particular poem he gives his name as the author:

'O daw gofyn pwy a ganodd hyn/llywelin ap Hwl ach car ddwbwl', where *Hwl* rhymes with *ddwbwl*; v. *Canu Rhydd Cynnar* 21-25. One of his poems is included in the *Oxford Book of Welsh Verse*, number 109.

Examples of using Hwlyn as a hypocoristic for Hywel/Howel occur in the Morris Letters, 1. 301, 303, 307, 381, 452; 2. 209, 2. 578. The example found on 1. 183 refers to Howell Harris; the example in 1. 307 refers to Howel Lewis, a doctor in London who attended upon Richard Morris. W. Roberts in *Ffrewyll i'r Methodistiaid* (1745) also refers p.35 to Howel Harris as Hwlyn.

Examples of adding *-ta* and *-ca* as suffixes to *Hul-*:

CaernQSR 5. Henricum ap Lli ap Hulta. 196. John ap Ieuan ap Hulta. 198, 199. John ap Ieuan Hulta. 179. Thomas ap Ieuan ap Pulta (occurring also in RCA 301, Car-narvon). CaernCR 56. Gruffydd ap Dafydd ap Hulka; 83. Dafydd ap Hulka.

Abundant examples of *Hugyn* occur in the med. texts. There are several forms in Reaney which could be the sources of Hugyn and variants, Huggin(s), Huggin, Huggon, Hewkin, etc.

B13. 224. SR 1292. Hugyn de Leinthale. B15. 287. Aberyst – Cardn, 14th century. Hugyn ap Weyrvil, Yvor ap Hugyn. Brut y Saeson 148. Hugyn vab Randwlf (footnote variants, Huw; translation, 149. Hugh Ffitz Ranulf). PWLMA, Index, Higon (or Hugon) or Hugo, a number of examples. InvECP 58. Griffin Hygon of New Carmarthen (Carms 1544). 53. Griffith Hyggons. BBStD 182 has the form Joh'es Hugelyn; cf. Reaney under

Hewlins, Huglin etc., with examples of Hugelinus etc., originating in OFr Hugelin, Huelin.

SHROPSHIRE REGISTERS

Chirbury, Index, Hulins, Hulings, Huglings. Pontesbury, Higgins, Higons, Hughlin. Hanwood 23, ap Higgins.

Cf. the following surnames:

Hewkin, Caernarfon, Ynyscynhaiarn, Western Ward. Hewkins, Torfaen, Cwmbrân, St Dial's.

These possibly are the E forms mentioned in Reaney, rather than E versions of W *Huwcyn*, for the W *Huwcyn* is a phonetic version of the E name. ALMA 968 has the form Hucyn David Siôn; this stands for Huwcyn. But it would be right to regard *Huwcyn* as a Welsh name by adoption, because there is a 'complementary' form *Huwco*, e.g. the bardic name of Hugh Evan Thomas (1830-89) 'Huwco Meirion'.

Huwcyn is used as a personification of sleep or sleepiness, especially of a child; Fynes-Clinton 219; this is probably connected with the word for lullaby, 'hwiangerdd', and the sound 'hwian' used to send a baby to sleep; *v.* WG 450 (Interjections), *'hu, huw,* DG/D 148, used to lull a baby to sleep, later *hwi* (short proper diphth), *hwi/an'*.

I

Ieuaf ('junior')

The superlative of *ieuanc* was used for the youngest child and became a personal name. It may have been used at times to distinguish between two bearing the same name within the same family group and placed as an epithet after a personal name, the following seems to be an example:

CaernQSR 195. John Hyna ap Thomas ap Ieuan ap Grono, John Yeva ap Thomas ap Ieuan: *hynaf* is the superlative of *hen*, 'old'. Generally the examples of *Ieuaf* do not function to make a distinction between two; it is a normal name.

The final $f(v)$ of the superlative termination – and of verbal forms, first person sing. present tense – is hardly ever sounded in natural speech: we always say *gwela*, ('I see'), *mwya* ('biggest'), and *ieuaf* often appears without the *-f*. The other sound change is dealt with alongside the change of Ieuan, i.e. becoming *Iefan*, *Ifan*, *Efan (Evan)*; the adjective, (positive) *ieuanc*, becoming *iefanc*, *ifanc*; the superlative would become *iefa*, *ifa* colloquially. [If *Iefa(f)* as a name went a further step on the lines of change which made *Iefan* into *Jevon*, one would expect to see in the border counties forms such as *Jeva*, *Jeeva*, *Jevo*; these need no longer be hypothetical for the name *Jeavas* occurs in the Bristol TD, with a Bristol address. There is a *Howel ap Jevah* in Chatterton's 'Battle of Hastings'.] The confusion of *Ieuan* and *Ieuaf* in med writing has been mentioned before; this is inevitable in script using *u* for the $f(v)$ sound. Another possibility of confusion could arise from the use of a horizontal mark above the 'preceding' vowel as a substitute for the letter *n*, so that 'Ieuan' would be 'ieuā'; an indistinct mark could lead to reading 'Ieua'. B13. 142. Bonds of peace 1283, 1295. First bond 142. Ieuaf fil Ririd; second, 143. Yeuaf ab Ryryth. B13. SR 1292. 220. Howel ab Ieuaf. B5. 60. Lleyn late 13th century jewa gwyth. B15. 57. AS 1406. Je ap Je ap Jeua gam. B23. 166. Arundel Charters – Chirk. Ieva Llwyd ap Ieva ab Madog. B24. 188. Fasti Cist Camb., Cadwgan ab Ieva; 1276-97. Abbot of Cwmhir; 226. Iewaf Talrein. BBStD 220. Howel ap Ienaf ... l'ewel ap Ienaf (= Ieuaf). AnglPleas 8. Gruffith Yena (? Yeuaf) ap David (obviously = Iefa). Mer LSR 24. Ieuaf; 25. Madoco ap Ieuaf; 77. Ken(eric) ab Ieua, Ieuan ab Ieuaf; RecCa 115. Cad' ap Jeuaf; 253. Ieuan ap Ieuaf (Index quotes examples of *Jeua* and *Ieuaf* as forename). CalACW 21. Einion ap Ieuaf of Kerry; cf. 155, 227. Einion ab Ieuan. Bartrum 300-985, 72. Examples of *Ieuaf* following *ap*: Hywel ap Ieuaf; 73. Ieuaf ap Ieuaf; 74. Maig ap Ieuaf; in frontal position, six examples. 985-1215. 132-3. seventeen examples (cf. 133-5, Ieuan fiftyfive). CaernQSR 108. William Iva ap John ap William; 114. ditto; = 188. William Yva ap John ap William. 144. William Yeva ap Ieuan ap Llywelyn. JEG 5. Penhesgin, Llanfaethlu, Gwenhwyfer, d. of Jevah ap Cynwrig Efell (end of 13th century).

The superlative *ieuaf* has the suffix added to the comparative *iau*; there is another superlative form, used colloquially, *iengaf, iangaf*: Bartrum 1215-1350. 270. Gruffudd Iangaf ap Hywel ab Einion; 1350-1415. 525. Dafydd Iangaf ap Bedo ap Hywel.

There are two compounds of *ieuanc* and *gŵr*: the improper compound (i.e. joining the words in their normal syntactical order, noun and adj.) is *gwryang*, plural 'gwreng'; the proper compound (adj. preceding noun) became *iangwr*; this form was used as an epithet and looks like a surname:

B6. 262. Lleyn 1350. David Iangor. B12. 165. AnglRent, 16th century dros dir y kor jangwr. RecCa 30. Dauid Yangor.

Ieuan, (Ifan, Evan, John, Siôn, Jac, etc.) *Johannes* borrowed in the Roman period became *Ieuan*: the first syllable has consonantal *i* and diphthong which sounds like E *eye*. In the med. period, *John* was borrowed, and in the New Testament of 1567, Salesbury, with the motive that Welsh orthography should display the connexion with Latin, (e.g. *eglwys* printed as *eccles*), chose the form *Ioan*, so that we refer to the Fourth Gospel as 'Efengyl Ioan'. But throughout the earlier periods it would be 'Efengyl Ieuan', and although 'John' was borrowed and used fairly extensively, one must be prepared to see 'Ieuan' generally throughout the earlier period where 'John' would be used in English. They are now regarded as quite separate names. [Index A of the DWB shows men in the nineteenth century called 'John' adopting Ieuan as bardic name; others named 'John' adopted Ioan; one used *Iocyn*; most of those with the bardic name of Ieuan had the registered name Evan.]

InvECP 83. Denbs 1533, Thomas ap Ieuan ap David ap Blethyn alias Thomas Jones, of London, merchant taylor. 84. 1537, Thomas ap Ieuan etc. alias Thomas Johns of London, merchant tailor. 151. Monts 1551. John Warden alias Ieuan ap David of London. 169. Breck 1547. Roger Jones, son of Roger Evans (in English called Jones). 194. Glam 1529. Richard ap John Mellyn, Richard ap Ieuan Meleyn.

The adj. *ieuanc* 'young' can be used alongside *Ieuan* to observe sound changes. The adj. changed to *iefanc*, *ifanc*, and the name to *Iefan, Ifan*, and lines of verse in cynghanedd, such as the identity of *rhif* and *ifanc*, show that the change to *ifanc* goes back at least to the fourteenth century, and one may safely infer that the same change took place to the personal name at the same time, *v.* WG 104-5. Morris Jones states that the dialects now 'have *if-*, as Ifan, ifanc, but *ienctid* for *ieuenctid*'. That is true of most dialects but in East Glam a man whose registered name is 'Evan' is called 'Iefan', and attention is drawn to this for the consonantal *i* must have remained to become the *j* of *Jevan, Jevons* in English speech. [The entries of a parish

register will of course vary according to the date of the registration and the writing habits of the clerk concerned. The PR of Llantrithyd in East Glam has 32. 1577. Katerin Jevon; 61. 1571 Jevon ap Jevon; 62. 1594, Margare Jevan, 63. 1608. Morgan Yeavan; 36. 1605. Elizabeth Yevan.] One cannot rely upon med writing to tell us when the *f(v)* sound appeared because *u* (or *v* or *w*) was used for *f(v)* as well as for the vowel sound. And med orthography is liable to mislead in another respect: the superlative of *ieuanc* is *ieuaf* (although it is now regarded as archaic), and this in med script is *ieuau*: the superlative adj. was used for the youngest son and served as a personal name, this fact, added to the difficulty of being certain whether the final letter is *n* or *u* (= *f*), leads to confusion of the two forms or the two names, *v.* p.6. The use of *f* or even the omission of the final -*f* of the superlative removes any doubt: Mer LSR 24. Ieuaf; 25. Madoco ap Ieuaf; 45. Ieuaf ap Ieuan; 77. Ken(eric) ab Ieua. CalACW 21. Einion ap Ieuaf, of Kerry; 155, 227. Einion ap Ieuan.

The examples occurring in the SR of 1292 will illustrate the various forms of spellings of Ieuan/Ifan:

B13. 215. Juan ap Lewelyn; 216. Yuan ab Adam ap Kneytho; Yuan ap Seyselt; 217. Yeuan Abreboget; Ihewan ab Howel ab Gronou, Ihewen ab Harry; 218. Iwan ab Huren. Cf. also RadsSoc XLIII.81. Assessment 1293. Youan de Strende; 83. Yuovan ap Wyn. It is possible that some of the examples above such as 'Iwan' represent, not the labio-dental 'Ifan', but a bilabial 'w', i.e. the modern Iwan. Cf. CatAncDeeds 111. A.6030. Hereford ? Henry III. Iorword ab Iwan. A reason which undermines the view that Iwan was an early variant of Ifan is that no such form as 'Biwan' came out of it.

It is important to show examples of *ief-* (i.e. *iev*) with the consonantal *i* remaining, and the vowel *e*; from the conson. *i* comes the *j*, as already mentioned, and the vowel *e* surviving accounts for the Evan/Bevan version, the other form *Ifan* giving the S.W. Wales pronunciation which is 'Eevan', 'Beevan'. CatAncDeeds IV. A.6573. Hereford, 15 Edw.I. Zevan son of David ... (Z = cons.i) CAP 476. 1418. Hereford border: Richard Yevanes. WPortBooks 95. David ab Yevang-bage; (cf. 104, David ab Ieuan of

Carmarthen; 105. David Bevan of Carmarthen). B14. 50 (2nd vol. St David's regs) William Ieuans (prob. Ievans/Evans). Star CP 172. Wm Evans als ap Ievan. 186. Ricd ap Robert ap Ievan, Ievan ap Ricd, his son, alias John Roberts. InvECP 221. Monm 1533 John Yevans. [224. Monm 1533 William ap Eyvan, probably for Yevan.] CRHaverford, Index has four entries of Ievan; 212. John Ievanes; 210, 228, 232. Thomas Ievanes. HM. i. p.45. Llangattock V.A, list of tenements in 1606, includes name of Hugh Ievans; p.47 Ped. of Evans (Herbert) of Llangattock V.A., note Ievan and Evans amongst the sons of Ievan: Ievan ap Thomas Herbert, his sons: Thomas ap Ievan, William Evans, clk LLB, vicar of Llangattock V.A., and Treasurer of Llandaff, ob. 5 Jan. 1589-90, John Evans, clk, vicar of Cwmdu, . . . John ap Ievan, James Evans.

In these examples one sees *Ievan* changed to *Evan(s)* and the latter becoming the standard name and surname of the anglicised classes. The spelling *Evance* disguises Evans: CaernQSR 90. Robertum Evance; 92. Robert Evance, dean of Bangor, signed, Rob't Evance. H Asaph i. 360. Cursal Canons. John Evance, Rector of Llanmerewig, 1660-88, 'He was of the Evances of Treflech Hall'; i. 536. John Evance, All Souls College, Oxford . . . son of Nehemiah Evance of Hanwood; further refs. 546-7. RadsSoc XXXVI. 27. Chancery Papers: John Evance.

The following examples are given to show variations in the final vowel: B5. 63. Lleyn, late 13th century jevin (69. jevan ap y llall). B5. 144. Caern 1293. jeven ap madoc da (147. jevan ap llywarch). CatAncDeeds V. 13604. Anglesea [sic] 8th of Henry IV. Couus ap Jevaun Lloyt (misreading of Conws; the spelling Jevaun is repeated). PWLMA 276. Deio ap Ieuan ab Adda ab Yevons. RadsSoc VII. 13. Will 1559, Presteigne, Richard ap Jevin ap Madoke. Glam Cartae 1543. Joh. Bevyn. The texts of wills published in the transactions of RadsSoc have frequent examples of *Jevn* alongside examples of *Jevan*, e.g. XL. 61, Painscastle 1573, David ap Jevn Goch . . . Lewis ap Jevan and Jenkin ap Jevn my brothers; *v.* other examples below p.134, and also the examples of a colloquial Jenn. InvECP 30. Mer. 1547. Robert ap Yevin ap

Getyn (31. Mer. 1553 Yevan ap Rese ap Bened). 99. Denbs 1551 Hugh ap Beven ap David . . . 112. Flints 1518 Bennet ap Even son and heir of Even ap Lewellen. 252. Marches 1533 David ap David ap Iven (Evan) [editor's explanation in brackets]. CRHaverford, examples of Beavan (82) and Beavans (69, 133, 149). cf. 155. Dorothy Beavens.

SHROPSHIRE REGISTERS
There is a great quantity of relevant material in the Shropshire registers; although the large number of variant forms includes many examples which are due to bungled or incompetent spelling, the curious spelling may be the explanation of surnames which have survived and are still used; only representative examples are quoted.

Many early examples seem to show by the spelling the version *Iefan* (i.e. consonantal *i*) before changing to Evan(s): Ford 6. 1620. Owen Yeavans; 9. 1628. Hugh and Gwen Yeavens; 10. 1631. Hugh and Gwen Evans; 11. 1634. Hughe Evans and Gwen; 10. 1629 . . .d. of Howell and Christian Appeyeavan. Neenton 17. 1673. Joan Eouans; 17. 1674. Sarah Eouans, d. of John and Margery, cf. 17. 1671. C. d. of John Evans and Margery; 18. 1676. T. s. of John Evans and Margery. Ludlow 229. 1574. John Yevance. High Ercall 242. 1689. Henery Yeuans = 261. 1695. Henricus Evans. Norton-in-Hales, 25. 1630. Yevan Gryce = 28. 1634. . f. Evani Grise. Oswestry 39. 1564. Thomas ap Thomas Jeuans; 40. 1564. Elizabeth vz Ric' Jevans; 49. 1566. John ap Richard Jeuans; 64. 1579. Doritie vz Thomas Jeuens.

Examples showing variation of final syllable: Hughley 6. 1611. Catherina Beevans, fillia ffrauncescus Beevan; 7. 1611. Catherina, fillie ffraunciscus Beevens. Hanwood 22. 1606. Debora Eevons (?) – editor's query. More 21. 1639. . . . Ap Heven = 22. 1643. ap Evan. Edgton 11. Beven; Greete index, Bevan, Bivean, Bivon. Habberley, Alberbury, Chirbury – all have Evance. Cleobury Mortimer 31. 1624. Bevans; 55. 1676. Bevon; 57. 1696. Beavon. 236. 1772. Jevins = 240. 1776. Jevens. (Index includes Giffons, Gavans.) Claverley 4. 1570. ab evon; 27. 1588. Abbevon; 6. 1572. Bevone, 42. 1602. Abbevone; 314. Jos. Jeven. Westbury

29. 1655. John ap Biveon. Ludlow 667. 1711. Beavand; 685, 692. ditto. Oldbury 3. 1599. Richard ap Evan = 6. 1614. Richard Byvain. Kinlet 24. 1675. Bivane; 27. 1679. Bivon = ib. ib. Bevon = 29. 1681. Beven. 36. 1687. Beavons = 37. 1688. Beaven = 40. 1691. Beavane; 54. 1701. Bivan (prob. same person). Lee Brockhurst 3. 1601. Yevands. Moreton Corbet 53. 1791. Bevarn; 53. 1792. Bevern. Wrockwardine 202. 1767. Bevorn = 231. 1785. ditto = 206. 1769. Bevan. Condover 236. 1747. William a base son of Eliz. Bevin alias Bevan, a Vagrant woman. Shrewsb. St Chad's, Index, Jevens etc. . . . Jevin. Edgmond 14. 1689. Jevins = 16. 1694. Jevon. Waters Upton 41. 1763. Bevern. [This kind of spelling might have been suggested by the pronunciation and spelling of the river Severn; cf. PR Bromfield 138. Severn; 105. Sevorne.]

Examples of initial J:
One cannot rely upon early orthography and feel sure what the letter *j* stands for; one can assume that initial *y* stands for consonantal *i*, and that initial *j* in the early modern period stood for the modern *j* sound; the use of letter *g* is evidence that the initial sound is *j*. Leebotwood 19. 1612. Margerye, d. of Geavan and Elizth ap Robert. Cleobury Mortimer 236. 1772; 245. 1781 Jevins = 240. 1776. Jevens. (Index includes Giffons, Gavans). Claverley 314. Jos. Jeven (Index has Jenks, Ginks). Neen Sollers 40. 1798. Sarah Javon. Kinlet 128. 1770. William Jeovans. Non-con. Shrews. High St 15. 1754. Titus Jeavens. Shrews. St Mary's Index, Yevens, Yeven, Jeven, Javen. St Chad's, Index, Jevans, Javens.

There is no need to explain examples quoted above which have *ab* with *Bevan* etc., this is faulty writing, since the *b* of *ab* has been transferred to be the initial of Bevan. The following denote *p* although there is no reason for the provection of *b* to *p* in *ab* + *Ifan*: Ford 10. 1629. . . . Appeyeavan. Ludlow 90. 1583. Howell ap Pevan; Shrewsbury St Mary's, 1743. Pevan.

One thing calls for comment, that is the addition of genitive *s* to the *ab*- formation, *v.* examples above *Beavons*, and amongst the examples taken from CR Haverfordwest. This could only happen in a community that was not Welsh-speaking: in the Welsh-speaking community it is either 'Evans' or 'Bevan'. The proper English counterpart is 'Evanson': Wem 436. 1715. George Jevanson; 439. 1719. Edward Evenson p. Preece. Non-con, Dodington – Whitchurch 75. 1760. Sarah Evanson, Wem Chapel St. Ind. Ch. 300. 1833, Evison = 301. 1835 Evanson = 303. 1837. Evison; Claremont Bapt. Shrewsbury 149. 1807. Evanson.

PRESENT-DAY REGISTERS
The ordinary versions Evan(s) do not need to be quoted. The following example of *Ievan* as christian name deserves mention: Conway, Conway Marl Ward, Ievan Lloyd-Mostyn. There are occasional examples of *Ifan* and *Ifans* to be found; they are twentieth century conversions of 'Evans': the poet William Evans used 'Wil Ifan' as his bardic name; Cardigan, Llanbadarn Fawr, Dafydd Ifans; Preseli, Letterston, Ifans (Cenn. Jacqueline, probably Kenneth Evans); Aberystwyth, Ward 3, Mererid Ifan (student). *Jeavon(s)*: Ludlow, Alveley; Wrekin, Albrighton; Ketley – Wellington Rural; Leominster, town; S. Gloucs, Winterbourne; W. Gloucs, Aylburton. *Jevon(s)*: S. Hereford, Goodrich; CT, Fairford; Dumbleton; Kidderminster, Baxter, Oldington; St. and Hyde, Dukinfield East; Nantwich, Hatherton; Barrow-in-Furness, Salney, Hindpool; Newport, Central 4. *Jevans*: Times 19.9.77, Obituary of Mr Jevan Brandon Thomas (second son of Brandon Thomas, author of 'Charley's Aunt'). Times 29.9.78, p.10. Deborah Jevans (British under 21, tennis player). *Javans*: Wrexham, Wrexham Boro, Grosvenor Ward. *Givvons*: Newport, Central 5, Victoria 3. *Givons*: Newport, Allt-yr-yn 5. *Givens*: City of Gl. Tuffley Ward p.6; Monmouth, Wyesham (Given). *Beavan*: CT, Snowshill; Bromsgrove, N.W. *Beaven*: S. Hereford, Llanveynoe; S. Gloucs, Almondsbury; Filton, Northville; CT, Leckhampton; Stroud, Shipton Moyne; Crewe Central; Newport, St Woolos 6. *Beavon*: Ludlow, Highley; Oswestry, M.Drayton; S. Worcs, Croome-Kempsey. *Bavon*: Oswestry, East. N.W.; Wirral, Ellesmere Port, Central, Victoria, Whitby. *Bevin*: Oswestry, Ightfield; W. Gloucs, Newnham; Nantwich, Chorlton-Cuddington, Nantwich, N.Rural, Haslington 1 and 3. *Beavin*:

Chester, Ch. Rural – Barrow; Torfaen, Cwmbrân – Oakfield. *Beavand*: Preseli, Hayscastle. *Bevans*: Ebbw Vale, Tredegar West; Abertillery, B.G.South (0); S. Pembs, St Issell's South; Preseli, Camrose, Goodwick. *Bevens*: Knutsford, Hale – West. *Bevins*: Knutsford, Over Ward, Wilmslow, Morley; Westmorland, Windermere.

HYPOCORISTIC AND COLLOQUIAL FORMS OF IEUAN

Ifan, Iefan, Evan, the naturally developed forms of Ieuan, have a hypocoristic form which is still in colloquial use, namely Ianto: a boy or young man named Evan may be called 'Ianto' by his acquaintances and equals in the Welsh community; we can testify for SW usage, *v.* Fynes-Clinton 230 for Gwynedd. It has been suggested above p.33, that the *-to* ending comes from Guto: there seems to be no evidence that 'Iantyn' has ever been used. Although Ianto is one of the most widespread hypocoristic names, examples in records are hard to find; an early instance is B5. 144. Caern 1293, Gwyn ap Yanto.

The form Ifano is also known in the modern period although rare: e.g. the name of the well-known Cardiff librarian, the late Ifano Jones. Examples in early texts might be deceptive, for the final *-o* might be the dative or ablative of a latinized version, but the spelling in the following shows that it is unmistakeably the hypocoristic version, Mer LSR 32, Ivanou ap Madoc. However it is difficult to find evidence that Ianto and Ifano became surnames as happened in the case of Guto, Gutyn, Bedo etc.

Seeing how very common a name Ieuan, Iefan, Ifan was in the med period, one would expect to see a hypocoristic form other than one which made use of a 'borrowed' suffix; hypothetically one would expect *Ianno and *Iannyn/*Iennyn. It is a pity that so many texts use abbreviations which possibly fail to reveal interesting formations, but there may be reason for the belief that these hypothetical forms may be confused with the borrowed Breton-French *Janyn*.

Reaney under Jennings, Jennans, Jennins etc. quotes early examples such as Janyn le Breton 1332 (= SRLancs), Jenyn de France 1379 (= Yorks Poll Tax); cf. also this example from a Welsh source, B15. 53. AS 1406. Janyn ffrank, which means 'Janyn the

Frenchman'. The locale and context of the following indicate they are probably of Norman-Breton origin, BBStD 136 Ianyn Martyn; 156. Ianyn Takul. The texts of the LpOswestry and of BYale have the forms Ienna, Janyn; the Shrewsbury BR has examples of Genno; the Shropshire registers have many variations of Genno/Genna. A possible explanation of the Jenna/Genno name is that, in the bilingual community, it is the complementary *-o* version of Janyn/Jenyn. If Jenkyn/Siencyn can have the *-o* counterpart Sianco/Shanko (v. p.138) Jenyn/Jennyn can have the *-o (-a)* counterpart Jenno/Jenna.

LpOswestry 30-31, Names of 'Gwelyau': Ienna ap Ithel (in 1393) = Ieuan ap Ithel, in 1586 and 1602; ibid 163, 164, 165 Janyn Lloyd; 168. Atha ap Jenna pader.

BYale, date 1315, explanatory note 26, the editor deals with the difficulty of deciding whether the letter in names such as *Houa, Eigon,* and *Ienna* is *n* or *u(v)*, 'In eight instances in the text it is written Ienaf or Iennaf . . . In one case only is the name written Ieuan, *v.* p.68 of text; and in fifteen instances it is spelt in full unmistakeably as Ienna'. It is possible that some of these examples are of *Ieuaf* ('the Younger') and what appears to be the superlative ending may suggest this reading; it is far more likely that the scribe misread his copy, turning *n* into *-af*, as if *-a* were colloquial. Anyhow one can feel quite sure that most of the examples referred to, especially those that have the double letter *-nn-* stand for Ienna. The *-a* ending may be compared with the variants Guta, Deia, etc. instead of Guto, Deio, etc. It is reasonably certain that these Ienna forms are the same as the Genno/Genna versions which one finds later in the Shropshire – West Midlands area.

Shrewsbury BR, Genno, four entries 1595, 1598, 1598, 1616. Shropshire PRs have: Genowe, Genns, Gennoe, Genner, Genna, Gennah, Genoa, Gennough, Ginner. (Some forms may be connected with 'Gwenhwyfar'.) Shrewsbury-Hereford TD, Gennoe, two; West Midlands North, Gennoe, four; Genna, two; Birmingham, Ienna, one; Gennoe, six. For comparison: Shrewsbury BR 164, Geoffrey of S. smith, s. Jenen ap Yolyn of the Heldre in Caus, 1529; Griffith of S. s. Jenen ap David ap Res.

The roll has examples of Jenyns, Jennings, Jens. The PRs have plenty of examples of Jennings, Jenings, Genyns; and note the spelling Janence in PRPontesbury. There are many examples of Jennyn etc. in the records of Rads especially close to the border: RadsSoc VII. 13. 1559. Presteigne, Robert Jenyns, Robt Genyns. XXVII. 20. 1550. Old Radnor, Robert Jenins of Prestend. 22. 1551. Norton, Richard Jenyns. 23. 1552. Prestene, Roberd Jenyngs. XXVIII. 13. Robert Jeninges. XXX. 52. 1568. Lewes Jenyns of Walston. XXXII. 58. 1581. John Genyns.

Early examples of Jennings etc. in Wales, far from the border, are only occasionally found: cf. InvECP 48. John Jenyn of Carmarthen; Richard Jenyn, Carms 1533. The numbers of Jennings and variants in the English border counties are very high, and it is curious that there is no evidence of Jennin(gs) being borrowed and becoming 'Siennyn/Shennin', and this contrasts with Jenkin/Siencyn. [Forms and numbers taken from TDs illustrate: Shrewsbury-Hereford, Jennings 70; West Mids North, Jennings 1½ columns; Jennens four; (Jenn, one); West Mids South, Jennings, one column; Gennings, one; (Jenns four); Birmingham, Jennings 2½ columns; Jennens twenty-one.]

Reliable examples of forms such as Ienno/Ienna are hard to find at a distance from the border; the following is unusual: CalACW 183 Einion ap Jana, sheriff of Anglesea, 1323. The location of Ienna, and of later Genno/Genna etc. seems to prove that this form developed in the Shrewsbury – Oswestry area, and suggests that it is related to Janyn/Jennyn as the complementary -o form. The puzzling question still remains, i.e. the apparent absence of hypocoristic forms of Ieuan, other than 'Ianto', which one would expect to find with as much frequency as (if not more than) Guto, Gutyn and the versions derived from these.

The texts of wills published in the transactions of RadsSoc are by their nature more colloquial in the way they name persons and therefore contain versions which represent natural usage, uninfluenced by familiarity with literary Welsh. Alongside Ieuan, Ievan, Jeuan, Jevan, there are frequent examples of Ievn, Jevn, and there can be no doubt that Ievn is a version of Ievan: e.g. XL. 61. Pains-castle, David ap Jevn Goch . . . Lewis ap Ievan and Jenkin ap Jevn *my brothers*; 62. Nantmel 1573, Rees ap Ievan . . . To Elen vch Ievn *my sister*. There is another version, Ienn, Jenn. This we suggest is a contracted colloquial form of Ieuan, with the vowel *e* of the diphthong *-eu-*, i.e. Ie(ua)n. There need be no doubt about the validity of the form Ienn, Jenn, as if it might be the result of misreading the text, for the surname Jenn, Jenns, survives; and Ienn, Jenn cannot be a scribal abbreviation like 'Lln' for Llywelyn; a surname would not come into use through a scribal abbreviation. The form *Jenn* is found in documents besides wills and it is obvious that it was normal usage in Rads in the late med and early mod periods.

Examples of Jevn:
VI. 9. 1544. Llu (correct to Lln) ap Jevn and Jevn ap . . . 10. Jevn ap Rs. 10. 1545. Rs ap Jevn ap Dd. 11. 1545. Jevn ap Rys ap Meryck . . . in Llanbaddern Vynyth. XXXVIII. 44-45. 'Glascumbe' 1543, Jevan ap David ap Jevn Goch; 45. 'Clirowe', Jevan, ap Jevan and Jevn, in the same will. 47. Llowes 1570. Roger ap Ievn . . . Thos Holl ap Jevn Duy.

Examples of Ienn, Jenn:
XXIX. 32. Patent Rolls 4 Eliz. Jenn ap Dd ap Howell. Jenkyn ap Jenn ap Meredd. Jenn ap Dd Lloyd. XXXI. 6. 6 Eliz. Several examples of Jenn. XXXV. 38. 1527. Griffith ap Jenn Lloyd, David ap Jenn ap Morgan. XXXVI. 38. 1558. Jenn ap Lewis of Ryslipp, co. Midx. 40. 1633, Oliver ap Jenn and James ap Jenn his son. XLI. 61. Divers Ministers' Accts, 1383-4 Jenn ap Dd ap Gwilym Gethyn. Jenn ap Rez Cachepoll.

PRLudlow has one example of *Jenns*, 73. 1575. It was pointed out above that the name survives and is to be seen in TDs:
Jenn: Ludlow, Much Wenlock; Newport, Beechwood 2. *Jenns*: Kidderminster No. 2. Baxter; No. 5 Park; No. 4. Rowland Hill. Cf. *Joenn*: Newport, Beechwood 4, Malpas 2 (*v.* examples below from PRClunbury and PRPontesbury, Johens, Johanes).

Further close investigation may determine whether Jenn(s) merged with Jennin(s) in the border area of Radnor-Hereford. [It is worth adding the following examples of Jenno, Jenn, Jenns from TDs of the London area: London Postal Area, Jenno 2; West Mddx, Jenno (Feltham); Lond Postal, Jenn 7; West

Middx, 2 (Ruislip); N.W.Kent 3; S.Herts and Mx, 1 (Kings Langley); N.E.Surrey, Jenns 6; N.W.Kent, 7.]

In the Hereford-Gwent area, and in Gower, there is a surname variously spelt, Jeyn, Jeyne, Jayne. It is not the woman's name Jane, although it may sometimes have that spelling, e.g. RadsSoc V. 4. Leet Courts 1688. Manor of Ugre, List of Constables ... Jane [sic] Owens (contributor using *sic*). Clark 305 has a short genealogy of Jayne of Brockweir, together with the genealogy of a branch. The first generation is Jevan Herbert (of Coldbrook, living at Brockweir 1562), and his son is John ap Ievan, als John Jayne of Chepstow, 1547 and 1562; and his son is John Jayne or Jane of Brockweir. The pedigree of the branch has the same evidence: Thomas ap Jevan Herbert, alias Thomas Jayne of Tintern in 1548: the children and descendants are Jayne. If we accept this evidence that Ieuan is the original source of Jeyn etc. we must assume that there was a colloquial pronunciation not very much different from the Ienn (Jenn) above: i.e. Ieu'n or Iei'n; in SW pronunciation there would be no difference between -*eu*- and -*ei*-, and the source therefore would be *Iei'n*.

B25. 485. Accts Earl of Worcs 1530. Jeyn ap John. CatAncDeeds V. 12510, Hereford, John ap Jeyne. A. 12135, Hereford, 5th Henry VII, Thomas Jeyn. Star CP 10. Monm. Arnold and Edward Jayne. InvECP 225. Monm. 1538. John Jeyn. HM iv. p.10. Caldicot, ll'n ap Jeyne ap Hoiskin; p.11 Court Roll 1716. Llewelyn Jeyne ap Hoyskin. PRLlanbadoc 1586. Moris John Jein. Bradney has a footnote: 'Jein, often written Jane, Jeyn, Jayne, etc. is a softened form of Jenkin'. The word 'softened' does not convey any real meaning, but Bradney may have seen Jenkin spelt as in the following: MLSW 119 (Brechonia 1503) Jankyn ap Price ap Jeynkyn = 121 Jankin ap Rice ap Jankin; 128. Jeynkyn ap Guilim.

The TD of Cardiff and S.E. Wales shows that the name is fairly common, more especially in Gwent, in the forms Janes, Jayne, Jaynes, Jeanes, Jaynes; the TD of Swansea and S.W. Wales has a few, the Gloucester TD has the following: Jane 4, Janes 20, Jayne 14, Jaynes 12, Jeynes 18.

FORMS OF JOHN

The name *John* would be borne by Anglo-Norman settlers in Wales; it is certain that native Welshmen were given the name as early as the thirteenth century.
B13. 215. SR 1292. John Bras (jurors of 'Brentlys' and Glasbury), 218. John Bongam; 221. John Tandy; 225. John Baner; 229. John Beg. (The roll has a large number of Ieuan/Ifan variants.)

The versions *Johannes, Johanne* in Latin documents probably stand for 'John', although they could be for 'Ieuan' since there was an awareness of the identity of the two names, but when a document has both forms one assumes that *Johannes* etc. represent 'John':
B2. 253. Brec-Llandov 13th century Johanni Pres, Johanni Loweys ... Ievano Benlloyd, 254. Johannes Havard. B2. 77. 1301. De Yeuano ab Madoc; 81. Johannis Wogan (note that 'Ieuan' is followed by 'ab', and that 'Johannis' is not).
Even after the surname 'Jones' came into use, the original 'Johannes' may affect the spelling:
CaernQSR 133. Morgan Johans. Star CP 15. Monm Robert Johans (cf. next but one entry, Robt Johns). InvECP 93. Denbs 1547. Owen Johans, a servant in London. 239. Monm 1551. William Joans of London, son of John ap Jenkin. PRClunbury 25, 26. Johens, Johanes, Johands. PRPontesbury 183. 1668. Edwardus Johens.
Note example from present-day register, S. Worcs, Bredon, *Johan*; and note also the form *Joenn* quoted above.

The change that took place to E *j* (= dzh) and initial *g* (= dzh) in words borrowed in the early med period is dealt with in EEW 226-7 and the personal names Jasper, Jerome, John, Joachim, Jonas, Joseph, Jenkin, George are quoted. As the sounds of E *j* (and E *ch* and *sh*) were not included in the Welsh system of sounds the *j* became *si* − not merely as a matter of orthography; the *si* represented the Welsh pronunciation, a normal *s* sound given the palatal quality of *i* but without making a vowel of it. Two lines are quoted from the poems of Dafydd ab Edmwnt in which the name 'Siôn', written in the E form *John* makes consonantal identity with the *s* of *eisiau* and *swllt*: 'Eissiau neb i John abad' (s-n-b = J-n-b), 'I'r byd swllt yw'r abad John' [r-b-d-s- = r-b-d-j; obviously the *j* is meant to be sounded as *s(i)*]. Despite this spelling, the standard form of the med period was *Siôn*, the *i* being the palatal quality of the *s*, the name being a monosyllable, and it is worthy of special notice, that the vowel *o* is long and closed, the *o* expected before a single *n*. English words with initial E *sh* and E *ch* were treated in the same way, *shop/siop, chalk/ sialc*. In the early modern period a change took place which was the converse, Welsh developed the sound of English *sh*. Therefore the borrowed 'John' went through these stages, becoming *Siôn* (normal *s* with just a touch of *i* sound), then becoming *Shôn*. This form of name appearing in an English context or document is bound to become 'Shone', and a mixture of 'Siôn' and 'Shone' will at times become 'Shione'.

Sannan 1668. Gwen Siôn; 1684. David Shion . . . Da. of Shion ap Richard; Margt Shion; 1690. Shon David . . . Shon Peter; 1691. David Shône; 1699. William Sionas; 1706. Richard Sion Bedward. PRConway 1727. Gaynora Sion; 1750. Elen Shione; cf. RCA 62. Angharrade *Vershone* (= 'verch-Shone').

In Wales, *John* and *Jones* prevailed as standard forms, and the use of *Siôn* as standard form was discontinued, so that examples of 'Shone' now found in Wales probably have their source in the border counties. The following are a selection of the various versions in the Shropshire registers: Oswestry 456. 1627. Owen Sion; 662. 1668. Owen Shone; 495. 1633. Lowry ach Shone Bach; 518. 1635. Elin vz John Bach; Claverley 35. 1596. Richard Apshone = 66. 1626. Richard Shone (same person). 62. 1622. Roger Shone; cf. 115. 1658. Roger Shaune; 108. 1653. William Shaune. Ludlow 599. 1699. Thomas Ap-shone. Church Preen 24, 25, 1789. John Shone; 28. 1789. John Shones (not the same person). Grinshill 2. 1606. William Apthone [sic] of West Felton. Wrockwardine 140. 1739. Milbrom d. of William Shoan. Wem 43. 1618. Jane d. of John Shone; 139. 1619. Margrett d. of John Shoone. Hodnet 85. 1707, 87. 1710. Ralph Shone; 131. 1740. Mary d. of John and Mary Shone; 134. 1743. John and Martha Shorne. Shrewsbury St Mary's, Index, Ap John (Apjohn). Evan ap Jones (early period),

Shone, ap Shone. St Chad's, Index, Shone (Shane); 1874. 1802. Eliz Sions. Edgmond 195. 1803. Joseph Shones. Selattyn 36. 1590. Nathanael s. of John Apson. 257. 1730. Shane Dafydd; 258. 1731. Shone Dafydd. Llanyblodwel 40. 1727. David Shion.

There is no need to plot examples of *Shone* in present-day registers: it is widespread throughout the border constituencies, and in certain wards in Northwich (Northwich Rural, Delamere) and Nantwich (e.g. Tushingham-cum-Grindley) the instances abound. An unusual version is found in Workington, Keswick town, namely *Shons*.

Mention has already been made of the hypocoristic or colloquial form *Sionyn*, this is confined to N. Wales (the SW *Sioni* is taken from E *Johnnie*). There is also a form *Sioncyn*, cf. Sannan 1724, Robert son of Thomas Sioncyn of Llan. . . . This looks like 'Siôn' + dimin. suffix *-cyn*, but it is more likely to be a borrowing of *Jonkin*, a variant of Jankin/ Jenkin; cf. Morecambe and Lonsdale, Grange, Jonkin.

Examples have been quoted of *Ap John, Ap-shone* etc. These two elements do not make a compound in Welsh, but the natural tendency in E speech is to put main stress on 'ap' and make an improper compound, *Apjohn*. This form, although not common, occurs as a surname, e.g. Cardiff TD; D. Tel 13.9.77, Deaths. The variant *Upjohn* is also found, e.g. S. Gloucs, Filton, Conygre Ward; Macclesfield, Henbury; Islwyn, Cefnyfforest East; D. Tel 6.9.77, Deaths. Cf. also D. Tel, 6.4.84, Marriages. Henry *Upshon*, Chichester. There are occasional instances of 'translating' Ap-John: InvECP 128. Flints, 1553. John ap John alias Johnson of London: cf. Angl Muster Book 32. Will'm ap Hugh Johnson.

In the process of turning the father's name to be the fixed surname of the son and descendants, two versions (in addition to the *ap*-formation) came to be used, the form 'John' unchanged and the *s* form, Jones. It has been observed before, e.g. in the case of David (Davies) that certain areas were inclined to use the christian name unchanged, notably S. Pembs, and a simple count in some of the wards will prove the point: S. Pembs, St Issell's South, John (30), Johns (4), Jones (32); Amroth 17; 4; 9. The difference in the spelling is significant: the vowel of 'Johns' is the same as in 'John', but the vowel of 'Jones' is the vowel of Siôn, Shone.

A few simple examples will show the process of making the surname Jones:
JEG 1. Owen Jones alias Owen ap John (late 17th century). InvECP 241. Monm 1556 Christian Johns, alias Crislye ver John; PRWhittington 134. 1637. Thomas Johnes alias Thomas ap John, of Francton.

In the Welsh-speaking community it should be either the *ap*- form or '*s* genitive; cf. example from an area losing, or having lost, its Welsh idiomatic usage:
PRAlbrighton 11. 1585. Thomas, s. of Davye ap Jones, repeated 14. 1592; 16. 1596; but 19. 1600, Marye d. of Davye Jones; cf. Shrewsbury St Mary's, Index, early period, Evan ap Jones.

Examples quoted above show 'Jones' spelt 'Johans'. The following curious spellings could possibly provide clues to explain unusual variants:
InvECP 191. Glam 1528. William Jhonys. 222. Monm 1533. Thomas Jonys. 235. Abergavenny, 1547. Wenthlyan Johnez. 241. Monm 1556. Hugh Joynes alias Sare.

COLLOQUIAL FORMS OF 'JOHN'
Examples of *Jack* are found in Welsh records.
B15. 46. AS 1406. Ken ap Jack ap bled; 51. Gron ap Atha ap Jack; 55. William ap dd ap Jac; Dd ap Jack ap Diarmed. B15. 288. Aberyst-Cardn 140. Jack ap David. BBSt D 142. Elena Iakke. CaernHS 26. Bolde Rental 37. Ken ap Jake.

We have relied upon the vowel *a* in putting the above examples together and keeping them separate from forms that have the vowel *o*. There do not seem to be Welsh derivatives from Jac (by adding *-yn* to give 'Jacyn', or 'Jecyn' by affection), and we presume the initial sound was *dzh* or as near as Welsh speech got to it; the colloquial form of 'Jackie' in West Wales is *Siaci*. (Although there is no derivative using *-yn*, the hypocoristic *Jaco* is occasionally heard.)

The name found in the form 'Jokyn, Yockyn' in early records looks as if it is derived from Jock, a variant of Jack; but this is doubtful; it differs from *Joc* in that the initial sound is consonantal *i*. The 'j' used is often misleading, or unhelpful, but one can rely upon the instances which use 'y' to prove the

sound, and infer that in the examples which use 'j', it is meant to be capital '*i*'. The name survives in place-names: JEG 23 Bryn Iocyn and Acton; Rec Denb/Lordship (1860 edn) 84 Edward Aylmer of Pant Yokin; p.138, Common Burgesses in 1678, Lloyd of Croesyockyn. (It is worth pointing out that Jokyn/ Yokyn is abbreviated *Joc'* in med. records, with a mark of abbreviation generally but not always, e.g. B4. 155. Ardudwy 1325- Jock' ap Meilir, 158. Eva filia Jock'.) One piece of evidence proving the connexion of John and Iocyn is the adoption by John Richards (1795-1864) of the bardic name 'Iocyn Ddu'; *v.* DWB *s.n.*

B6. 261. Lleyn 1350. Jokyn Goch. B6. 360. NW 1326. Meuric ap Jockyn. B7. 144. Caern 1303. Yockin duy. B13. 225. SR 1292. Stephen Iokin. B15. AS 1406. several examples; e.g. 42. Jockin ap dd ddu. Rec Denb Lp (1860 edn) 40. Yockin Duy ... Yockin, Groom of the Foresters. JEG 38. Dafydd ap Llewelyn ap Dafydd ap Iocyn. 124. temp. Edw. IV (1465) Sion and Iocyn = brothers. Bartrum 1215-1350. 337. Iocyn ap Cynwrig Fawr ap Rhys; 1350-1415. 643. Iocyn ap Einion Sais.

Example of '*s* genitive: ADClun 131. John Jokins.

Examples of using the -ws suffix:
B15. 51. 1406. Yockus ap Meurig. CatAncDeeds iii. C.3516. Merioneth. Tethyn Jokus Coydyn ('Tyddyn . . .').

FORMS OF IONCYN, SIONCYN, JANKIN, JENKIN
The name *Sioncyn* has been quoted above, with the suggestion that it might possibly be *Siôn + cyn*, i.e. a formation in Welsh; but the existence of Jonkin makes that less likely; it is probably a borrowing of Jonkin, a variant of Jankin. But the form represented by Ioncyn is essentially different from the others, for these, whatever the initial letter in medieval records, have initial *dzh* sound which came to be pronounced Siencyn (Shenkin) in Welsh, whereas Ionc- has consonantal *i*, often written *y*, and it remained Ionc- as shown in the examples below, and as it survives in dialect. It may be a form fossilized from an earlier period. There are examples of *Ioncyn* and *Ioncws*:
RadsSoc XLIV. 64. Assessment 1293, Yuor fil(ius) Jonkyn. B11. 167. Boro' of Bala C.1350, Quotation, . . . Johannes fil.

Jonckyn. CaernQSR 7. John ap Gruff' ap Thomas ap Yonckus; 220. Gruffydd ap Hywel ap Gruffydd ap Jonckws; 220. John ap William ap Hywel Jonckws. Mer LSR 24. Ionkin (cf. 14. Ieuan Jankin).

Example occurring in place-name: Western Mail, April 20, 1978, Notice of Sale, Smallholding, Yonkin Farm (Kinnerton, near Presteign).

In the dialect of Swansea Valley, *ionc* and *ioncyn* are used as common nouns, in a contemptuous, derogatory sense, meaning 'silly fool, lumpish idiot': these words would be used by young men only; comparison with the hypocoristic forms Iolyn and Lelo (*v.* p.140, 149) makes it fairly certain that the common noun comes from the personal name Ioncyn. Because of the difference between Ioncyn and Jenkin/Siencyn, one ought to look possibly for a different source and it may be that the following provide a clue:

PRDiddlesbury 76. John Yonke; 81. Susan Yonke. PRWrockwardine 240. 1791. John Ianks, aged 74, bur.

The form *Jankyn* which became *Jenkin (Siencyn, Shenkin)* occurs frequently in med records:

B11. 62. Broniarth 1429. Iankyn ap Yollyn; 73. Iankyn ap Gr loit. B22. 2. Jankyn Vaghan, Catchpoll (of Swansea mid 15th century). BBStD 20. David Ianckyn; 168. Iankyn Tancard; 306. Iankyn ap David. HM iv, 7. Chepstow, Philippus Janckin; ibid. 97. 'the above John who is also after the Welsh fashion called Jenkin'. CaernHS 26. Bolde Rental 43. John ap Jevkyn; 44. Gruf ap Ievkyn (? Jenkyn). B13. 100. 16th century Pembs estate, Willm Jankyn; 102. Jankyn ap John, Jankyn Nicholl. Cf. examples also of *Jeynkyn* in footnote.

There are examples of using the suffix *-ws*, instead of *-yn*. One expects the vowel of *-yn* to affect the vowel *-a-* that precedes it, since this vowel affection is almost a universal rule in Welsh (*adar, aderyn*); but for *-ws* to cause affection would be against the rule, yet the examples show the version 'Jencws': one must infer that the *-ws* has been added, not to *Janc-* but to *Jenc-* which had received its vowel affection from suffix *-yn*.

B11. 58. Broniarth 1429. Hol' ap Jenkos. 61. Hoel ap Ienc' ap Ieuan; 66. Hoel ap Iencous ap Ieuan. 71. Hol' ap yenc'. ADClun 180.

Iencus Goch. Bartrum 1350-1415. 656. Jenkws ap Gronwy ap Iorwerth.

If this survived in English-speaking areas and especially in England, the initial *i* would become *j*, as in Ieuan > Jevon; and in fact the Birmingham TD has an example of *Jenkus*.

In the modern period the E version Jenkin(s) is regarded as 'standard' in Wales, with Siencyn as the 'phonetic' and self-conscious Welsh version. The version spelt *Shenkin* survives, e.g. Radio Times 3.1.78, Supermind, taking part in Quiz game, David Shenkin, from Newport, Salop, Brain of Mensa 1977, Mastermind 1977. The register of Newport has Shenkin, Hyman M. and Vera H. D. Tel 26, 8, 80. Ruby Weddings, Luxton-*Shinkins*, at Waltham Abbey, Sussex; this exactly represents the pronunciation of 'Jenkin' in many SW dialects.

There is a hypocoristic *Shanco* used colloquially; cf. HM i. 159. parcel of land called Cae Shanko. The celebrated Lewsyn yr Heliwr of the Merthyr Riots of 1831 had a literary name, 'Lewys Shanco Lewis': his father's name was Jenkin Lewis; *v.* DWB *s.n.* Lewis Lewis 1793. The name *Janko* occurs in CT. Bishops Cleve. The name survives in a peculiar phrase in the colloquial usage 'man-a-man â Shanco', meaning, 'it makes no difference, it is all the same in the end'.

Ifor

This name, although not as common as Ieuan or Iorwerth, was not confined to any one part of the country. The examples quoted below are intended to show the widespread distribution. It occurs in the compound name *Cedifor*, the vowel of *Cad-* being affected and changed to *-e-* by the *-i-* which follows.

B13. SR 1292. Several examples; 216. Iuor ap Adam; Yuor ap Wronou. B15. 287. Aberyst-Cardigan 14th century. Yuor ab Hugyn. B24. 196. Fasti Cist. Camb. Gilbert Ivor (of the Forest of Dean) Tintern 1320. Mer LSR 37. Iuor; 38. Heylin ap Iuor; 47. Griffid ap Iuor. BBStD 316. Ieuan ap Eynon ap Iuor, Euor ap Iuor, 318. Yuor ap Ph'. L & P, iii (part 2), Grant 2587, p.1101, Pardon for murder to Oliver ap Ever alias Pever, a carpenter of Middlewich, Cheshire (dated 1522). MLSW 198. Philippi ap Ievour. InvECP 186. Rads 1556. David ap Evor Phelpot, (cf. RadsSoc VIII, 51, Will, John Apevor Phelpot.) 205. Glam Cowbridge 1544

John Griffiths alias Evors. 262. Marches 1556. ... on behalf of Yevor Bedwas. RadsSoc XXXII. 60. 1587. Will, several of ap Evor; XXXV. 33. 1593, Will, John Evor of Ednoll; ibid 38. Star Chamber, Yevore ap Rees David; XL. 61, 1573. Painscastle, Will, Rs ap Gwilym Bevor. Glam Hearth Tax, Cadoxton psh. William Evor. St David's Diocese, Index of Marriages – Llandingad 1703 David Ivour and Jane Williams.

The only example picked up from a Shropshire register is Claverley 62. Yevers.

The name in the E form *Ivor* and in the W form *Ifor* has been in vogue for a few generations, and this may be attributed to the attention given to the medieval Ifor Hael, patron of Dafydd ap Gwilym, and the name of the Friendly or Sick Benefit Society, Yr Iforiaid, 'The Ivorites'. But it is probably correct to say that before this nineteenth century revival of interest, the name had fallen into disuse, for it is very significant that it is difficult to find surnames derived from it, coming into use during the period of adopting permanent surnames.

Iorwerth

There is a good variety in the spelling of this name, especially the final syllable, but there appeared to be great uncertainty how the first syllable should be spelt; it is *Ier-* so often that it is necessary to determine what the standard form should be. Texts of early poetry such as Hendregadredd have Iorwerth, e.g. in the title of poem p.192; and the internal rhyme of ang*or*/y*or*uerth is the best form of evidence, p.158, *aryf taryf toryf angor yoruerth* (= arf tarf torf angor Iorwerth). The following selection illustrates the variety of spelling: B2. 54. 1301-2. yorworth ab Madok. B2. 150. Cricieth 1320. Gveyervil uxor Ierueriod; 151. Ieruerod ... Ieruod. B3. 151. NW Boroughs, 1295. Zereward Voyl. B6. 258. Lleyn 1350. de Yarward ... B7. 291. N. Pembs 1599 Ioroth ap Ieuan. B13. 142. 1283. Yorwerth ... Yorwarth ... Yorward; 1295. yerward ... Yerford. B13. SR 1292. 216 ... ap Ierewaru, Yereuarth, 218. Ioreuerth, 220. Yereuerth, 221. ab Yeruorth, Yereuoth, Ioruert, 222. Yareford, Yereuart, 223. Yoruard, 224. Yareuord. B15. 289. Aberyst-Cardn. 14th century. Joruth Gleys. B16. 118. temp. Edw I. Yerwardi. Glam Cartae, a few examples taken from the index: Yeruerd,

jerewrth, Jeruard, Jerevad, Yoruard, Joruard. BBStD 22. ... ab Ioru'th, 146. ... Iorueth. CAP 73. David ap Youet. Mer LSR 4. Iorword; 80. Iarword. LpOswestry 32/33. Ioweth; 144. Irwerth, Ierwerth, 155. Iewerth. ADClun 208. ... ap (Eorath ?) (obviously, Iorath). MLSW 129. ... ap Ierwith. CalChancProc. 85. ... Yaruort. CatAncDeeds VI. C.6243. Chester ... Yarward. C.3927. Chester ... Yarvard. DLancaster 151. Jorothe Nicholas; 164. Yorrowe Smith. 192. Henrici Yerith, Harry Yeroth. 199. ... Yrroth; 204. Yearoth. CalACW 49. Ereward ap Leuca. Glam Hearth Tax, Lysvane, Evan Yarrowthe; Siginston psh. Rd Yarrow. Star CP 191. Jno Yorath son and executor of Yerorth Wm.; 191. Christopher Yerrorth. HM iv. Chepstow, 12. Alice Aberoth. PRCaerwent 1570. ... ab yeroth. InvECP 5. Anglesey 1533. ap Erwerth.

There is a good example above of *ab* – *Iorwerth* changing in colloquial speech to give *Aberoth*.

RCA 11. Anglesey, Robert ap Barworthe ap Howel. Cf. PRConway 1615. Mary David ffilia Davidi ap Hugh ap William Borwarth. ML 2. 296, W to R. Iorweth Berwerth (converted in William's facetious style from Ned Edwards).

As *Iorwerth* fell comparatively into disuse, and was replaced by Edward, especially in N.E. Wales, there are only rare examples in the Shropshire registers. In the Whittington register, 129. 1635, there is mention of a place-name, Fernhill yerwarth. The Shrewsbury BR, 321. 1713 has Yorward – one entry. In present-day registers one occasionally finds examples of the correct or near-correct form: *Iorwerth*: Wrexham, Allington. *Yorwerth*: Knutsford, Congleton – Church Hulme; Wrexham, W. Boro – Caia Ward, Offa Ward. *Yorath* occurs oftener: City of Hereford, St Martin's; City of Glouc, Tuffley p.6, Podsmead 17; Newport, Michaelstone-y-Vedw; Monmouth Mardy – Llantilio Pertholey, Monmouth, Overmonnow. Cf. Br Radnor, Cynlais Ward, Name of Street, Gwernyorath: Gwernyorath House, lived in by Yorath G. Earland. *Yarworth*: S. Gloucs, Lydney Alvington, Awre 1, Tidenham; West Gloucs, Newland, Newnham, West Dean; S.

Worcs, Malvern East – Langland, Malvern South No. 1. Cf. also, Times 11.11.76, In Memoriam (p.32) Green, Arnold Yorwath.

The name Yearwood occurs in Ludlow, Bridgnorth St Mary Magdalen (Not in Reaney), and Yarwood (not in Reaney) which may be the same name, occurs oftener: Oswestry Urban, Castle W.; City of Hereford, St Martin's; W. Gloucs, Tidenham; – City of Gloucs, Longlevens p.4; Nantwich, Cholmondeston; Northwich (widespread throughout constituency): these two merit further investigation.

The replacement of *Iorwerth* by *Edward* and the idea of the equivalence of Welsh *Iorwerth* and English *Edward* have been dealt with above. In the med period the name *Gervase* was used occasionally in official papers for Iorwerth:

CalACW 97. Gervase son of Llywelyn, Elias son of Dafydd, Gervase his brother . . . to the King of England, 1281-97. 87. and master Gervase, Llywelyn's clerk and vice-chancellor, 1277. 198. Gervays Caerowys, chaplain, 1393. 148. Gerveys son of William. ? 1295. DWB 416. Iorwerth (or Gervase), abbot of Talley and bishop of St David's 1215-1229. *A Description of Caernarvonshire* (1809-11), Edmund Hyde Hall, 1952, p.152, Bishop of Bangor, Griffith ap Ierward, or Fitz Gervase.

HYPOCORISTIC FORMS

The hypocoristic forms are *Iolo, Iolyn*; cf. Bartrum 1350-1415, 645, Iolo ap y Teg Fadog; 647, Iorwerth ap y Teg Fadog ap Madog. The *l* is really double *l* and the pronunciation ought to be as in E 'dolly'. As the use of *Iolo* in the modern period is mainly due to a revival of archaic forms the presence of the single *l* in the written version has influenced the pronunciation, to make it like E *polo*. Attention is drawn to this in OIG 25 but the correction is not likely to bring about a changed pronunciation for *Iolo* with the sound of 'polo' has become far too common to be altered. The form *Iolyn*, especially as a common noun meaning 'silly fool, lout', has the correct double *l* sound: there has been no break in its usage and it has, because of the continuity, retained the original pronunciation. In early documents written by English and Norman clerks the names usually have double *l*, 'correctly' written according to E

values: the use of *ll* in Welsh for the 'unilateral hiss' has forced Welsh writing to use single *l* for the sound of single *l* and for the sound of double *l*.

The numbers of the examples in Bartrum's Genealogies are probably a fair indication of the social status of the hypocoristic forms: period 1215-1350, Iolo, three; Iolyn, ten; followed by eleven pages of Iorwerth, 337-347. Many of the examples quoted will have -*en* in the final syllable, which is the E tendency to give the vowel of the final syllable the neutral sound.

B13. 227. SR 1292. Griffyt Keneu Iollyn. CaernQSR 30. Joh'es ap Rythergh ap D'd ap Iollyn. RecCa 261. Jollyn ap Eign Gymmen. B15. 42. AS 1406. Iolyn Goch; 43. Iollo ap Gruffith; 45. Iollyn ddu, Jolyn Pwrs; Jollyn ap Jeu(an) Dew; 47. Iollo ap Ior ap Ho(well); B11. 57. Broniarth 1429. Iollyn ap Eyno(n) ap gr. CaernCR 119. Iolyn (MS Jollyn) ap Dafydd Ddu. CatAncDeeds V. 13319, 1556. Salop. Thomas ap David ap Yollin. Shrewsbury BR 74. under Davies . . . Geoffrey . . . s. David ap Yolin, of Alberbury 1495. 164. Geoffrey, of S., smith, s. Jenen ap Yolin, of the Heldre, in Caus 1529. InvECP 83. Denbs 1533. John ap David ap Jollyn. 86. Denbs 1538. . . . Alice his wife, late the wife of Robert ap Yolen, Complainants, John ap Howell ap John (John ap Yolen) and Katherine his wife, Defendants; Lands . . . formerly of David ap Yolen, father of the said Robert. (Here it is obvious that *Yolen* has become a fixed surname, but there is nothing to show how John ap Howell has the alias of John ap Yolen.)

SHROPSHIRE REGISTERS

The evidence of these registers shows the development of *ab-Iolyn*, giving *Biolin, Byollin*. As the *i* or *y* in this form is consonantal, with the accent on -*òll*-, there is an inevitable simplification giving *Boylin* or *Bollin*. The -*in* will become *ing* in some cases; the genitive *s* will be added to give *Bolling, Bollings*; in others the vowel of the final syllable will be neutral, indicated by -*en*, as in the examples of *Yollen* above.

Whittington 599. 1777 . . . and Jane Biolin of the p. of West Felton. Kinnerley, Index, Byolin (Boyling): 224. 1784. Edward s. of John Byolin and Mary; 229. 1787. Richard, s. of John Byolin and Mary; 277. 1788.

William s. of John Byolin = 302. 1780. Marriage register, John Boyling, of Kinnerley, widr. and Mary. Oswestry 225. 1601. Katheringe vz Thomas Biollin of Utton. St Martin's, Index, 9.11.93. Jn Biolyn. Hordley 45. 1811. Esther Byollin, spinster . . . Wit(ness) William Byollin. Shrewsbury St Mary's, Index, Ballance, Ballins, Ballince, Bollins – put together. Index puts Bealling (Beolin) separate from the above. 200. 1691. Thomas Beolin and Catherine Bowers, marr. 449. 1771. Catherine Bealling, bur. (Hardly the same Catherine). Shrewsbury BR, Index, Thomos Byllyon of S. Shereman, 1450 (surely this is meant to be Byollyn).

Instances are given above of the change to *Boyling*: cf. Knockin 29. 1782. Boyling, probably the same family as the family of Byolin/Boyling of Kinnerley above: Whittington 577. 1757. Mary Boyling. Pontesbury 511. 1790. Richard and Abigail Boyling; Ludlow 1. 1559. John Boylinge.

Examples of Bollin, Bolling, Bollen
Selattyn 117. 1639; Thomas Bolyn, a base child. Chirbury 81. Bollin. Church Preen 18, 20. John Bollen; 26. Mary Bollen; 27. John Bollins. St Chad's, Index, Bollin (Bollen, Bolling, Bollings, Bollins).

Of the two hypocoristic forms *Iolyn* predominated in mid- and N.E. Wales (and N. Wales generally), and this probably explains the absence of names which represent 'ab-Iolo'.

PRESENT-DAY REGISTERS
Iolyn taken over into English speech should become Jollin, Jolling: this single example demonstrates that this took place: Runcorn, Appleton, South Ward, *Jollings*.

No example of *Biolin* was picked up during scrutiny of electoral registers, but the name *George Biolin* occurs on a tablet in the porch of St Alkmunds, Shrewsbury, dated 1910, commemorating muffled bells for the death of Edward VII, G.B. being one of the bellringers. There is no lack of instances of *Boylin* or *Boyling*:
Shrewsbury, Belle Vue, Castlefields, Harlescott, Monkmoor. Ludlow, Broad St., East Hamlet, Much Wenlock.

Iestyn
The name of Iestyn ap Gwrgant, King of Morgannwg in the second half of the eleventh century is Jestin in LL 273, and Gistinus in

271-2; but in spite of the *G-* version, the initial was consonantal *i*. The name was not much used in the med period, but it may be the source of the surname *Jestin*, occurring in East Flint, Buckley, Bistre West, Ewloe Wood, Hope (JA). The TD of London has one Jestin and one Jeston. The name of the 'township' of Hope was Estyn, *v.* WATU 67.

If *Ieuan* could become *Evan*, *Iestyn* could conceivably become *Estyn*, cf. ADClun 174 Estyn Cado; 195, 196, Estyn Cadw (abbreviation of Cadwgan). Estyn is found occasionally as a man's first name.

Ingham, Inghan *v.* Einion
Inion, Inon *v.* Einion
Iolo, Iolyn *v.* Iorwerth

Ithel
An earlier form is Ithael: the OW form was Iudhail (= iüd-hail), as it is set out in WG 32; the *ae* of the final syllable tends to give *e*, as in gafael/gafel, gadael/gadel. The index of LL provides several examples of the primitive version, *Judhail*. The following represent the versions of the medieval period:
B2. 151. Criccieth 1320. Itel Vawr. B10. 256. West W., Llewelyn ap Griffith Eythel. B13. 221. SR 1292. Ythel ab Houa; 226. Ithel le Mercer, Ithel ap Iuor; 229. Ythel Bola.

Example of the name latinized: Glam Cartae – Index – Itellus fr. Wasmihaggel. The following single example shows that a derivative form was in use, Mer LSR 47. Ithaelin.

Examples from early modern texts:
CatAncDeeds VI. C.7806. Flints 21 Eliz. Richard ap Thomas ap Jethell. C.7916. Flints 26 Eliz. Richard ap Thomas ap Ithell. Star CP 73. Flints Jno Bythell of Sceifiog. InvECP 84. Denbs 1537. Griffith ap Ethell. 84. Denbs. 1537. (another case) Griffith ap Ithel. PRConway 1669. . . . d of Nithael Johns (?). 1718. Catherina filia Gulielmi Bethel . . . Bithel, supra dict. 1725. Gulielmus Beethel. 1775. Ellin Beithel . . . Biethel.

SHROPSHIRE REGISTERS
Bitterley 5. 1664. Gulielmus Bithill. Alberbury 80. 1622. Catherine verch Yethell. Ludlow 38. 1631, Richard Eythall. 402. 1644. Bethel, s. of Matthew ap Edward and Jane. Uffington 12. 1627. Margrette Ithill. Hodnet 139. 1745. Thos. s. of Thos. and Abigail Ethell. Whittington 287. 1720. Thomas Eathel = 293. 1726. Thomas Ethel. 319. 1745. Gwen Beethol; 452. 1752. Edward

Ithiel (a quite common spelling of the name).

The name in its various forms is still fairly common, especially in North Wales and in the E counties which would receive emigrants from N.W. Dialect variations can be expected, e.g. final -*e* becomes -*a* in Gwynedd. The following selection represents the variety:

Ithel, Wrexham, Brymbo Vron Ward; West Flint, Rhyl West cc50. *Ithell*, City of Chester, Ch. Rural, Wervin, Dunham Shiffnall. *Ethell*, Knutsford, Hale Central 1, Hale SE 2, Bucklow Rural, Rostherne. *Ethall*, Caernarvon, North Ward A. *Bithell*, Ludlow, St Leonard; S. Hereford, HC Walford; Kidderminster, Kiddr. Foreign. *Bythel*, BrRadnor, Brynmawr Central. *Bythell*, Ludlow, Morville, Wrekin, Wellington, Wellington Regent. *Bethile*, City of Glouc, Hucclecote p.29. *Bethel*, S. Gloucs, Winterbourne; Shrewsbury, Castle Foregate; Ludlow, Broseley; S. Hereford, Kingstone. *Bethell*, Shrewsbury Westbury; Ludlow, Bridgnorth Oldbury; Knutsford, Bucklow Rural, Plumley. *Bethall*, Ludlow, Madeley.

Irian *v.* Urien

J

Jack *v.* Ieuan
Jane, Jayne, Jeyne *v.* Ieuan
Jankin, Janko *v.* Ieuan
Jenions *v.* Einion
Jenn *v.* Ieuan
Jenyns, Jenyngs *v.* Ieuan

Jevans, Jevons *v.* Ieuan
Jevanson *v.* Ieuan
Jockyn *v.* Ieuan
John(s) *v.* Ieuan
Jollings *v.* Iorwerth
Jones *v.* Ieuan

K

Kadegan *v.* Cadwgan
Karenion, Kyrynion *v.* Introd. Place-names
Karlyon *v.* Caerleon
Keelan, Kellan, Kilan *v.* Cilan
Kefanbauche *v.* Bach
Keiling, Kewelling, Kyellin *v.* Cuhelyn
Kenefick, Kenfig, Kennifeck *v.* Cynffig
Kendrick, Kenrick, Kenwrick, Kenwright *v.* Cynwrig
Kemeys, Kemmish, Kemys *v.* Cemais
Kendal, Kendell *v.* Cynddelw
Kenevin, Kenvin, Kenvyn, Kenwyn *v.* Cynfyn
Kerry *v.* Ceri

Kethine, Kething *v.* Cethin
Kibbey, Kibby *v.* Cybi
Kidwelly *v.* Introd. Place-names
Kiffin *v.* Cyffin
Kindellan *v.* Cynddylan
Kinner *v.* Cynyr
Knayth, Kneath *v.* Cnaith(o)
Knethell, Knythell *v.* Cynddelw
Knevet, Knyvet *v.* Ednyfed
Kydogan *v.* Cadwgan
Kydwaliter *v.* Cadwaladr
Kyffin *v.* Cyffin
Kynan, Kynon *v.* Cynan

L

Lamphey
This place is a civil parish in South Pembs; in Welsh *Llandyfái*:
Surveys GK, 128. Jennet Lamphey; Badminton Manorial Papers, 2628, Gower Survey 1594-5, Robt Lanfey. Glam Hearth Tax, Reynoldston. Dd Lamphey. Fenton 235-6 uses the form Lamfey and provides a derivation which is very different from Llandyfái corrupted.

Landeck, Landeg *v*. Glandeg

Landimôr
This place is a hamlet in the Gower peninsula; no original W version of the name is given in WATU or in the Gazetteer. Ekwall 286 has a place-name Landermere, and an early example in the form of *Landimer*, from OE *landgemaere*. If the Gower place-name is a version of the English word, one can easily account for the change to the final vowel, that, in a place not very far from the sea, it would be influenced by the W *môr*, 'sea'. D.E. Williams 52 quotes 'Ego Philippus Davy Filius David De Landimor', 1315. The surname Landymore is found in Wrekin, Dawley – Horselay. Cf. also Times 12.1.84, Forthcoming Marriages, P.J.A. Landymore, Geneva and Gendon, Bucks.

Lanyon
This is not given as a place-name in Gazetteer and WATU had no reason to mention it. Examples of Lanyon as a surname occur in Newport, St Julians 3, Victoria 2; Monmouth, Llanfoist Fawr; and the form *Lonyon* is found in Macclesfield, West Ward.
It may be a difficult place-name to explain, but there can be little doubt that the surname is derived from the Pembs place-name, the examples of which show the variation LL/L, and variation of the vowel Lan/Lon. TYP 47, text, *Ac yn Llonyon ym Phenvro*; variant readings

49 include *llouyon, Llovian, llofion*, obviously the result of misreading. The note on p.52 has 'Perhaps Lanion near Pembroke', and quotes examples in LL 124.26; 255.12, which speak of 'Din guennhaf in lonion'. Amongst the numerous refs. given to us by Major Francis Jones are:
the manor of Llanien, NLW MS 1602D. fo 171, circa 1600-1610. Wm Holcombe of Llanion, Esq. NLW Bronwydd deeds no. 1569. Wm Holcombe of Lanion, parliamentary voter 1760; his will dated 31 March 1763 at Lanyon, NLW Probate wills.

Laugharne
The original W name is Talacharn; the use of this form is still favoured by some, but the W version generally used is *Lacharn*, the unaccented first syllable being lost in natural speech. *Laugharne* in the first place is obviously meant to be an English disyllabic version of Lacharn, but the -*gh*- has become silent and the name is pronounced as a monosyllable, 'Larn'.
WPortBooks 92. John Lagharn. Ex Pro James I. 310. 311. Laugharne (as surname). CRHaverford, Index, Laugharn(e), six entries as surname. There are thirty entries in the Swansea TD; examples outside Wales can be found in Stroud, Hardwicke, Minchinhampton North. *Larne* is also found in Hubberston, Milford Haven: this is probably a simpler spelling of Laugharne, and not the Irish *Larne*.

Leader, Ledder *v*. Elidir
Lellew, Lello, Lelow *v*. Llywelyn
Lewis *v*. Llywelyn
Ley *v*. Lleiaf
Leyshon *v*. Lleision
Lia *v*. Lleiaf
Lidnerth
Glam Hearth Tax *c*. 1672 (PRO

E179/221/297) has John Lidnerth and Lidnerth John both dwelling in St Fagan's. A similar list of almost the same date (E 179/375-6) spells the latter name as Lydnarth John, reflecting the local pronunciation of the name. Lidnerth is rare and unusual as name or surname, and is not to be confused with the name Idnerth.

L.J. Hopkin James and T.C. Evans, *Hen Gwndidau* (Bangor 1910) give a number of Glamorgan poems of the Tudor period which refer to the parish or land of Lidnerth and to St Lidnerth, and in their notes (ibid., 247-8) identify Lidnerth both with Llidnerth son of Nudd Hael and brother of Dingad (according to Rees's *British Saints*) or to St Leonard, and identify the parish of Lidnerth with Newcastle on Ogmore, near Bridgend, *v.* also Baring-Gould and Fisher, *Lives of the British Saints* (1911), iii, 376 for the saint. The identification of the parish of Lidnerth with Newcastle on Ogmore is accepted by G.J. Williams in TLIM 122.

It is possible that the Lidnerth family of St Fagan's came from Newcastle on Ogmore or from the Hundred of Newcastle.

Lilwall *v.* Llywelyn

Lleiaf

This is the superlative of *bach*; it was used as an epithet for the smallest or youngest member of the family, like *Minimus*, the examples taken from Bartrum (below) seem to prove that the epithet was applied to the grandson who had the same name as his father and grandfather. There is one example below of the epithet used as forename, as in the development of *Ieuaf*. The final *-f* would not be sounded in colloquial speech, and one should expect *Leia*, variously spelt in early records.

Glam Cartae 1448. Wenllian v. Res Leya. PWLMA 295. Dafydd Leiaf; 344. John Leia (1497, Reeves, Carmarthen). 454. Y Moel ap Gruffydd Leia. CatAncDeeds V. 13319. Salop. Oct. 1556. David ap John Lya. MLSW 107. Philip David Lia; 108. Philippus David Luya; 112. Gwilym David Lya, Philip David Lya; Bennett Pedigrees MS Ped 72. . . . Gladys vz Lln ap Dd Leya of Nantyclays. Bartrum 1215-1350. 211. Cadwgon Leia ap Cadwgon Fychan ap Cadwgon. 303. Hywel Leia ap Hywel ap Hywel. 315. Ieuan Gadarn ap Dafydd Leia ap Dafydd. Surveys GK, Kilvey 107. 1583. Georgius David Morgan

Luya. 228. 1632. Mawd Lia. 347. 1686. Tir Tom Lya. InvECP 81. Denbs 1533. Lya ap Meredith.

The name *Ley* (rhyming with *pay*) is found in the Swansea area; there are twenty-five entries in the Swansea TD, most of them on the left bank of the river Tawe, and the examples of *Lya* above in the Kilvey Survey which covers the same area raise the question whether *Ley* has its origin in *Leia*.

Lleision, Leyshon

The surname *Leyshon*, although not much used outside, is well-known in Glam. Clark has the pedigree of Lleisan of 'Aberpwrgam', and Lleisan of Baglan, and cadet branches, with odd references elsewhere. The charters of Glam have Leisan (Leysanus), Leyson, Lleyson, Leissan, Lleison, Leison, Lyson. Amongst the persons represented by these references is Lleision ap Tomas, the last abbot of Neath. Because the name is always pronounced with initial *l*, in other words, as the sound of initial *ll-* is never heard because the Welsh version has become obsolete, one felt it necessary to establish that the name in Welsh had initial *ll-*. WG 208 quotes 'Y Lleisioniaid' from LGC 100 (as an example of adding pl. term. to a personal name to denote the 'tribe'); and G.J. Williams throughout his TLIM has 'Lleision, ap Lleision, y Lleison-iaid'. The late Professor Williams has interesting quotations which refer to the Lleision family of Baglan, and to residences of theirs; the first on p.24 from John Leland, 'The Lysans . . . say, that theire familie was there afore the Conquest of the Normans'; the second in a footnote on the same page from Rice Merrick, ' . . . an ancient house . . . where Ieuan gethyn ap Jeuan ap lyson dwelt'; the third from Rice Merrick in a note on p.128, ' . . . near unto ye same church and passage lysson ap ryce ap Ieuan hath builded a fair new house'.

Cf. B13. 218. SR 1292. Res ab Leysan. PWLMA 375. Lleision ab Owain (1485. Catheiniog). Star CP 28. Morgan Leyson, of Llantwit iuxta Neath; Jenkin Leyson. 78. Glam, Wm Lysonte. InvECP 50. Carms 1538. Greffyn Leyson, doctor of the court of Arches. CRHaverford 74. Wm Lysan. HM. iv 6. Leishini ap Morgan, 13c. Hundred of Caldicot. 7. Leyson ap Morgan, Jurors 1361. The *-s-* of *Lleison*, given the quality of the vowel -i would become sh in colloquial Welsh, and be written Leyshon. There are seventy-six entries in the Cardiff TD and fifty-six in the Swansea TD. There are occasional examples in the border counties, West Gloucs, Longhope, West Dean; City of Hereford, Bartonsham; a stray example in Anglesey, Llangefni. The form *Leyshan* (hyphenated) is found in W. Gloucs, Long-ford, and the spelling *Layshon* in Runcorn, Mersey Ward 2.

Examples of *Lysons* occur in the con-stituencies of Ludlow, Wrekin, Oswestry. This name is probably not related: Reaney has a Norman origin, *Lison*.

Llello v. Llywelyn

Llewellen, Llewellin v. Llywelyn

Llifon v. Introd. Place-names

Llowarch v. Llywarch

Lloyd v. Llwyd

Llwchwr, Loughor

Llwchwr is the name of the river which serves as a boundary between W. Glam and Carms; the W name of the village close to the ancient castle near the estuary is *Casllwchwr*, the *cas-* referring to the castle. *Loughor* (as an English version of Llwchwr) is used for the river, the village and the former Urban district. The pronunciation needs a special note, for unlike Laugharne and the 'silent' *gh*, the pro-nunciation of *Loughor* retains the guttural *ch*, although the initial sound is single *l*. D.E. Williams 64 quotes the example Philip ap David Delozur, 1322 (Glam Cartae IV. 618), which is a good example of using *z* for the *ch* sound.

One finds relatively early examples of Loughor, Lougher attached to pers. names, or virtually as surnames. Clark 93-5 has *Loughor* pedigrees, with branches in Tythegston, in the Vale of Glamorgan, in Pembs and around the Bridgend area: today it does seem that the biggest concentration is found in the Cardiff area.

WPortBooks 88. William Lougher of Tenby. Star CP 7. Henry VIII. Glam, Watkin Loughour. Ex Pro James I. Rice Lougher of Wallwinge Castle, Pembs. HM iv pt 3, 166. Watkin Lougher.

Llywarch

Lugumarcos is given as the British version, v. Jackson, LHEB 442. B13. 143. Bonds peace 1283. Anyan fil Lywar'; yleward ab blethin;

(yl = ll). B13. 220. SR 1292. Eynon ab Louargh; 222. Leuwergh ab Alan. 226. Anable Wreyg Louarch. B4. 351. AnglCourt 1346. lowargh' ap y barth. B5. 57. Lleyn, late 13th century. loar ap seysyll. B5. 146. Caern. 1293. lowar; B6. 258. Lleyn 1350. terre Madoci ap lowar. B9. 68. Treflaward (Foot-note, Trelywarch). Mer LSR 44. Kenuric ap Louard . . . Yerword ap Loward. BBStD 256. Eyno ap bowarth [sic[; Cadogan ap Lowarth. RecCa 91. Bellyn ap llowarch; Index, Lowar, 20; Lowarth 1, Llywarch 1; Lywarch 18. Glam Cartae 2366. . . . ap Thlowarth; 2362. . . . ap Thlewarth. 544. Lourarth ab Was-dewi; Index, variant spellings, include Luarch, Luarh. ADClun 16. Eynon ap llowarth; 142. Map Lowergh; 143. Map Louargh. DLancaster (Fforrenry . . . Kidwelly) 231. Thomas Llwarch; 288. Llowarche Redderch. Rec Denb Lp (1860 edn) 32. David ap Lauwargh, Lanwarth ap David; 39. Lawargh Gogh. PRCaerwent 1596. Sibyll dau. of James lloarch. BYale 112. Thewertk ap Madoc (trans. Llywarch) cf. 114. Lloargh. Surveys GK. 1687, 334. Phillipp Llowarck. B25 – Accounts . . . relating to lands of Earl of Worcester in the 1530's; p.304, Footnote 1, Text containing 'Johanne Loargh' struck through. p.306, Footnote 7, (Johannis Lloughers) refers to the forms of the name occurring in the text. InvECP 239. Monm 1553. Philip Loarghe. late of Chepstow. [? 241. Monm 1556. late the wife of Richard Large]

The Shropshire registers do not yield many examples, Westbury 350. 1810, Joan Llowarch, 355. 1812. William s. of David Llowarch and Sarah. If it is not a mistake of reading or printing the following example showing metathesis is an example of some interest: St Chad's 1909. 1811, *Llowrach*.

In present-day registers *Llywarch* is found in Monts, Castle Caereinion, Llanfihangel, Llanrhaeadr-ym-Mochnant.

Llowarch, Oswestry, Wem Urban; City of Chester, Ch. Rural, Upton by Chester. Wirral, Ellesmere Port, Westminster Ward, (several), Grange Ward; Monts, Guilsfield. *Lowarch*, Oswestry, Ellesmere Rural – Dudleston Heath; Cheadle, Hazelgrove and Bramhall East 1; Cheadle (AA) Adswood. Penrith and Border, Eden District, Appleby (Appleby Ward). Monts, Llansantffraid

Deythur.

Llywelyn

Lugubelinos is given as the British form which became Llywelyn, *v.* LHEB 414, 440. The first element is seen in the names Llywarch, Lliwelydd, the second element is that seen in the name Belyn, p.50. It is perfectly obvious that it has no connexion with *llew* 'lion', but the attraction of 'llew' could not be resisted so that 'Llewelyn' became normal spelling. The point has been made before that the sound of the second syllable would, to English ears and according to English values, require *-ell-*, resulting in the spelling 'Llewellyn', which is so misleading because the sound of the initial *ll* and the sound of the medial 'll' are different. But this, unfortunately, is the usual spelling of the surname, and to make things worse, ignorance and slovenliness quite often turn the initial *ll* into a single *l*. The idea that the first element meant 'lion' no doubt helped to produce the anglicised version *Leoline*.

Sir Leoline Jenkins (1625-85), DWB *s.n.*; B3. 147. Glam Loyalists 1696, Leolin John; HM i, 52. Vicars of Llangattock V.A., 1683, Leoline Williams of Llantwit Faerdre.

The name was much used in the med period: it was borne by two of the greatest and most powerful princes, and one may judge how popular it was by the numbers in Bartrum, of Llywelyn as first name: period 985-1215, pp. 143-147; 1215-1350, pp.357-371; 1350-1415, pp. 666-681. Below it will be shown that it was later replaced, to a great extent, by Lewis, as an English approximation. Examples of unusual means of spelling the name in the med period and early mod period:

B6. 354. NW 1326. Leuelin rouca; 358. Howel ap Leulini. B13. 143. Bonds peace 1283, 1295. ab yleuelyn; leulyn ab yerward; Tuder ab yleulin. [Obviously, *yl* is meant for *ll*, as there are other examples, yleward (for Llywarch), Cadugan yloyd (for Llwyd).] ACW 49. Elilevelin ap Phelipe (1283-90 ? 1299-1303 ?) B14. 241. temp Edw 1. ap Leulyn. PRLl.Ystern Llewern, 17. 1729. Anna filia . . . Leoloni John de Tre Castell y lluel. PRCaerwent 1704. . . . a servant of Lawellins.

The main difficulty of the English scribe was the way to represent the sound of initial *ll*. B13. 216. SR 1292. Thelwelinus ap Meweric,

Howel ap Thelwelin. (other examples in the text have Lewelyn, leulyn). B15. 130. temp Edw I. . . . ap Thlewelyn. InvECP 40. Cards 1553, Jenckyn Swellin alias Griffeth, . . . Swellin ap Griffeth. 112. Flints 1515, John (–) Apswellen. 153. Monts 1553. William Llewelyn (Fowellen), citizen and salter of London. 208. Glam Flewellin and David Gytto. 209. Glam Fluellen ap Roser . . . Margaret Fleuellen. 216. Monm . . . ap Fluelyn. 235. Monm Thomas Davy ap Thellyn. L'Estrange Ewen 255 gives *Thelen* as a version of Llewelyn.

SHROPSHIRE REGISTERS

There is no difficulty in finding instances in the Shropshire registers, of unusual versions, and especially of *Fl-*, *Fll-* for the initial sound: Pontesbury 40. 1574. Eliz. Thewelling. Westbury 362. 1759. Llallin Jasper. (husband's name). Ludlow 327. 1623. Gwen Fluellin. More 3. 1591. . . . Thos Llewelline; 5. 1597. Thomas Llewellen. 9. 1606. William Lewelling; 10. 1610. Robert Llewellinge. 21. 1638. Elizabeth Llewillin. Munslow 6. 1546. Alles Lawellen. Norbury 27. 1629. Humfrey Lluellene. (The only entry of this name as such but there is a possibility he is the Humfrey Wellings of earlier entries). Myddle 66. 1609. Nup. Leweni Tayler, vel Lodovici Tayler, rectoris de Morton Corbett. 239. 1768. Mary Leweuilin. Albrighton 160. 1785. Francis, s. of Mary Lewilin. Donington 29. 1640. John Llewen and Judyth Nittingall. mar. 29. 1641. John s. of John and Judyth Fluellin. Moreton Say 3. 1693. Joan Fluellen was buried, wife to Rich. Fluellen. 4. 1694. Richard Lluellen, bur. 38. 1737. Elizabeth, a base child of Mary Fluellen. Wem 156. 1637. John Flewellin; 667. 1768. A infant of Thos. Fluelling's, of this town, . . . bur. 658. 1761. Hamelia Fluelling, of this town. Hanwood 42. Flwellin. Wolstaston 4. 1625. Edward and Anne Flawelling. St Chad's, Index, Fluellin, Ffewellin, Fllewelin, Flueline etc. Llanyblodwel 25. 1712. Martha W. of Edward fflellen.

PRESENT DAY REGISTERS

The variant spellings are found in present-day registers:

Llewellen: Conway, Deganwy Ward; Leominster, Middleton-on-the-Hill, as christian name. Llewhellin: S. Pembs, Cosheston – Nash; Preseli, Fishguard N.W., Milford,

Hakin Ward. Llewhelyn: Preseli, Fishguard N.W. Flewellen: S.Gloucs. Bitton; Hanham Abbots 3. Flewelling: W.Gloucs. Lydbrook; Bl.Gwent, E.V., Rassau North, Beaufort Ward. Fluellen: Crewe, Crewe 1, Central. Cf. Sunday Times 24.7.77, News item concerning Bill Flewellyn, the Australian hang-gliding champion, also D. Tel, 23.6.83. Deaths, John C. Fuelling, Kew.

A name which occurs with great frequency throughout the border counties is *Welling(s)*; it is possible that this name and its variants have a source in an English place-name: what is certain is that *Welling* can be traced back to *(Lle)wellyn, (Lle)wellin*: the examples quoted below are conclusive evidence and the high frequency of the instances in the border counties is additional circumstantial evidence:

B6. 256. Lleyn 1350. ada ab Welyn. RecCa 250, 251. Welyn ap Mad'. CatAncDeeds V. 12941, 1575. Salop. Edward ap John ap Ewelyn (name repeated at the end of document). Glam Cartae 294, 308, 310, 317. archid. Wellen. Star CP 207. Pem. Thos Lln als Whellen. PWLMA 413. Henry ap 'Welyn' 1322. Serjeants, Elfed. RCA 296. Caernarvon, John ap Ewlyn.

There are examples in some of the parish registers of Shropshire of *Welyn* following *ap*: Ludlow 57. 1563. Alice ap Welyn [cf. 6. 1571. Lewis Bewlyn; 243. 1583. John Bewlen]. Munslow 48. 1608. Elizabeth d. of Rice ap Wellys, of the Bishops Castle (this is entered in the index as Ap Wellings). Whittington 52. 1623. . . .d. of Thomas Pawelin, weaver, of Ebnall. 47. 1626. Thomas s. of Thomas Llewelin, of Ebnall, weaver. Wem 443. 1708. Benj. Bewellin, p. Ellesmere.

Examples of Wellin, Welling, Wellen, etc.
Shipton 29. 1657. William Wellings; 30. 1664. Wellins (same person). More, 23, 33, 50, 51, 62, 68. Wellings (Wellins). Lydham 2. 1606. John Wellens; 7. 1613. John Wellens; 14. 1639. Margaret Wellings. Neenton 13. 1645. Richard and Eave Wellings; 13. 1646. Eave w. of Richard Wellins. Stanton Lacy 20. 1590. Yevan Wellines: Chirbury 5. 1631. Richardi Wellynes; Index: Wellynnes, Wellins, Wellings, Welings, several entries, compared with very few of Llewellin. Ludlow 77. 1577. Charles and Laurence Wellyns. Diddlesbury 1. 1583. Johes filius Wm

Wellens 9. 1587. Syman Wellence; cf. Simonis Wellens. 28. 1687. Wellens = 29. 1690. Wellings (same person; this variation continues through the records). 150. 1735. Anne Wellins = 156. 1737. Ann Wellens = 161. 1740. Ann Wellings.

PRESENT DAY REGISTERS

The forms *Welling, Wellings, Wellen, Wellon*, etc. are found well-distributed through the border counties:

Welling: City of Hereford, Bartonsham (16 examples); S.Hereford, Fownhope; Leominster, Stretton Sugwas; S. Gloucs, Siston-Oldland; CT, Ashchurch. *Wellings*: Shrewsbury, Abbey Foregate, Belle Vue, Monkmoor, Condover (15), Berrington, Dorrington, Pimhill-Fitz, Preston Gubballs; (there are far too many locations to plot them in detail). *Wellens*: Ludlow, Madeley, Ironbridge; St and Hyde, Dukinfield West, Duk. East, Central; Knutsford, Wilmslow, Fulshaw Ward 2; Torfaen, Cwmbran St Dial's. *Weallens*: Knutsford, Congleton Bradwell. *Wellon*: S. Gloucs, Sodbury, Ch. Sodbury, Chaceley, Down Hatherley; West Gloucs, Forthampton (many); CT. Ashchurch, Lechlade, Walton Cardiff.

HYPOCORISTIC LLELO (LLELLO, LELLO)

In the hypocoristic name the *l* is double *-l*; Welsh writing is forced to use single *l* for obvious reasons; therefore in Welsh one uses *Llelo/Lelo*; in an English context, as it has the sound of *fellow, bellow*, the spelling is almost invariably *Llello, Lello*.

It has already been observed that the final *-o* of these pet names was liable to become *-a*, so that the examples of *Llela* need not be regarded as incorrect.

B15. 57. AS 1406. llello ap dd. AnglPleas 36. Gruffith ap Llewelin ap Jevan ap Llela. MLSW 274. Monts. Bedo ap Llello. Bartrum 1215-1350, 356. Llelo ap Llywelyn ap Madog; 379. Madog ap Llelo ap Llywelyn. 1350-1415, 609. Hywel ap Madog ap Llelo; 627. Ieuan ap Hywel ap Llelo. 633. Ieuan ap Llela ap Rhys; 666. Llela ap Rhys ap Einion. RadsSoc VI. 9. Will 1544. Moryce ap Lellowe. InvECP 22. Caern 1553. Edward Llyllo. 179. Rads. 1538. Llella Mores, saddler. ML 2. 185, 191. Llelo Gwtta = Llewelyn ap Meredydd.

The form *llel* in CaernHS 26 Bolde Rental 38, *llel ap y bille* may be nothing more than a written abbreviation, but the writers once knew a person named Llewelyn called 'Lel' colloquially. The form *Llellye* appears to be a genuine variant of the pet form, CaernQSR 150, Meredydd ap Rhys Llellye of Caernarvon.

There is not much evidence of a form made up of *ap* + *Llelo*; the following is an oddity of spelling: RadsSoc XXXII. 58. Will 1581, Willm ap Plello.

SHROPSHIRE PARISH REGISTERS
The registers provide a considerable number of examples of *Llelo*, *Llallo*, *Lello*, with other variant spellings. There are no examples of adding *'s*. Examples of initial *Ll-* are not necessarily proof that the *Ll* was pronounced as in Welsh, but it is interesting to mark the example in Burford 22. 1607, *Richard Flello* for the *Fl-* is the attempt to pronounce the Welsh *ll'* of the initial. Note should be taken also that there are examples of the ending in the -*a*, *ah* form.

Clunbury 16. 1616. Henricus Lelowe; 17. 1618. Katherina Llello = 28. 1631. Catren Lellowe; 20. 1624. Johannes Llellewe = 23. 1623. Johannes Lellow; 30. 1634. Elnor Llello; 31. 1635, 32. 1635. John Llello; 46. 1648. Lewis Lello; 138. 1737. Sarah Lellewe; 147. 1745. Sarah Lellew. Alberbury 482. Lellowe; 617. Lullow. Chirbury 217. 1767. Eleanor Lelow. Ludlow 9. 1576. William Llello; 20. 1594. Margery llallow. 44. 1636. Anne Lelloe; 314. 1617. Richard Lello; 204. 1640. Henry Lelo. Diddlesbury 28. 1687. William Lealoe; 39. 1711. John Lealoe; 62. 1668. William Lelloe. 63. 1669. William Lello = 69. 1676, 71. 1678. William Lella. 72. 1678. Mary Lella; 96. 1696. Mary Lealoe. 114. 1710. William s. of John Lealoe and Mary. Munslow 157. Lelloe; 138. Lealoe. Burford 22. 1607. Richard Flello; 240. 1690, 244. 1797. William Lello. Stokesay 144. 1790-91. John Lelo. Meole Brace 70. Eliz. Lellah.

PRESENT-DAY REGISTERS
Lello: Shrewsbury, Castle – Stone, Belle Vue. Ludlow, Broad St, Corve St, Old St, East Hamlet, Clun, Clunbury. Llanfair Waterdine, Bromfield. *Flello*: Bromsgrove, Alvechurch, Hopwood Ward. Kidderminster, Abberley, Astley, Kenswick, Kiddr. Foreign, Lingridge, Martley, Wolverley 1. *Flellow*: Bl. Gwent, Abertillery, Blaina

Coedcae (Q) Nantyglo.

The account given by Theophilus Jones, HBr 284 has been mentioned above, that as *Lelo* was used as a 'cant term' for a fool or simpleton, families named *Lelo*, *Lello* adopted the name *Lilwall*. The name *Lilwall* is found in several places in Herefordshire and elsewhere, e.g. City of H, Bartonsham, Holmer, St Martin's; South H. Eaton Bishop, Much Dewchurch, Llangarron, Cusop. It would be very difficult to demonstrate that any of these families were originally *Lello*. (There are early examples of *Lilwall*, e.g. CatAncDeeds V. A.12553, Hereford, John Lillwall ... Kington, Meredith Lillwall).

LEWIS FOR LLYWELYN
The equivalence of these names is probably due in the first place to the deliberate policy of medieval clerks of using Anglo-Norman names as substitutes for Welsh names. The first syllable of *Llywelyn*, especially if it was *Llew-* (and possibly pronounced *Lew-*) was quite sufficient to bring about an identity with *Lewis*, and justify the use of *Lewis* instead of Llewelyn. There are examples as early as the thirteenth century, e.g. CAP 505, Lewys the son of Gryffin, 1277-78 (= son of Gr. ap Gwenwynwyn); cf. also 527, Lowys Duy (1402, Carmarthen, text French). [It is surprising how often one finds *Lewis* spelt *Llewis*, e.g. CatAncDeeds VI. C7443, Monts, Owen ap Llewis ap Owen; HM iv, 9 Chepstow, Rent Roll Lordship of Chepstow, Thomas Llewis Hopkin; InvECP 70. Pembs 1544. Llewys Mathews, late prior of the Black Friars of H'west; 207. Glam 1552. Edward Llwys, esquire, (prob. Lewis y Van); Ex Pro James I, Index of Lewis, Lewes etc. includes Llewes; PRChirbury, Index of Lewis, includes Llewis.]

This equivalence has two aspects, first the aspect of interchangeability, so that it would be common practice for a man whose proper name was Llywelyn to call himself, or be called, Lewis; and later, in occasional instances, for a man whose proper name was Lewis, to call himself, or be called, Llywelyn; and second, the abandonment of Llywelyn as a traditional name and the adoption of Lewis in its place. This second aspect makes Lewis the official name and that is the reason for the wide-spread use of Lewis as surname in Wales.

Generally one is unable to determine in the

case of early examples of Lewis, Lowis, whether the name is the man's proper name or whether it is being used as a substitute for Llywelyn. In the case of the poet Lewis Glyn Cothi (fl. 1447-86), his other name was Llywelyn y Glyn (see DWB *s.n.*); Lewys Morgannwg (fl. 1520-65) was the bardic name of Llywelyn ap Rhisiart (DWB *s.n.*). One suspects that PWLMA 494 Lewis Arthur (1442) is the same person as 511, 526 Llywelyn Arthur. Apart from this the index of PWLMA has a few entries 'Lewis (or Llywelyn) . . .', although the actual text does not show up the interchangeability. The records of the chancery proceedings show the change from *Llywelyn* to *Lewis* although it is not quite certain that the official clerk is responsible for the change: InvECP 29. Mer 1538. Morice Lewes, alias ap Llewelyn of Putney. 79. Denbs 1530. Thomas ap Lewis alias Thomas ap Ll' ap Dd' goz. 106. Denbs 1537. Thomas ap Llewelyn ap David Goz, alias Thomas ap Lewis. 147. Monts. 1547. John Llewelyn alias John ap Lewys of Wendover, co. Buckingham, labourer, son and heir of John ap Lewys.

Long after the name Lewis, as christian name and as surname, had become established in Wales, the awareness of an identity with Llywelyn remained, but only amongst the cultured and knowledgeable, like the Morrises of Anglesey. Lewis Morris is often called Llewelyn Ddu or Llewelyn Ddu o Fôn; William tells his brother that his baby son's name is Lewis, 1. 79, Lewis yw enw'r etifedd yma; later 2. 100, he refers to the child as 'Llywelyn fach'. In ALMA 35 King Louis of France is called 'Llewelyn Ffreinig'.

During the scrutiny of various texts one naturally kept a look-out for early examples of Lewis or Loweys as christian name, in order to see the change over. The text in B6 of Lleyn Minister's Accounts 1350-1 has instances of Howell and Llywelyn (of uncertain spelling) but not one of Hugh or Lewis. The following suggests that one must wait until the fifteenth century to see Lewis being used: B24. Fasti Cist. Camb. 183-4 '. . . the monastic usage as a christian name of Lewis does not come until 1399, and Morgan does not appear before 1443. Another name of interest is Llywelyn, borne by six religious of Cymer, Strata Florida and Whitland, it is limited to the period 1274-1380, which saw the closing years of Prince Llywelyn's life, and was a time when his memory was probably still vivid in Welsh minds'.

Bradney has an example of Lewis, early in the fourteenth century; in the pedigree of Morgan of Llangattock Lingoed, HM i, 257, there is mention of Eurydd, daughter and heir to Lewis ap Rhys ap Rosser. And in the pedigree of Morgan (Llewelyn ab Ifor) of Llangattock in i. 254 one sees Lewis coming into the pedigree as replacement for Llywelyn. This information should be linked to Part iv, 75 Chepstow, 'St Pierre was possessed by Sir David ap Philip, which Philip was younger son of Llewelyn ab Ifor by Angharad daughter and heir of Sir Morgan ap Meredydd of Tredegar . . . His son Lewis ap Sir David is, in 1430, described as a lord of a parcel in Magor. Thomas ap Lewis the son of Lewis ap Sir David, was killed at the battle of Banbury in 1469 . . . His son was the first to adopt Lewis as a permanent surname, and in 1487 was lord of the manor of Raglan alias Denis Court in Redwick'. The pedigree of the Lewis family of St Pierre is given in p.76: summarized, the great-grandson of Llewelyn ab Ifor becomes Lewis ap David Philip: this Lewis and his son Thomas ap Lewis, and grandson William Lewis become the forebears of a great host of Lewis families.

All books of pedigrees provide the same evidence. Clark 23, Mathew of Talygarn, has an example of 'Lewis (or Llewelyn)'; the same on p.63; pp.34-5, Lewis of Rhiwperra, shows the sequence, Llewelyn → Thomas ap Llewelyn → Lewis ap Thomas. The pedigree of Lewis of Van has Llewelyn recurring until one reaches Edward Lewis (p.46) 'the first of that place and surname'. One further example, 118, Llewelyn of Rhydlafar shows the change to Lewis.

The pedigrees of JEG have similar examples: p.2 Rhosbeirio Ucha, Family name Kerver, this page shows Lewis replacing Llewelyn. P14 Chwaen Hen, Llantrisant and Llanddyfnan, Llewelyn, living 1485, his second son is Hugh Lewis. P64 Llewelyn of Presaeddfed, one of his sons is a Hugh Lewis and his descendants became the Lewises of Presaeddfed (not the same family as p.14). P.292, Llangïan in Lleyn, Margaret, d. of Hugh ap Lewis ap Howel ap

Llewelyn.

The following notes are based on the pedigrees in Dwnn:
1. 16. Krisli v. Ieuan ap *Lewis* ap Ieuan ap *Llewelyn* vychan o Abermaed. 1. 27. Gelli Aur, ... Thomas *Lewis* ab Dd ab Phe ab *Lln* ab Ivor ab *Llnn*. 1. 253. *Lewis* becoming family surname, greatgrandfather, *Llewelyn*. 1. 266. *Llewelyn*, grandsons = John and *Lewis*. 1. 272. *Lewis* ap Evan ap Evan ap *Llewelyn*. 1. 363. Pedigree, showing use of *Lewis* and *Lodwick* : *Llewelyn* – Meredith ap *Llewelyn* – *Lewis* – Maurice, *Lewis* – *Lodwick Lewis* – Maurice *Lewis* – *Lodwick Lewis* (*Maurice* probably meant to be subsitute for *Meredith*). 2. 24. Part of pedigree of Thomas Lewis 'o Dre'r Delyn' = Harpton, Rads. : Thomas ap Hyw ab Dd ab *Lewis* ab Hyfyn ab Dd ab *Llenn*. 2. 199. Footnote, Hugh (or Hugh *Lewis* as he is called) *ap Llewelyn*. 2. 291. Pedigree showing *Llewelyn* being replaced by *Lewys*. It is hardly necessary to say that records of the sixteenth century which have lists of names, e.g. the Anglesey Pleas, the Anglesey Muster Book, have many examples of Lewis, and hardly any of Llewelyn.

As the name Lewis was in use before the patronymic system was discontinued it is difficult to understand why 'ab-Lewis' did not result in a surname 'Blewis';
B7. 286. Toll Books N. Pembs 1599 Elys ap Lewis of Llanelltyd, co. Merion, (ditto 287, 288, 289); 318. Lewis ap Lewis of Egloss-erowe. B10. 84. Kemes, Pembs 16th century, Lewis ap Lewis William. PWLMA 294, 408, 417. Dafydd Llwyd ap Lewis (second half 15th century). Star CP 90. Eliza ap Lewis, als Felyn. Pontesbury 59. 1588. Johannes ap Lewis. Great Ness 23. 1625. ... John ap Lewis; 50. 1663. John Uplowis of Hopton, bur.
The following examples are exceptional: Ludlow 539. Ann Blewis. RadsSoc XIII. 22/23, 1697. Hugh Blewis, John Blewis.

There was one other substitute for Llewelyn, which came about through using Lodovicus for Lewis.

RecCa 1938. Leodovicus ap Hoell; 303. Lodouicus. Glam Cartae 1863. Lewis Thomas abbot of Morgan = 1920. Lodowicus Thomas ultimus abbas dicti nuper monasterii. PRConway 1586. Williemus Lewis fil Lodovici Owen. PRLlanbadoc

1638. Alicia, filia Lodovici Morgan. Alse Morgan, dau. of Lewis Morgan. PRLlantilio Cr. et Penrhos p.2. 1612. Blaunchia, fil' Lodovici p'ger (Footnote, 'Lewis Proger was a younger son of John ap William Proger of Wern-ddu'). p.3. lodouicus wm p'ger gen' sepultus fuit. Ex Pro James I. Caerns 52. John Ludwick. StarCP 221. Church Stoke, Lodowick Lewis. Cwtta Cyf. 3. Lodovicus ap Edward.

There is a sprinkling of Lodwick as surname in S. Wales, the Swansea and S.W. Wales TD has fifty-four entries; Cardiff and S.E. Wales has seven and three of Lodwig. The form Lotwick (one instance in the Cardiff TD) shows the 'hardening' of *d* > *t* character-istic of the dialect of Glam and Gwent. Fifty-four entries may be more than 'a sprinkling'; compare that number with nearly twenty columns of Lewis. Lodwick is not confined to S. Wales, e.g. East Flint, Holywell East; Oswestry, O. Urban, Castle W, North W, Wem Urban, Oswestry Rural, Maesbury.

Llwyd (Lloyd, Floyd etc.)

Llwyd is usually understood as the adjective 'grey', but just as *glas* may include the meanings 'blue, silver, green', *llwyd* also includes shades of brown: 'dŵr llwyd' refers to the brown waters of a river in flood, 'papur llwyd' refers to old-fashioned wrapping-paper or 'brown paper'. It is very likely that when used of younger men 'llwyd' referred to brown or mouse-coloured hair. But 'llwyd' could of course be used also to refer to the grey hair of old age, and was occasionally found in compounds with 'gwyn' (white): WM 127 (Peredur) gwr gwynllwyt, 146 y gwr llwyt. Cf. the tale of Macsen Wledic, ibid. 191, where the young boys who had joined in the campaign were become 'grey men' because it lasted so long: *y gueisson ieueinc ... yn wyr llwydon rac hyt y byassynt yn y guerescyn hwnnw*. However, in general it is likely that the adjective 'llwyd' referred to some sort of brown hair when associated with a personal name. HBr 495 is wrong in stating 'the third son was called David Llwyd, I presume, from his grey hair early in life'. By the time the pedigree in question had evolved, the adj. had long ceased to have the literal meaning 'grey'.

The surname *Llwyd* retains the radical consonant after the personal name, masc. and fem. alike, i.e. Dafydd Llwyd, Morfudd

Llwyd, because in the medieval period *llwyd* had yet another meaning, that is, 'holy', and with that connotation the adj. lenited; *v*. examples quoted in TC 115-6, especially those in which the *cynghanedd* of consonantal identity removes all doubt: Beuno lwyd o Ben y lan, GG1 xv.ll; Diwyl lon, myn Dewi lwyd, IGE² 3.20; O Dduw lan i Ddewi lwyd, ibid. 242.14. There was nothing in the 'meaning' to justify the retention of the radical, for the compounds of 'llwyd' meaning grey or brown, such as 'mynglwyd' (brown-maned) or 'penllwyd' (brown-headed), lenited, *v*. *infra*, and 'llwydwyn' (compound of grey and white 'gwyn') the reverse order of 'gwyn-llwyd', lenited, *v*. TC, 115. If the published text reproduces the MSS the following examples are mixed:
B 15, 43, AS 1406, Ior llwydwyn; Ie[uan] ap Ior llwydwyn; ibid. 47, David lwydwyn; ibid. 51, Tuder ap dd lwydwyn; ibid. 57, Ho/we/ll ap dd llwydwyn. RecCa, 253, – ap Mad' Lwytwyn.

Llwyd was sometimes used as a forename or christian name, just as *Gwyn* was e.g. Llwyt uab Kil Coet, WM 79, PKM 64, notes 247, in the third branch of the Mabinogi; and although the note casts certain doubt over the name because the Red Book version of the text has *llwydeu*, there are examples of *Llwyd* as the forename of historical persons:
B10. 83. West W. 1352. Lloid ap Kadymore.
B10. 151. Kemes Pem., Lloyd ab Ieuan ap Eynon. BBStD 214. Elloyd' ap Eynon (?).
The evidence concerning the use of the radical consonant after masc. and fem. personal names is dealt with in the introduction to GDG (xlvi-xlviii), to account for the radical consonant in the name of Morfudd Llwyd. As the usage of the med. period was to employ the mutated form of this adj. to convey the sense of holiness, the unmutated form had to be used even after a woman's name. Morfudd Llwyd (not Lwyd) had perforce to be used in order to avoid the connotation of 'holy'. (The lists of names referred to are of little value, for the editors concerned failed to appreciate this and printed 'loyt', not realising that the defective writing of the texts would not differentiate between *Llwyd* and *Loyt*). The other aspect of the discussion asks whether the use of Llwyd, having become a fixed surname, was 'carried forward' from one

generation to the next, which is evidence that Llwyd had become a fixed family name as far back as the fourteenth century. There can be little doubt that Llwyd was a fixed name and the editor gives examples of 'huiz' (= chwith) and 'goch' which confirm the view that they were becoming fixed epithets or family names. But the vast majority of names through the med. period using the patronymic system (both *ap* and *ach*) render the small number of families using fixed and unchanging epithet names such as Llwyd, Goch, Chwith, very exceptional.

There is a derivative using the suffix -yn, *llwydyn* : there are examples of *llwydyn* as a personal name, and of its use as an epithet:
B10. 94. Kemes Pem. . . . tir lloidin ('the land of Llwydyn'). AnglPleas 53. Tyddyn Lloydyn ('Llwydyn's cottage'); ELlSG 35. Tyddyn Llwydyn, Mer LSR 10. Loydin. CaernCR 36. Llwydyn ap Penmarch. 28. Ieuan ap Llwydyn [MS Loydyn]. RecCa 283. Dd ap Lloydyn. Cf. farm name in p. of Llan-gyfelach, *Tŷ-lwydyn* (for lenition of proper name, genitive case, after *tŷ*, *v*. TC 109-110). Examples of *llwydyn* as epithet; maybe as surname:
CaernCR 19. Ieuan Llwydyn [MS Loydyn]. 48. Dafydd Llwydyn [MS Lloydin]. Glam Cartae 1717. Will. Loydyn, rect. de Lamays. DLancaster 291. Kidwelly, Rice David John Lloydin; 295. Harry David Lloydin. RCA 6, Anglesey. Rice ap Lewes Lloydyn. [There must have been a derivative form in the source or original of the following:
PRBitterley 137. 1787. *Benjamin Loidan* (the same person, if the wife's name Susannah is proof, as the *Benjamin Lloyd* of 139. 1789). Wirral, Ellesmere Port Poole Ward 3, *Loyden*; Stanlow Ward ditto; Whitby Ward ditto. A further example, the name of Edward Loyden, who was M.P. from 1974 to 1979.]

The Anglo-Norman scribe would not be familiar enough with the medieval Welsh orthography to know that *ll* was used for the 'unilateral hiss' and generally used *l* for the initial *ll* and its lenited version, single *l*, except that occasionally attempts were made to show that the sound was *l* with a difference. The diphthong *ŵy* was not within the scribe's own system and the nearest was *oi*, *oy*. Therefore the version one finds oftenest is Loid, Loyd (sometimes Loyt):

B2. 150. Court Criccieth 1320. ieuan loyd; 151. Ieruod Loyd; 159. Egnon Loyt. B4. 152. Court Ardudwy 1325. Gruffudd Loit, Ieuan Loit ap Madoc.

This use of *l*, and a knowledge that adjectives generally lenite when fixed after a pers. name, have together misled textual editors into a belief that *lwyd* or *loyd* (of the English or Norman scribe) stands for the lenited form so that they have printed *Lwyd* in their modernised versions, i.e. failing to realize that *llwyd* is one of the exceptions.

AnglCourt 1346. 45. Einion Lwyd ap Dafydd. CaernCR 19. Goronwy Lwyd; 122. Ion ap Dafydd Lwyd.

Examples of orthographic devices to convey the *ll*' sound:

B13. 143. Bonds Peace 1295. *Cadugan yloyd* The *yl* obviously stands for *ll*, there being examples in the same page of *ab yleuelyn, yleward*). B13. 223. SR 1292. Eynon Thloyt. B15. 129. NW. temp Edw 1. Rees Thloyt. BBStD 214. Elloyd ap Eynon. CalInquEdw III, 661. Griffith Thloyd ap Rees.

The versions found in official papers and other records of the Tudor period and later are worth quoting because they provide the evidence that curious versions found today are in fact corruptions of *llwyd*:

RadsSoc XXIX 47. Presteigne. Hugh Alide 'My Kinsmen Richard Lide and John Lide'. XXIII. 46-7. Presteigne 1535. William Luyde, Peers Luyde. XXIV. 34. New Radnor. Thomas Llowyde ... Llowyd. WPortBooks 63. John Thllewyd of Penone, co. Glamorgan. L & P i 707. John Lloilld (for Lloid, Lloyd = Floyde, 1143 = Lloyd 3335); 2684 (23) Roger Thloyd. vol. 1. 438 (3.m.5) p.237. Maurice Flood or Ll'd, of London, alias Maurice Walshman, late of Elsyng, Norf. alias Maurice Apowell, late of – (blank) co. Oxon. yeoman. InvECP 20. Caern ... ap David Lloyed. 30. Meirion. 1547. John ap David Lloud ... of London. 38. Cards 1538. Rice ap Fludd (Floyd) of the commote of Creuddyn. 73. Pembs 1553. John Flude (H'west). 80. Denbs 1553. ... son and heir of Gryffyn Fflowede. 103. Denbs 1556. Thomas Llud of Llangwyfan. 157. John Hewes alias Lloied of Burford, co. Oxford. RCA 179, Anglesey, Davy Flodd, yeoman of guard; 301. Carnarvon, Lewis Flude (Flud in index).

Edward Lloyd (*c*.1570-1648) the Recusant, of Llwyn-y-maen, near Oswestry had his name variously spelt Ffloyd, Floed, Floud, Fludd; *v*. DWB *s.n.* John Lloyd (1480-1523) the musician, born in Caerleon, 'Bachelor of Music and a gentleman of the Royal Chapel, temp. Hy VIII', was also known as Floyd. [Cf. Dom. A. Hughes and G. Abraham (eds), *Oxford New History of Music*, iii, *Ars Nova and Renaissance 1300-1540*, London, 1960, p.331, note. The famous mass of 'O Quam Suavis' was long a mystery, and it was prefaced by a puzzle antiphon written by one '*Johannes Maris*'. Thurston Dart showed that this was John of the flood, literally, and was a pseudonym of John Fludde, Fluyd, Floyd or Lloide or Lloyd, the Caerleon composer of the courts of Henry VII, VIII, Wolsey etc. No reference is given for Thurston Dart's article.]

SHROPSHIRE REGISTERS

It is difficult to summarize the versions of the Shropshire registers. Little is gained from quoting instances merely to show initial *Fl*: examples will be included below in any case. There are entries of *Ll* or *L* varying with *Fl*- for the same person or within the same family. Whittington 20. 1695 (error for 1675), Mary w. of Eavan Floide = 22. 1694, Yeavan Loyde. Sheriffhales 26. 1628. Abigell d. of Richard and Elizabeth Llwyed alias Blockley. cf. earlier entries, e.g. 22. 1619. Lloyd; and in the burial register: 50. 1605. Margaret d. of Rycharde and Elyzabetha Floyde. 51. 1610. William Lloyd alias Blockley; 53. 1619. Sara Lloyde, alias Blockley. 36. 1647. Thomas s. of Evane and Elizabeth Flyde; 38. 1652. Evan and Elizabeth Flyde. 61. 1653. Yeavane Flyd. 55. 1624. Elizabeth w. of Richard Llued alias Blockley. 58. 1639. Richard Flued alias Blockley. 67. 1626. Richard Lloyd alias Blockley.

The versions of the diphthong -*ŵy*- show greater variety; it is usually *oi* or *oy* and there is no need to quote especially to illustrate. But many examples show attempts to transcribe 'ooee' sound, and the 'oo' sound in particular:

Shipton 7. 1551. ... filii Aliciae fludd. 30. 1665. Susan Flooyde d. of Evan Flooyde. Bitterley 79. 1732. ... Edward Flewett (the same marriage is entered again, lower down the page, with the spelling Fluet; Index has

Fluett, Fluat also; and Floyd, Floyde are indexed separately). Pontesbury 41. 1574. Elenora fflowd. Oldbury 48. 1791. Mr Manning Flewett, of Bridgnorth. Sheriff-hales, *v.* entries above, Llwyed, Flyde, Flyd, Lloud. St Chad's 5. 1617. Loulld (one entry, Richard Jeb of Tilley (as christian name). 540. 1750. Martha bastard d. of Catherine Lloud. St Chads 5. 1617. Loulld (one entry, probably following the pattern of 'would, could', etc).

PRESENT-DAY REGISTERS
(FLOYD TAKEN FOR GRANTED):
Loydd: Bl. Gwent, Tredegar Central. *Flewett*: Oswestry, Whitchurch Urban; Bromsgrove, Stoke Prior, Hagley. *Flewitt*: Runcorn, Mersey Ward 1; Chester, Chester (AA) Boughton; Knutsford, Wilmslow, Morley Ward. *Flowitt*: Wirral, Neston-Burton, Ness Ward. *Flood*: Northwich, Northwich No. 1. Castle 2; Stroud, Uley; S.Hereford, EA Bridstow; Preseli, H'west Hamlet St Thomas, H'west St Mary. *Flude*: Cheadle Hazelgrove and Bramhall, South Ward; Ch.Hulme North.
Cf. D. Tel 26.7.80, Deaths, Gladys Olive Flude, Ringmer.

Lloyd has long been the usual version of the surname in Wales, in all parts, with the *Ll* pronounced as single *l*. The use of the single L in the spelling (as in the example from Tredegar above) is rare, cf. D. Tel 29.6.77, Deaths, *Lloyd* and *Loyd* in close proximity; D. Tel 22.8.79, Births. The form *Llwyd* has not often been used in the modern period: the list of subscribers of the second edition, 1898, of the HBr has the name Mrs Llwyd, Pantglas. *Lloyd* has been deliberately changed to *Llwyd* in a number of cases in our own time.

The sixteenth century antiquary Humphrey Llwyd was the son of Robert Llwyd (or Lloyd); he also used the form *Lhuyd*. During the sixteenth century, grammarians and authors experimented with Welsh orthography and sometimes *Lh* was used for *ll'*. The great Celtic scholar, Edward Lhụyd (1660-1709), Keeper of the Ashmolean, was the son of an Edward Lloyd. The antiquary Angharad Llwyd (1779-1866) was the daughter of John Lloyd.

The form *de Lloyd* is known in Wales, e.g. David de Lloyd, one-time professor of Music at Aberystwyth. The information was given to us long ago by a fellow professor of de Lloyd's that this form in origin was 'delahoyde' and was the same name as Deloite; cf. ALMA 382 Hugh Delahoyde (the 381 of the index is incorrect) p.753; index to supplement, Hugo Delahoyde, letters 425, 426, 430.
Lodowick, Lodwick *v.* Llywelyn
Lougher, Loughor *v.* Llwchwr
Lowarch *v.* Llywarch
Loydan, Loyden *v.* Llwyd
Luc, Lucas, Luke
If the biblical *Luc* had been fully taken into the language in the early period, (i.e. borrowing from Latin) the initial would certainly have become *Ll-*; there is very little evidence on the point, and the Huw Lluccas of ADClun 225 is exceptional. A few examples collected are appended:
B13. 227 SR 1292. Sums paid at 'Bergauenny') Lewelin ap Luccas. B9. 244. Early Caern 1321-1390. Edenyfed ap Lucas. Mer LSR 47. Map Luges.
We have been conditioned by the form 'Luc' of the Welsh version of the Bible to say 'Luc' in Welsh, i.e. *l* and *k* sounds, when speaking of the third Gospel. The name has not been much used as a christian name, and when it does occur, it is in the E form *Luke*; or in the form *Lucas*.
PRConway 1731. Dorothea Wms als Luke; 1732. Dorothea Luke; 1752. Elizabeth Luke. The surname *Lucas* has been in the Gower peninsula for several generations, *v.* the Index to Clark; they were probably settlers and do not represent native nomenclature.

In modern registers, the name *Luke* occurs in Preseli, Wiston (six entries), West Flint, Ffynnongroew (nine), Trelogan; East Flint, Greenfield – Bagillt Road. The name *Lucas* also occurs in East Flint, Hawarden, Mancot and Moor, Shotton, Sandycroft. There is also the form *Pluke* in East Flint, Flint, Trelawnyd (AB), Starkey Lane; and one surmises that this is a recent application of *(a)p* to 'Luke'.
Lullow *v.* Llywelyn
Lya *v.* Lleiaf
Lyson, Lysons *v.* Lleision

M

Mab

There are examples of using *Mab/Fab* 'son' as an epithet attached to a pers. name, not as in a pedigree but as an epithet used to distinguish. The usage was not general, it looks as if it were peculiar to certain areas; and the usage being so restricted and the use of *mab* in this way being so unusual, one hesitates to believe that it is the word *mab*; and yet what else can it be? In the place-name *Llanddaniel Fab*, Anglesey, it is certain that *mab*, lenited, is used to distinguish. Reaney has early instances of *Mabb*, *Mabbs*, (*Mabbys*) as surname, 'a pet-name for Mabel'; it cannot possibly be this; and note especially that *mab* is usually in the lenited form.

Glam Cartae 2351. Margam Charters, middle of 13th century, Signature of Witness, Meurich Vap. BBStD 74. Joh'es Mab ... Johes Fab; 76, Walt Fab ... Walt'us Mab; 78. David Fab; 82. Rob'tus Fab, Joh'es Mab ... Walt Mab. Bartrum 985-1215. 117. Gruffudd Ddu ab Ieuan Fab ap Ieuan Las. 1215-1350. 267. Gruffudd Fab ap Gruffudd Gŵyr ap Cydifor. 375. Ieuan Fab. 387. Maredudd ap Gwyn ap Gruffudd Fab. 490. Hywel ab Gruffudd Fab.

One may feel reasonably certain that *Mabe* occurring in S.W. Wales represents this use of *mab*; there are eleven entries in the TD of Swansea and S.W. Wales, seven of these in Pembs; the Cardiff TD has only one. Cf. also Exch Proc Wales 356, Hereford, 8th Elizabeth, John Mabb, goldsmith of London, note the context.

Mabon (Modron)

The mythical *Mabon fab Modron* is brought into the story of Culhwch and Olwen. Dr Bromwich TYP 433-36, conveys that Mabon in origin was a Celtic deity by translating 'the youth (god) son of the mother (goddess)'.

There is a church, Llanfabon, in Mid-Glam. There is some evidence that the name was used in the early period. It occurs in the Book of Taliesin, more than once, as the name of a great warrior, pp.38, 39, *v.* CT 96 and Dr Bromwich's note.

Bartrum 985-1215, 147 has two examples; and the RecCa 78 has 'David ap Mabon', the index shows three instances as first name.

There does not seem to be evidence that it continued in use in Wales through the med period down to the early modern period. It became well-known in the modern period as the eisteddfodic name of William Abraham (1842-1922), MP and first president of the SW Miners' Federation.

Dr Bromwich sees good reason for associating the cult of Mabon with the Scottish border country and mentions two place-names that seem to preserve the name, the village of Lochmaben in Dumfriesshire and the megalith known as the Clochmabenstane near Gretna. The surname 'Maben' is found today in Wrekin, Wellington, Park-East.

Locations of *Mabon*: Stroud, Kingswood, Wotton-under-Edge; Stalybridge and Hyde, Longendale, Hollingworth; Cheadle, Hazelgrove and Bramhall, East Ward 1; Carlisle, Staidans.

One has to ask whether the former usage in Wales was sufficient to explain the presence of these examples or whether one should suggest that they have come from another direction. The following is no doubt a version of *Mabon*: PRLudlow 728. *Mawbone*.

There seems to be a surname representing *Modron*; cf. Glam Cartae, Index, *Ric. Maderun*; Wirral, Hoylake, Grange and Newton Ward 2, *Maddrann*.

The name *Madrin*, *Madryn*, found as a surname, e.g. in Ex Pro James I, Index, came from the 'estate' surname of the Madryn family in Lleyn, Caernarvonshire: *v.* Introduction, place-names.

Machen

Machen is a village in S.W. Gwent. HM i. Skenfrith 26, examples of *Machen* as surname. In ibid. iii 283, Llanddewi Fach, Bradney gives 'Names of Incumbents . . . 1858, John Edward Jones, M.A., Jesus College, Oxford, son of Daniel Jones of Cardiff, clk, assumed the additional surname of Machen'. Footnote: 'The son of the Rev. John Edward-Jones, Machen is well known as an author as Arthur Machen'. This information and the knowledge that Llanddewi Fach near Caerleon is in Gwent lead one to a mistaken inference. 'In fact the author was born plain Arthur Jones and it was his clergyman father who added his wife's Scottish family-name Machen . . . His mother was Janet Robina daughter of Captain Robert Machen, R.N., a Scot whose mother, however, was of Welsh stock', D.P.M. Michael, *Arthur Machen*, pp.1-2. Welsh speakers, innocently unaware of this, are naturally inclined to pronounce the name as if it were Welsh, just as if it were the same as the name of the village.

An example of surname *Machen* occurs in Cheadle, Gatley Ward 2; but one cannot tell what the source of this is.

Madog

In the early native texts one expects to see the form *Madawc*, e.g. H. p.5, in the title of the poem *madawc m. maredut*; in the text, p.16, line 7, *madawc*. This changes to *Madog* although the final consonant in many examples is written *c* or *k*, just as *Caradawc* changes to *Caradog*, often written *Cradoc, Cradock*. The continued use of *c* in native Welsh texts is a survival from earlier orthography, but it is normal for E. scribes to use *c* or *k* because final *g* in Welsh strikes an English ear as *c* or *k*, and *vice-versa*: e.g. place-names *Defynnog* written *Devynock, Llangadog, Llangattock*; *Meurug* > E *Meyrick*; *E. billhook* > W *bilwg*. Therefore Welsh *Madog* became *Madoc, Maddock* in E contexts: with the *'s* added, this became *Maddocks, Maddox*.

B1. 264. NW 1304. De Madok Thloyt; ibid. De eodem Uadok. B13. 143. Bonds Peace 1295. Tuderus ab Madoc. B13. 217. SR 1292. Madauc ap Kediuor; 222. Ririth ab Madoc, Madoc ap Griffri (cf. 217. *Meydoc ap*

Gorgeneu; on the same page, *Creidoc*, obviously for 'Cradoc'; the form is *Madoc, maddoc* or *madauc* elsewhere in the text).

The following are unusual spellings: CatAncDeeds V. 12144, Hereford, Madouch and Milo sons of Wronou son of Retherech. DLancaster (LpCaldicot 1613) 149. terras Johannis Modoche = 154 . . . Madok.

The combination of *p* and *m* in 'ap Madawc' etc. produces *Amhadawc, Amhredydd, v.* WG 184; Rice Merrick's name written in Welsh is *Amheurug, v.* index of TLlM. The following may be added to the example given in WG 184: ML 1. 251. Llewelyn Amhadog, (the 'Llew Amhadwy' of the index is incorrect). InvECP 80. Denbs 1533. David, Howell and Mores Hamhaddocke; 83. Denbs 1536. John ap Damhadocke and Griffith ap John ap Damhadoke; 85. Denbs 1543. David ap Madoke (Hamhaddok).

The following variants occur in the Shropshire registers:

Ford 6. 1621. John Madokey. 24. 1712. Charles Maddox. (Note: the name *Dax* occurs, e.g. p.31; can there be a connexion?) Clunbury 57. 1666. Anne Maddaux. Chelmarsh 122, 123. 1787. Richard and Mary Mattox (Index includes with Maddocks). Clive 8. 1709. William Maddax = 9. 1709. William Maddox.

These forms are still found in present-day registers:

City of Hereford, Bartonsham, Maddox; Islwyn, Pontllanfraith East, ditto. Islwyn, Pontllanfraith East, Maddax, Penllwyn, ditto.

In certain border dialects the vowel of the second syllable became *i*:

Maddick, S. Gloucs, Winterbourne, Macclesfield, Bollington East 2, West. *Maddicks*, Macclesfield, Congleton North 2; Newport, Alway 3; West Flint, Gwernymynydd. *Maddix*, S. Gloucs, Winterbourne.

The change to *i* in the final syllable is also seen in *Dimmick, Bantick*, Macclesfield, Congleton West 2.

There is also a form *Maddy*, fairly common in the border counties: it may be derived from some form of *Madog*; the forms *Madyn* and *Baddy* will be dealt with below. Here are a few locations of Maddy:

Hereford, City; S. Hereford, Eaton Bishop, Cusop, Michaelchurch, Crasswall, Michaelchurch Eskley; Leominster, Bromyard, Middleton-on-the-Hill; West Gloucs, Dymock, Tidenham; Bl. Gwent, Tredegar, Georgetown; Monmouth, Llanddewi Sgyrrid.

The hypocoristic form or forms of *Madog* are problematic. We do not know of any area where there is a pet form in actual use today with an awareness of its connexion with *Madog*, the reason probably being that *Madog* has not been in continuous use except to a limited extent, that is, as a popular boy's name. There are quite a number of forms which may in origin be pet versions of Madog. *Mato, Madyn (Medyn), Matw, Matws, Madow-gyn, Bady, Bato* (these forms with *t* are almost invariably Matto, Mattw, Mattws, Batty, in early records); it is possible that the form *Maddy* quoted above should be added. There is the possibility that one of these forms stands for *Matthew* which in some dialects (West Glam for instance) is pronounced *Matho*. [The name Matthew (Mathew, Mathews) is very common in East Glam, there are several entries in PRLlantrithyd; occasionally it is written Matho, e.g. 3. 1604. Christian Matho the d. of Thomas Matho, 4, 1609. John Matho tayler; 4. 1611, Mathew the son of Wm Matho; Alic the daughter of Matho ffrancis.] The form *Mattws* looks like *Matthews*, but the date and context make that unlikely, and in any case there is a hypo-coristic suffix -*ws*. Unfortunately one does not find examples which quite firmly make them '*alias* Madog', but it is fairly certain that *Mato, Madyn, Matw, Matws, Madowgyn* belong to *Madog*. Although not an 'alias' there is one piece of evidence which links *Bady* with *Madog*, the statement in CaernCR 124 (in translation) 'amerced . . . because he did not sue Madog called Bady for debt'. There is a similar statement on p.131 with no mention of 'Madog': 'John Bron amerced 3d because he did not sue Bady for debt'; and on pp.141, 151, there is a 'Madog Bady'. Ifor Williams in B5.41 mentions *y Badi* and calls it 'a nickname the same as y Guto (for Gruffudd), y Bedo (for Meredudd), and it remains in the place-name Allt y Badi, in Llangollen . . . I am not sure as to its origin but I suggest it is a nickname for Madyn, Madog', and the next sentence invites readers to give their opinion. Melville Richards refers to the matter in B18. 180 in a

note on *Allt y Badi* and provides evidence from the seventeenth century that people named 'Baddy' lived in the district, there is nothing to substantiate Ifor Williams's conjecture that it was a pet form of Madyn, Madog.

There are examples of *Bado, Bato, Baty* below, taken from Bartrum's pedigrees, but the usual form is *Badi* or *Bady*. Because of the presence in early periods of the pers. name *Ade, Ady*, one naturally thinks of the pos-sibility of *ab-Ady*, and of suggesting that the def. art. sometimes preceding *Badi* is the vowel of *ab*. A strong objection to this is the use of *(y) Badi* as a forename at a time when one would not expect *Bevan* or *Bowen* or *Powel* as a forename.

To turn to forms such as *Matto, Bato, Baty*, the provection giving *t* for *d*, should not present a difficulty for the pattern of *Guto* would be a sufficient explanation. And the interchange of *m* and *b* is not difficult to under-stand, for it is seen in *Bedo, Bedyn* for *Maredudd*, and there are many words which show this interchange, *bawd* and *modfedd* ('thumb' and 'inch'), *morddwyd/borddwyd* 'thigh' etc.

The various forms are set out below:

Madowgyn: CaernCR. 99. Dafydd ab M. *Madyn*: B5. 146. CaernLSR, Madyn hagr; 147. Angharat filia madyn; 148. jevan ap madyn; B6. 360. NW 1326. Rees ap Madyn Esspyn. B10. 168. AnglRent 16c, dros dir madyn tusw. RecCa, Index, Madyn, ten entries; 289, 291. Madyn Kalche, 84. Madyn Troyne. CaernCR 46. Madyn ap Cuhelyn; 134. Madyn Hedde. There is no example of *Madyn* in the index of Bartrum 1215-1350, or in the index of 1350-1415, to follow pages and pages of Madog; but there is one example of Metyn in 1350-1415, p.699; this *Metyn* appears as if it was the 'complementary' form of *Mato*. In BYale one finds *Madyn* and *Medyn* 86, Madyn ap Madoc, 132, Madyn le Pulter, 74, Medyn ap Cadogan. Attention has already been drawn to the point made in CD 41 that the pers. names *Cadno* and *Madyn* were transferred through a process of personific-ation occurring in natural speech to be common nouns meaning 'fox', *v.* above p. 62.

Mato: B15. 43. AS 1406. Matto ap Meurig; Matto ap Ie(uan) ap Philip, Matto ap Je(uan) ap Ken; 44. William ap heilyn ddu . . . Matto filius eius. AnglPleas 7. Thomas ap David ap

Jevan ap Matto. Note: cf. 8. David ap Griffith ap Matto, late of Trevor, co. Anglesea: ? Matto or Mathe; the name *Matheo* occurs on p.16, Robert ap David ap Matheo; the name also occurs in the AnglSubm 1406, B15. 49. Matheu ap Konws. RecCa, Index, three examples. CaernCR. 112. Mattow ddu; 115, 136, 166. Matto ap Conyn. JEG 17. Matto; father's name Madog. InvECP 99. Denbs 1551. Matto ap Tedre.

Matws, Matw:B15. 45. AS 1406. Mattws ap dd lloghwyn. 46. Mattw Tew; 49. Mattw ddu ... Matto Gwydd. Cf. ML 1. 217. W to R, Mae'r Fadws; 1.463. W to R, *dacw'r Fadws hwnnw* yn yr Iwerddon. Compiler of index states 'cf Madog'; there is nothing in the context to help; the mutation of the masc. personal name is an instance of William Morris's whimsicality.

Badi, Madi, Bato, Batty: B2. 253. Brec Llandov. 13th century. Waltero Bady. BBStD 78. Ph'us Bady. B23. 338. Mawddwy Court 1415. Daicws ap y Badi; Lleuqu verch y Badi. Bartrum 1215-1350, 208. Badi, four examples ('See also Madog'; there is no example in the long list of Madog that proves Badi = Madog). 1350-1415, 519. Badi, ten examples ('see also Madog'. One example has Madog in brackets, this means Madog occurs in one of the sources, but does not necessarily prove equivalence). 705. Nicholas ap y Badi. 763. Dafydd Goch ap Badi ap Madog. 804. ... y Badi Cethin ap Mwstwr, Corwen. 827. Badi o'r Rhuddallt ap Madog. 783. Llywelyn ap Ieuan Madi. 1215-1350. 444. Gwyn ap Bado. 820. Bato ap Madog ap Gruffudd (cf. CatAncDeeds VI. *c.* 6318, Henry VI. Batto ap Madoc ap Gruffith). 826. Lleucu f. Bato ap Madog. InvECP 140. Monts. 1538. Hugh Batty. MLSW 192. Willelmo Baty.

The following must be a variant of Bady: RCA 81. Bromfield, John David ap Evan ap Badyw.

SHROPSHIRE REGISTERS

Oswestry 219. 1600. John ap Richard Bady. Ratlinghope 8, 10. Bady (Beady). Alberbury 152, 153, 155. Badie, Baddie. Worthen, Index, 1618. John Bady Mathews, bur. (indexed as if *alias*) Many other entries under Bady, Badey, Beady.

The DWB has an art. on Thomas Baddy, a religious writer who died in 1729; there is a quotation in which he is called 'Mr Thomas Baddie of Wrexham'; his brother Owen Baddy was a schoolmaster in Wrexham. The author of the article, the editor R.T. Jenkins, states 'It is said that Baddy is a colloquial form of Madog'.

The possibility should not be excluded, that the name found in Wales and in the border counties goes back to an English source, and that because of its form, it was attracted and became attached to Madog.

RadsSoc XLIII. 84. Assessment 1293. Willielmus Badde; XX11. 43. Court Rolls, Presteigne/Norton, Roger Badde. ELS Cumberland, 6th Edw III. Kirkbride p.26, Ranulf Badde.

Maddran *v.* Mabon

Madryn *v.* Introd. Place-names

Madwyn, Medwin *v.* Maldwyn

Madyn *v.* Madog

Maelog

This name is included in the place-name *Llanfaelog*, Anglesey; and with the prefix *Ty-* in *Llandyfaelog*, Carms and Brecs. It appears to form part of the place-name *Mynydd Garthmaelwg* near Llantrisant, Glam. It obviously is the same name as the OBret *Mailoc*, and is derived from British Maglacos, LHEB 464. *Maelog* was not at any time in general use; Bartrum 985-1215, 152 has one example: Glam Cartae, Index has a few entries of *Meyloc, Mailoc, Maeloc, Mayloc*, and Clark 539 has the pedigree of Maelog of 'Lystalybont' [sic] a small manor between Cardiff and Llandaff; the name in the case of some members of the family is *Mayloc* or *Maeloc*, and one member is named Ralph. (17 Edward II. m. Gwirvil, d. of Llewelyn, and had William and Roger).

The following example of the name was picked up:

Maylock, Ralph, proctor of the Abbey of Lyre, *Lancastrian Kings and Lollard Knights* (K.B. McFarlane, Oxford 1972) p.192.

Maelor

Two commotes in medieval Powys were called Maelor Gymraeg and Maelor Saesneg. The examples of surnames in the E border counties, derived from *Maelor*, are spelt *Maylor, Maelor*. It is remotely possible that the personal name Meilyr could be concealed in some of these, but it would be more reasonable because of the location, to regard them as forms of Maelor, given originally to persons as labels of their place of origin when they came as strangers to a new place.

Maylour: InvECP 79. Denbs 1553. Richard ap Griffith Maylour. *Maylor*: Wirral, Stanlow Ward 2, Hoylake – Greasby Ward 1, Neston, Little Neston 1, 2, Neston – East Ward, Wirral Gayton Ward, Haswall, Pensby. *Maelor*: Knutsford, Wilmslow, Fulshaw Ward 2; Wirral, Ellesmere Port, Poole Wards 1, 2, 3, Grange 2, Sutton Ward 3, Whitby Ward.

Maesmor

Maesmor is a compound (improper in formation)< maes-mawr, 'great field'. There is a Maes-mawr (loosely combined) in Llandinam, Monts; *Maesmor* is in Tywyn, Merioneth: it is a typical example of the name of the residence being adopted as surname: *v.* JEG 220, John Maesmor of Maesmor, p.244 Maesmor pedigree.

Rec Denb Lp 137. Common burgesses in 1671. Maysmor of Maysmor (John Maesmor, gent). PRSannan 1682. Jane Maesmor.

PRESENT-DAY REGISTERS
City of Chester, Newton Ward Part 3, Maysmor; Trinity Ward 2, Maysmoor.

Magor

Magor is an anglicised version of W. *magwyr*, from L *maceria*. As it merely means 'wall', one might expect to find it in place-names fairly often; but the only *Magor* that is well-known is the village and district in S.E. Gwent.

B24. 186. Fasti Cist. Camb. Richard Magor. Present-day examples:
Stroud, Hardwicke; City of Hereford, Bartonsham; Torfaen, Cwmbrân – Northville, Cwmbrân – Fairwater/Henllys; Caernarvon, Pwllhelli – North.

Main, Mayne, Vain, Vayne

Main 'narrow, thin' was used far more as an epithet after a pers. name than the adj. normally used for 'thin', namely *tenau*. It was the rule to use the lenited form after masc. and fem. pers. names. Examples of the unlenited form are found in the early modern period and in the Shropshire registers; this is prob. due to conscious restoration, for which there would be a strong motive in this case since 'Vain', spelt or pronounced as in English was not an attractive name. In the standard orthography of early med. Welsh one expects to see *mein, fein, vein*.

B15. 48. AS 1406. dd vain; 52. gron ap Je(uan) vain. B24. 187. Fasti Cist. Camb. William Vayn; 262. David Veyn. ADClun 114. David ap Griffith Veyn. CatAncDeeds VI. C 7893. Monts. 1585. John ap Gruffydd ap David Vain. cf. 7894. 1858. Gruffydd ap Vain – obviously 'David' is missing. Ex Pro James I. 93. Cards, Humfrey ap Griffith ap Llin Vain. 98. Mefenydd, Jevain Vaine. Star CP 5. Flints, Robert Mayne. HBr 337. Ped. of Gunter family '. . . Margaret m. Gwilym Vain or the slender'. HM iv, 71. Mathern, List of Vicars, Philip Veyn, in 1535.

The examples from the Shropshire registers are mixed, some have the lenited form, others the radical:

Clunbury 58. 1667. John Vaines (?) editor's query. 67. 1678. John Vain; 74. 1695. Thomas Vain; 81. 1704. Anna Vaine. Alberbury 46. 1612. Catherina Gough Vayne (?) editor's query. 87. 1624. Gwena verch Roger als Vayne. Ludlow 210. 1558. Agnes Main. 1008. 1780. Ann d. of William Main and Christiana = 1023. 1784. Hannah d. of William Mayne and Christiana; 1028. 1785. ditto. = 1202. 1779. William Main and Christiana Draket Jones (signs, Christiana Draycott Mayne late Jones).

Main is still found in the border counties and occasionally in Wales:
S. Hereford, Eaton Bishop; BrRads, Builth; Monmouth, Abergavenny Castle and Priory; West Flints. Caerwys; East Flints, Flint – Coleshill; S. Pembs St Mary's 'D' Llanion 1.

Mainwaring, Mandry

Although the 'Mannering' pronounciation is heard amongst people who have been taught that it is the correct way, generally the pronunciation in a Welsh or bilingual context is 'phonetic', i.e. 'Main-waring'. However the colloquial pronunciation in some areas such as Swansea valley is *Mandry* – obviously -*nr*- becoming -*ndr*-, as in 'Hendry'. An example of *Mandry* occurs in S. Pembs, Monkton, Pembroke West; there are two entries in the Swansea and S.W. Wales TD, one in Cardigan, the other in Pontyberem; and one entry in Cardiff and S.E. Wales, in Treharris; D. Tel 9.5.79, Deaths, no address, W. Mail 28.5.84, Deaths, Edward Mandry Evans, Llangynwyd.

Mâl *v.* Melinydd
Mandry *v.* Mainwaring

Maredudd, Meredith, Bedo, Bedyn

The OW forms are *Morgetiud, Margetiud, v.*
LHEB 346; the final element 'iudd', found in
other names such as *Gruffudd, Bleiddudd*,
became *udd* as a noun meaning 'lord'. The
forms found in native Welsh writing of early
poetry is *Maredud* standing for *Maredudd*. In
Welsh the accent is on the penult, and this
leads at times to the elision of the vowel of the
first syllable, to give 'Mredudd':
B15. 43. AS 1406. Mredyth ap Je(uan) ap
Cradog; other examples 46, 54; and this form
abbreviated, 53, Deicws ap Mredd grydd.

In texts written by Anglo-Norman scribes the
vowel of the first syllable is generally *e*, and the
final cons. is generally *th*.
B13. 143. Bonds Peace 1283. Maredud grach;
B15. 45. AS 1406. Bedyn ap Maredudd. B13.
225. SR 1292. Mereduth fil' Hwitelou. B10.
72. Crown Lands West W. 1352. Meredith ap
Kenwric ap Choel; 74. Meredith ap Madoc
Leia.

The name is frequently disguised in the
records written by non-Welsh scribes and
takes the form *Mereduc*. There was another
name, *Moreiddig*, e.g. B2. 151. Criccieth
Court 1320. Adam ap Meredic . . . Adam ap
Moredic. Confusion of these two names
might be part of the reason, but the general
use of 'Mereduc' owes more to its suitability
for taking Latin case-endings:
B14. 306. Accts temp. Edw I. Mereduco filio
Griffini. B9. 52. de terra Lewelini filii Mered-
uci = 69. Lewelini ap Mereduth. B1. 263.
1304. De Mereduco ap Lewelin; 264. De
Wyn ap Mereduc. 265. De Mereduco ap
Madok. B13. 143. Bonds Peace, Maredud
grach (First Bond, 1283), ibid. Griffin ab
mereduc (Second). B13. 220. SR 1292.
mereduc ab Kedyuor. B26. 81. Welsh Roll.
Edw I. David Vyol [sic] ab Yerward ab
Merduk. BBStD 168. in manu M'educi ap
Gourwared. CAP 438. 1318 Anglesey.
Mareduk ap David. Glam Cartae 525. Howel
Amereduk. RecCa (as a rule the abbreviation
M'ed is used); 209. Mereducus ap Edeneuet
Gam. ('Moreiddig' is in the forms Moredik,
6; Moriddik, 4; Morithik, 1.)

Maredudd/Meredith is liable to confusion with
other names. In the dialect of Dyfed, final *dd* is
almost invariably lost: CRHaverford 44
Meredy Jordan is a simple example of this. With
the accent on the penult, *Meredith* could

become '*Redith* in colloquial speech, and if one
can rely on the text and the editing, the following appears to be an example:
InvECP 78. Denbs 1529. John ap Meredyth
(Redith) Lloyd. (We take it that these two
versions are used in the case papers.)

One hesitates because in the following
example 'Reddith' is not a version of Mered-
ith but of Rhiryd, often through dissimilation
Rhiddyd, or with metathesis Rhidydd; the
Middleton family of Chirk Castle have per-
petuated the name of Rhiryd Flaidd: ibid 142.
Monts 1538. Robert ap Reddith alias
Middilton.

There are also examples in the chancery
papers of equating Meredith with Merrick,
Meyrick, Moryce, presumably on the basis of
the 'Mer', although it is possible that Maurice
was adopted as an approximation:
InvECP 139. Monts 1533. John Moryce, son
and heir of Meredith ap John. ibid. Hoell ap
Meryk alias Meredith, gentleman. 145.
Maurice Thomas son and heir of Thomas ap
Meredith. 164. John Meredyth ap Richard
alias Moryce, son of Richard ap Howell.

If 'Redith were preceded by *ab* one would
expect 'Bredith', since it is *R* not *Rh*; on the
other hand analogy could make it 'Predith'. If
Redith stood for *Rhiryd*, it would decidedly be
Predith. But then there is another possibility,
that Predith is a version of *prydydd* 'poet'. The
editor of the Subsidy Roll 1292 in B13. 212
makes the following point: 'Cadwgan Predith
and Eynon Predith were bards of Glascwm
and Elfael, unless, indeed, their father was a
Meredith'; the names occur on p.221, and
one may add 217, Yuan ap Gronnou ap
Predith; 218. Cadugan ap Predet. We would
not expect *ab* in the form *b* or *p* in 1292, nor to
find a colloquial form of *Maredudd*, since the
text has Mereduth and Mereduc, *v.* above. In
the first example of the following, prydydd is
used as an epithet; in the second, it is the name
'Rhiddyd', the variant text showing -*r*-; B15.
54. AS 1406. Je(uan) lloyd brydydd; Je(uan)
ap Preded Voel, text B, prered voel.

The following appear to show that Pridie etc.
is a form of Pridith:
WPortBooks 35. Richard Pridie . . . Pryddie
. . . Priddie. 132. Rice Priditt of Dale. 314.
Phillip Pridith (Tenbie – Manorbeire).

SHROPSHIRE REGISTERS
Hanwood 20. 1602. Margareta Mredith; 21.

1605, ... Thome Mredith. Tasley 1751. Medereth (? misreading); the same family in 1754 = Meredith. cf. 32. 1791. Maredith. More 64. 1748. Sarah Meredeath. Clunbury 37. 1641. Merideth. Cleobury Mortimer 31. 1624. Meredite = 38. 1637. Meredithe (cf. 35. 1625. Griffite, 37. 1627. John Smite). Diddlesbury 6. 1586. Philipe Maredyth. Onibury 21. 1609. Merddith ap Evan; 25. 1615. Miredith ap David. Norbury 5. 1579. Merydethe (surname). Norton-in-Hales 44. 1672. Johannes f. Johannis Remedy, alias Meredith. Wrockwardine 37. 1663. Meriddeth Marpale. Hodnet 46. 1685. Elizabeth w. to Thomas Remedith. The version used by Anglo-Norman scribes, *Mereduc-* (*v.* above p.160), survives in the eighteenth century as a christian name: Westbury 153. 1716. Mereducius, s. of Mereducius Thomas and Mary, bap.

The following are quoted at this point because, judging by appearance they seem to be from Meredith: Chirbury 2. 1629. Johannis Rydeath (placed with Rerrid etc. in index). Ludlow 5. 1569. Anne Apredith; 330. 1630. John Pridethe. Shrewsbury St Mary's 3. 1585. Margaret Preaddethe.

In spite of appearance there is stronger reason for believing that the above are versions of Rhiryd, or Rhiryd having undergone changes, for the equivalence is actually seen within the same family.

No present-day examples of Meredith are being quoted: the name is still well-known in Wales and elsewhere. There is a remarkable survival of the medieval 'manuscript' version *Mereduc-*, found surviving above as a christian name in the eighteenth century in the PRWestbury, date 1716, Mereducius: the following is found today in Wrexham, Cefn Mawr, Cefn Ward, Meredyk. The corruption Merredy is found in Leominster, East Nor.

HYPOCORISTIC, BEDO (BELLOW, BEDDOE, BEDDOES ETC) BEDYN

The hypocoristic form of Maredudd is Bedo; if the difference in form appears to be very wide one should call to mind that these forms have their origins in baby-talk, and that the consonants *b* and *m* are liable to interchange. The genealogy in Clark 118 has 'Bedo alias Meredith' twice. The pedigree of Surdwal of Aberyscir in Theophilus Jones, HBr 270 includes 'Meredith alias Bedo bwch or Bedo bach'; cf. also RadsSoc IV. 3. Will 1608, Meredith als Bedogoch, Jevan. In Bartrum 1350-1415, in spite of the cross-reference under Bedo, 'see also Maredudd', definite proof of the identity is difficult to establish, but there are two good examples: the example under Bedo of Bedo ap Ieuan Gethin ab Einion Llwyd occurs also as Maredudd, and is listed under Maredudd; and also, 695 Maredudd ap John Goch ap Gruffudd Llwyd = 520 Bedo ap John Goch ap Gruffudd Llwyd.

Examples in early records: Bartrum 1215-1350, 208 has three examples: 1350-1415, twenty-eight.

The following few specimens show it as a christian name, as second or third name in a pedigree, and later as a surname: B11. 73. Broniarth Court 1429, Bedo ap Ieuan ap Ieuan Gethin. ADClun 207. R. ap Bedo Due; 208. John ap Bedo; 225. David Bedo. RadsSoc XXIV. 31, Will, Old Radnor 1540, Rees Abedo ap Rees. Star CP 11. Monts H.VII. Bedo ap Thomas; 12. Rads H.VII Howel Abedo; 43. Carms Eliz. Dd Bedo of Llandybie; John Dd Bedo. InvECP 38. Cards 1538. Rice ap Hoell Beddo. 54. Carms 1537. Thomas ap Bedo. 169. Brecs 1547. John Abedo. 179. Rads 1538. Howell Obedo.

With the def. art.: JEG 321. 16c. Howel ap y Bedo ap Deio. Bartrum 1350-1415. 823. Y Bedo ap Tudur ap Dafydd Goch. InvECP 147. Monts 1547. David ap y Bedo.

L'Estrange Ewen 125 includes the form *Peddowe* in the list of surnames occurring in PRO papers. This is the only example we have come across. It might of course be a clerical error in the first place; on the other hand, *Bedo* after *ab* ought to produce 'Pedo', and there must be a reason why 'Pedo' does not occur oftener than the single example mentioned; the use of the def. art., probably, is the reason, or at least plays a part in the explanation.

Examples of Bedos, Bedowes are found in Ex Pro James I, 244, 269, 279.

Judging by the number of examples, the form with the suffix *-yn*, Bedyn, must be a derivative from Bedo, to make a pair like Guto, Gutyn:

B15. 48. AS 1406. Bedyn ap Maredudd; 49. Bedyn person llan babo; 50. Bedyn ap Eign. ap ho-ll. ML 1. 128, 131, 142 (W to R), y Bedyn.

SHROPSHIRE REGISTERS

There are examples without the addition of s; and of the final vowel becoming -a, -ah, v. p.34. If one took a count, most would have the 's added, and this version tends to have the neutral vowel, Beddus etc. The form Bedhouse is almost certainly an attempt to provide an etymology that gives meaning. It should be mentioned that the fairly common place-name in Wales, Betws, is derived from OE bede-hus, 'house of prayer'; and GPC actually quotes one example of bethouse under Betws. There is one instance of the surname Betthouse in the Ludlow register, 979. 1773, Ann d. of James Betthouse; but this piece of evidence loses its value when placed against the many examples in the register, one and two generations earlier, of Bettoe, Betoe, Beatoe:

435. 1665. Elinor Bettoe; 436. 1665. Edward Bettoe = 441. 1668. Betoe. 531. 1687. Henry Bettoe; 655. 1709. Hen. Betoe. Similar entries 674. 1712; 678. 1713; 682. 1714; 694. 1716. 787. 1730. Edward Beatoe; 838. 1739.

An 's can be added to Bettoe to give Bettoes, which is afterwards changed to Betthouse; one cannot do the reverse and make Betthouse to be the origin of Bettoe. What really calls for an explanation is the consonant t, Bettoe (for the d of Bedo). This is probably due to the 'harden-ing' of g, b, d into c, p, t, which is a regular feature of the dialects of Glamorgan, Gwent, and Brecon, without altering the quality of the vowel: e.g. bedw, 'birch' becomes bētw, mis medi 'month of September' becomes 'mis mēti'. [The dialect of Rads, or parts of Rads must have had this 'hardening', e.g. the parish of Llandegley (Llandeglau) is written 'of Llandecley', in a New Radnor Will 1548, RadsSoc XXV. 30.] A man named Bedo moving from Breconshire to Shropshire could quite conceivably pronounce his name as Bēto. Shipton 24. Carolus and Jane Beddo. Hopton Castle 18. 1636. Joan Bedhouse = the Jone Bedowes of 7, 8. Edgton 12. 1764. Hill Beddus; 14. 1772. Obed Beddose = 26. 1772. Obed Beddoes (Index has Beddos and Beddoe) Stanton Lacy, 28. Johane ap

Beddowe. Bitterley 7. 1667. Willihelmi Beado (Index, Beddo also). Cleobury Mortimer, Index, variant forms include Beddus. Pontesbury 362. 1760. Beddah = 365. 1761 Beddow. (Index, Beddow, Bedda, Bedow, Bedowe). Westbury 364. 1763. Mary Beddass. (Index has the usual variant forms). Diddlesbury 50. 1744. Samll Beddas. 211. 1782. George s. of George Beddoes bap. June 30; George Beddies, infant, bur. Aug. 6. Burford 145. 1729. Edward Biddow; 146. Richard and Martha Biddow (Index puts this with Beddow etc). Neen Savage 125. 1776. Nicholas Bedo = 131. 1781. Nicolas Bedos = 135. 1788. Nicolas Baddoes = 140. 1794. Nicolas Beddoes. Wistanstow 41. 1692. Beddas; 45. 1695; 46. 1696. Bedas. Al-brighton 89. 1699. Sarah Bedhouse. 95. 1707. William Bedhouse and Margaret. 97. 1709. William Beddowes and M. 99. 1712. William Bedhouse and M. Donington 24. 1614. Jone d. of Davy Abeddowe. Selattyn 48. 1600. John ap Llewelyn Dab bedow of Llansilins p. [Footnote, David ab Bedow, i.e. Bede; this explanation should be ignored.] 48. 1601. . . . ap llewelyn Dab bedo. 49. 1601. . . . d. of John ap llewelyn David bedow.

PRESENT-DAY REGISTERS

The forms Beddoe, Beddow, Beddoes, Beddowes are so common in Shropshire and Herefordshire, plotting them can be dis-pensed with. Examples of the original Bedo are found occasionally, e.g. BrRadnor, Llan-badarn Fawr; Newport Central; and one example was picked up in Leominster, Holmer, of Bedding which could be a form of Bedyn.

Amongst the examples above from the Shropshire registers, there is an example from the Diddlesbury register of Beddies = Beddoes. A good number of examples of Beddis are found towards the southern border and one may surmise that this kind of change to the final vowel belongs to the speech of Gloucestershire. The examples found in Gwent have probably come from the neigh-bouring English county.

S. Gloucs, Awre 1, Aylburton, Cinderford 1. W. Gloucs, Cinderford (several), Littledean – Longhope, Lydney (several). Ruspidge (several), Westbury-on-Severn, West Dean (several), Broadwell. Torfaen, Cwmbrân – Fairwater and Henllys. Islwyn, Crumlin

High Level, Trinant 2. South Pembs, St Mary's 'D', Llanion 2.

Maldwyn, Madwyn, Bodwyn

Maldwyn is the W version of Baldwin; the town of Montgomery is Trefaldwyn, and the former county was Sir Drefaldwyn.

There is an English pronunciation of Baldwin which, to Welsh ears, has no *l* sound, and this probably is the explanation of Madwyn.

B10. 173. AnglRent 16th century dros dir Madwyn. LpOswestry 159. Madwyn (forename occurring several times in the text). InvECP 260. ... heirs of Dackyn ap Gittyn ap Madwyn, of Camberwell, co. Surrey, (context, Marches). PRConway 1597. Hugo filius Davidi Bodwen.

Mantach

This obsolete adj. means 'toothless'; it was used as an epithet after a personal name; it was generally lenited, but the documents of Clun have a number of examples of retaining the radical. There are examples of the adj. being used, after the def. art., with no pers. name, as if it were a nickname.

B13. 228. SR 1292. Meuric vantach. B15. 59. AS 1406. Dd ap gruffith vantach. PWLMA 535. ... Maredudd ap Cadwgan Fantach. B10. 70. West W. 1352. Ieuan ap Eignon Vantach. ADClun 34. guttyn vancach [sic]; 35. griff' mancach [sic]; 36. Guttyn Mantach; 37. Guttyn Mantath [sic]; 98. Tudur Mantagh; RadsSoc XLIII. 80. 1293. Joh(ann)es Manthac. RecCa 115. Bleddyn ap y mantach. B10. 167. AnglRent 16th century, dros dir gwas Lewys long ar mantach yn amloch. Reaney has an example of *Vantage, Vanntage*; one cannot refrain from suggesting that the W. epithet may be the origin.

Marychurch *v.* Introd. Place-names

Mato, Matws *v.* Madog

Maur, Maure *v.* Mawr

Mawer *v.* Mawr

Mawr

Mawr 'big' is also used in the sense of 'great', i.e. *Llywelyn Fawr*, prince Llywelyn ab Iorwerth. When used after a pers. name it generally lenites, but there are many quite valid examples, early and modern, of using the radical form, and it is very difficult to find a consistent rule for the two usages. It was proposed in TC 115-118 that when it was used, originally, to distinguish between two

men with the same name, it was proper to use the lenited form, but it could also be attached to a man's name to describe his size or greatness without reference to another, and that this construction used the radical form; these two usages could not be kept apart; but although the usage of the lenited adj. prevailed, examples of the other usage remained in certain dialects. Rhodri King of Gwynedd was Rhodri Mawr; D.J. Williams has a character called *Morgan Mowr*, StTG 84, and these represent the early usage of the radical and its survival in the Carmarthenshire dialect. Therefore the examples below of *mawr* need not be regarded as wrong; on the other hand it is quite possible that in a bilingual context, *mawr* might be entered in a record instead of *Vawr*, as a restoration.

These few examples of *Vawr* will suffice:

B6. 355, NW 1326. gweirvyl uxor madoci vawr. B2. 151. Criccieth Court 1320. Itel Vaur. B4. 156. Ardudwy Court 1325. Ieuan Vawr; 160. Grono Gogh ap Ririd Vawr. BBStD 48. Moris Vaur; 66. Joh'es Vaur; 114. Nest Vaur. MLSW 95. Griffith Vawr. RadsSoc XXVI. 25, Will, 'Prestene' 1544, Hew Vaur; cf. 31. 1550 Margaret Vaure of Norton; XXXIV. 40, Will 1590, John Vaure. Bartrum 1215-1350. 540. Dafydd ap Ieuan Tew Fawr ap Jenkin.

Examples of mawr, (sometimes alongside examples of *vawr*):

B15. 44. AS 1406. Deia Mawr; 46. Jor ap dd ddu fawr; 49. Tegwared vawr; 50. Twtta Mawr; 53. Deikws vawr. CatAncDeeds VI. C.5075, 21 Henry VII. (Glam Pendoylwyn Aradur) David ap Jenkyn ap Gr(ono) Vawr ... William Llywelyn alias William Maur. InvECP 200. Glam. 1538. Thomas ap Howel, alias Thomas Maur. Star CP 4. Denbs Edmd More (possibly = Mawr). 8. Glam (Llandaff) Thos Levy, als Mawr. MLSW 55. Willelmi More (poss. = *mawr*).

The following may be the E *mower*:

HM iv, 98. Portskewet, Tenants of Barony 1569. Rice Mowere. Cf. CRHaverford 238. Mr. Vawer; 44. Jenkyn Vawer (149. index must be at fault, 196. *v.* index for other entries and variants, Vaure, Vaur. PRHopton Castle 7. 1593. *Henricus Maure*. Shrewsbury St Mary's, Index, under *Goures*, there are two very early entries 'alias Vaure'; there are a few early examples also under *Vaure, Vawre*.

T.E. Morris, 117 gives the following versions: Maher, Mawer, Mayer, Mayers, Mairs, Moir, More, Moore. No textual evidence is provided and most of these forms are surmises.

Mayler *v.* Meilyr

Maysmore *v.* Introd. Place-names

Mayvot *v.* Meifod

Meddyg

Meddyg 'doctor' is found attached to a pers. name, sometimes with radical cons., at other times with lenition.

B13. 228. SR 1292. David Medik. B15. 44. AS 12406. Eigian ap dd vethig; 55. Jollo vethig; 57. Holl ap Je(uan) ap Mad feddig. B7. 292. Toll Books N. Pembs, Ieuan lloid Methig. PROswestry 19. 1560. M'gret vz Dd Lloyd veddyg. InvECP 112. Flints 1515. . . . Geoffrey ap Edward ap Howell Vythig, Elyn ap Howell Vethike. PR Ll. Crossenny et Penrhos 1623, p.8, Catherina fil. Caroli harry, fethig;

Without personal name:

BBStD 224. Gruff ap Medic. ADClun 100. Ieuan loyt ap Methig.

The surname *Meddick* found occasionally in present-day registers must be a version of this noun epithet; examples were noted in the following locations:

Cheadle, Heald Green Ward 1; Denbigh, Llandrillo-yn-Rhos, Eirias Ward; Monmouth, Abergav. Cantref and Grofield.

Meifod

The *Gazetteer* names only one Meifod, a parish and village in Monts; WATU lists two other places or 'townships' in Denbs.

CAP 486. Lewes Mayvot, parson of the church of Llanvechein, 1407-8. CatAncDeeds V. A 12556, Denbs, Flint, Henry Mivod; ibid 111. C 3481 Merion. Robert Meyvot (Edward IV), 3484. Robert Meyvote. RCA 156. Ellis Myvod. Cwtta Cyf. 100. 1623. Harry Myvod gent (father of Thomas Myvod); 130. 1629. John Myvod. PRPontesbury 229. 1697. Edwardus Myvert; 234. 1700. Euardi Meivers; 238, 1702. Edward Myvert, paup. sep.; Anna f. Eduardi and Joanne Myvart; 287. 1727. Myvart; 382. 1769. Mivort.

Meilyr

The composition of this name is shown clearly in the constructed Brythonic form *Maglorix*, the *maglo-* of *Maelgwn, Maelog* etc. and the *-rix*

of *rhi*, 'king, lord', and forms such as *Tudri*; but with only the *-r* remaining of the second element, as in *Tudur*. The first of the Gogynfeirdd poets was named *Meilyr*. It was in general use in the med. period:

B13. 143. Bonds peace 1295. Melirus ab Heylin. B13. 218. SR 1292. Meiler du; Kedyuor ab Meiller; 219. Meiler ab Tancard; 220. Gronow ab Miler; 220. Yuan ab Maillier; 221. Meilerus parvus; Richard fil' Meileri; Mailler ab Worenou. B15. 45. AS 1406. Ednyvet ap Meilir ap y Kethin; 52. Deikws veilir (unusual construction). Mer LSR 11. Meilor ap Ada; 32. Morur(an) ap Meiller. BBStD 18. Ph'us Meyler; 46. Meylor ap Ph', Ieuan ap Ll ap Meyler. 84. Gurgen' ap Myler, 86. Gurgen' ap Meyler. LpOswestry 40. Gavell Mylir; 147. Cecilie Meiler. ADClun 35. Ieuan Meillur; 81. Willim ap Meiler. CatAncDeeds 111. D 401. Pembs Henry V. Joan Meyler, daughter and heiress of David Meyler, of Meyleriston. [D 934, Hereford, Henry IV. David Meyler . . . in Rosmarket . . . The Hereford location must be wrong; cf. the following entry: D 1101. Pembs Henry V. . . . Richard . . . son of John Meyler of Rosmarket.] Star CP 132. 135. Pembs Robert Meyler. 209. Pembs Ricd Megler (misreading). WPortBooks 87. John Meyler (? Milford), 121. John Mayler (Milford). JEG p.1 Trefeilir, Trefdraeth (Anglesey). CRHaverford, Index, Twelve entries under Meyler, with variants Meyllor, Mayler, Maylor, Meyller, Maylar, Meylard, Meyler.

The name fell into disuse and only a few scattered examples were picked up in present-day electoral registers:

Meyler: Runcorn, Appleton North Ward; Crewe South 4; BrRadnor, Llangorse; South Pembs, St Issells South; Cardigan, Aberystwyth Div. 1. Ward 1. Mayler: E. Vale, N. Central Willowtown.

Like Gwyther, Gwion, Wogan, the name survived mainly in the English-speaking parts of Pembrokeshire, and the examples to be found in Dyfed and West Glamorgan have probably come from S. Pembs.

Melinydd, Mâl

One expects to find this occupational epithet, 'miller', attached to the pers. name:

B13; 227. SR 1292. Seysil Melinyt. B15. 47. AS 1406. Jockyn Vylinydd; 50. Dd ap

Blethyn velinidd; 53. Matto velinidd. AnglPleas 28. Hoell ap Llewelin ap Jevan Velenyth (*Velenyth* occurs three times). Mer LSR 29. Gurg(enu) Melinnith. CaernQSR 65. Gwalchmai ap Ieuan ap David Velenyth of Dwygyfylchi, miller. 79. John Ieuan Felinydd; 195. Grono ap Llywelyn alias Grono Velynydd. PRSelattyn 23. 1571. Thomas ap David, velinidd. 25. 1573. David ap Jeuan alias velinith.

NOTE CONCERNING 'MÂL, VÂL'

The following examples, although scanty, show that there used to be an epithet *Mal* fixed after the pers. name; one example showing the lenited form *Val*:

Mer LSR 77. Madoco ap Gryffyd Mal (footnote, no solution); 78. Madoco ab Iarward mal; 81. Wyon Mal. BBStD 218. Joh'is Val.

Mâl as a noun is used in the abstract sense, the process of grinding; in a concrete sense, the mill itself; cf. the place-name Ffrwd-fâl. There are strong objections, but this may be the word in the above examples. It is also possible that the lenited form *Val* is to be seen in the following:

CRHaverford 39 date 1592. John Valle, tailor; 214. 1591. John Vall; 232. 1596. John Vale; 207. 1589. Thomas Vale; 209. 1588.

Examples of *Vale* as surname also occur in the Shropshire registers, e.g. Bromfield 93, 94, 138.

Melyn

Melyn 'yellow', fem. *melen*, probably, as an epithet attached to a pers. name, referred to the colour of the hair; there is a compound adj. with *pen* 'head', *penfelyn*. The noun meaning 'mill' is *melin*, but the examples below of 'melin' are really mis-spellings of *melyn*. The adj. is usually used in its lenited form, *Felyn*, *Velyn*, but there are far too many examples of the unlenited form to believe that they are mistakes. Usage must have varied from place to place; on the other hand it is probable that in a bilingual context the use of 'Melyn' unlenited is due at times to 'restoration'. If the published text properly represents the original, the following appears to be an example of deliberately restoring the radical for the two instances refer to the same person:

CaernQSR 58. Gruffydd ap Rhys ap Hywel alias Gutyn Felyn; 217. Gutyn ap Rhys ap Hywel alias Gutyn Melyn.

Specimen examples of the lenited form:

B13. 216. SR 1292. David ap Wronu Velyn; [219. John Melym, At Penbroc]. 226. Iuan Velyn; 227. Wronu ap Ririd velyn. RadsSoc XLIII. 80. Assess 1293, Alicia Velin. LpOswestry 87, Ros David Velyn (89. Ros David Welyn). 144. Extenta 1393. Agnes filia Ricardi Velyn. . . . Ierwerth Velyn. Star CP 90. Merioneth. Eliza ap Lewis, als Felyn.

Examples of the unlenited form:

BBStD 154. Rob'tus Says melyn; 156. Ieuan, Seysmelyn; 182. Joh'es Melyn. Glam Cartae 1738. Dav. Melyn prepos. Swaynesey; 2018. Rees Melyn; 1889. Ric. Melyn. B2. 253. Charters Brec. Llandov. Ievano Melin. MLSW 132. Walter Melyn.

The Shropshire registers have many forms: Selattyn 20. 1582. . . . ap Thomas ap William Velyn. Oswestry 89. 1582. Sina Velen.

Here the fem. form is correctly used; the examples one finds later of *Mellen* are not really the fem. form, but examples of the discolouration of the vowel in the final syllable in English speech:

More, Index, several Mellings, e.g. 45. 1701. James Mellings. Clunbury 162. 1790. William Mellings; 183. 1812. Rebecca Mellins.

The above summarize the various examples of the registers, and only specimen examples (and locations) can be given of the very large numbers found in present-day registers.

In Cheadle, Gatley Ward 3 there is a family named *Vellins* which certainly appears to be a version of the lenited form. *Mellin*: Stalybridge & Hyde, Dukinfield East, Central; Bl. Gwent, Tredegar – Georgetown; West Flint, St Asaph; S. Pembs, St Mary's 'D' Llanion (2). *Mellins*: Bl. Gwent, Tredegar, Georgetown. *Mellen*: Wirral, Ellesmere Port, Central Ward 1; Westminster Ward 2; Newport, Alexandra 2, Bettws 3; Shaftesbury 2. 4; St Julian's 5. *Mellens*: Monmouth, Caldicot East (V). *Melling*: Shrewsbury, Meole Brace; Chester, Newton Ward Part 3. *Mellings*: Shrewsbury, Kingsland; Bromsgrove N.E.; Wrekin, Newport.

Mendus, Mends

The name *Mendus*, although not numerous, is associated with Pembs. It occurs in the records of Haverfordwest, CRHaverford 192. Mendous, one entry, no forename, date 1582; also, WPortBooks 222. John Mendus (?

Milford); B7. 284. Toll Books, N. Pembs Fairs 1599. Gr' Mendus of Capell Mihangell. Examples in present-day registers: S. Pembs, St Mary Pembroke East; Preseli, Fishguard N.W., N.E. Dinas, Newport. S. Gloucs, Filton, Charborough. *Mends*: S. Pembs, Jeffreyston, St Mary 'D' Llanion (1), St Mary 'A' Pennar, Pembroke; Preseli, H'west, Hamlet St Thomas, Neyland.

The explanation of the French *Mendès* in Dauzat is probably applicable: 'n. d.'Israélites venus du Portugal vers le XVIes'.

Meredith *v.* Maredudd

Merfyn, Mervyn

This occurs in the name of the ninth century King of Gwynedd, *Merfyn Frych* 'Merfyn the Freckled'. For some curious reason it did not become a favoured name in the med. period; it does not show up as a first name in any of the three indices of Bartrum's Genealogies. The explanation may be that Merfyn had come, according to bardic tradition, from the Isle of Man; HW 323; i.e. the name may not have been native Welsh or British. Merfyn Frych's grandson was given the name Merfyn fab Rhodri. The RecCa 257 records the name Rodri ap Mervyn.

The name seems to have survived in the Hereford – Brecon area: CatAncDeeds VI. C.4841. Hereford, John Mervin, 4830. Nicholas Mervin. C.5122. repeated; C.5172. repeated. Mervin (Nicholas, Roger, John, Sibyl) in C.5677, C.5954, 6416, 6515, 6516, all located in Hereford, 6515 being 21 Edward III. Cf. also MLSW 147, Hugh Mervyn, Brecon 1525; RCA 199. Brecon, Hugh Mervyn. There is no example in HBr.

The name has been used in S. Wales in the twentieth century as a boy's christian name. A quick glance at the names in the list of Guild of Graduates under any well-known surname, Davies, Evans, Griffiths, Jones, will show several named Merfin or Mervyn, and sometimes Merfina. The following examples place it at least as far back as 1890-1900: D. Tel/W. Mail, 31.10.79, Deaths, Myrfyn Thomas . . . (Rhiwbina, Cardiff) aged 90; D. Tel, 9.11.79, Deaths, Mervyn Gurney Talbot Rice, (Abingdon), aged 80.

Merrick *v.* Meurig

Methig *v.* Meddyg

Meurig, Meurug, Meyrick, Merrick, Morris, Morys

Welsh *Meurig* is derived from L. *Mauricius*, WG 106, which is itself a variant of *Mauritius*, Withycombe 95. Generally, when *i* and *u*, or *u* (eu) and *i*, follow each other, the first vowel (or diphthong) yields to the second and takes over its quality. The reverse may happen occasionally, so that *Meurig* may become *Meurug*, WG 112. This must be regarded as exceptional for the examples in most cases show *-ig, ic*. In English *Mauricius* became *Maurice, Morris*. The form *Morys* is in use quite early in Welsh contexts and it does appear that the identity of *Meuric* and *Moryce* (Morys) was known. This would not be due to a knowledge of the derivation but to the search for 'approximations' and the overt appearance of *Meuric* and *Maurice* was a sufficient basis. Examples were given above of *Moryce* being used in official records as a variant of Meredith. Under *Madog*, *v.* p.156, it was shown that *ap* + *M* could become *Amhadawc, Amhredydd*, and that this can affect *Meurig*, for the name of Rees Merrick appears as *Amheurug*; cf. also ML 1. 220, 285, Gwilym Amhorys, and examples below of *David Amorice, Griffith Amorice*. In the examples below *Meurig* and *Morys* etc. are not kept separate:

B13. 215. SR 1292. Alexander Ammoris, Meurich ap Yeuan, Madoc ap Meirich; 216. Meurik ap Keynolf, Thelwelinus ap Meweric; Yereuarth ap Meurich; B15. 42. AS 1406. Morus ap Prioryn; 54. Morus ap de Crwnn; 60. Meurik ap dd Hakney, [cf. 55. Mattw ap Je(uan) Bodfeurik; 61. Je(uan) ap Je(uan) Bodveurig = place-name]. RecCa, Index, several entries Meur, Meur^c, Meurik; cf. 16. Gogan ap Meuris. ADClun 100. Meuric ap David ap Cadwalader; 208. Muric ap Ieuan; 211. Huw ap Muric Bach. Ex Pro James I. Index, Meiricke, Merick, Merrick, Mericke. RadsSoc VI. 11. 1545. Jevn ap Rys ap Meryck . . . in Llanbaddern Vynyth. InvECP 3. Angl 1529. Morice ap Inghan. 77. Denbs temp Henry V. Maurice Pentelyn; ibid Lowes Moreys. 111. Flints 1515. David Amorice, son and heir of Griffith Amorice Tona. . . . lands . . . late of Morice Tona. 138. Monts 1518. David Myryk (living in Kent) son of Meryk ap Ineon. 215. Monm. temp Henry V. Muric and Ieuan ap David ap

Thomas. 220. Monm 1529. son of ...
Gryffyth ap Jehan Myryke. 234. Monm
1547. Margaret verch Meroke. 241. Monm
1556. Meryke Grefyth. 248. Marches 1504.
Maurice Kiffyn, of Oswestry.

SHROPSHIRE REGISTERS

Shipton 14. 1587. david ap morize ap
Griffiths. Claverley 9. 1575. Catherine Ap-
morres. Kinlet 6. 1658. Mairick (surname,
occurring three times). Stokesay 26. 1634.
Sara fa Richardi Mearicke. Wem 93. 1590.
Thomas Meiriche.

PRESENT-DAY REGISTERS

Meyrick: Ludlow, town, Broseley, Willey,
Madeley: Wrekin, High Ercall. *Merrick*:
Ludlow, Bishops Castle, Ludlow town,
Willey, Madeley, Much Wenlock. *Merricks*:
Wrekin, High Ercall. *Myrick*: Newport,
Caerleon.

Meyler *v.* Meilyr
Meyrick *v.* Meurig
Meyvot *v.* Meifod
Modron *v.* Mabon
Moel

Moel, 'bare, bald' is also found in the compound *penfoel*; *moel* is also used as a noun, for
bare hilltop, and in this sense is often found in
place-names. It is usually used in the lenited
form as an epithet attached to a pers. name,
but there are examples of the unlenited form.
There are texts which have lenited and
unlenited in close proximity:
BBStD 218. Th Voyl ... Ieuan Moyll; 284.
David Moil, next para. David Voyl. B10. 74
West W. 1352. Ieuan Moyl ap Eynon Goche;
76. Ieuan Voil. B13. 306. NW. temp Edw I.
Theawayret Voyl; cf. CalAncCorr 4. 119
Tegwared Foel, (1292). B13. 216. SR 1292.
Eynon Voil, Creddac ap hwetheleu voil. B26.
80. Fragment Roll 1294. Lewelinum Voyl ab
Yginon ab Lewelin; 81. David Vyol [sic] ab
Yerward. B3. 151. Personnel Criccieth Castle
1295. Zereward Voyl.
Examples of the unlenited form:
BBStD 268. Meur^c Moyl. B15. 45. AS 1406
dd ap Deia Moel.
One can only repeat suggestions already
made concerning other epithets which have
the two usages, that although the lenited form
was normal construction, there was an urge to
use the unlenited, especially if the epithet was
becoming a fixed surname. It is strange to see
Moel, unlenited, after a woman's name, e.g.

Bartrum 1350-1415, 813 Gwladus Moel f.
Hywel ap Dafydd Llwyd. Was it a surname as
Llwyd was in the case of Morfudd Llwyd? *v.*
p.151-2. Another use of *moel* would have
helped to establish the radical form, namely,
using *moel*, without a personal name, as a
nickname, after the def. art.:
B6. 357. NW 1326. Adaf ap y moel. PWLMA
454. Y Moel ap Gruffydd Leia. B10. 166.
AnglRent 16th century, dros dir y moel
chwyth [cf. ibid. dros dir y Ko(ch) moyl; 170.
dros dir y Koch moyll; CaernHS 26. Bolde
Rental, 45. Y Coch Moel].
From the two usages, two surnames were
produced, although it is not easy to decide
when it is proper to regard the epithet as
surname. Cf. B13. 92. Some records of a 16th
century estate, pp.92-3. 'the Pembrokeshire
family of the Voyles who were direct
descendants of Dafydd Foel ap Owen who
lived in 1320 at Trewern in the parish of
Nevern'.
This evidence suggests that *Foel/Voyle* in the
fourteenth century passed on as a family label
to Dafydd's descendants.
The name Voyle is typical of
Pembrokeshire:
WPortBooks 82. John Voyle, Haverfordwest:
87. David Voyle, H'west. CRHaverford,
Index, Voell, Voyell, Voyle, several entries
with these variants, but no entry of Moyle.
Cf. examples of Moyle:
AnglPleas 11. John Moyle. InvECP 88.
Denbs 1538. Robert Moyle of the commot of
Denbigh. 88. Denbs 1543. Thomas Moyle.
StarCP 17. Flints. Ricd Moyle als Day.

SHROPSHIRE REGISTERS

The Shropshire registers have *Moyle* and
Voyle, with varying spellings including *Foile*;
and of *Moyles*.
Wolstaston 16. 1725. Joan Moil. Sibdon
Carwood 13. 1744. John Moyl. Clunbury
113. 1741. Nicholas Moyle = 114. 1741.
Moyl. Eaton under Heywood, Index, variant
forms including Moyal. Wem 490. 1729.
Thomas s. of John Moyles. Stanton Lacy 10.
1576. Edmonde Voile; 12. 1580. ... Voyle.
Sidbury 6, 10, 11, 12, 13, 14, 18. Voile,
Voyle. The forms Voile and Foile occur
c. 1600; mark especially 6. 1598. Nicolas
Voyle; 6. 1600. Voile = 1603, 7. 1606.
Nicolas Foile, cf. 10. 1664. Nicolas s. of
Richard Voyle, buried; 7. 1604. Richard

Foile.

Moyle: Shrewsbury, Welsh Ward, Frankwell and The Mount; City of Glouc, Linden Ward p.4. *Moyles*: S. Gloucs, Winterbourne; Preseli, H'west, St Thomas; S. Pembs, Kilgetty. *Voyle*: Stroud, Dursley; Newport, Malpas 3; Shaftesbury 5; S. Pembs, Slebech, Robeston Wathen, Tenby, Penally, New Moat. [Richards's Dictionary, having given the meanings including Eidion moel, 'an ox that hath no horns', states 'Hence MOYLE, the name of a family in Cornwall, who bear in their coat of arms an ox wanting horns'. Cf. the following reference: CatAncDeeds IV. A9997 John Moyle (Cornwall).]

There is a derivative using the suffix *-yn*, corresponding to *cochyn* and *llwydyn*, BBStD 150 Will's Moylyn; Bartrum 300-985, 62 Bledrus y Moelyn ab Aelan; RecCa 104. dd' ap Moelyn. The dictionary of Thomas Richards has 'Moelyn, a person having a bald head', and quotes 2 Kings ii, 23, Dôs i fynu, moelyn (Go up, thou bald-head).

Moel made a number of compounds with other adjectives denoting physical appearance, B23. 166, Arundel Charters, Chirk; Einion ap y Moelfrych (with *brych* 'speckled, spotted'); JEG 223. Evan Voelfrych; BYale 108 David ap Ken Voylgam (with *cam* 'bent, bandy' ? cross-eyed'), B23. 341. Mawddwy Court, David ap Moel Gloff – this probably was 'Moelgloff' ('bald and lame'). The compound one finds oftenest is Moelwyn 'bald and white': this could be an epithet following a personal name and it could also be used as a personal name itself:

B15. 50 and 60. AS 1406. Kynddel ap Ho(we)ll Voelwyn. CaernCR100, 102. Dafydd Moelwyn. B13. 221. SR 1292. Yuan ab Moelwyne. B10. 70. West W. 1352. Mohlwyn ap DavidGelymor . . . eidem Moilwyn. CaernHS 8. 14. Early Hist. Conway, Moylewyn faber. PWLMA 492. Ieuan Llwyd ap Moelwyn.

The surnames *Moelan* and *Moelon* were found in electoral registers.

Moelan: S. Gloucs, Berkeley; Wrexham, Cefn 2, Acrefair and Penybryn; Newport, Betws 1. *Moelon*: BrRadnor, Llanelly – Darren Felen; Newport, Shaftesbury 5.

Moesen *v.* Moses

Moia *v.* Mwyaf

Moil *v.* Moel

Morgan

The OW form was *Morcant*, the *-nt* becomes *-nn-* in *Morgannwg*, 'Glamorgan'. The name became Morgan in the med period, just as *ariant* changed to *arian*, but there are examples, relatively late, of Morgant, e.g. RecCa Index, Morgant, two instances, Morgan, one; BYale, text in several places retains final *-t*: 58, Morgant, twice; 106, Morgant ap Madoc; 116, Morgant ap Hona [sic]. Cf. the following versions: LpOswestry 155. Ricardum ap Morgraunt ap plleu'; ibid. Morgraunt ap Ieuan ap plleu'; 166. Four sons named . . . of . . . ap Morgraunt. InvECP 229. Monm 1538. Rowland Morgayne; 242. Thomas Morgaine, Knight. It has already been noted that *ap + m* may become *am*-; cf. MLSW 132. Morgan ap Ieuan Amorgan.

High Ercall 458. 1759. Jane Morgon. Astley 3. 1703. . . . d. of Peter Morgin; ditto 4. 1704; 4. 1705; 5. 1707. 7. 1713. William Morgon; 7. 1715. William Morgin. Wem 530. 1745. Thomas Morgin; 646. 1749. Thomas s. of Morgin Vaughan = 676. 1775. Morgan Vaughan.

The following explanation of the name *Seaborn* is interesting – not of its origin, of course, but of its application in a special case: H Asaph 109-110. Committee of Approvers during the Puritan period, includes the name of (8) William Seaborn (Morgan), seaborn being a name intended to translate 'Morgan', the translation based on the mistaken view that Morgan means 'môr-gen-i' (stem of *geni* 'to be born', being *gan*-). Thomas Richards, *Puritan Movement in Wales*, 105-6 is very sceptical and implies that this 'translation' is a surmise; Thomas Richards believes that the approver's real name was Seaborn and that there is very little evidence for identifying him with a William Morgan of the period. Similarly the first syllable, taken to be *môr* 'sea', accounts for the use of the name *Pelagius*: here are actual examples:

PRLlanfihangel Ystern Llewern, p.13, 1723, Jacobus, filius Morgani, alias Pelagij, Paske. 14. 1724. Susanna, filia Pelagij, alias Morgani Paske. 15. 1726. Laetitia, filia Morgani Paske; Anna uxor Morgani Paske.

A myth had developed that the great heretic Pelagius was a Welshman named Morgan. According to Theophilus Evans, DPO[2] 219, he came from Gwynedd, and was named Morgan because he was born near the sea ('ar lann y môr'), but changed his name to Pelagius when he settled in Italy; the running headlines from 219 to 237 are 'Heresi Morgan'; also on p.85. Art. 9 of the Thirty-Nine Articles in the Welsh Book of Common Prayer, the Pelagians are called 'y Morganiaid'.

In certain dialects a colloquial form *Mocyn* is used; cf. CaernCR. 80 *Mokkyn*. Also, RadsSoc VII. 13, Presteigne 1559, Mekin ap Dd; should this be 'Mokin'?

Morrice, Morris *v.* Meurig

Moses, Moesen, Moy

In med W the biblical Moses is always *Moesen*. In the translation of the Bible, *Moses* was used and we have become accustomed to this version. Like other O.T. names Moses was used as a christian name in the protestant period (i.e. not necessarily puritan and non-conformist) and this occurred early enough to make *Moses* a surname. What is surprising is to find occasional instances of *Moesen* surviving as surname, e.g. Denbigh, Llangollen Rural, Trevor Isa; Wrexham, Cefn 2.

Quite apart from Jewish families named *Moss*, it is the case that 'Moss' is well-known in Wales as the colloquial form of Moses or Mostyn as christian name. It is found as a surname in certain parts of Wales, e.g. Wrexham, Bersham, North Ward, Broughton, Cefn Ward, Gwersyllt, West Ward – fairly common in all these places; can it be the colloquial form of Moses in these cases?

The name Moses has been changed to *Moy* in the case of a well-known family in Swansea. The son of D.L. Moses, a literary figure of some importance in Brynamman at the end of the nineteenth century, became a prominent solicitor in Swansea; the mother's name was Evans and the son adopted the name Moy Evans, and his children have kept this name.

In North Wales, *Moi* is a common pet-form for the christian name Morris, e.g. *John Moi*, the popular appellation for Sir John Morris-Jones.

Mostyn

Pennant in his *Tours*, 1, pp.17-18 (*Rhys* edition) states that 'Thomas ap Richard ap

Howell ap Jevan Vychan, Lord of Mostyn, and his brother Piers, founder of the family of Trelacre (= Talacre) were the first who abridged their name', and then proceeds to tell the story of the occasion when Rowland Lee, president of the Council of the Marches, sat at one of the courts on a Welsh case and became so exasperated by all the *aps* in the names of the jury that he directed 'that they should assume their last name, or that of their residence . . .'. This story of the origin (with none of Pennant's *aps*) is given in *The Mostyns of Mostyn* pp.82-3; it is right to say that the authors use the words 'by a decree, *so it is said*, of Bishop Rowland Lee'. If the surmise of the authors is correct there is a MS source not later than 1596, for this kind of explanation. The note derived from the MS source gives the year of the great session, the occasion of the decree, as 1539.

Mostyn became the surname of several members of the family in succeeding generations. [*v.* A.D.Carr 'The Making of the Mostyns', Cymm Trans 1979. Thos[s] and Piers were the first to adopt Mostyn as a surname. Tho[s] appears first as Thomas Mostyn *alias* Thomas ap Richard ap Hywel in a deed of 1544 (U.C.N.W. Mostyn MS 1016).] The sixth baronet Sir Thomas Mostyn who died in 1831 was unmarried and the baronetcy lapsed. The estates passed to Sir Edward Pryce Lloyd who became the first Lord Mostyn in 1831: his son, the second Lord Mostyn, added Mostyn to the Lloyd of the surname.

Mostyn as a place is a sizeable town, so that in the case of the various examples of Mostyn as surname, it is difficult to decide whether they possess the name as descendants of the original Mostyn families, or whether they acquired the name as label of their place of origin.

PRAlberbury 313. 1705. George Mostin, of Criggion, labr. bur. 323. 1708. Ellinor Mostin, of Criggion, bur. PRSheriffhales 2. 1559. Walter son of Thomas and John Mostinn.

PRESENT-DAY REGISTERS

Mostyn : Cheadle, Hazelgrove and Bramhall, South Ward 2; Cheadle Hulme North; Denbigh, Ruthin, Llandyrnog – Llanbedr. Monmouth, Abergavenny – Hereford Rd.

Moy *v.* Moses

Moya *v.* Mwyaf
Moyle(s) *v.* Moel
Mwyaf
This is the superlative of *mawr* 'big'. It is used as an epithet to distinguish when father and son have the same name, as an alternative to using *Fychan* or *Leiaf* for the son (or grandson): PWLMA 449, 453, Ieuan Llwyd ap Ieuan Fwyaf (= B10. 143. West W. 1352. Ieuan Loid ap Ieuan Veyaf, misreading); not all examples will show the function of differentiating. The final *-f* tends to disappear and *oy* for *wy* in medieval Welsh is not unusual. Some examples keep the radical consonant, although in most cases the adj. is lenited: B13. 225. SR 1292. Yuan Moya. BBStD 204. David ap Ieuan Voyaf; 260. Cadogan Voiaf. ADClun 204. Ieuan Voya. MLSW 109. Ieuan ap David Voya . . . Griffith Moya.
If *Leia* could become *Ley, v.* p.145, one could expect *Voy* or *Moy* theoretically. We have found one family named *Moye* in Torfaen, Croesyceiliog, but we have no means of proving what this represents, but *v. Moses (Moesen, Moy)* above.

Mwyndeg
This compound adjective should be compared with *glandeg, v.* p.100. *Mwyn* meant originally 'of gentle birth and upbringing', and later 'gentle, tender, sweet-natured'.

There are examples of using *mwyn* as an epithet: Lp Oswestry 164. Willelmum ap Ieuan moyn. PRSelattyn 42. 1595. Lewis ap Richard, alias mwyn (footnote, i.e. 'kind, gentle'). 66. 1614. Elen Lewis, mwyn (– the editor's unnecessary comma).

Examples of Mwyndeg:
Bartrum 1215-1350, 539. Dafydd ap Ieuan Fwyndeg; 629. Ieuan Fwyndeg ap Ieuan ap Dafydd. Cwtta Cyf. 86. 1621. . . . sonne of Edd ap Hugh ap Rees Moyndeg gent deceased; cf. RCA 405. Flints, Hugh ap Rees Mondege; in another reference, H. ap R. Moindege, H. ap R. Moyndege. Cf. H Asaph VI. 371. Parish of Cilcain, Vicars . . . 1521 Mondek (Mwyndeg) Sir Geffrey (addition in brackets is the editor's).
In *Parochialia* Part 1, 79-83 Kilken (i.e. Cilcain), Lhuyd's informant sends a list of unusual names in use in the parish, p.81; the list includes, Mwyndeg Hughes Llongwr sydh yn Ll. Hasaph . . . Mwyndeg Edwards, mae tri ne bedwar o'r enw yn Llan Hasa. ('A sailor who lives in Llanasa; . . . there are three or four of this name in Llanasa').
Cf. also examples of *Mwynwyn*: JEG 265, Margareth Moyn Wynn (mid-eighteenth century), in pedigree and in footnote, this probably ought to be a joined compound.
Myvod, Myvert *v.* Meifod

N

Nanney *v.* Introd. Place-names
Narberth, Narbett
(*v.* also Introd. Place-names) The original Welsh is *Arberth*, on the border line of the division between Welsh-speaking and English-speaking parts of Pembrokeshire; the *n* is either the *n* of the Welsh preposition *yn* 'in', or from the English preposition.
Cf. variant spellings, Narburth, e.g. CR Haverford 82; Narbeth, ibid 135. WPortBooks 56. David Narberth (Milford); 89. David Nerbert. B7. 289. Toll Books N. Pembs. John Narberth of Bygelly, co. Pemb. Swansea TD has eleven entries of *Narbett*. Bl. Gwent, Beaufort, Narbett; Monmouth, Chepstow, St Mary's, Caldicott. Bl. Gwent, Nantybwch Sirhowy (Dukestown) Narbed. Cf. W. Mail 6.9.80 In Memoriam, Narbed, Rhymney (in Welsh).
Nash: *v.* Introd. Place-names

Nest
This fem. pers. name was popular in the med. period, found in the form of *Nest* and latinized as *Nesta*; both forms have been brought back into use, more especially the -*a* version.
B2. 254. Brecon – Llandov. Neest Scolayke. B5. 144. CaernSubsidy 1293. nesta filia madoc da; 146. nesta uxor adgyn. PRCaerwent 1573. Neast, dau. of William Wiriet. PRLl. Crossenny 5. 1616. Nestia ux' Joh'is Hughe Gwynedd.
In the position of mother in a pedigree, i.e. after *ap* or filius:
B13. 225. SR 1292. William fil' Nest. RadsSoc XL111. 82. Assessment 1293. Thom(as) fil(ius) Nest. AnglPleas 22. Angharat verch Llewelin ap Nest verch Tanno verch Jevon Gogh.
As surname:
PRHopton Wafers 30. Wm Nest; 90. Marg. Nest. PRWestbury 4. 1639. Richard ap Owen and Margery Nest. CRHaverford 143, date 1653. Will[iam] Neast.
The TD of S. Herts and Middlesex has one example of *Nest*, (Rickmansworth).
Nevett, Nevitt *v.* Ednyfed

O

Oinyans *v*. Einion

Oliver

Judging by the examples this name came to be used in Wales in the late med period:
Star CP 122. Monts Eliz. Oliver ap Oliver; 124. ditto; InvECP 137. Flints 1515. Morris ap Oliver; 155. Monts Oliver ap Morris.

Sibdon Carwood 10. 1705. John ap Oliver, alias Boliver (cf. 11. 1717. John Olivers, – not the same person as the wives' names are different). Stanton Lacy 159. Hest. Bolliver. Chirbury 95. 1694. Jana Aboliver; cf. 150. 1729. Eliza ap Oliver. Worthen, Index, Aboliver, A'Boliver (with A'Boliner) – abundant. Hopesay, Index, Bolliver, Boliver, ap Oliver. Myddle 316. 1817. Mary Bolver; 318. 1822. Jno Bolver. Selattyn 391. 1799. William Bolver. Whittington 462. 1763. Jonathan Bolvir. Kinnerley, Index, Boliver, Bolliver, Boylever.

The forms *Boliver* and *Bolver* are still found in the N.E. on both sides of the Welsh border: *Boliver*: Wrekin, Oakengates; Albrighton; Oswestry, Baschurch, Myddle-Baschurch, Loppington; Leominster, Walton; Crewe, West 1. *Bolver*: Oswestry, Weston Rhyn; Monts, Llandyssil; Llanfair – Rhiwhiriaeth, Llanerfyl; Runcorn, Aston, and mark especially that *Olver* occurs, three times, in Runcorn, Appleton, North Ward.

Onian, Onians *v*. Einion

Orwarod *v*. Gwrwared

Owain (Owen, Bowen, Ednowain)

The derivation of the name is discussed in TYP 477; one explanation is Latin Eugenius > OW Ou(u)ein, Eug(u)ein ... 'variously written in Ml.W. as Ewein, Owein, Ywein. LL gives the forms Euguen, Iguein, Yuein, Ouein. The corresponding form in Irish is Eoghan'. The alternative explanation is also given that it is Celt. Esugenos, 'engendered of Esos'. Dr Bromwich favours *Eugenius* as the origin, 'But it is to be noted that W Owein is normally latinized as Eugenius ... and it seems most natural to regard both the Welsh and Irish forms as derivatives of the Latin'.

In the early poetry texts it is generally *Ywein*, e.g. Hendregadredd 12, 15, and the associated name is *Ednywein*, G 439-40. The diphthong *yw-* (= pronunciation of E *how*) is very unstable and easily becomes *ow-*; the words *cywydd, bywyd* often occur as 'cowydd, bowyd'; and *bywyn* (the part of the loaf inside the crust is *bewyn* in certain dialects). Therefore one must expect *Owein, Ewein*, in med. texts; if anything, *Owein* is the standard version, e.g. the hero in the story *Iarlles y Ffynhawn* in the WM and RM texts is *Owein*, which stands for *Owain* in later Welsh. The diphthong *-ai* in the unaccented final syllable changes to *-e* in colloquial speech, *llefain* 'cry' is *llefen* in SW dialects; and the change to *Owen* is similar. It is rather surprising however to find quite early evidence of the change to Owen. (It is difficult to keep the name *Ednowain* separate: it appears to be a name constructed by a reshuffle of the naming elements, i.e. taking *Edn-* from *Ednyfed* and putting it before *Owain*). Boys' named Owen (in NW especially) are generally 'Now' colloquially; is this < (Ed)nowen?

In the note above p.90 on *Bened, Bennett*, it was suggested that *Bened* might possibly conceal the name *Ednyfed*. An example of *Benett* was the entry, InvECP 85 Da ... ap Benett of Llanfair, co. Merioneth, tanner, son and heir of Benett Owne (alias Smyth). This may very well conceal 'Ednywain' or 'Ednywen'.

A few specimens are given:
B13. 217. SR 1292. Elidyr ap Oweyn; 222. Oweyn ab Wronou. BBStD 76. Oweyn Cheke; 84. Oweyn fil Enote. ADClun 34. Lewelin ab Oweyd (misreading); 35. Lewelin ab Oweyn. B4. 155. Ardudwy Court 1325. Edenoweyn ap Grono; 159. Edenoweyn ap Adaf; B7. 144. Caern 1303. Iorwerth ap Edenewein. B15. 46. AS 1406. Gron ap dd ap Ednywayn, Dd ap Ednywain. B13. 142. Bonds Peace 1283. Owen fil Anyan. B10. 258. West W. 1352. Owen ap Owen. B11. 72. Broniarth 1429 Owen ap Ieuan ap Dd Hudol. Mer LSR 5, 33, 46. Edenowen. MLSW 124. Jankyn Apown ap Watkyn. RCA 3. Anglesey, Gavel Edenoyn.

In BYale 56 there is a *David Oen*, and the translation has *Oen*: it is prob. an odd spelling of 'Owen', but one would expect 'ap Owen'. In the same text, 88, Kydyvor et Madoc ap Edenewyn; in certain dialects final *-ain* changes to *-in*, e.g. *cymain*[t] *cymin*[t].

There are latinized versions other than Eugenius; Glam Cartae, Index, Audoenus, Audonus, used for Owen; also Oenus, Oeneus, for Owain, Owen. PRSannan. 1710. Audoenus filius Ellisei Jones . . . bapt.; 1712. Owenus ap William Ellis; PRConway 1695. Oudoenus filius illegitimus vl spurius Owini prichard. 1701. Johannes filius Audeoni Owen. PRLlanddewi Rhydderch.

21. 1717. Aoedenus, fil Jacobi and Aliciae Price.

The form Bowen hardly needs illustration: JEG 60. The sons of Owen ap Hugh (17th century): (1) Thomas ap Owen, whose son is William ap Thomas ap Hugh; (2) Edmund Owen, died without issue; (3) Hugh Bowen. CRHaverford 191. Griffith Abowen; 174, 176. Owen Abowen; 214, 227, 231, Phillip a Bowen; 173. Thomas Abowen. (Many entries of Bowen but no instance of Bowens.) RadsSoc VII.12, Will, has *Beowen* twice; this may indicate a local pronunciation of Owen as (I)Owen.

Neen Savage 5. 1581. Thomas ap Owyne, s. of Morice ap Owyn. 6. 1581. David ap Bowyne; 33. 1623. John Bowynne; 33. 1624. John ap Bowynne = 39. 1634. John Bowin. Bitterley 64. 1720. Stephanus f. Johannis ap Owen, alias Bowen = 65. 1721 Stephen ap Bowen. Stanton Lacy 24. 1596. Thomas Bowinne; 143. 1741. Owin the s. of Mary Gough. Worthen, Index, Apowen. Westbury 39. 1660. Margery Abowen. Lydham, – Index treats Bowing as if it were a variant of Owen.

The TD of Swansea and S.W. Wales has long lists of Owen and Owens; the Cardiff and S.E. Wales is the same. Cf. electoral reg. of Cheadle, Marple, Central-West, Bowins.

Oynions *v.* Einion

P

Pailin(g), Palin, Payling v. Heilyn

Pannwr

Pannwr, 'fuller', occurs very frequently as an epithet attached to pers. names; in some examples the radical cons. is retained, in others lenition is shown. Selected examples are given below:
B13. 225. SR 1292. Knychton ... John Baner. B15. 47. AS 1406. Je(uan) ddu banwr. Mer LSR 67. Heylin Pannor. CatAncDeeds V. 12694, Brecon 1586. Jenckin ap Jevan Bannour. V. 12685, John Bannour. LpOswestry 50, Survey 1602. Edward ap Thomas bannar. CaernCR 154. Llywelyn Pannour; PRSelattyn between 7. 1561 and 111. 1635 has several examples of ... Bannwr. PROswestry between 21. 1560 and 170. 1596 has ... Banur, Banor, etc. PRWhittington 16. 1597. Harrie Pannour; 103. 1616. ... wife of David Loid, Bannwr, of Daywell. Mer LSR 16 has *Pengour, Houa ap Pengour*, this version is difficult to explain as a compound of *pen* and *gŵr*: is it possibly a form of *pannwr*?

Parbert, Parbot, Parbut(t) v. Herbert

Parry v. Henry

Pasgen

This name is discussed in TYP 487; *Pascen(n)* < OW *Pascent* < L *Pascentius*. There are early records of the name, in inscriptions and written texts. The following may be added to the examples quoted in TYP, B13. 229. SR 1292, *David ab Pasken*.

It does not occur with frequency in the med. period but various versions occur in the parish register of Chirbury, v. index: *Peskin, Paskins, Peskyn, Pasekyn, Paskyn, Paskin*.

Paskin(s), Paskyn v. Pasgen

Peascod, Peasgood, Pescod v. Pysgod

Pelin, Pella, Pellin, Pellyne, Penllyn v. Belyn

Pembrey v. Pen-bre

Pembro, Pembroke v. Penfro

Pen – compounds

Pen, 'head', combines with simple adjectives to give compound adjectives, e.g. pengoch, penddu, penwyn, penfelyn, i.e. with *coch, du, gwyn, melyn* ('red, black, white, yellow'). *Pen* is a masc. noun but the gender does not matter in the structure of a proper compound: in proper compounds the initial consonant of the second element lenites regardless of the gender of the noun contained in the preceding element. TC 20-21, 100. In the case of adjectives with initial *ll* and *rh*, the consonant -*n* of *pen* would cause provection, *nl* > *nll*; *nr* > *nrh*, penllwyd, penrhydd; TC 27; provection could also occur to change -*ndd*- into -*nd*-, TC 26.

In the classification below, attention is given mainly to those compound epithets which occur oftenest, especially those which are potential surnames, and which also make good comparison with the usage of the simple adjectival element as epithet, i.e. *penwyn* with 'gwyn, wyn'; *pengoch* with 'coch, goch'. The initial *p* of the compound epithet following a pers. name generally lenites, e.g. the names of the poets *Dafydd Benfras, Dafydd Benwyn*; but many of the examples below from early texts show an unlenited form; and in some examples, no lenition is shown within the compound itself, e.g. *penbras*. In some instances the compound epithet has no pers. name before it; with the def. art. it stands for the person whose proper name is omitted, e.g. *Y Penwyn*.

Pengoch, (cf. forms of *Coch* above, *Goch, Gough* etc.):
B5. 58. Lleyn, late 13th century: y pengoc

(probably for 'pengoch', if it meant 'head cook', it would be 'pen-cog', i.e. improper compound). HBr. 289. Pedigree: Meredith Bengoch; 293. Walter Bengough, incumbent Llanganten 1682; p.311, ditto. HM iv, 136. Caerwent, Lower Llanmelyn, 19 century, property of Bengough. ALMA 878, Malan goch = 941 ... falan bengoch (i.e. William Morris's maidservant). PRLudlow 684. 1714. Mary Bengough. PRNeen Savage 7. 1583. John s. of Henry Bengoahe; 21. 1604. John Bengoch.

The following example deserves special notice: ELS Cumberland, 46 (Bowaldeth), 6th Edw. III, Robert Benghok. Examples of *Bengough* noted in present-day registers: S. Worcs, Beckford, Overbury; S. Gloucs, Cinderford 3; S. Hereford, Ross-on-Wye; Cardigan, Llandygwydd.

Penddu

B15. 43. AS 1406. Jor ap Je(uan) pendu (var. ap pen duy). 45, 47. Je(uan) Penddu. Mer LSR 21. Madoco Pendwy. BYale 62. Ithel Penduy. PROswestry 26. 1561. Elinor vz John Benddu. Cf. Bl. Gwent, E. Vale, N. Central, Willowtown, Pendey (?).

Penwyn

B1. 264. NW 1305. De Iorwerth Penwyn. B5. 143. Caern 1293. david ap y penwyn. B13. 222. SR 1292. Lewelyn ab Penewen. B14. 311. NW, Edw I. Yereward Penwen. B15. 47. AS 1406. Dd ap Je(uan) ap Je(uan) penwyn; 52. Matto Benwyn; BBStD 58. Kedivor Benwyn. CAP. 85, 396. Grono Loit ap y Penwyn (1330). MLSW 16. Meurig ap Thomas Penwyn; 33. Howell Benwyn. PRFord 3. 1599. John s. of Rees Penwen. PRSidbury 7. Benwin. PR Ludlow 15. 1586. Cadwallader Benwyn (Placed in index as a variant of Benyon). PRRuyton 69. 1781. Elinor d. of John Williams (alias Penwyn). ShrewsburyBR 229. Penwyn, Hugh s. David ap Mores Penwyn, of Wittington in Powys, 1504. The following is contrary to the normal and grammatically correct usage, and is difficult to explain: RadsSoc XLIV. 59, Will 1575 Nantmel, Howell Bengwyn's lands.

Pengrych ('curly headed'; after a fem. name it should, strictly speaking, be Pengrech. The examples below show the Welsh *ch* sound disappearing in English speech). B13. 221. SR 1292. Meuric Pengrich. BBStD 322. Tegwared Pengrech (fem. form not intended,

but due to defective writing). Mer LSR 10. Wm ap David Pengreck (footnote, 'It is not known which Pencraig is referred to'; probably this represents 'Pengrych'; cf. ibid 31, Madoco Pengrek; ibid 54, Eynon Pengrek). PWLMA 472, 541. Hywel Pengrych. RadsSoc XLIV. 59, Will 1575, Nantmel, Philip David Bengrich. [Cf. RadsSoc XLI. 58. Misc. Ministers' Accts, Mad' ap Ipengrith; 64 ... ap Pengreth. XXVII. 23, Will, 1552 'Prestene', Hoell Bengrethes wife.] HM iv, 273. Robert Pengrith (probably Pengrych). PRClunbury 64, 1674. John Bengrey; 65. 1676. John Bengre; 100. 1727. Bengry. PRStanton Lacy, 199. 1794. Bangry.

PRESENT-DAY REGISTERS

Bengry: Shrewsbury, Battlefield; Ludlow, East Hamlet, Bitterley. *Bengree*: Ludlow, Ludford, Madeley, Munslow; Wrekin, Wellington Park – East, Chetwynd; BrRadnor, Glyntawe – Penwyllt. *Bengrey*: City of Hereford, St Nicholas.

Cf. D. Tel 28.6.80, Marriages, ... Williams + Pengree, Chichester, (widow of E.G.C. Pengree): as seen in PRCleobury Mortimer 135. 1718, Martha Pengree.

Penllwyd

B2. 253. Brec-Llandovery, Ievano Benlloyd. B13. 143, Bonds Peace 1295. Eygnon penllwyd. CaernHS 26, Bolde Rental 38. llin ap Penlloyt. AD Clun 208. Dio Penloed. CatAncDeeds V. 12358, Brecon. John ap Rees Been lloid. PWLMA 436. Hywel Ben Llwyd 1525. (read 'Benllwyd'). HRads 333, Appendix, 33 Henry 8. Nuper Monasterium de Comhere, Dd Benlloid.

Pengam 'head-bent', 'not straight'.

BBStD 30. Johes Pengam. Mer LSR 55. Wion Pengam; 65. Pengam. RecCa 55. Hoell Bengan (?). PR 87. 1582. Elen vz Thom's als Bengam.

Penfras 'fat-head, big-head'.

B5. 62. Lleyn, late 13th century Eynion penwras. B15. 43. AS 1406. lln Penvras. BBStD 284. David Gogh ap Ieuan Penvras. CaernHS 26. Bolde Rental 48. Gavell Trahayarne Penbras. Mer LSR 18. Adaf Penbras; 20. Win Penbras.

Pendew 'fat-head, possibly stupid'.

B5. 59. Lleyn, late 13th century ... uxor pendew. ADClun 87. Philip Pendew's lands. Bartrum 1350-1415, 718. Rhys Bendew (var.

Benddu). JEG 5. Ednowain Bendew.

Penhir, Penfyr 'long-head, short-head'.

The two elements of *penhir* also have the order, *hirben*; but the pattern of the proper compound is 'penhir', *v.* TC 21.

BBStD 314. David Penhir; 320. D. Penhire; [ibid 310. David Penvir]. JEG 5. Meredydd Ben Hir. Bartrum 1215-1350, 390. Maredudd Benhir ap Maredudd. PRMunslow 71. Penir.

Penarw, 'rough-head', < *garw*'.

B4. 160, Ardudwy 1325. Map Penarw. Mer LSR 59. Ierword mab Penaro. Bartrum 1215-1350, 252. Einion ab Owain ap Gwion Benarw.

OTHER FORMS

Cf. B5. 69, Lleyn, late 13th century y pengalot (? pengaled, caled = 'hard'). Mer LSR 91. Ieuan pengul (*cul* 'narrow, thin'), *v. cul, cule,* above. CaernCR 21. Ieuan Pethledan (must be *Penllydan, llydan* = 'wide, broad'; *thl* being the scribe's attempt at *ll*'; *nl* would give provection, *nll*). Bartrum 1215-1350. 261. Gruffudd Bengu (*cu* 'dear, gentle'). PRLlanyblodwel 27. 1713. Sara d. of Robert Penfrith ... (*brith,* 'speckled, mixed-colour, multicoloured'). PROswestry 185. 1596. Anne vz Robert Benvelyn a beggar (*melyn* 'yellow'). B15. 43. AS 1406. dd tew ap Pensith (= *syth,* 'stiff, upright'). Mer LSR 38. Eynon Penteg (*teg* 'fair', read 'Pendeg' or 'Bendeg'; cf. RecCa 99. Mad ap Pendeken, ? derivative of 'pendeg'); Cf. ELS Cumberland 30, Brampton, Andreas ffairhare.

v. also separate art. on *Penoyre.*

The compound *penbwl* means (1) 'stupid, blockhead'; (2) river fish 'bullhead'; (3) tadpole; a large head is prob. intended in the following:

B13. 228. SR 1292. Iuan Vachan Penbul; 229. Dauid Penbole. BBStD 220. Ieuan Penboul. GlamCartae 960, 2322. Eniaun Penbul.

Pen followed by a noun to make a normal genitive construction, can result in the forming of an improper compound, e.g. pen march, 'horse's head', becoming 'pen-march' attached as an epithet to a pers. name. CaernCR 36. Llwydyn ap Pen march; 34. Pen march; 38. Cyfnerth Pen march; ibid 62. Gwenllian Pen Hwch, *hwch* 'sow, pig'. Mer LSR 74. Pendauat, *dafad* 'sheep'. Cf. also Mer LSR 16. *Pengour, Houa ap Pengour. v.*

Pannwr above. B13. 226. SR 1292. Craddoc Bentan, (*pentan*, 'fireside hob'). B15. 59. AS 1406. Deicws ap Penntan. (var. Pwntan).

Penath *v.* Bennet

Penbow *v.* Benbow

Pen-bre, Pem-bre

Pen-bre which is to the west of Llanelli is pronounced 'Pem-bre' in the speech of S. Wales, just as 'gan bwyll' becomes 'gam-bwyll'. The following surnames may have come from this place-name:

CRHaverford 86. Samuel Penbray. S. Gloucs. Winterbourne 2. Pembry. Bl. Gwent, Tredegar – Georgetown N. Pembrey; Sirhowy S. ditto, Vale Terrace, ditto.

Pendey *v.* Pen

Pendrey, Pendry *v.* Henry

Penet *v.* Bennet

Penfro, Pembroke

The proper W version is *Penfro,* Sir Benfro; but the colloquial W of SW is 'Sir Bemro'. [WATU 173 mentions a 'township' Penfro in Caerhun, Caern.] The following examples show the E Pembroke, and this version in lenited form, in addition to the W Pemro or Pembro:

Pembro. Ludlow, Bridgnorth – St Leonards. Pembroke. Cheadle, Bredbury South 2; S. Hereford, Fownhope. Bembroke, C. of Hereford. Tupsley.

Pennaeth

This is derived from *pen* and means 'chief'.

B13. 228. SR 1292. Iuan ap Seysil Pennayth. Mer LSR 25. Eynon Penath. CAP 145. Hugh Bennaythe of Pembroke (twice). Text editor quotes refs. to Richard Bennayth of Pembroke, and Richard Hugh of Monkton, alias Richard Benet, although not absolutely clear one may presume that in this instance, Benet is a variant of Bennayth. PWLMA 309, 430, 431, 513, 548. Philip Benneth (or Bennyth, Bennayth). 426. Dafydd ap Gwilym Bennyth. The following were found in present-day registers:

Caernarfon, Criccieth, Benneth; Conway, Conway – Eidda Ward, Benneth Roberts (i.e. christian name).

Pennant (*v.* also Introd. Place-names)

The celebrated traveller and zoologist Thomas Pennant, in his *History of the parishes of Whiteford and Holywell* (London 1796) pp.34-5, sets out the origins of the Pennants of Bychton, Flints. They were of pure Welsh origin, known to be living in the locality in the eleventh and twelfth centuries. David ap Tudor of Bychton, in the middle of the fifteenth century, was the first to take the name Pennant: he was the father of the Pennant abbot of Basingwerk abbey, the patron of the poet Gutun Owain. This David ap Tudor (David Pennant) was also the first of the family to marry an Englishwoman, from just across the border. Thomas Pennant believed that David ap Tudor took the name Pennant because his old house at Bychton was at the head of the little dingle leading down to the shore of the Dee, *pen y nant*. JEG 214, Downing and Bychton, reproduces this explanation.

Star CP 5. Henry VIII, Flints, Dd Pennant; 33. Eliz. Caern William Pennant, of London, gent. Ex Pro James I – Index, many examples, mostly from Holywell. Cwtta Cyf. 54. 1615. Hugh Pennant; 72. Grace Pennant widow (the late wief of Hugh Pennant, gent, deceased).

The name is still found in West Flints, Tremeirchion.

The Gazetteer names eight places named Pennant, with Pennant Melangell making nine; there is no example located near Holywell; if Thomas Pennant's account is correct, the place-name did not exist independently, it was a made-up name. WATU has a total of nineteen examples.

Pennoyre
Also spelled Pennoyer, the surname is associated with Brecon and border areas, and also there is an American line of the family. The surname of a gentry family, Pennoyre of the Moor in the Golden Valley, Herefs, it has been explained as from W *pen-aur* (literally 'golden or yellow head') possibly referring to 'the head of the Golden Valley'. Branches of the family came into Breconshire, later giving their name to Pennoyre House near Brecon. W *Pen-aur* would be in SW dialect 'pen-our = pen-oir', but a compound adj. attached to a person would normally lenite and become *Ben-aur* (or in SW dialect Ben-our = Ben-oir). Such a form exists in PRMillum (Cumberland) p.224, 1720 'Henry Benoyre, a poore man; p.227, 1727, Frances widow of Henry Benoire ales Benyon, poore' (given in index as 'Benyon [Benoyre]').

Penrice
The Gazetteer names two places called Penrhys, one in the Rhondda still called Penrhys, the other in the Gower peninsula generally called Penrice. The use of *-rice* for *-rhys* is exactly the same as with the pers. name Rhys, Rees, Rice, Price, Pryce; but the *-rhys* part of Pen-rhys cannot be the pers. name for it makes no sense in a place-name: there must be another *rhys*, as in *rhysfa* 'fortress' (or 'slope' which would go well with *pen*).

PWLMA 241. John De Penrees (1277, constab. Dinefwr) = Penrice, Gower. Examples of Penrice are found far and wide and it is remarkable how often it is found in the constituencies of N.W. England:

Penrith and Border, Dalston; Boro' of Copeland, Gosforth; Carlisle, Trinity. Allerdale, Cockermouth. Bromsgrove, NE; No.2 SW; Newport, Alexander 1. TD of West Midlands – South, six entries; Birmingham area, nine.

Penry *v.* Henry
Perbert *v.* Herbert
Pernad *v.* Bernard
Pibydd
Examples of Pibydd 'piper', unlenited and lenited:

B15. 47. AS 1406. dd ap Rhobin bibidd. CaernCR 153. Llywelyn Pibydd (MS Pybyth); 156. Llywelyn Bibydd (MS Pybyth). Bartrum 1350-1415, 820. Jonet Bibydd. L & P, iii. pt.2. Grant 2214 p.941, March 1522, Pardon for stealing given to Gryffyth Pybyth, a weaver of Kyngton in Marches of Wales: it appears to be a surname, not an epithet giving Gryffyth's occupation. PRLudlow 302. 1611. Joan Bibbith.

Picton (*v.* also Introd. Place-names)
Picton is a well-known surname in S.W. Wales; it is fairly obvious that the source is the place-name seen in Picton Castle, Pembs; cf. BBStD 86. Will'mus Pyketon: there are over fifty entries in the Swansea TD.

Pill
Pill or *Pyll* is best known as the name of one of Llywarch Hen's twenty four sons. Some of the following examples show how difficult it was for the Anglo-Norman scribes to write the name:

B13. 142. Bonds Peace 1283. Yorwarth fil Pyll; 143. 1295. pethil Cryck. CAP 189. Hova ap Pilth; 190. David ap Pilth; *c.* 1391-2. French text, context, see of Bangor; 202-3.

Bleddyn ap Pill, 1276-77; (B) Lodyuit ap Pyll, 1301-07, Flints CalACW. 227. Pilthle ap Ednyfed. RecCa 100. Dd ap Pill (cf. 63. Gilth ap Pridith; 59. Greth ap Prydy ap Gorndur; 60. Hoell ap Gilth; ? misreadings). CaernHS 26. Bolde Rental 47. Gavell Pill a Grono; 49. the same under Table of Gavaelion (in brackets, Extent dated 1352, Pilth & Grou).

It is possible that the following represent the same name, pronounced no doubt as in English:

PRCleobury Mortimer 305. Jno Pill.

It is found today in Wrekin, Lawley – Wellington Rural, Copeland, Millom.

It is important, though, to remember that Pill is a place-name element found especially on both sides of the Bristol Channel, meaning 'a tidal creek, a pool in a river'; the OE *pyll* is generally considered to be a borrowing from Welsh, *v.* Pierce, *Placenames of D Powys* 116. An example of a place-name is *Cogan Pill*: D.E. Williams 64 quotes examples of *Pill, Pyll* which are obviously taken from the place-name: Nicholas Pill, 1542 (CarRec. 1. 234), John Pyll, 1558 (IV. 126); William Pill, 1575 (Ill. 25). A few examples are to be seen in the Cardiff TD.

Piscog *v.* Hiscog

Pleavin, Pleithyn, Plethyn, Plevin(s) *v.* Bleddyn

Pluke *v.* Luc

Pobydd

This is W for 'baker':
B15. 46. AS 1406. Eign ap dd bobydd (repeated). CaernCR 48. Simon Bobydd (Bobith); 105. Simon Pobydd (MS Pobith). HBr vol. 2. App.4. Bailiffs, 1560. Thomas John Bobydd. (One cannot be too sure of this for Theophilus Jones may have translated from 'Baker'). PROswestry 7. 1559. John Bobydd; 15. 1559. Robert Bobyth. 183. 1596. Lowrie Bobyddes. (= fem form).

Poiskin *v.* Hoskin

Pomphrey *v.* Humphrey

Popkin *v.* Hopcyn

Porthmon

W for 'drover', a borrowing from E portman, EEW 52.

B13. 228. SR 1292. Iuan Portmon. B5. 146. Caern 1293. y porthmon. B10. 150. West W. 1352. Ieuan Borthman. B23. 344, Mawddwy 1415. Tegwarot ap Ieuan ap y Porthmon.

Porthor

W for 'gatekeeper, doorman'.

Mer LSR 33. Griffid Porthour. RecCa 284. Eign' Porther. PROswestry 135. 1589. Nicholas ap Thom's Borther.

Povah, Povey *v.* Hwfa

Powel, Powell, Powles *v.* Hywel

Poyskyn *v.* Hoskin

Pragnall, Pragnell, Prangell *v.* Rheinallt

Pralf, Praulf *v.* Ralph

Prandle, Prendle, Prondle *v.* Randell

Prawling(e) *v.* Rawlin

Praynold *v.* Rheinallt

Preddy *v.* Maredudd

Predith *v.* Prydydd

Preece *v.* Rhys

Prendergast *v.* Introd. Place-names

Price *v.* Rhys

Prichard, Prickard, Pritchard, Pritchett *v.* Richard

Priddy, Priddie, Pridett *v.* Maredudd

Probert, Probin, Probyn *v.* Robert

Proger, Prosser *v.* Roger

Prothera(h), Prothero(e) *v.* Rhydderch

Prydydd

This was widely used in the earlier periods for 'poet'. There is possible confusion with forms which have come about through metathesis *etc. from Rhiryd* (*v.* p.183) one may feel reasonably certain that it is *Prydydd* in the examples affixed as epithet after a pers. name, especially if there is a lenition; the examples which cause uncertainty are those which follow *ap*, RadsSoc XLI. 66. D'd ap Pridith, for in spite of the version in the document, this may still be 'ap Ridith' wrongly set down.

Mer LSR 28. Eynon Pridith. B13. 212. SR 1292, text editor's remarks: 'Cadwgan Predith and Eynon Predith were bards of Glascwm and Elfael, unless, indeed, their father was a Meredith' (text 221. Eynon Predith ... Cadugan Predith). 217. Brakenok, Yuan ap Gronnou ap Predith. 218. Cydweli, Cadugan ab Predet. B15. 45. AS 1406. David y prydydd; 54. Je(uan) llwyd brydydd. BBStD 284. Dauid Gogh ap Predith = Surveys GK, Clase and Landewy 1326. 192. Dauid Gogh ap Predyth.

Prynallt *v.* Rheinallt

Pryse *v.* Rhys

Prytherch *v.* Rhydderch

Pugh(e) *v.* Hywel

Pullin *v.* Hywel

Pumphrey *v*. Humphrey
Pwlkin *v*. Hywel
Pysgod
Originally a collective noun from L *piscatum*, it became the normal plural for 'fish'. The following example shows it as a trade epithet, CaernCR 118. Goronwy Bach Piscod.
Note: There is a name, with variations, in English contexts which has striking resemblance to *pysgod* but which is unconnected, namely *Peascod, Peasgood* etc. The E surname is from 'peas-cod' (i.e. pea pod), a nickname for a seller of peas. Bardsley 333-4, including Footnote, mentions street-cries as origins of surnames, giving 'Fresh fish', 'Coloppes', 'Fresh-herring', 'Mackerel' and 'Peascod' as examples; p.485 (nicknames) includes 'Nicholas Pescodde' and the index names Godwin Pascodde.

Reaney has Peescod, Pescod, ... Pescud, Peasegoed, Pescott, Peskett and Bisgood, and for comparison quotes 'Richard pesemongere'. Very little purpose would be served by adding instances, early and contemporary, to Reaney's (there are families of *Pescod* in Tredegar – Georgetown North and Picton St.). One is struck by the evidence that the typical street-cries and nicknames include 'Fresh-fish', 'Fresh-herring' and 'Mackerel'.

Powys
The new division of Wales into counties has brought back the name Powys; in the med period it was the name of the princedom of N.E. Wales. The proper spelling is Powys, the final syllable having the diphthong *ŵy*, rhyming with *pwys, dwys*; but this diphthong is inclined to become *wŷ*; e.g. the adj. *tywyll* 'dark' should rhyme with *twyll, pwyll*, but is now virtually *tyw-yll*. Thus the -*y* becomes a vowel following consonantal *w*; and this leads to the form and spelling *Powis* which is the form generally found in the surname. Like *Gwynedd* and *Gwent* it was used as label to show a person's place of origin.
CalChancProc 481. 1318. John de Powis (no

Welsh context); 223. 1305. John Powys the King's yeomen. CaernCR 129. Lleucu Powys. ADClun 175. Meredith Powis; 183. Moylagh and Deye Powys. PRLudlow 853. 1742. Saml Powess, Phoebe Powess; 856. 1743. Saml Powis. Index, Powis, Powes, Powess, Powice, Powiss, Powys. PROswestry 26. 1561. John Powis.

It is fairly common in modern registers, e.g. *Powis*, Shrewsbury, Berrington; Ludlow, Broad St; Monmouth, Mitchell Troy United. *Powys*, CT, Up Hatherley.

Pride, Pryde
Reaney in the first place gives an E origin, 'No doubt often a nickname or pageant-name from ME "pride", but also clearly an adjective' (i.e. since early examples are of the type John le Pride). It is then stated that the surname appears particularly in the Welsh border counties and may be from Welsh *prid* 'precious, dear'. Frequent examples in the Welsh border counties would be a good reason for the surmise, but there is no evidence that *prid* (used only in SW for 'expensive') was used as a personal epithet. The *pr*- should lead one to look for a Welsh name such as 'Rhyd', so that 'ab Rhyd' would give 'Pryd', the nearest one can get to such a name is Rhiryd, *v*. below p.183, but this is only a remote possibility, and we much prefer believing that the name is the E *pride*, and would suggest that the source of the surname is a character in a morality play.

There is some evidence in Welsh sources for the presence of the name in Welsh border counties: MLSW 51. Ricardi Pruyde; HM i. 125. Pedigree of ... Styant of Cefn Llytha and Pride of the Cwm; with the statement that the Prides are located in Caerwent and Llanfair Discoed. PRCaerwent 1779 has a Thomas Pride; and PRLl. Discoed p.56 1776 has a footnote, 'Thomas Pride was a Gloucestershire man'.

Puskyn *v*. Hoskin

Q

Quellyn *v*. Introd. Place-names   **Quilt** *v*. Gwyllt

R

Raglan

Rhaglan or Raglan, originally a hundred in Gwent, it is now the name of a parish, a town, and a castle. The surname is found oftenest in east Glam and one wonders whether there was a Rhaglan other than the Gwent place-name: the early examples of Raglan given by D.E. Williams 65 show that it was adopted by a branch of the Herberts 'adopting the name of a country seat', and this implies the Gwent Raglan.

Star CP 8. Henry VIII, Glam Sir Jno Ragland. InvECP 207. Glam 1547 Thomas Raglonde, ... messuage in Llanilltyd Faerdre, late of John Raglonde. PRLlantrithyd 33. 1580. John sonn to Thomas Raglon (index has Raglan).

The pedigrees of the Raglan families of Glam are given in Clark 274-5. The following references of the eighteenth century are taken from the MS diary of William Thomas of Michaelston super Ely (Cardiff MSS):
Harry Raglan, workman at Cottrel, 1767. Sarah Raglan his wife buried 1767. Thomas Raglan buried Michaelston from Fishwear nr Wenvoe 1787 – he was aged 76 and the last of that ancient family.

Raglan as a surname is today found in Monm, Abergavenny, Cantref and Grofield.

Ralph

The examples below justify the inclusion of this name:
B13. 217. SR 1292 (at Brekenok) John ap Rauf. 219. (at Penbroc) ... jurors ... David Rauf. B4. 227. NW Boroughs. David ap Rauf. B2. 150. Criccieth 1320. David ap Rauf; 158. David ap Rawff. AnglPleas 25. Margaret verch Roff. Bartrum 1350-1415, 611. Hywel ap Ralph ap Hywel.

WPortBooks 5. James Praulf (Swansea); 20. Henry Praulf; 21. Jacob Praulf. InvECP 78. Pembs 1518. Ranwlph ap Eden ap Ieuan. Cwtta Cyf. 14. Mathewe ap Raphe Wyne. B3. 140. Glam Loyalists 1696. David Praulse (? misreading of Praulfe).

Randell, Randle, Rondle

The following versions were noted in Welsh sources:
Star CP 5. Flints Henry VII. Randall Jenkin; 222. James I. Jno Lloide Rondle of Llanvorda, gent. JEG 3. Randle Hanmer. CaernHS 6. 1945, p.60. (Early Caern Seamen, compiled 1589) Randell Cooke. Cwtta Cyf. 48. Rondle Lloyd.

SHROPSHIRE REGISTERS

Selattyn 313. 1777. Elizabeth Prondle; 329. 1774. Thomas Prandle. Oswestry 11. 1559. Ieuan ap Rondell. 212. 1599. Hughe ap Rindle ap Owen. 673. 1668. Margaret the daughter of Josephe ap Rondle. St Martin's, Index, Prondle, Prandle, Prendle. L'Estrange Ewen 255. Prandle (ap Randal).

PRESENT-DAY REGISTERS

Randall: Wrexham Boro Caia Ward. Randle: Wrexham Boro Caia Ward; East Flint, Buckley, Bistre West, Greenfield. Rendle: Cardigan, North H 1. Rondel: Newport, St Julian 1. Rondell: Wrexham Boro, Cefn Ward. Randles: Wrexham, Burton, Allington, Wrexham Boro, Cefn Ward; West Flint, Dyserth; East Flint, Marford and Hoseley; South Pembs, Manorbier. Prandle: Nantwich, Weaver Ward; Runcorn, Frodsham South (next door to Randles). City of Chester, Ch. Rural – Upton by Chester; Wrexham, Llay, Wrexham Boro – Maesydre, Cefn, Caia; West Flint, Rhyl S.E; East Flint, Buckley Bistre West; Bangor, Overton.

Rawlin

Reaney gives *Rawlin* and several variant forms. The name is found occasionally in early W sources.

B15. 290. Aberyst – Cardn, 14th century Rawlin Piscar. Bartrum 1350-1415, 747. William ap Rawling ap Dafydd. CaernQSR 97. Elsabeth ferch Rulinge of Rywe; 210. Rowling ap Llywelyn. InvECP 128. Flints 1553. Thomas ap Rowling. Star CP 112. Monm Eliz. Proger Rawlins. PRLl.Crossenny et Penrhos, Intro. p.iv speaks of Watkin Powell Prawling, son of Howell ap Rawling of Penyclawdd . . .; other branches of the same family settled on Prawling (ap Rawling) and Rawlins; 1575, p.25. . . . fil's Watkinni Powell Prawlinge . . . fil's Thome Powell Prawling. 1630, p.43. Anna uxor Thome Powell Prawlinge.
The following seems to be a surviving version: Prowlin. City of Hereford, Bartonsham, St Nicholas.

Rederick *v*. Rhydderch
Redyth *v*. Rhiryd
Reece, Rees *v*. Rhys
Rendle *v*. Rendell
Rerrid *v*. Rhiryd
Rice *v*. Rhys
Riddith *v*. Rhiryd

Rheinallt

Reaney gives several variant forms including *Reynell, Renaud, Renaut, Rennell*; the OFr *Reinald, Reynaud*, OG *Reginald*, . . . latinized as *Reginaldus*, 'Some of the numerous instances of *Rainald* in England may be from ON *Ragnaldr*, but most were introduced from France and Normandy where both the OG and ON forms contributed to its popularity'. The following from Withycombe is relevant: 'In the 15th century such forms as *Raignald, Reignald, Reignolde, Reginalde* came into use. The reappearance of the *g* after several centuries of disuse may have been an early example of the effect of antiquarianism on names'.
The following examples from Welsh sources represent the variations shown above, and some of the examples will show the change of -*ald* into -*allt*; a few examples of this in borrowings from E are given in EEW 244, such as *Oswallt*, 'Oswald', seen especially in *Croesoswallt*, 'Oswestry'.

BBStD 140. Walt'us Raynold. B7. 285. 1599. N. Pembs, Rinold ap Res of llysyvran co. Pemb. B10. 167. AnglCrown Rental. Rynallt ap Hugh ap Hwylkyn. B11. 66. Broniarth 1429. Reinalld ap Ieuan. Star CP 4. Denbs Henry VII. Reynold ap Jno ap Griffith; 57. Denbs Eliz. Raynallt ap Evan, . . . 204. Monts James I. Solomon Reynalles. PRSannan 1701. Edward ap Rynallt. PRConway 1583. Hugh ap Jo( ) fil Jo( ) ap reignalt. PRLl. Yst. Llywern 34 (end 18th century) several instances of Rannells.

SHROPSHIRE REGISTERS

The registers abound with examples of *Reynold* and its variants and derivatives and only a summary can be given:
ap Rainold, Hanwood 11. ap Raynold, Alberbury 289. 1698; ap Reignald, ibid 219. 1676; Prennald, ibid 192. 1666. ap Pragnald, ibid 198. 1668. Prunell, Cleobury Mortimer 112. 1670. Prunnald, Westbury 270. 1780. Prenal, High Ercall 538. 1786. Prynalt, Noncon, Oswestry Old Chapel 18. 1810. Prinold, Great Ness 43. 1656. Prineaux, Tong 57. 1721 = Prenals 59. 1724 = Prenocks, 95. 1764. Prenhals, Wroxeter 82. 1726. Prenut, Prenault: Shrewsbury St Mary's Index. Prenaut, Prinnott, Prennett: St Chad's Index. Proynal, Edgmond 189. 1792. Prignald, Oswestry 639. 1665. Prinall, Whittington 206. 1677 = 210. 1687 Preynold = 211. 1687 Prinalt = 217. 1693 Preignold. Rennots, Hodnet 22. 1690. Prynnoc 106. 1724, Prynnot 113. 1728. Brinallt (several entries) in St Martin's Index, together with Prinallt, Prynoll, Prynolt etc.

Some of the above forms survive in the electoral registers:
Reynallt (as surname) BrRadnor. Llanddetty, Llangynidr. Prinold, Wrekin, Rodington. Prynallt, Wirral, Hoylake – Meols Ward.

The following versions are quoted although there is an element of uncertainty:
Pragnell, S. Hereford, Hentland, Whitchurch; West Gloucs, Drybrook Div. 2. *Pragnall*, Denbs, Llandrillo-yn-Rhos, Glyn Ward. *Prangnell*, West Gloucs, Longlevens 2; CT, Cirencester 4; Preseli, Puncheston, Little Newcastle. *Prangell*, Islwyn, Risca Waunfawr. Cf. also Prangle, City of Glouc, Podsmead p.8. Pringell, West Gloucs, Longlevens 2 (unless < *Rhingyll*).

Rhingyll

The texts of the ancient laws mention *rhingyll* frequently: he was an official or servant of the court. There are examples of using it as an epithet attached to a personal name: there are others in which it is used as an occupational name instead of a pers. name. The word is taken from OE *ringild*. B13. 223. SR 1292. Bishops Castle, Cadogan Ringild. B4. 152. Ardudwy 1325. Gwyn ap Adaf Ringildus. AnglCourt 1346, 35. Goronwy Ringyll. PWLMA 480. Ieuan Du Rhingyll. HBr 439. David Ychan ap David y Rhingyll.

An example of Pringell is quoted with forms of Pragnell etc., under Reynold, Rheinallt.

Rhirid, Rhiryd

Rhiryd is a well-known name in the med period. The two *r's* in the name produced dissimilation and the form *Rhiddid* is found quite early in standard texts, e.g. if one compares the texts of the Chronicles of the Princes edited by Thomas Jones, one finds *Rhiryd* in the Peniarth 20 version, and *Ridit* in the RB version, which Professor Jones turns into *Rhiddid* in the E translation, *v.* pp.102-103 and compare the indices of the two publications. An example of this dissimilation is found in the place-name *Llantrithyd* in the vale of Glamorgan: originally Nantrhiryd (anantririd) *v.* TC 104. But there must also have been a further change, the metathesis which turned 'rhiddid' into 'rhididd', cf. Glam Cartae, Index...Lanririd ... *Lanritith*. The Middleton family of Chirk castle have perpetuated the name of their ancestor Rhiryd Flaidd, cf. InvECP 142. Robert ap Reddith alias Middilton, 1538; Ex Pro James I. 157. Rhidudd Middleton.

B13. 215. SR 1292. Rired Apewyn, Maddoc ap Ririth. 223. Ririth ab Enyas; 225. Walter ap Pririth. B1. 263. NW 1304. De Ririt ap Wyn. B6. 274. Lleyn, terre Ririth. B15. 54. AS 1406. Tudur ap Je(uan) ap Rered (variant, prered) ibid. ... ap Preded voel (var. prered). LpOswestry 31/33. Rise ... (1393) = Rhirid ... (1586) = Rhydyd (1602 ibid 40. Rental 1607. Gavell Yr Yeered; 87. (1586) Gwely Reddit. CalChancProc 556. Rythit ap Carwet ... Riryd ap Carwet of the commote of Evyonyth; Ruryt ap Carwet ... Reryth ... Ririt ap Carwe. MLSW 201. Ieuan ap Rithed; 211. 212. Lewelini ap Ieuan

ap Ririd; 219. Rithede ap Madoc. InvECP 151. Monts 1551. Lawrence ap John ap Reryd.

SHROPSHIRE REGISTERS

The name virtually fell into disuse in Wales, but it survived into the early modern period in certain Shropshire parishes, and quite remarkably so in a family with the surname of Porter in the parishes of Alberbury, Chirbury, Pontesbury and Westbury, a family of lowly status, not the kind one expects to be aware of a pedigree. There does seem to be some confusion of the version Redith with Meredith, but as Redith occurs in the Porter family as an obvious variant of Rerith, Rered etc. one may safely conclude that Redith is not derived from Meredith; on the other hand, one can well imagine the name 'Redith' being regarded by a clerk making entries in registers as a colloquial form of Meredith.

There are so many entries one must try to summarize:

Alberbury, between 278. 1694 and 325. 1709, six entries of Rerid or Rered Porter. Chirbury, between 2. 1629 and 98. 1696, there are at least twenty-six entries, either as forename or surname, of the following versions: Rydeath, Rydeth, Rydyth, Ryrryd, Rerrid, Rerridus, Rerridd, Redith, Redyth, Ryddyth, Rerryd, Ryddyh, Rerdith, Riddith. Pontesbury 269. 1719. Rerid Porter and Martha Cook, banns. Westbury 99. 1689. Redith Porter and Martha Foord, mar.; with further examples of Redith as forename and as surname; including also p.72 *Isabell Meredith*, which may be a 'correction' of *Redith*.

The Shrewsbury BR 249 has: *Reryth, Reginald ap . . . s. of Reryth ap Gro. of Edgerley, 1451.*

Finally, Shrewsbury St Mary's 3. 1585 has *Margerett Preaddethe.*

It is not easy to detect examples in present-day registers: the following appears to be a much changed version: Wirral, Ellesmere Port, Grange Ward 2, *Ryrie*.

Rhydderch

One of the North British rulers of the sixth century was called Rhydderch; his epithet at times being *Hen*, but generally *Hael*; for early references to *Rodarchus, Rodercus, Rederech v.* LHEB 658, 662, 668, 710, and TYP 504-5; in Nennius he is *Riderc hen*, in other genealogies *Retherc hael*; Dr Bromwich gives a number of quotations from early poetry which refer to Rhydderch. It was a fairly common name in the med period, and it was the kind of name which by its very nature brought about a variety of adaptations and spellings. It would be best at this point to describe the changes that took place and to quote afterwards. The simple straightforward development would be to have an 'English' spelling, *Rhytherch*, and for *ab* + to give *Prydderch, Prytherch*. The other changes took place in the final syllable, in the writing system of English scribes, and one can sense that the pattern as regards sound and spelling, of English words such as '-burgh, borough, boro, thorough' produced *Rothero, Protherough, Protheroe*, so that the pronunciation, in the English and official context came to follow the spelling. As a result *Prydderch (Prytherch)* and *Protherough, Protheroe* have quite different pronunciations. And one may surmise that the first syllable came to have -*o*-, as in 'mother, brother'; but instead of keeping the quality of the -o- in 'brother', it tended to change to the quality of 'bother'. Quite apart from the orthographic adaptation on the pattern of 'borough, boro', the sound of -*erch* as pronounced in Welsh was extremely difficult to put into writing and scribes seemed to have heard an epenthetic sound between *r* and *ch* which is shown by such spellings as 'Retherech'.

The other change was the use of *Roderick* to replace *Rhydderch*, so that it came to be regarded as the standard form. Phillimore 210-211 suggests that *Roderic* came to be used in the first place for another name, i.e. *Rhodri*. George Owen uses Roderic for Rhodri, and he probably was following Powel's *History of Wales* 1584. 'The custom of calling persons named Rhodri "Rodericus" or Roderick doubtless partly came from falsely equating the Welsh name with the similar Gothic one . . .', then follow other examples of 'equation' such as Edward and Iorwerth, and actual examples of treating Roderick as anglicised from Rhydderch: 'A good instance of the Anglicisation of Rhydderch into Roderic in the course of the last century, is given in Meyrick, in the *Hist. of Cardiganshire* p.401. He there says, *à propos* of Pen Glais, near Aberystwyth, "The present house was built by Roderic Richards. His father was Richard Rhydderch".' Phillimore's other example is

Siôn Rhydderch (1673-1735) the publisher, who was also known as John Roderick. The footnote has the clue to the confusion of Rhodri and Rhydderch in early texts, 'Perhaps the confusion of the two names points to the earliness of the habit of Latinizing both alike into Rodericus. An early instance of Redricus for Rodri is found in the Life of St Cadoc (*Cambro – British Saints* pp.86-7) where the same person is thrice in the nominative called *Rodri*, and once in the dative *Rodrico*'; *v*. above for use of *Mereduc-Maredudd*. [It is strange how infrequently the name Rhodri occurs in the medieval period; as it virtually disappeared, the following example as surname in the nineteenth century is most surprising: Census Returns 1861, PRO, Llangyfelach Lone, William Rodry born at Llangyfelach and his family. It has now become one of the most popular christian names.]

Examples in early and early modern texts:
B13. 229, SR 1292, Treharn ab Retherech. B24. 187, Fasti Cist. Camb. 204. John Rodryke/John Rotherith (Rotherhithe) – text editor suggests they are the same. BBStD 50. Rether ap Cadogan. CatAncDeeds V. 13268, Anglesea [sic] Rederych ap David. V. 12144, Hereford . . . sons of Wronou son of Retherech. VI. 4273, Chester date 1333, Thomas son of Rothoric. CAP 1455. Rethergh . . . Retherg, Rethregh ap Rees. B6, 73, Eliz. Docs. Rotherche dd ap Rotherche alis Gwyn. B10, 85, John ap Rutherch suber = 86. John ap Ryddz syber, Kemes Pems 16c. DLancaster (Kidwelly 1609) 181, . . . Redderch; 230, David Pretherake. Star CP 158, Cards Ievan ap Rudder, 161, Php Protheroth. WPortBooks 222, Owen Rotherugh = 224 Rotherghe. InvECP 17, Caerns 1538, John ap Redragh. 29, Merion 1538, Ritharche . . . CRHaverford 22, Henry Preddergh, 186, Harry Retheraughe.

A few examples from the Shropshire Registers will represent the astonishing variety found in them:
Ludlow 14, 1585 John ap Rothers. 17, 1590 Elnor Throwtherege. Wistanstow 39, 1691, Pothero. Eaton-under-Heywood, 1, 1627 Prothro 4, 1663 Prutherock. Condover 89, 1637. Pritherg 165, 1706 Putheror (Index, Putheroe).

A special note should be made of another variation.

Hodnet 79, 1717-18. John Protherah. 231, 1780 Martha Protheroe. 156, 1756 Mary Prothera. Edgmond 173, 1766 Pruthery.

Here are a few examples apparently beginning with *B*:

Meole Brace 216 Broderick. St Chad's, Index Braderick.

In the following examples one sees an attempt being made to provide a *B* form with an etymology:

Wrockwardine 187, 1756 Ann. d. of Robert Brotheroe; 190, 1758 Elizabeth d. of Robert Brotherwood and Mary.

Four other children are baptised 193, 196, 199 and 202, and the parents are Brotherwood on each occasion. In the Index, Brotheroe is put with Brotherwood, Brethwood, Brotherhood and Brothwood.

The modern electoral registers provide the following examples, and those with -*e*- in the first syllable are consistent with the explanation given above.

Rederick, from Ludlow, Much Wenlock, Cheadle, Heald Green Ward 1. Rotherick, Leominster, Eye. Broderick, fairly widespread: Ludlow, Much Wenlock; Wrekin, Stockton – Albrighton, Tong – Albrighton; City of Hereford; Stroud, Chalford 3, Painswick, Stonehouse etc. Brodrick, CT, Coln St Aldwyn; Stroud, Nailsworth; Bromsgrove No.3 S. West. Bretherick, Bromsgrove, No.3, West; Wirral, Barnston, Haswell; West Flint, Rhyl East; East Flint, Hawarden – Manor and Rake. Boderick, Bl. Gwent, Abertillery, Nantyglo. Brotherhood, Monmouth, Trelech United (*v.* PRWrockwardine above). Brotheridge (? may -*idge* be from -*erch*); CT, Chipping Camden, Chipping Camden Lower, Upper, Leckhampton; Kidderminster, Tenbury. Cheadle, Marple, South Ward 1. [Variants of Broderick occur frequently, and the *Br*- form is difficult to explain at present. The same difficulty arises with names like Brobben, Brobbin, etc. occurring side by side with Proben, Probyn, etc.]

Rotheray is not frequent, Runcorn, Lymm – Booths Hill; Copeland, Ennerdale and Kinniside; South Worcs., Malvern East – Langland; *Rothery* is widespread and frequent in the constituencies of Barrow-in-Furness,

Copeland, Workington.

Because of the frequency of the name in N.W. England, it would be safer to conclude that it is indigenous to the area, although it could still be of British origin, but the name is best left to scholars approaching from another direction. We also find that it occurs fairly early in the records of the North West:

PRGreat Orton 10. 1612, George Roddery = 11. 1617, George Rotherie = 13. 1622; 76. 1617, ... Rothery; PRPenrith 1559, Roddery; PRPenrith (St Andrews) Index, Rodderie (several); PRBridekirk, Index, Rothery (several) and Rohherie.

Rhys (Rees, Reece, Preece). Rice, Price, Pryse, etc.

Rhys is one of the commonest Welsh names; the version *Rees* and the form *Price* are especially typical of parts of SW It was transposed into Rees (sometimes *Res*, or *Reez*) by med scribes: the -*ee*- is an accurate spelling, in English, of the sound in SW dialects which have long ceased to give to -*y*- its peculiar quality; in any case the -*ee*- comes near to the original sound. The version *Rees* does not show the aspirate quality of the native *Rhys*; the fact is that Welsh writing in the early med period fails to show this and uses *r* for both the lenited and unlenited sound. One sometimes finds *Rh*, e.g. B15. 287. Aberystwyth – Cardigan 14th century: Rhis vach Walter (? misreading of 'vab'). It is unusual to find *Rh* with -*ee*-, cf. B10. 181. Llanuwchllyn 18th century: Edward Rhees. It is latinized as Resus:

B10. 64. West W. 1352. Jeuan ap Resus; 72. ... Resi ap Res.

It is possible that AN scribes observed the peculiar quality of the vowel in the name *Rhys*, and the use of *Rice* may in origin have been an attempt to represent the sound; it is far more probable that, seeing the Welsh version Rhys, Rys, they pronounced as if it were the E *y*, and that this led eventually to the spelling *Ryse, Rice*. This was very widely used and this is the version seen in *Price*. There were other spellings, Pryce, Pryse (pronounced the same as Price, and not as in Prys, which represents the correctly developed W version). The Rice form was latinized into Riceus, e.g. Sannan 1668, *Dowsa filia Ricei*. Needless to say, *ab-rhys* became *Pr*- (Prys, Preece, Price, etc.): these few examples illustrate the *ap*- formation and the survival of the vowel *a*-:

Star CP 4. Denbs Robt ap Price = 5. Robt Aprice. 169. Denbs Katherine Price of London daughter of Thos ap Rees Wyn. HM iv, 71. Mathern, List of Vicars, 1560. David ap Rees (also called David Price). Cwtta Cyf. 96. 1623. one Richard Price M'cer son of John ap Rees.

The following represent the various forms and spellings in med. and early modern texts: B13. 217. SR 1292. Res Kethin. B6. 147. Caern 1303. Griffini ap Rys; B6. 360. NW 1326. Rees ap Madyn Esspyn. AnglPleas (the spelling throughout is 'Res') 31. Meredith ap Res. LpOswestry 51. Rice Kayn (i.e. the poet Rhys Cain). DLancaster (Dom de Monmouth 1610) 86. Lawrencii ap Prise. PRConway 1618. ... ap Hugh Rice. InvECP 3. Angl 1529. ... ap Rise. 158. Monts 1556. Richard Uprise. 186. Rads 1556. Richard Aprece. 254. Marches 1538. Thomas ap Ryse Melyn. CRHaverford, Index, Rees, with variants, Reece, Rice, Rise, Ryse, Reese. L'Estrange Ewen, 255, gives Press (ab Rhys).

Although the usage may not be widespread we can provide local evidence from certain parts of West Glamorgan of the use of 'Rhysyn' as a colloquial form of Rhys; the following appear to be examples:

RadsSoc XLI. 57-8, Builth 1343-49. Resen ap Griffith. InvECP 197, Glam Senghennydd 1533. Thomas, Resyn and William, Treharn.

SHROPSHIRE REGISTERS

Hanwood 34. 1628. Rise (?) ap Propert (editor's query). Hopton Castle 7. 1594. Lodovicus Ap Preece. Clunbury 38. 1641. Reise Preise. 57. 1667. Anne Reice. Claverley 18. 1581. Yeven Apprise. Worthen, Index, Appres. Pontesbury 364. 1761. Preest, probably = 372. Preece. High Ercall 64. 1617. Rice ap Richards. 106. 1634. ... David ap Rize ap Williams. Acton Burnell 19. 1603. Richard Rise. Tong 48. 1707. Robert s. of John Priest or Price. Sheriffhales 2. 1558. ... Margaret Ryse. 10. 1584. Howell and Agnes Ap Ryce.

One has to ask whether Breeze and Brice are related. These versions can be dismissed outright. The *zed* quality of the consonant rules out Breeze at once, quite apart from the difficulty of reconciling *Br*- with a *Pr*- form. Breeze occurs quite often in the Shropshire

registers and occasionally -*s*- is used, e.g. Waters Upton 56 -1789, Joseph Brees; 60 -1792, Joseph Breeze, but in the majority of cases it is written Brees or Breeze, e.g. Billingsley, Index, Brees, Bres, Breeze.

Brice, Bryce also occurs quite often in the registers but the occurrence of Brice in English contexts is not in favour of a Welsh origin, e.g. Lay Subsidy, Cumberland, 6th Edward III, Penereth p.67 Thomas son of Brice; the form Briceson also occurs in the document; to quote only two examples, B Yale (Survey 1315) 45, Ricardus Brice occurring amongst non-Welsh names.

Cf. also Bown 3012 brice o vristeu (= Brice of Bristol), *v.* note 245, an AN baron (= Brise de Bretoue).

Richard

Reaney has a number of variant forms such as *Ricard, Rickerd, Rickert, Ricket*. Although the forms Richard, Richards, Prichard are recognized as the correct or standard forms in Wales, the colloquial pronunciation in the Welsh-speaking communities in SW is (using English spelling) 'Richet' or 'Ritchet, Ritchets'. As the sound represented by -*ch*-, -*tch*- did not exist in Welsh originally, -*si*- took its place in Welsh to give the med. Welsh *Rhisiart*; the DWB has two poets of the sixteenth and early seventeenth centuries, Rhisiart Fynglwyd and Rhisiart Owen ap Rhisiart. A derivative form using suffix -*yn* is seen in the name of the fourteenth century poet Rhisierdyn.

The following, including *Pr*- forms, represent the various versions found in Welsh sources:

B2. 68. West W. 1301. Ricardo Wroth. B10. 152. West W. 1352. Richett. B15. 61. AS 1406. Meredyth ap Rigert. ADClun 67. Laurence Priket. B14. 135, 2nd vol. StD regs. Ieuan Pricker ... Ieuan Prycker (?). WPort Books 96. Richard Priccard of Tenby; 128. Rice Prickhard; 140. Rice Prychard; 205. Rice Prickett. RadsSoc XLIII. 27 Jan. 1574-5, Will, Cefnllys, To Ellen vz Ricarte ... William Priccart. XLVIII. 79. Will, Nantmel, 1576. Riccard ap Edward. XLIV. 46. 16 cent. David ap Gwelym Prikerd of Paynscastell. Star CP 84. Glam Eliz. Jenkin Dd Rickett ... of Gelligaer. HRads 399. Prickards of Dderw ... 'the family of the Prickards, ap Prickard, ap Richard, and of

Rycard, as the name appears to have been spelt interchangeably in old times ...'. CRHaverford 193. Reese Prichet; 183. William Ricard.

SHROPSHIRE REGISTERS

Because of the effects of dialect changes the variety seen above is extended in the Shropshire parishes:
Ford 16, 18. ap Richard, Aprichard. Clunbury, Index, Rickards, several entries. Chelmarsh 94, 95 (1746) Mary Prichards. Alberbury, Index, 265. Prichett – one entry of husband and wife compared with hundreds of Prichard, Pritchard. ChStretton 118. 1776. Delabere Pritchett. Cleobury Mortimer 321. 1810. Prickett; 336. 1799. Pritchard or Pritchitt. (Index also gives Pritshard) Westbury 30. 1655. Thomas ap Ellis aliter Prichatt; 33. 1657 ... ap Prichatt; Moreton Say 50. 1753. William Pratchet; 61. 1769. Mary Pratchett; Wroxeter 89. 1732. Mr John Prachett, p. Harley.

PRESENT DAY REGISTERS

There is no point in plotting the ordinary forms in present-day registers but the version with *Up-* should be noted:
Uprichard, St. and Hyde, Langendale – Hollingworth; East Flint, Sealand (H); *Upritchard*, Northwich, Tarvin Rural – Wellington. *Rickets*, Preseli, St Dogmaels. *Rickard*, Wrekin, Wrockwardine; Islwyn, Crosspenmaen; Monmouth, Mathern. *Rickards*, West Flint, Rhyl East – Central. *Rickus*, Wrekin, Hadley (several). *Prickett*, Ludlow, Ch. Stretton; Oswestry, Baschurch; S. Glouc, Winterbourne 3, *Pritchette*, CT. Cirencester 2. *Prickard*, BrRadnor Ll. Cwmdauddwr. *Pratchett*, Monmouth, Overmonnow.

v. above p.11, examples of Crichett, Crichard which may be derived from *verch* or *ach* – *Richett/Richard*.

Robert

Reaney has the variants *Robart, Robarts, Robberds* etc., and the still earlier versions *Rodbertus, Rotbert*. The best-known pet form is *Robin* (giving *Robins, Robbens* etc); there are a number of other derivative versions including *Roblin, Robelyn*.
Cf. the following from Welsh sources:
B13. 220. SR 1292. Deffrin Brueyn: Roppertus ap Howel. 224. 'Kery and Kadewing', Ropperd Voel. 226. paid at 'Bergauenny',

Iuan ap Roppert; 227. Dauid ap Wronu ap Roppert. B6. 359. NW 1326. Howel ap David ap Rotpert. B15. 287. Aberyst-Cardgn. 14th century Jeuan ap Rotperd. CatAncDeeds iii. C3234. Monmouth, Thomas ap Roppert (master-serjeant of Bergeveny, Edw III). B3. 71. Criccieth, 14th century. Willelmi ap Robyn. B15. 47. AS 1406. dd ap Rhobin bibidd. CaernQSR 239. Hugh ap John ap Hywel ap Robyn and James Robyns. CaernCR 18. Robyn ap Roppert. B10. 91. Roll of Wards, LMKemes, George Owen's entries, Jevan Ropperts wiff. CRHaverford 128. Alce Properte; Elizabeth Properte. 46. Robert Propert; 46. William Propert. HM i. 29. Skenfrith. Ped. of the Family of Probyn. ibid. iii (Part 2) Usk, 116. James Probins, end of 17th century. JEG 23. Son of Robin Norris becomes Henry Robinson. InvECP 96. William Robynson, alias Robertes of London (twice, Denbs 1533).

SHROPSHIRE REGISTERS

Hanwood 34. 1628. Rise (?) ap Propert. Lydham 41. 1757. Griffith Probart; 44. 1764. Griffith Probert. Church Preen 17. 1730. Elizabeth Probot. Neen Sollars 3. 1716. Probberts. Hopesay, Index – one of the variants, Probut. Myddle, 19. 1564. Humf'redus Probin. 41. 1586. Sep. Morgani ap Probarde. Acton Burnell 102. 1736. Martha Probat. Great Ness 53. 1677. John Probutt; 55. 1679. Faith Probut. Wem 63. 1632. Hommfrey Probin; 168. 1646. Humphrey Probinne. 71. 1636. Ellis ap Probat; 100. 1608. Jone ap Probarte. 147. 1627. John s. of John ap Probate. 150. 1630. Anne w. of Oliver ap Probatt; 372. 1695. Probats. 151. 1632. Allis Probin.

Only representative examples from present day registers are given below; no examples being given of the usual forms *Roberts* and *Probert*:
Propert: S. Gloucs, Filton. *Proberts*: S. Worcs, Malvern East/Langland. *Probett*: S. Worcs, Evesham East/North; Evesham East/West. *Probin*: Nantwich, Burland, Cholmondeley; Northwich, Tarporley South. *Probyn*: Ludlow, Bridgnorth – St Leonards; South Hereford, Fownhope.

Robin *v.* Robert

Roddericke, Roderick, Rodryke *v.* Rhydderch

Roger, Rosser, Proger, Prosser

There has been occasion more than once to explain that the Welsh sound system originally did not include the sound of *j*, or the *-g-* of Roger; when words containing this sound were borrowed the nearest sound in Welsh was *s* or *si*, so that Roger became Roser, usually written Rosser; with the initial *r* given the aspirate quality, Rhoser, occasionally Rhosier is used.

B13. 217. SR 1292. 'jurors of the commote of Peruet', Cadugan ap Roser. BBStD 64. Gurgen ap Rosser. ADClun 23. Lewelin ap rosser. Star CP 8, Glam Henry VII. Rosser Kemeys; 195. Monm Jas I, Rhytherch Rosser, yeoman, son and executor of Roger Rhytherch. InvECP 169. Brec 1547. John Rogers alias John Rosser Thomas.

An example of Rhosier is the name of the Catholic author, Dr Rhosier Smyth, whose name also appears as 'Dr Roger Smith, Smithe Roger, Rogerius Smythus Wallus', v. pp.vi-vii of *Theater du Mond*. The *-si-* of borrowed words and even of native Welsh words became *-sh-* in the spoken language of the early modern period, and this change produced *Rosher*, cf. RadsSoc XXXVI. 37, Chancery case 1558-79. Thomas ap Rosher of Clero; HM i. 243. Pedigree of Rosher of Trewyn. There are three entries of the name *Rosier* in the Cardiff and S.E. Wales TD; this may be from a different source; five in Gloucester TD, five in Bristol, two in Shrewsbury – Hereford. There is one entry of *Rosher* in the Bristol TD (in Cleveland); D. Tel 30.10.78, Deaths, Roshier (Exeter). The educated classes of Gwent would be able to pronounce Roger properly before the patronymic system of naming was discontinued, therefore in Gwent and the border counties, the *ab* + gave *Proger*; whereas in other areas, *ab* + gave *Prosser*. Roger became a popular name in Wales so that Rogers as surname is found in abundance.

Star CP 112. Monm Eliz. Proger Rawlins; 117. Monts. Eliz. Lloyd ap Roger; 192. Monm Jas I. Walter Proger. HM i. 199. Pedigree of Family of Herbert, became Proger, Roger ap John → John ap Roger → William ap John Proger. InvECP 209. Glam 1553. Fluellen ap Roser. 237. Monm 1551. Thomas Aproser.

SHROPSHIRE REGISTERS

Clunbury 38. 1641. William Procer = 42. 1645. Gulielmi Procer = 44. 1647. William Prosser. Stanton Lacy 75. 1671. Progers; 82. 1682. John Procer. Ludlow 406. 1662. Hugh |Progers = 412. 1666. Hugh Proger (later examples of both forms). Neen Sollars 3. 1714. Prodgers.

Rondle *v.* Randell

Rosher, Rosier, Rosser *v.* Roger

Rothera, Rotheray, Rotherith, Rotheroe, Rothery *v.* Rhydderch

Ryrryd *v.* Rhiryd

S

Saer

Saer means 'carpenter'; *saer maen* (*maen* = 'stone') is used for mason; there is an example below from PRSelattyn.

B13. 227. SR 1292. Seysil Saer. B7. 143. NW 1303. Madoci Sayr. BBStD 216. Ieuan saer, Ieuan Sayrhir (i.e. I.S. Hir 'the tall'). 226. Cristina sayr, (wife taking husband's occupational name, or daughter taking her father's). Star CP 203. Monts Roger ap Jno als Sayer, of Berriew, Carpenter. DLancaster 10 (Monm) Thomas Sare; 23. Heredes Nichole Sare ... 40. Nichole Sayer. InvECP 140. Monts 1538. Owen ap John Sayer = 143. Owen ap John Zare, brother and heir and executor of Bedowe ap John Zare. 254. Marches. Humphrey ap Davy alias Sawyer. PRWestbury 3. 1639. Saire (surname); 8. 1641. ditto = 12. 1643, Sayer; 51. 1665. Sayre. PRSelattyn 135. 1651 Jonathan s. of Robert, saer mane, of Llangollen; (cf. 230. 1703. Owen ye Carpenter). PRWhittington 1. 1643. Margarett the daughter of Robert John Sayer.

The relation to E *Sawyer, Sayer, Sayers, Sayre, Saer, Sare*, etc. (Reaney) is difficult to establish. There is no suggestion in LP 17, 26, that the W *saer* is a borrowing; the Irish *sáer*, mod. Irish *saor* is evidence that the W and I forms have a Celtic origin, but the similarity of *saer/sayer* means that in the border areas (and registers) the names merged and the spellings became confused and interchangeable. According to Reaney the various E forms have more than one source; the possibility of a W source in some cases might be considered.

Saethon *v.* Introd. Place-names

Sais, Sayce, Seys

The usual meaning of *Sais* is 'Englishman'; fem. *saesnes*, pl. *saeson*; but as an epithet attached to a pers. name it probably meant 'able to speak English'; in the early period this was a rare enough accomplishment to be distinctive. There is no reason to believe that it had any meaning of contempt: one of the twelfth century court poets was called Elidir Sais (his poems are printed in MA 240-245). B13. 210, SR 1292. '... Griffith, Cantington alias Griffith Hir Sais ...' B1. 263. NW 1305. De Kenwrico Seys. B15. 47. AS 1406. Ho(we)ll ap Je(uan) Sais; cf. 50. Je(uan) Englis. [Cf. ADClun 44. Tybot le Englys; 51. Eynion le Engleys. InvECP 250. Marches 1518. ... daughter of Thomas Englishe, alias called Thomas ap Griffith Tuppa. DLancaster Lps 87. William James David John Yrish (there must be more than one person here). Reg C of Marches 176. David ap Lewis Comro.] RecCa, Index, Says, five; Seis, four; Seys, five. Glam Cartae, Index, Sais, Sayce, Seys, Saise, Seyse. Surveys GK, Reynoldston 1665, 267. Edward Seyes; 269. William Seyes. Millwood 1641, 288. Roger Seys and Richard Seys.

The following appears to be a derivative using the *-yn* termination – BBStD 266. Ieuan Seysyn.

Examples in Shropshire registers:
Lydham 21. 1696. Richard Sais; 24. 1708. Sarah Sayse; 24. 1707. ... Sayse. Alberbury 321. 1708. John Smyth, alias Says, of Westbury. Chirbury 13. 1635. Margarita Saysse. Whittington 168. 1647. ...d. of Thomas Kingricke alias Sais of Daywell. Oswestry 108. 1585 has an example of the fem., Anne Saesnes, and Alberbury and Ludlow have examples of the plural. [Cf. RadSoc XXV. 30, Will, New Radnor 1548, Anne Sasnes; D.E. Williams 48, footnote, quotes from

Bradney's examples of nicknames found in Monmouthshire, 1785 Bessy Saesnes (Betsy the Englishwoman) = Elizabeth Powell.] Alberbury 497. Sayson. Ludlow 323. 1622. Richard Season and Jane; 325. 1622. Margaret Season; 338. 1626. Anne Season. Representative examples from present-day registers:

Sayce, Shrewsbury, Cotton Hill; Ludlow, More; S. Worcs, Berrow; further examples found in S. Gloucs, W. Gloucs, City of Glouc, City of Hereford, S. Hereford, BRad, Monts, Newport.

Saice, Bromsgrove, No.4, S.E. *Saies*, Preseli, Llangwm, Herbrandston, Steynton. *Seys*, S. Gloucs, Lydney – Alvington; W. Gloucs, Lydney 2; Monmouth, Chepstow – St Christopher's.

Sandde(f)

This name in the form *Sande* (= *Sandde*) occurs in the tale of *Kulhwch ac Olwen*, WM 462-3; this shows the loss of final *f*, for it is *Sandev* in LL 279, and also shows it was not just a name used in a myth or primitive story: CaernQSR 168 John Santhey; ibid 228 David ap Sander (? = Sandev); Mer LSR 28 Ieuan ap Landeu (a name difficult to identify, probably 'Sanddef'); JEG 80 . . . ap Sandde; Bartrum 300-985, two examples in addition to the character in *Kulhwch ac Olwen* 985-1215, 110, Elfan ap Sandde; 172, Sandde as first name, five instances. Many families claimed descent from the forefather *Sandde Hardd*, *v.* Bartrum 300-1400, 821-830.

One sees the forms *Sandy, Sandey, Sandie* in various registers; these probably come from colloquial forms of 'Alexander'; is it possible that in some cases, e.g. *Sandie*, in Denbigh, Llantysilio, the name is a survival of 'Sandde'?

Sant

L *sanctus* became *sant* in Welsh; the *-nct* in modern W 'sanct, sanctaidd' is due to the latinizing orthography of William Salesbury, *v.* OIG – Index. In the pedigree given to the patron saint David, he is said to be the son of Sant, in which case 'sant' is used as a personal name (i.e. as 'noun'); usually *sant* is used as an epithet following the pers. name; it is true that the saint's pedigree uses 'uab Sant', *Dauyd uab Sant, vab Keredic*; B Dewi 1, the saint is usually called Dewi Sant: Professor D. Simon Evans in his note p.25, doubts whether this 'sant'

was a historical character, for his name does not appear in the royal pedigree of Ceredigion; and one may justifiably suggest that the epithet has been converted into a pers. name.

BYale 40. Johannes Sant. B15. 45. AS 1406. dd Sant. RecCa, Index, three. AnglPleas 18. John ap Jevan ap David Sant, late of Aberalawe. 45. Morvith verch Gruffydd ap David Sant. PWLMA 393. Ieuan Sant ('may be identified with John Sant'). PRBitterley, Index, Sant (Saunt, Sunt).

The surname *Sant* still survives; it is found in abundance in Nantwich, Middlewick, Wards East, North, West; cf. also, W.Mail 20.12.77, News item mentions David Sant, Abermule.

Sayce *v.* Sais
Saycell, Saysell *v.* Seisyll
Sayre *v.* Saer
Sayson *v.* Sais
Scholick, Scollick *v.* Ysgolhaig
Scourfield *v.* Introd. Place-names
Scurlage

CatAncDeeds iii. D112. Pembs, and D242. Herbert Scurlag (Henry III). Scurlage is a manor in Llanddewi in the Gower peninsula. Cf. Clark 502-3, Pedigree of Scurlage of Scurlage in Gower, and note especially, 'William Scurlage, to whom Richard, Earl of Clare, about 1250, granted a manor, no doubt that known as Scurla Castle, or Trecastle, near Llantrissant, where the grantee seems to have built a strong house. Probably both manors, that in Gower and that near Llantrissant, took their names from the family'.

Later, Lucy Scurlage is referred to as 'of Scurla Castle in Gower'. Next, 'A branch of this family migrated in 1184 to Ireland, of whom was Capt. Oliver Scurlock, who served with the Irish at the siege of Boulogne in 1544. His son Aristotle Scurlock was physician to Queen Mary, and had from her Rosslaw Manor, Co. Wexford. His numerous children settled in Caermarthen, where a granddaughter married Sir Richard Steele, Addison's contemporary.'

The name *Scurlock* is well-known in Swansea and in Pembs and there are five entries of the name in the TD of Cardiff and S.E.

Scurlock *v.* Scurlage

Seisyll, Seisyllt, Cecil

The form with -*ll* and the form with -*llt* are found in early texts; this variation occurs in other words, *gwyllt, gwyll; cyfaill, cyfaillt, v.* GPC. If the scribe had no distinct method of writing the *ll*' sound he might use a single *l*: that would make three variant forms; the *llt* is sometimes *lld, llth*, and even the initial -*s*- may vary. The poems of Seisyll Bryffwrch (1160-1220 ?) are printed in MA 235-6, and the verses of his bardic dispute with Cynddelw in H 180-81.

B13. 215 SR 1292. Seisild ap Adam, David ap Seysil. 216. ... ap Seisil, ... ap Seycild, ... ap Seyselt. 223. ab Seicil = ab Seisil; Secil ap ...; ... ab Ceicil. B2. 77. ab Madok Seithild. CAP 39. Griffin and Dyddgu Seisyllt, Index; text = Seyisyllt, 1323. BBStD 92. Trefseyssel; 98. Trefseysil (Place-name). 100. ... ap Seyssil; 286. gwele Seyssillth ap Gwyann. GlamCartae, Index, Seisil, Seisill, Seisild. RadsSoc XLVI. 31, Pat Rolls 1403, David ap Saisall. DLancaster (man. de Albo Castro) 116. Robert Cicilt; 127. Thome Cicile. HAsaph V11.62. Oswestry, vicars, 1217. Seysyllt Porcionarius. InvECP 207. Glam. 1551. Morgan and John Syshelth (Cicholth) of Bristol. HM has many references, and his version throughout is 'Sitsyllt', until it becomes 'Cecil'. i. 82. Ped. of Fam. of Cecil of the Dyffryn, one of the branches of Cecil. 97. Ped. of Fam. of Powell (de Bredwarden) of Ll. Crossenny, mentions Cynfyn ap sitsyllt Fychan, Ralph ap Sitsyllt. In Part iv. 98. Portskewet there is a *Cycill Griffyth* in the record of tenants of the barony 1569; but the most important examples are connected with the family of Alltyrynys: Part ii. 242, ped. of family of Wynston of Trewyn mentioning Thomas Sitsyllt of Alltyrynys, 'A quo Cecil of Alltyrynys'; and on p. 242 is the evidence for the belief that the great Cecil families of England came from this source. P. 245 'The name of Cecil is not extinct in the county. More than one labouring man can be found with this surname, and in the parish of Welsh Newton near Monmouth, is a most respectable family of farmers named Cecil, who assert their claim to be considered kinsfolk of the noble family in England. [T.E. Morris p.108 gives a pedigree, starting with 'Gilbert Winston ...', then four generations of Sitsilt, leading to 'William Cecil, Baron of

Burley ...'. The following information is added: 'Boswell, a writer on Armoury, states that he had seen the names Sitsilt and Sitsylt "in documents in the possession of the Right Honourable the Lord of Burghly, to whom in blood the same belongeth, whose name being written Cecil at this day" (1572), and he adds that the original home of the Cecils, "Alterynnis remaineth near Abervanny".']

The name *Cecil* survives in Gwent and in a few places on the border according to present day registers:
Monmouth, Chepstow St Mary's; S. Gloucs, Awre 1; West Gloucs, Awre, Blakeney, Lydbrook, Lydney, West Dean; Ludlow, Bridgnorth St Leonard.

There is also a name spelt *Saysell* or *Saycell* very much like the *ap Saisall* quoted above; *Saysell*, Newport, Malpas 2, Malpas 3, St Woollos 2; Monmouth, Chepstow Larkfield, Newcastle – Ll. Vibon Avel, Shirenewton, West Newchurch – Shirenewton. The spelling Saycell is found in Cardigan, Goginan – Melindwr (two families), Llanbadarn Fawr, Vaenor Upper.

Selyf, Sely

Selyf is the early W version of 'Solomon', derived from *Salomo, v.* WG 91. It is a common feature for final -*f* to drop; the final syllable is sometimes -*au*, or -*ef*, giving -*e*; *v.* TYP 507.
Mer LSR 45, Map Sely; 49. Ioreword ap Seleu. B15. AS 1406. Ho'll ap Jockyn ap Seli (variant Sela). Bartrum 985-1215, 173. Selyf, five examples; 1350-1415, 801. ... Hywel Sele ap Meurig Lloyd.
Reaney gives Sealey, Sealy, Seely etc., and offers an OE derivation, *saelig*, 'happy, blessed'. The W *Sely* might be considered as a possible source of some of the examples quoted.

Seys *v.* Sais

Shenkin, Shinkin(s) *v.* Ieuan

Shone, Shoone *v.* Ieuan

Skeyviocke *v.* Introd. Place-names

Stackpole, Stackpool

We have received detailed notes from Major Francis Jones concerning the place-name and surname, some of the information drawn from the MSS muniments of the Earl of Cawdor, Golden Grove. The name derives from the stack at the entrance of Broadhaven, the house and the village standing at the head of a fiord; Charles, *Non-Celtic Place-names in Wales* 26. Stackpole House stands in the parish of St Petrox; Cheriton was known as Stackpole Elidor, and Bosherston as Stackpole Bosher. The earliest owner of Stackpole had the Welsh name of Elidor/Elidir; *v.* account in Fenton's Pembrokeshire 231 (2nd ed) of the younger brother who went to co. Clare during the invasion and occupation of Ireland and established a branch of the Stackpoles in Clare. There are various references in documents of the med period to families from the area of Stackpool, with the surname Stackpole, not necessarily of the same family; and the name survived for some centuries in S. Pemb, e.g. George Stackpull witnessed grant at Easter Trewent to George Lort of Stackpool in 1589. The name of the novelist de vere Stackpole probably comes from the co. Clare branch. For another spelling: D. Tel 26.8.80, Deaths, Stacpoole (in Sidmouth).

Sully

Gazetteer gives Sully as an E version of the W *Sili*, for the village between Cardiff and Penarth; WATU 199 has 'Sully (Sili) [Abersili]'. A long list of early refs. will be found in G.O. Pierce, *Place-names of Dinas Powys* 290-293, such as Waltero de Sulie, Sulley, Sullyn, Scilly, etc.; despite all these references Professor Pierce has to admit that the origin of the name remains obscure, 'the difficulty lies in seeking to establish whether the family of *de*

Sully who held the manor from the last decade of the 12th cent. . . . derived their name from the place, or whether the place was named after them'. It is sufficient for the purpose of this work to show the existence of the place-name and the surname in the early med period. Sully is given in L'Estrange Ewen 242, in the list of W place-names used as surnames. Also D.E. Williams 62, referring to De Sullis, and example quoted of Johannes Sylly, 1537, from Glam Cartae VI. 2151. The TDs of Cardiff and of Swansea show that Sully is well distributed throughout South Wales.

Swrdwal

This is best known as the name of the poet Hywel Swrdwal (fl. 1430-60); cf. MLSW 89, 116, Philippi Surdwall (location 'Wenllouk'). It is generally considered that this name represents 'de Surda Valle', found in the name of the Norman 'Robertus de Surda Valle' who went on a crusade at the end of the eleventh century. The poet may be a descendant of Sir Hugh Swrdwal who was given the manor of Aberyscir for his service to Bernard Newmarch during his conquest of Breconshire. The pedigree of Surdwal of Aberysir (read 'yscir') is given in HBr 270. The name *Serdiville* in East Flint, Hawarden, Manor and Rake might possibly be a version of *Swrdwal*, or of 'Surda Valle'.

T

Taffe, Taaff(e)
v. above p.30.
PRLudlow 348. 1631. Thomas Taffe.
PRMeole Brace, Index, Taff (husband and
wife). Non-con. reg., RC Mawley Hill, 18.
1799. James Taff, son of William and Rachel
Taff. Bromsgrove, Redditch S. Central,
Taaffe; D. Tel 3.12.78, Taaffe, address,
Balham.

Tal
The adj. *tal* is borrowed from E 'tall'; the
vowel in W is short, and the *l* in fact is double
-*l*, i.e. as in Pall-Mall. As the adj. for height
(of a person) it has displaced *hir* 'long'. In
some of the examples below the adj. after the
def. art. stands for the person unnamed, i.e.
'the tall one'.
B15. 46. AS 1406. Kyn ap y Tal, Je(uan) ap
dd ap y Tal; 57. Jockyn ap Ithel ap y Tal;
probably the def. art. is missing in the
following through elision: 50. Je(uan) ap
Kadr ap Je(uan) vab tal.

An example could be given of a colloquial
usage of *tal* in the lenited form distinguishing
between two cousins with the same name, *Sei
dal* = 'Isaiah the tall', TC 117; no lenition is
shown in the following:
B15. 56. AS 1406. Je(uan) Tal. CaernHS 26,
Bolde Rental 35, 36. Ievan Tale; RecCa 5.
Ieuan Tal. Bartrum 1215-1350, 227. Dafydd
ap Gwilym Tal ap Rhys [Ddu]. Surveys GK
276, 277. Jurors ... William Tale; 283.
William Talle.

Tâl – compounds
The meanings 'forehead, front, end' are
given in WG 68; one must add 'head', just as
pen means 'end' and 'head'; in most of the
examples below the word refers to the hair. A
note in WG 68 explains that *tâl* (with long
vowel, single *l*) changes to have a short vowel
in place-names such as *Tal-y-bont*. *Tâl* was
used, as *pen* was, to make proper compounds
with adjectives describing hair or complexion
or shape of head; the name *Talhaearn* probably
means 'iron-faced'.
B15. 47. AS 1406. Deikws Talgoch. B15. 288.
Aberystwyth – Cardigan 14th century Jeuan
ap Talgoch. RadsSoc XLI. 66, 1383-4. Mur'
ap Gruff' Dalgoogh. BBStD 140, 156. Will's
Taldu (= 'Talddu'). ADClun 23. Lewelin
talduy. Bartrum 1215-1350, 348. John Dal-
ddu. 1350-1415, 808. Dafydd Tal-llwyd of
Ardudwy. B13. 229. SR 1292. Yewan
Talloyd. (= 'Tal-llwyd'; the second element
of the proper compound should lenite to give -
lwyd but there is a strong tendency for the
contact of *l-l* to reverse the process and
become *l-ll*, as in *ail-llaw* 'second hand', *v.* TC
41, 142). Mer LSR 16. Meurico Dathloyt (?
thl = *ll*'). Bartrum 1350-1415, 732. Talgrych
ap Dafydd Fychan (crych, 'curly'; cf. *Pengrych*). Glam Cartae 1511. Dafydd ap Jev.
Dalgron (one expects 'dalgrwn', 'round-
head') ADClun 66. Eignon Talgron. RecCa
285. Cochyn ap Talboeth, Ieuan ap y
Talboeth ('hot-head', from *poeth*). BYale 94.
Ienna Talvoyll ('bald-head', *moel*); cf. Mer
LSR 55. Tale Moel; CaernCR 18. Dafydd ap
Adda Tal-y-Foel [MS talemoil]; the editors
have taken this to be a place-name, 'Top of
the bare hill', a quite reasonable interpretation; it could also mean 'Baldhead'.
B13. 220. SR 1292. Phillip ab Talcan (?
Talgan, from *can* meaning 'white, shining').
[It is possible that it should be the noun *talcen*
'forehead'; which is used as an epithet in the
following: CaernCR 34, 55. *Dafydd Talkyn*;
81. *Ieuan ap Dafydd Talken*. Cf. ELS Cumberland, Thoresby, p.21, John Talkan.] Mer
LSR 68. Cad(ugan) ap Talbant. ADClun
184. David ap Talbant (? from *pant* 'hollow,
dent'). B3. 37. Ithel Dalfrith (from *brith*,

'greyhaired'; quoted in CA 145 in the note on *talvrith*). Cf. B13. 224. SR 1292. Yereuarth Talren (At 'Cloun'). ADClun 15, 17, 19, 25, 32. Willelmi Talryn; 183. Dac' Talrayn. BYale 78. Madoc Talren. RadsSoc XXV. 25. Old Radnor 1544. Roger Talren; 26. New Radnor 1545. Also Taldren, (*lr* > *ldr*; cf. cafaltri, 'cavalry', Dem. Dial. in EEW 234). Is this a place-name in or near Clun; or from *rhyn* in the sense of 'stiff'? *v.* CA 92; if a place-name, it should be compared with Penrhyn.

Tannat (*v.* also Introd. Place-names)
The source of this surname is the river Tannat, and the name of a residence which included the river-name and then adopted as the surname of the family, e.g. H Asaph i. 488. Griffith Tannat, M.A., Jesus College, Oxford (of Glantanat, date 1589); V. 253, Llansantffraid-ym-Mechain, vicars, 1579, Griffith Tannat.
JEG 200, shows the marriage at the end of the sixteenth century of one of the Nanney daughters to Edward Tanat, 'of Neuadd Wen Co. Monts'. Star CP 12, Henry VIII, Miscell. Thos Tanat . . . Jno Tanat. PRMyddle 186. 1735. Joseph and Elizabeth Tannet. 309. 1810. Ann Tunnatt.
PRESENT-DAY REGISTERS
Bromsgrove, Broms. S.E. Tannett. C. of Hereford, Tupsley, Tannatt Nash. Monts, Llanwrin-Is-y-garreg, Tannatt.

Taylowe *v.* Teilo
Tecca, Tecco, Tecka, Teckoe *v.* Teg
Tedder *v.* Tudur

Teg
Teg 'fair, beautiful' was once in common use as an epithet attached to a pers. name. There is no need to question this or look for another explanation or meaning for it occurs as an element in the compounds, also used as pers. epithets, *glandeg* (*Landeg*), *mwyndeg*, *v.* above p.170; cf. also the following examples of *haeldeg* (*hael* = 'generous'), B2. 250, Charters Brecon-Llandovery, Griffino Hayldeke (var. Haldek); 253 (other inspeximus) Johanni Hayldoke (sic), 254 Griffino Hayldeke. Note also the unusual way of linking two adjectives (rather than by making a proper compound): HM i. 339. Gruffydd ap Howel, called Tew a theg (Fat and fair), slain by Gilbert de Clare, 1282. The adj. is found in the compound named *Tegwared*, *v.* below and Bartrum has examples of the compound *Tegwas*, in which

gwas would mean 'youth': 985-1215, 173, Selyf ap Irfelyn ap Tegwas; 174, Tegwas ap Gwyn ap Aelaw. An example also of having *teg* placed before the pers. name, thus – grammatically – making a proper compound: 1350-1415, 645, Iolyn ap y Teg Fadog; 647, Iorwerth ap y Teg Fadog (probably the same person, Iolyn hypocoristic for Iorwerth); cf. Dwnn 2. 110. Y teg Vadog in the Brogyntyn pedigree. Used in combination with *pen* (as in *Pengoch, Penwyn* etc. *v.* pp.174-5) it ought to be 'pendeg': the only example collected fails to show *d*: Mer LSR 38. Eynon Penteg.

In some of the examples quoted below it is written with a *k*: this kind of orthography is quite usual in native med W texts; it has been observed before that final *g* of Welsh words and names strikes the English ear as *k*, Llangattock for Cadog, *v.* p.62; the use of 'Teke' is probably intended to convey a long vowel. There are examples of using the spelling *teague*: this may occur in place-names, e.g. InvECP 229. Monm Philip Gwillim of Panteague (i.e. Panteg, or Pant-teg, near Pontypool): StarCP 189, 195. Monm Panteagne (miscopy or misreading of 'Panteague'); HM i. 428. Mamhilad, Gravestones having on them the 'parish of Panteague'; 454, altar-tomb in Penygarn Baptist Chapel, with the words 'Parish of Panteague', as late as 1832.

The Irish *Taidhg* is sometimes spelt 'Teague', and there are examples in a Welsh context of the Irish name being spelt Teague, Teage, so that there is a possibility of mistaking the Irish name for the W epithet, and *vice versa*, e.g. WPortBooks 1. John Tage (Chepstow), 188. Teage Plaine (Waterford), 192. Teage Fflachy (Waterford, probably = Flaherty'); 315. Tege Flemyng; PRCaerwent and Ll. Discoed, Ll. Disc 1696, Margaret, wife of Tegg O Brian, p. 59 Xnings Elizabeth daughter of Tegg OBrian was baptized . . . 1681; John son of Charles Obrian; the name O Brian removes doubt that this is the Irish forename; cf. also PRLl.Crossenny 1632 . . . fil's Rich'i Brian – Footnote, 'The name has continued in the parish until recently'. The presence of 'O Brian' settles the matter in these examples, but there may be other examples which, because of the identity of sound of W. *teg* and Irish *Taidhg*, will be difficult to determine what they really are in origin.

A point of grammar needs to be explained: the forms of comparison of *teg* are as follows, equative *teced*; comparative, *tegach* in med W *tecach* in mod W; superlative, *tecaf*. The terminations of the equative and superlative were -*hed*, -*haf*, so that the *h* changed the *g* into *k* (the change in the comparative in mod W came about through the force of analogy). The superlative *tecaf* was used at times as an epithet; the dropping of final *f* (*v*) in natural speech gave *teca*. It is entirely contrary to the phonetic law of the provection *g* + *h* >*k* , to have 'tega' in the superlative epithet; there appear to be such exceptional examples.

Examples of *teg* or *deg* as epithet attached to personal names:

B13. 227. SR 1292. Ririd ap Lewelyn Tek. B10. 164. AnglRental 160. . . . ap Ieuan teg. RadsSoc XLI. 58. Builth 1360-67, Morgan Tec. AnglPleas 46. David ap William ap David Deck. CatAncDeeds V1. 07835. Monts. John ap Llywelynn ap David Tege (16 Elizabeth). CaernCR 48. Einion ap Ieuan Teke [? = Teg] editor's query; 102. Hywel Teke. InvECP 40. Cards 1553. Gwillim ap Ieuan ap David Tege. 51. Carms 1544. Thomas David Tegge. 104. Denbs 1556. Hugh ap David ap Ieuan Deke. 142. Monts 1538. Thomas ap David Deygge, gentleman of Keweylok.

Examples of the superlative, tecaf, teca', deca', etc.

B15. 49. AS 1406. lln ap Je(uan) Teka. (Text editor's footnote refers to evidence in JEG *Pedigrees* . . . Gwenhwyfar d. of Ifan Decca.) JEG 41. Ifan Decca . . . (the example quoted above). 75. Decca alias Deio, 15th century. 275. Roger Decca of Ryton; 286. Hanmer co. Flint, . . . David Deccaf Vychan of Rhwytyn. Bartrum 1215-1350, 212. Cadwgon Deca ap Iorwerth ap Cadwgon Ddu. ibid. Ieuan Deg ap Dafydd. 617. Ieuan Deca ap Dafydd ap Iorwerth. [Cf. BBStD 142. Johnes Plubel; Dauzat's *Dictionnaire* includes *Plubel*, 'de Plus belle, soubriquet'.]

Examples of tega:

BBStD 220. Ieuan Tega. AnglPleas 5. Llewelin ab David Tega.

SHROPSHIRE REGISTERS

The Shropshire registers have such an abundance of examples and such variety of form only specimen examples are given:

Selattyn 5. 1559. Margett verch Ieuan teg . . . Oswestry 250. 1604. . . . Hugh Tege of Poole. Non-Con. and RC, Oswestry Old Chapel 121. . . . Susanna (Tegg) i.e. mother's name before marriage. Hanwood 11. 1583. Jonna Tege; 12. 1585. Willielmi Teage. Chirbury 37. 1651. Ellena Teage; 186. 1750. Anne Degg. Pontesbury 14. 1551. Elisabetha Tege f. Willmi de Lea. 16. 1552. Willimus Teage de Lea. Westbury 22. 1650. . . . Felis Tegue. Ludlow 30. 1604. Thomas Teage = 132. 1605. . . . Teigue = 138. 1609. Teague. 389. 1644. Thomas Tegue. 499. 1676. Catherine Degg. Munslow 49. 1610. . . . d. of David Teeg. 105. 1663. Catherine Deage. Wistanstow 173. 1810. Tague. St Chad's Index, Deag (one family); Teague, Tage, Teag, Teage, Tege. St Mary's, Index, Teague, Teage, Tayg.

The form *Teague* occurs frequently in the eighteenth century, e.g. Stanton Lacy 141. 1739 Anne Teague. The following example shows it being used as forename: Alberbury 273. 1692. Teague, s. of Teague and Joan Williams.

In addition to *Tecca*, the superlative in origin, there are variant forms such as *Tecco*; this change of final -*a* to -*o* is seen on other names, *Batha*, *Bathawe*, *Batho*, *v*. p.41; cf. also the interchange of -*o* and -*a* in hypocoristic names, *v*. p.34. Examples below make it quite certain that *Tecco* = *Tecca*.

Alberbury 150. 1651. matrimonium inter Johannem Tecca de Criggion . . . 203. 1670. John Teccoe, of Criggion . . . bur. 231. 1680. Margarett Tecco, of Chriggon, widd. bur. Acton Burnell 5. 1578. Griffyth Tecka. 6. 1579. Elizabeth d. of Griffyth Teckin (*v*. below). 7. 1582. Thomas s. of Griff. Teckah. 53. 1654. Mary Teckeo of the Township of Frodsley. St Mary's, Index, Tecka, Tecco, Teckoe, Tecker. St Chad's, Index, Teckot, Tecco, Teccoe, Tucko, etc. Selattyn 412. 1802. Elizth Tako.

Tegyn, Teggin etc.

It will be best to list the examples first:

InvECP 124. Flints . . . of the demise of Robert ap Richard Tegyn Monmouthe alias Robert Tegyn, 1547. 125. Richard Tegyn of Pelham Furneaux, co. Herts. . . . Close of pasture called 'Cae Tegyn' in the Hope (owen), late of Richard Tegyn, grandfather of complainant. Star CP 1. Flints Edwd T ᵥn

... Robt Tegyn. 55. Denbs Edwd ap Madock Tegyr (? misreading). PRActon Burnell 6. 1579. Elizabeth, d. of Griffyth Teckin (the other examples, as shown above, are Griffyth Tecka or Teckah). PRRuyton XI towns, 28. 1744. Thomas Teggin. PRSt Chad's, Index, Teggin, Tagine, Teggint, Tegin, Tegine, Teygine. PRWhittington 472. 1768. Elizabeth d. of Edward Teggen and Sarah his wife. = 475. 1769. Teggan; 483. 1772. Teggen; 489. 1774. Teggen, = 503. 1777. Teggin. 623. 1794. Sarah Teagin.

The name *Tegyn* may be a derivative of *Teg*, with the suffix *-yn*, similar to *Cochyn, Llwydyn, Moelyn*. One cannot feel really confident in making this suggestion because *teg* is not now used colloquially as an epithet (as far as one is aware). The other possible explanation is that it is a corruption of *Tegeingl*, the name of a commote in N.E. Wales, virtually the same as Flintshire. Early records of the name *Tegeingl* are given in *Flintshire Place-names* 160. On p.115, *Mynydd Tegan* or *Tegen* is given, with a quotation from *Paroch.* 1.72, and a statement that *Tegan* is a shortened form of 'Tegengl, Tegeingl, the ancient name for part of Flintshire'. It will be observed that the examples of *Tegyn, Tegin*, come almost entirely from Flintshire, and there is evidence above that 'Teggin, Teggen, Teggan' are variants of the same name, which is argument in favour of Tegeingl. One very puzzling piece of evidence is the entry found in PRActon Burnell above, which shows 'Teckin' as variant of superlative 'Tecka'.

Summary of examples in present-day registers:

Tegg, Stalybridge – Hyde, Stayley Ward Part 3; Cheadle Hulme, East Ward 1; Swansea TD, three entries in Llanelli. *Degg*, Bromsgrove, Hunnington; S. Worcs, Malvern East – Langland; West Flint, Rhyl S.W. *Degge*, S. Gloucs, Churchdown 1; City of Glouc, Kingsholme Ward p.29. *Tague*, Macclesfield, Disley 1. *Teague*, the most widespread version, e.g. Ludlow, Ch. Stretton; Bromsgrove, N.W.; West Glouc, Ludbrook 1 (abundant); Monmouth, Raglan; S. Pembs, St Issells, South Ward. *Teggin*, Shrewsbury, Harlescott, Meole Brace, Westbury. Oswestry, O. Urban, West Ward. *Tegan*, Preseli, Llanrhian; Swansea TD, one entry. *Teckoe*, is found in several places in Shrop-

shire, *v.* TD for Shrewsbury-Hereford, and for West Midlands.

Teggan, Teggin, Tegyn *v.* Teg

Tenby (*v.* also Introd. Place-names)
Torfaen, Cwmbrân, Fairwater and Henllys, *Temby*; Oakfield, ditto; Cwmbrân – Ton Rd. ditto; next page *Tenby*. Cwmbrân, Croesyceiliog, *Teanby*.

Teilo
This is the name of the saint found in the name of the several parishes in Wales called *Llandeilo*. The name does not seem to have been in common use at any time, and if the examples given below do represent the name *Teilo*, it may be that the use as surname came from the parish name in a community that was aware that the pers. name in the church or parish name was Teilo not 'Deilo'; but there is also an example below obviously representing 'Deilo':
WPortBooks 74. Thomas Tylo, Gloucester. L & P, 1. 438(4) p.265. Thomas Taylowe or Teylowe, of Gloucester. 2402. Th Taylowe (mayor of Gloucester). 2055. Thos Taylowe of Gloucester, PRMontford 60. 1738. Eliz Tilo. PRTasley 4. 1606. Jane Dylowe.

In present-day registers:
Tayloe, S. Worcs, Malvern West – No.4; Newport, Liswerry 3. The correct spelling of the place-name is now generally used; a spelling based on English values, 'Llandilo', was in common use for a long time and may still be seen on occasion. The following versions of spelling Llandeilo (Grabban) should be compared with the surnames above: RadsSoc XVIII. 48. Llantheylaw, Llanteylawe, Llanteylo; XIX. 22. Llandeylou; XXXVIII. 45. 1565 ... of Llondilowe parish.

Tew
Tew 'fat, stout' remains unlenited in some examples, in others, it lenites, after masc. and fem. personal names alike.
B13. 227. SR 1292. Iuan Teewe. B4. 351. AnglCourt 1346. Eignon Tew ap David. B6. 358. N.W. Howel Dew. B2. 253, Charters Brec Llandov. Griffino Tew ... Johanni Tew; 254. Agneti Dew. (fem). AnglPleas 36. Jevan ap John ap Jevan Dew. B15. 42. AS 1406. Rees ap Tudur dew; 43. dd Tew ap Pensith.
A similar name, in sound and spelling, may have a quite different origin in England, e.g.

CatAncDeeds V. A 10815, Northampton, Tewe, (de Tewe), Tywe, etc.; but in view of the simple origin and natural usage of the W epithet, in the form *Tew* (*Tewe*) or *Dew*, there is a good chance that such names found in England, especially in the border counties, stem from the W adjective.

The entries in the Shropshire registers, on the whole, have the unlenited *Tew*, with variant spellings.

Shipton 7. 1551. Johannis Tew. Chelmarsh 108. 1765. Anne Tugh. Pitchford 48. 1584. Willm Teewe. Norton-in-Hales 1. 1573. Willmus Tue filius Richardi Tue. 3. 1575. Richardus f. Richardi Tewe. 6. 1585. Willmus Tewe. (several later entries of *Tewe* and of *Tue*).

Examples of *Tew* and of *Dew* are found in present-day registers:

Shrewsbury, Column Portion, Dew; Ditherington and St Michael, Tew. Ludlow, Bromfield, Tew. Torfaen, Pontypool, Conway Rd, Tew, Dew.

Thomas

The name was in common use in the med period; the following figures are a good indication: Bartrum 985-1215, nine; 1215-1350, eighty; 1350-1415, 187.

The following examples show the use of derivative forms and of colloquial forms (not necessarily Welsh in origin):

B5. 144. Caern 1293. thum, david ap thum, (prob. = the colloquial form now in use, 'Twm'); 145. thomyn. B10. 72. West W. 1352. walter ap Tomy; 65. Thomae Eynon; 262. per manus Thome Coyd prepositi eiusdem Burgi. B15. 50. AS 1406. Maredudd ap dd Tom. B22. 9. Swansea 1449. John ap Thomkyn. BBStD 220. Thomyn (not attachd to any other name). ADClun 39. Ieuan thomelet; 48. David Thomelet; 214. Roger Tomlyn. PWLMA 356, 554. Ieuan ap Tomkyn (1444. Reeves, Llanllwch). Bartrum 1350-1415, 743. Twmlyn Llwyd ap Madog Llwyd. HM iv. 43. Hundred of Caldicot, 'The daughter of Sir Thomas . . . married Thomas (in Welsh Tomlyn) [this remark should be disregarded] Huntly, whose son and heir, w. John ap Tomlyn, succeeded to lands in Beechly'. PRLl.Discoed, 46. 1717-18. Tacy, wife of John Tum; 1732-3. Elizabeth wife of John Tumm; cf. weddings 1688, John Tum . . . Tarsey Harris. InvECP 151. Monts

1551. David ap Ieuan ap Hoell Tome. PROswestry 18. 1560. David Tumkin.

Tither *v.* Tudur

Tona, Twna, Tunna

Reaney has *Tunna, Tunnah*, with the explanation 'person making tunnes "barrels" '. It is difficult to accept that this is the origin of the various versions found in records of W context. There is a dialect adj. *twna*, used in parts of SW, to mean 'morose, sullen'; it is not given in EEW. The great difficulty in trying to trace an origin is that in some examples it appears to be an epithet attached to a pers. name, and in others it has the usage of a christian name. Judging by the examples collected its usage appears to be largely confined to N.E. Wales, and it probably came from the neighbouring E counties.

B15. 54. AS 1406. Twna ap Ithell. Bartrum 1350-1415, 743. Twna ab Aren; 744. seven other examples of *Twna* as christian name; ibid 872. Twna ap Bleddyn ap Gruffudd. CaernQSR 210. John ap Kenner' ap Hywel Tona. InvECP 99. Denbs 1551. Hugh ap Bevan ap David ap Tone. 112. 1518. Howell ap Gryffyth ap Tona. 126. Flints 1551. Margaret verch David ap Res ap Tona of the city of London. 133. Flints 1549. Elizabeth ap William alias Elizabeth verch Ellys ap Tona, of the city of London. CaernHS 26, Bolde Rental, 39. Tona ap Eign Cam. Star CP 54. Denbs Edwd Edwds als Tunno.

Examples from Shropshire registers:

Edstaston 2. 1714, 3. 1715, 4. 1717. George Tunnah. 22. 1743. Thomas Tunnah. Newtown 3. 1786. John Tunnah. Oswestry 24. 1561. John ap Thomas, als Tona. 39. 1564. Roger ap Holl' Toona.

Towr

This is 'thatcher, or roofer', derived from *to* 'roof'; it could be disyllabic to start with, *tŏwr*, but through contraction it is now pronounced as a monosyllable with a diphthong.

B6. 359. N.W. 1326. Gronou ap Philip ap Tour. B10. 68. West W. 1352. Ieuan Dour. RecCa 101. Ieuan ap Toher. ADClun 40. Ieuan ap Tour = 94. Ieuan ap Toour. Dwnn 1. 33. Konstant v. John Towr. PRSelattyn 13. 1564. Edward ap Owen ap Gruffith dowr. PRWhittington 138. 1640. Marye, wife of John David y Towr, of Daywell. (182. 1651. John Davies the Thatcher). PROswestry 238. 1603. Anne the wyffe of Moris y Towre.

Trahaearn

The word *haearn* 'iron' occurs in a number of W pers. names, especially *Talhaearn, Aelhaearn, Cadhaearn*; the prefix *tra* 'over, excessive' probably conveys the meaning of 'powerful' in a compound of this kind.

The form Trahaearn, as it is correctly written in the name of the twelfth century poet Trahaearn Brydydd Mawr (poems RP 1222) will later change in more than one respect. The disyllable *haearn* as a common noun is very often reduced to one syllable in colloquial speech, to give 'harn': therefore 'Tra + harn' can be expected. It also appears that between the sonants *rn* an epenthetic sound was heard by some ears, and this may account for spellings such as *-heron*, *-haren*; or the explanation may be that the disyllable *haearn* was easier by transposing the *r* to give 'haeran'. The other change to the appearance of the name is due to the confusion with the common noun *tre'*, 'home, house, town', which occurs in so many place-names; this produced *Treharn(e)* etc.

B13. 217. SR 1292. Maddoc ap Treharne; 229. Treharn ab Rethrech. B2. 60. West W. 1301. De Eynono ab Traharn. B15. 51. AS 1406. Je(uan) ap Traharen; 56. Gruffith ap Tudur ap Trehayarn. Glam Cartae, Index, Trahaerne, Traharen, Traharn, Trahayne, Treharne. MLSW 23. Thomas Trahayren; 33. . . . ap Traheron. ADClun 27. trahar' ab Walter. CalChancProc 312. Traaharn Howell. HM iv. 125, quotes from a roll in Cardiff Free Library 1610. Thomas Treheron alias Somersett. CatAncDeeds V. 12246. Norfolk, George Treheyron. 12250. Norfolk, George Tryheron of London. 12724. Hereford, Thomas Treharne. VI. *c*. 7112, Hereford, Nicholas Trehayron of Burmershe. InvECP 38. Cards 1538. Trehayre ap Geoffrey. 39. Cards 1547. Treharyn ap Griffith. 48. Carms 1533. John Tryheron. 169. Brec 1547. John Trayne alias John ap Ieuan ap Trayne (Treheron). 210. Trahern Goz, Thomas Trehern. PRLlantrithyd 35. 1598. Anne Tyrheirne (editor has '*Query* Trehern' in footnote, and puts Treherne in the index, not the actual entry).

SHROPSHIRE REGISTERS

Kinlet 70. 1712. Mary Trehern, a poor wandering woman. St Chad's 1469. 1786. John Trehearn.

Summary of examples in present-day registers:

Trahearn, Kidderminster No.2 Baxter; Newport, Malpas 1; Bromsgrove No.7, North. Trayhern, S. Gloucs, Filton Northville; WG1. Tidenham Sedbury. Trayherne, WG1. Sedbury, Tidenham. Trayhurn, S. Gloucs Filton Conygre Ward 1, Thornbury; Stroud, Dursley; Islwyn Cefnyfforest East. Treharne, Wrekin, Oakengates; S.Hereford, Orcop. Trehearn, Leominster, Colwall; Bromsgrove, Stoke Prior. Trehearne, Wrekin, Wellington Park-Portion; CT, Ampney Crucis. Treherne, Shrewsbury, Welsh Ward, Shelton Portion; S. Gloucs, Winterbourne – Hambrook.

There is no example of *Cadhaearn* in G.; and it does not arise to be dealt with in TYP; but Bartrum 1215-1350, 95 has Cathaearn ap Blaidd ab Elfarch, and RecCa appears to have an example: Hoell ap Cathayron; cf. 68. Catharn ap Ken'. The structure of the name is simple, being compounded of *cad* 'battle or army' + *haearn*, 'iron'. For *Cadhaearn*, *vide* Cadarn, above.

Traharn, Traherne *v.* Trahaearn

Trefaldwyn *v.* Baldwin

Treharne, Treheron *v.* Trahaearn

Trevallyn *v.* Introd. Place-names

Trevor *v.* Introd. Place-names

Trewin, Winston

The second element must be the pers. name *Gwyn*; if it were the adj. it would be the fem. *-wen* after *re(f)*. WATU 215 lists four examples of places called Trewyn. The Tre-wyn of Crucornau Fawr in Gwent is said to be the source, through translation, of the name Winston; *v.* HM i. Abergavenny 242. Pedigree of Family of Wynston of Trewyn, and T.E. Morris's article pp.148-9. Cf. Trewin, Crewe, Sandbach West 1; Treywin, Crewe South 4. (These two examples may come from Cornish immigrants.)

Winston, Wynston, Winstone occur fairly frequently as surnames in N. Gwent, not far from Tre-wyn. The Christian name Winston is said to have been brought into the Churchhill family through a marriage of a Churchill to a member of the Winstons of Standish, Gloucs, a branch of Winston of Tre-wyn.

Trillo

Reaney gives *Trillo*, with one early example, Philip de Trillowe, 1279, with a Cambridge-

shire location; the explanation given is 'From Thurlow' (Suffolk)'. There must be another *Trillo* with a quite different origin. There are two parishes in Wales named Llandrillo, in Merioneth and Denbs; this has *ll*', not double *l*; cf. CaernCR 142 and 157, St Trillo's Day (16 June).
Bartrum 300-985, 79. Trillo ap Ithel Hael. PROswestry 95. 1583. John ap Holl Trillo; 465. 1629. Robert Tryllo. (cf. 119. 1587. Gruffith ap Ric. nuper Du . . . vixit de Llandrillo, obijt).
Examples are found today in the border counties; no doubt the pronunciation is double *l* (not Welsh *ll*'), *Trillo* in BrRadnor Knighton; City of Hereford; Shrewsbury, Belle Vue, Castle Foregate, Harlescott; *Trilloe*, CT. Moreton-in-Marsh. Cf. also D.Tel 6.6.84, News item p.19, the Rt Rev John Trillo, Bishop of Chelmsford.

Trwm
Meaning 'heavy', fem. 'trom'; the examples of *-Drom* below are not fem. but faulty spellings of *-Drwm*.
B13, 227, SR 1292, Meuric Trum; ADClun 168, Wellian daughter of Lewelyn Drom; CaernCR 57, Gwenllian ferch Ieuan Drwm (MS Trum), 68, ditto; WPortBooks 315, John Trom of the Dale; B13, 98, Recs 16th century estate Pembs, Thomas Drom, . . . John Drum.
Trygarn *v.* Introd. Place-names
Tudor *v.* Tudur
Tudur (Tudri), Tudor, Tither
The nominative form in Brythonic, *Totorix*, would give W *Tudyr*; an oblique form such as the genitive *Totorigos* became Tudri, LHEB 624. The standard W spelling has always been *Tudur*; needless to say this is the name which is Tudor in an E context.

The following show a great variety of ways of writing the name, including the approximation *Theodore*:
B15. 42. AS 1406. Rees ap Tudur dew; ib. Deia ap Tuddr. 43. Tudur Prydyn; 51. Tuder ap dd lwydwyn; 52. Tuder ap Ednyved marzog; 54. Tudr ap lln ap Eign velyn. B16. 117. temp Edw I. Tuder Vaghan; 131. Tuderi ap Kandalon. B14. 306. temp Edw I. Tudero filio Griffyn. BBStD 98. Ieuan ap Teder, David ap Tyder. B6. 73. Eliz. Docs. Richard Owen Teddir. DLancaster (Lp-Caldecot 1613) 145. Rosser Tedder. Star CP

20. Angl. Ricd Owen Theodore, of Pen-mynydd. CC. Tyder ap Robt; 66. Tydder ap Robt; 72. Tudder ap Robt. L & P i. 257 (71) Tedder, bailiff of Towcester. HM iv, 114. Caldicot, Rec. of 1665, signature, Will. Tydder of Shirenewton, yeom.
The collection made from InvECP has most of the above, including:
3. ap Tuder; 5. ap Tyther; 32. ap Tydyr; 82. ap Tudder; 89. ap Theder; 91. Lewis Tudder, alias Dedder, parson of Monkchurch; 99. ap Tedre; 158. John Tewder; 254. Marches 1538. ap Tither.
The form *Tewder* just quoted is probably not a version of *Tewdwr*, but a Welsh phonetic version of the E pronunciation of Tudor. With regard to the examples of Tither, we are able to provide a piece of oral evidence. At the end of a lecture given many years ago in London, one of the authors was approached by a member of the audience, who was a native of Flintshire, wishing to inform that in his childhood (in Buckley, we believe) a boy whose real name was 'Tudor' would be called *Tither* rhyming with 'hither'). This is entirely consistent with the variation *d-r/th-r* Clidro – Clitheroe. The PR of Clunbury 88. 1714 seems to provide this explanation in an odd spelling, *John Tydther*.
Ford 11. 1635, Abel Tither and Margaret are Abell and Margaret Tydder in 1636; cf. Acton Burnell 9. 1585, Roger Tither = 9. 1586, Roger Tidder; Smethcote 16. 1629, Thomas and Mary Tyther = 17. 1631, Thomas and Mary Tydder.
The Shropshire registers have the variants seen above:
Tither, Ford 11. 1635; Chelmarsh 87. 1735. Tidder, Lydham 28. 1715; Isaac Tidder, Alberbury 73. 1620 = Isaac Tydder, 88. 1624. Toudor, Chirbury 131. 1718 (Chirbury index, Tyther, Tydder, Tether, Tither, classified separate from Tudor etc.). Tadder, Wem 1599 . . . Evan Tadder = 20. 1602. Yevan Tydder.
As Whittington remained welsh-speaking for long, the register has Tudor or Tudur frequently; 258. 1698 John Tidor is unusual. Oswestry has an example of the 'approximation': 323. 1612. John the sonne of Theodore Sion of Mesbury.
Tudor in present-day registers does not call for close plotting; its frequent occurrence was

observed in the registers of S. Gloucs and in parts of Stroud, e.g. Slimbridge. Examples of the variants are here given:

Tuder, Ludlow, St Leonards – Bridgnorth. *Tidder*, S. Gloucs, Winterbourne. *Tedder*, S. Gloucs, Filton Conygre Ward; C. of Chester, Hoole Ward 1; Cardigan, Llandyfríog, Llandysul South, Town Ward. *Tither*, Oswestry, Weston Rhyn; St and Hyde, St. No.2, Millbrook Ward 1; Nantwich, Middlewick West; Runcorn, Grappenhall, North Ward; Westmorland, Kendal – Highgate; Monmouth, Chepstow St Mary's. *Tyther*, S. Worcs, Malvern South No. 3.

In some cases the surnames Tudor, Tither etc. might perhaps have been derived by analogy not from W Tudur, but from other W names Tewdwr, Tewdws or Tewdrig (which are in turn derived from Theodorus, Theodosius and Theodoric respectively). These names were of particular importance in medieval S. Wales, e.g. Rhys ap Tewdwr, last native king of Deheubarth. This may account for the relative frequency of the surname Tudor or its variants in the Hereford – Gloucestershire area, adjacent to S. Wales.

Topa, Twpa
Under *Topper* Reaney states, 'a derivative of ME *toppe*, a tuft or handful of hair, wool, fibre etc. especially the portion of flax or tow put on the distaff'. This word *toppe* is one possible source; the dial. meanings of *tup* 'ram' are more likely: the proper meaning of ram; one of the characters in a Christmas mumming play, a contemptuous or familiar term applied to a person, a stupid foolish person. The word *twp* is in general use, especially in SW dialects, for 'stupid'.
BBStD 276. Lewel Toppa; 278. Joh'es Top'. AnglCourt 1346, 34. Efa Tope. ADClun 24. Dauid toppa; 109. Lewelin Doppa; 170. Toppa. InvECP 250 Marches. Thomas ap Griffith Tuppa, 1518. Star CP 213. Rads Jas Duppa, of Michaelchurch; Thos Duppa of Colva his brother. HM iii, 218. Pedigree of descendants of Adam Gwent; fifth generation has Adam Dwppa. Bartrum 1215-1350, 205. Adam Dwpa; 332. Ieuan ap Madog y Twpa. 379. Madog y Twpa etc. PRClunbury 28. Duppa. PRBromfield, Index, Duppa, several.
Tugh *v*. Tew
Tyder, Tyther *v*. Tudur

U

Ungoed
This surname is found in Carmarthenshire; there are seven entries of Ungoed, Ungoed-Thomas in the TD of Swansea and S.W. Wales.
DLancaster (Kidwelly) 204. William Ungoed; 206, 227. John Ungoed.
A surname of uncertain origin, but if Welsh, could come from *Ynn – coed* 'Ashwood'.

Upjohn *v.* Ieuan
Uprichard *v.* Richard
Uren *v.* Urien

Urien
TYP 516- provides a lengthy note on *Uryen Reget*, the North British leader of the sixth century who fought against Hussa and his son Ida, and whose praises were sung by Taliesin. Following LHEB 439 the derivation of the name is given as Orbogenos > OW Urbgen > MW Urien, which could be given the meaning 'of privileged birth'; this being preferred to Thurneysen's suggestion that it goes back to Urbi-genus, 'city-born'. Dr Bromwich also refers to Ifor Williams's view that there was a variant form *Uruoen* (i.e. *Urfően*): in fact, Ifor Williams in CT xxxi states that the form Urfően should be restored to the text of the poems and that the trisyllabic form is needed to make better rhyme and scansion. This variant version, *Urfően* or *Urwően*, CT 37-38, might well be the explanation of the name Urwen; the incidence or frequency of Urwen in the north of England adds some support to this view, in the sense that it is at least a 'northern' name. There is no evidence in W literature or records that *Urfően*, giving *Urwen*, developed in Wales and this art. will be confined to Urien.
B13. 218. SR 1292. Iwan ab Huren; 229. Erduduil fil' Uryen. B4. 163, Ardudwy Court 1325. Urien ab Iorwerth ... predictus Urien.

Mer LSR 32. Urien Voyl. CalChancProc 58, 1295. Margaret late the wife of Urian de Sancto Petro has arraigned against Urian son of Joan de Sancto Petro concerning a tenement; references to Chester, Nantwich. CatAncDeeds, frequent refs, to Urian de Eggerton, town of Caldecote, location Cheshire, e.g. VI. C6314, 1330; C6316, 15 Edward II; C6300, 1346; C6311; 111. C3748; C3644. BBStD, Ieuan ap Uran; 200. Ll' ap Uryen; 276. David ap Uryen; 306. Marg'ia Yryan. Star CP 147. Sir Urian Leigh. InvECP 116. Flints 1533. Uryan Dymoke. JEG 271. ... of Hendre Irian, co. Merioneth; 283. Hendre urien. HM iv, 73. St Pierre, 'The name Urien closely associated ...', e.g. Urien de St Pierre; records of or references to a succession of people named Urien in 13th and 14th centuries; p.74, visitation of Cheshire 1580, Urien de St Pierre.
The name occurs in several forms in the Shropshire registers:
Urien, Whittington 362. 1724-5. Elizabeth d. of John Urien (= 366. 1726 ... Urion). ShrewsburyBR 291, two entries 1450, 1459. *Urine*, St Martin's, Index. *Urian*, Ch. Stretton 46. 1705, Urian Kyte yeoman; 48. 1706. Urian s. of Urian Kyte and Eliz. bap.; Worthen, Index (also Uurian, Urion); Ludlow 507. 1681. Mr. Urian Higgins, Pursuant; Eaton-under-Heywood 2. 1671. Urian s. of Urian and Jane Baldwyn; 2. 1600. Jane ... 3. 1663. John ... (ditto). *Irian*, Westbury 12. 1643. Robert Irian. 14. 1644. Robert Irian, alias Niccolls p. of Woorthyn. (cf. Pontesbury entry below). *Urion*, Non-Con. (Soc Friends Shrewsbury) 157. 1705. Elizabeth Urion of ye same place (= Ellesmere) ... wit. Roger Urion. Myddle 261. 1783. Eliz. d. of Charles Urion; 263. 1785.

Wm s. of Charles and Eliz. Urion (= 265, 1787 . . . Charles and Eliz. Urian); 294. 1802. Mary Urion.

Forms using 's:
Pontesbury 51. 1582. Thom. Urians; 139. 1640. Thomas Errians, alias Niccholls, sep. (cf. Westbury above); 141. 1642. Johannes Errians, alias Niccols, f. Thomas Niccols; 146. 1646. Richardus Irions.

The parish registers of Cumberland and Westmorland yielded the following:
Great Orton (1568-1812) 24. Susanna d. of James Urran, 1687, repeated 25. 1689; 26. 1691; 26. 1693. Penrith St Andrews, 1661-1713, Index, Urn, one entry.

The entries of the Oswestry register deserve special attention:
88. 1582. Richard ap Will'm Burian. 140. 1590. Thomas ap Wm Burian. 122. 1587. John ap Ric ap Wm Birrian. 127. 1588. . . . relict Willi' Brian. 176. 1595. Jeuan ap Tuder ap John ap Yrian. 206. 1599. Owen ap John ap Urian, buried. 228. 1602. Owen the sonne of John Burian . . . Crisned, Katherine the wiffe of John Burian, buried eodem die. 217. 1600. Janne the daughter of John ap Richard ap Urian. 230. 1602. Jane vz Wm Biriam of Mesbury. 255. 1604. Mary the daughter of John ap Irian. 343. 1614. Owen the sonne of John Birrian of Measbury.

It is of interest to note the *ab* forms, and the variation Biriam/Birrian; but it is of greater interest that Birian becomes Brian. There are other entries of this form, as surname and as christian name:
91. 1583. Ales Brian; 91. 1583. Brian ap Richard Gittens. 120. 1587. Brian ap Ric Gittins.

The form Briogn occurs in Whittington 136. 1638, shown in index to be = Brian.

Reaney, under Brian, . . . Brien . . . etc, mentions more than one source: a Breton name introduced into England by the Normans; 'In the north, it is OIr Brian brought by Norsemen from Ireland . . . to Cumberland and across the Pennines into Yorkshire. It is found in ON as Brjan'. The entries in the PR of Oswestry show that there was another source, Birian becoming Brian. This does not prove that ab-Irian is the main source of Brian; what it shows is that the version of W origin merged with the already existing names. It is interesting to note the fairly heavy incidence of Bryan in the following areas, as shown by the respective TDs:
Shrewsbury-Hereford, Bryan 47, Brian 3. Wirral-Chester, Bryan 38, Bryans 5, Brian 2, Brien, 1. West Mid. North, Bryan, whole column, Brian 6. West Mid. South, Bryan, none; Brian 3. The name Urian virtually fell into disuse in Wales, examination of the electoral registers of the N.W. English counties and of the Welsh Border generally shows that it survived in the forms Uren, Urion, Youren. The form Uren is widespread and only a few locations need be given.
Uren, Shrewsbury, Pimhill – Weston Ward; S.Gloucs, Winterbourne 3, Filton Northville Ward. *Urion*, Crewe, South 1; Wirral, Ellesmere Port, Grange Ward 2, Hoylake, Park Ward; Wrexham, Cefn Mawr, Cefn Ward; cf. Monts, Pennant, Pen-y-bont fawr, John Urion Roberts: Hirnant, Llangynog, Evan Urion Lewis. *Youren*, St. and Hyde, Stalybridge No.2, Stayley Ward; Nantwich, Wharton; Copeland, Millom; Carlisle, Denton Holme; Bl. Gwent, Tredegar West, Rassau South – Beaufort.

If *Urwin, Urwen, Irwin* are derived from the variant Urwöen, it can be stated with certainty that they are found in plenty in the same locations as the above. Another name found in the same areas, possibly in greater numbers, is *Wren* or *Wrenn*: is not this a form of Uren or Urien?

V

Vaghan, Vaghen, Vahan *v.* Bychan
Vain(e) *v.* Main
Vainow *v.* Introd. Place-names
Val(e) *v.* Melinydd
Valghe *v.* Balch
Vallender *v.* Cadwaladr
Vantage *v.* Mantach
Vaughan, Vaughn *v.* Bychan

Vaure, Vawre *v.* Mawr
Vayne *v.* Main
Vellins *v.* Melyn
Vethicke *v.* Meddyg
Voil, Voyle *v.* Moel
Voya *v.* Mwyaf
Vythig *v.* Meddyg

W

Walch *v.* Balch
Waliter, Wallet, Walliter *v.* Cadwaladr
Walter(s) *v.* Gwallter
Wargen(t) *v.* Gwrgan
Watkin(s) *v.* Gwatkin
Wellen, Wellin(g), Wellings *v.* Llywelyn
Wenlan(d) *v.* Gwenllïan
Went, Whent *v.* Gwent
Whitford *v.* Introd. Place-names
Whith *v.* Chwith
Williams *v.* Gwilym

Winston(e) *v.* Trewin
Winn *v.* Gwyn
Wiriet *v.* Gwriad
Wogan *v.* Gwgawn
Woolas, Wollow *v.* Gwynlliw
Woorye *v.* Gwri
Worgan, Worgen *v.* Gwrgan
Worvell *v.* Gweirful
Wyn, Wynn(e) *v.* Gwyn
Wyrill *v.* Gweirful
Wyriot *v.* Gwriad

Y

Yale *v*. Introd. Place-names
Yevan(s) *v*. Ieuan
Yarworth *v*. Iorwerth
Ynyr
TYP 412 deals with Ynyr Gwent in the note on Idon m. Enyr Gwent, and gives the derivation Ynyr < Honorius. The name was in regular use in the med period.
B13. 143. Bonds peace 1283. Dd fil enii (? enir), ibid 143, Bonds 1295, Eyner gooch. B13. 217. SR 1292. Ener vichan, Ener ab Iorwerth; Aron ab Ener; 218. Gronu ab Hener. B5. 145. CaernLSR 1293. Ynyr. B10. 80, West W. 1352. Enir ap Meredith. RecCa 55, 58. M'ad Bennyr (unexpectedly early *'B* version, might it be 'Befr' written *Beuyr* and misread?). 94. Euyr ap Cad' (correct to Enyr). BBStD 240. Ieuan Euer' Vachaun; 268. Gr ap Euer . . . Ieuan ap Euer (correct to Ener). CAP 508. Enyr Fychan, co. Merion. end of 13th century. CaernQSR 191. Hugh ap Inn' ap Ieuan = 193. ap Inner; BYale 140, several examples of Ever, e.g. Ever ap Ior, Ever Duy (= Ener, Ynyr). Bartrum 1350-1415, 747-8. Ynyr, eight examples. Star CP 198. Griffith Benner, gent. bailiff of Llanfyllin = 204. Griffith Byner. H Asaph V. 229. Llanfihangel yng Nghwnfa [sic], Rectors, 1588. Oliver Bynner; cf. 1. 329, 1373. Griffin ap Ienner (Ynyr) – the addition in brackets is the editor's; the consonantal *Ie-* makes this very doubtful and this may well be a misreading of Iennen = Iennyn, *v*. p.133.
SHROPSHIRE REGISTERS
Examples below from the Shropshire registers clearly show *Bonner* as a variant of Bunner (and therefore < Ynyr); cf. DLancaster (Dom de Monm. 1610) 24 Nathaniel Bonner.
It will help, before proceeding to the examples in the Shropshire registers, to state that the correct pronunciation of *Ynyr* means that the vowel of *Yn-* is the 'unclear' *y*, and that the vowel of *-yr* is the 'clear' *y*. Therefore, with the tendency of English speech generally to make final vowels neutral, the pronunciation *Bunner* is to be expected. In some cases the final *r* (trilled in Welsh) becomes *l*.
Ford, 36, 37, 38, 39, 40. Bunner. Alberbury 53. 1614. Willim's Bynner, peregrinus; 474, 630. Bunnear, Bunner. Worthen, Index, Bunner (Bonner, Brunner, Bunnar). Pontesbury 483. 1809. Susanna d. of Richard and Jane Bunner; 490. 1811. Thos s. Richard and Sarah Bunna (probably the same couple, it can be assumed the wife was 'Sarah Jane'). Westbury 297. 1791. Thomas s. of Joseph Bunner and Mary; 303. 1793. Mary d. of Joseph Bunner and Hannah. 327. 1802. Hannah Bunner. 328. 1802. Elizabeth d. of Joseph Bonner and Hannah. Ludlow 24. 1617. Richard Bonner; 63. 1567. Edward Bownner. Sheinton 1. 1688-1700, several entries of Binnell, namely the rector and his family. 3. 1716; 3. 1718; 4. 1720; 4. 1721, surname *Binner*; many later entries of the same form; 14. 1752. Hannah Binnel, bur., there is no previous entry of this person with this name, but she is probably Hannah Binner, bap. in 1718 (p.3). 22. 1784. Jane d. of Thomas and Ann Binner, bap. 25. 1791. Jane Binnal, an infant, bur. 21. 1780. William Binnel, bur; no previous entry of this person under this name, but there is one of William Binner, 15. 1758, bap. 16. 1763. Ann Binnals. Wrockwardine 3. 1595. John s. of John Bynnell; 116. 1718. Dorothy Binnell. Shrewsbury St Mary's, Index, Binnald, (Byndall, Binnell); Binner, one entry; Bunner, a dozen; Bynnell (Binnell, Bynnil) Shr. St. Chad's, Index, Banner, three entries; Binnall etc. several; Bunnir, Bonner, Bunna.

Whittington 458. 1760. John s. of Sidney Bunner and Elizabeth his wife. Kinnerley, Index, Bunnell, Bunnor (Bunner). Oswestry 526. 1636. Caddr Byner; 540. 1639. Cadwalader Beyner. 658. 1667. Cadwalader Bymer. 601. 1662. Bynner the sonne of Mr Thomas Owens of Aston. ShrewsburyBR Robert Bonor, 1472. Binnall, one entry, 1665. Bynner, Griffith, of S. grocer, s. William, of Lledrod, Montg. [sic] 1713.

PRESENT-DAY REGISTERS – SUMMARY

Benner, Barrow-in-F., Hawcoat 4; Barrow Island No.2. Binner, Bromsgrove N.W. Romsley; Wirral, Hoylake, Hoose Ward. Byner, Oswestry Urban Central W. Bynner, Monts, Montgomery (John Bynner Evans); Llansantffraid Deythur, Janet Bynner Evans; Llanwnog, Idris Bynner Jones; Tregynon, Eurwen Bynner Jenkins. Bunner, Shrewsbury, Shelton Portion; Ludlow, Worthen. Bonner, Shrewsbury, Abbey Foregate, Abbey Column; Pontesbury; Monts, Machynlleth. Binnall, Shrewsbury, Belle Vue Ward.

Yorath, Yorward, Yorwerth, Youarth v. Iorwerth

Youren v. Urien

Ysgolhaig

In mod W it means 'scholar'; it is a derivative of *ysgol* 'school'. The accent falls on the final syllable because it is a contraction of *-ha-ig*; it would fall on the penult *-ha-* before the contraction. A person disguised as an ysgolhaig (i.e. *yscolheic* in the text) appears in the Manawydan story of the Four Branches: he is followed by an *offeiriad* 'clergyman'; and then a bishop; obviously there is an ascending order. In his note PKM 244-5, Ifor Williams shows that it meant 'clerk', the lowest of holy orders, and in the context of the story the *yscolheic* no doubt was (in disguise) pretending to be one of the *scholares* (or *clerici*) *vagantes*, the wandering band of poets of the middle ages. One thing must be left unexplained, why it is

attached to a woman's name, as in 'Neest Scolayke' below.

B13. 229. SR 1292. Yoruerth Scolheig. B2. 253. Brec, Llandov. 13th century. Griffino Scolhayke; 254. Neest Scolayke. B15. 61. AS 1406. dd. ap Eign Scolhaic. Mer LSR 61. David ap Wion Scolheyk; 92. Ieuan Scoleyk. RecCa 114. Dd Scolaik. ADClun 157, Ieuan ap Philip Scoleye (?); 184. Philip ap David Scoleyk. PWLMA 526. Gruffydd ap Rhys ap Scoleig. CaernQSR 86. Gruffydd ap Ieuan alias 'Yscylaig Duy'; 218. Gruffydd ap Ieuan alias "Yscolaig Duy".

D.E. Williams quotes: Howel David Esgolhaig ap Ievan ap Meyric, *c.* 1440; Jevan Yscolhaig (ibid).

PRCaerwent-Ll.Discoed, Caerwent 1597, April 25, bur. Johan Clearte alias scholaige, a poore woman of the parishe of Skinfrith, w'ch came begginge to this parishe with ij litell childerne, was buried on saint Marke daie, beinge the XXVth daie of Aprill, her husband name, as she said was Richard Johnes, a lettice windo maker. [Footnote, 'It might be *Olearte*. Scholiage [sic] is for ysgolhaig (scholar) presumably a nickname'. One feels impelled to put forward the suggestion that the name is not Clearte or Olearte, but 'Clearke']

A surname which seems to be a version of the medieval *yscolheic* is found in the registers of Cumbria.

PRWarcop p.54, 1735. Thomas Martha Sckolek of Burton = 121. 1733. Thomas Scholekk. PRGreat Orton 127. 1792. Richard Scholick. PRBarton, Index, Scolick, Scholick, Scholicke, Scholik, Schollick, Scolough, Scollick; earliest entry 1707. PRSkelton 84. 1806. Mary Scholick; 176. 1796. Ann Scolick.

The surname *Scollick* was found surviving in Bromsgrove No.7, North. Reaney has no example.

BIBLIOGRAPHY

C. Baker and G.G. Francis,	(editors) *Surveys of Gower and Kilvey* (supplement to *Arch. Camb.*, London 1870)
C.W. Bardsley,	*English Surnames* (London 1875)
P.C. Bartrum,	*Welsh Genealogies, A.D. 300-1415* (8 vols. Cardiff 1974). *Early Welsh Genealogical Tracts* (Cardiff 1966).
W. Beaumont,	(editor) *Tracts . . . respecting the Legitimacy of Amicia, daughter of Hugh Cyveliok 1673-79* (Chetham Society, Manchester 1869).
E.G. Bowen,	*The Settlements of the Celtic Saints in Wales* (Cardiff 1954).
J.A. Bradney,	*A History of Monmouthshire* (4 vols. London 1904-1933). (editor) *Parish Registers of Caerwent 1568-1812; Parish Registers of Llanfair Discoed 1680-1812* (London 1920). (editor) *Registrum Antiquum de Llanbadoc 1585-1709* (From a copy made in 1839 by Lady Phillips) (London 1919). (editor) *Parish Registers of Llanddewi Rhydderch 1670-1783* (London 1919). (editor) *Registrum Antiquum de Llanfihangel Ystern Llewern in comitatu Monmuthensi 1685-1812* (London 1920). (editor) *Parish Registers of Llantilio Crossenny and Penrhos 1577-1644* (London 1916).
Rachel Bromwich,	(editor) *Trioedd Ynys Prydein; The Welsh Triads* (Cardiff 1961).
Bwrdd Gwybodau Celtaidd,	*Orgraff yr Iaith Gymraeg* (Caerdydd 1928).
J. Cayley and J. Hunter,	(editors) *Valor ecclesiasticus* (6 vols. London 1810-34).
B.G. Charles,	*Non-Celtic Place-names in Wales* (London 1938). (editor) *A Calendar of the records of the borough of Haverfordwest 1539-1660* (Cardiff 1967).
G.T. Clark,	*Limbus Patrum Morganiae et Glamorganiae, being the genealogies of the older families of the lordship of Morgan and Glamorgan* (London 1886). (editor) *Cartae et alia munimenta quae ad Dominium de Glamorgan pertinent* (6 vols. Talygarn 1910).
Albert Dauzat,	*Dictionnaire Étymologique des Noms de Famille et Prénoms de France* (3 me edition revue et augmentée par Marie-Thérèse Morlet, Paris 1951).
Ellis Davies,	*Flintshire Place-names* (Cardiff 1959).
Elwyn Davies,	(editor) *A Gazetteer of Welsh Place-names* (Cardiff 1957).
J.H. Davies,	(editor) *The Letters of Lewis, Richard, William and John Morris of Anglesey* (2 vols. Aberystwyth 1907-9)
Lewys Dwnn,	*Heraldic Visitations of Wales and Part of the Marches* (Llandovery 1846).
Ifan ab Owen Edwards,	(editor) *A Catalogue of Star Chamber Proceedings relating to Wales* (Cardiff 1929).
J. Goronwy Edwards,	(editor) *A Calendar of Ancient Correspondence concerning Wales* (Cardiff 1935).
Eilert Ekwall,	*The Concise Oxford Dictionary of English Place-names* (4th edition, Oxford 1960).
Henry Ellis,	(editor) *The Record of Carnarvon* (Record Commission, London 1838)

R. Ellis,	(editor) *The Parish Registers of Llansannan 1667-1812* (Liverpool 1904).
T.P. Ellis,	(editor) *The First Extent of Bromfield and Yale, A.D. 1325* (Cymmrodorion Record Series, London 1924).
D. Simon Evans,	*Buchedd Dewi* (Caerdydd 1959).
H. Meurig Evans and W.O. Thomas,	(editors) *Y Geiriadur Mawr* (Llandybie and Abersytwyth, 1958 and 1960).
J. Gwenogvryn Evans,	(editor) *The Black Book of Carmarthen* (Pwllheli 1907). (editor) *The Book of Taliesin* (Llanbedrog 1910). (editor) *The Text of the Mabinogion and other Welsh tales from The Red Book of Hergest* (Oxford 1890). (editor) *The Poetry in the Red Book of Hergest* (Llanbedrog 1911). (editor) *The White Book Mabinogion* (Pwllheli 1907) (editor) *The text of the Book of Llan Dâv* (Liber Landavensis) (Oxford 1893).
Theophilus Evans,	*Drych y Prif Oesoedd* (2nd edition, Amwythig 1740).
C.H. L'Estrange Ewen,	*History of the Surnames of the British Isles* (London 1931).
Olof von Feilitzen,	*Pre-Conquest Personal Names of Domesday Book* (Uppsala 1937).
Richard Fenton,	*A Historical Tour through Pembrokeshire* (2nd edition, Brecknock 1903).
Ralph Flenley,	(editor) *Register of the Council of the Marches of Wales* (Cymmrodorion Record Series, London 1916).
O.H. Fynes-Clinton,	*The Welsh Vocabulary of the Bangor district* (Oxford 1913).
H.E. Forrest,	(editor) *Shrewsbury Burgess Roll* (Shewsbury 1924).
J.E. Griffith,	(editor) *Pedigrees of Anglesey and Caernarvonshire families* (Horncastle 1914).
R.A. Griffiths,	*The Principality of Wales in the Later Middle Ages, vol. I, South Wales* (Cardiff 1972).
John Grigg,	*The Young Lloyd George* (London 1973).
R.T. Gunther,	*Early Science at Oxford, vol. XIV: The Life and Letters of Edward Lhwyd* (Oxford 1945).
Alice Hadley,	(editor) *The Parish Registers of Conway 1541-1793* (London 1900).
J.F. Haswell,	(trans.) *Parish Register of Wicham* (Cumberland and Westmorland Antiquarian and Archaeological Society 1925).
E. Hyde Hall,	*A Description of Caernarvonshire 1809-11* (Caernarvon 1952).
Dom A. and G. Abraham Hughes,	(editors) *Oxford New History of Music, Ars Nova and Renaissance 1300-1540* (London 1960).
Garfield H. Hughes,	*Iaco ab Dewi 1648-1722* (Caerdydd 1953).
H. Seymour Hughes,	(editor) *The Registers of Llantrithyd, Glamorganshire* (London 1888).
A.E. Hutton,	*The British Personal Names in the Historia Regum Britanniae* (California and Cambridge University Presses 1940).
Kenneth Jackson,	*Language and History in Early Britain* (Edinburgh 1953).
L.J.H. James and T.C. Evans,	(editors) *Hen Gwndidau* (Bangor 1910).
T.I. Jeffreys-Jones,	(editor) *Exchequer Proceedings concerning Wales in tempore James I* (Cardiff 1955).
J. Gwili Jenkins,	*Hanfod Duw a Pherson Crist* (Liverpool 1931).
Emyr Gwynne Jones,	(editor) *A Calendar of Exchequer Proceedings concerning Wales* (Cardiff 1939).

G.P. Jones and Hugh Owen,	(editors) *Caernarvon Court Rolls 1361-1402* (Caernarvonshire Historical Society Record Series, I, Caernarfon 1951).
G.P. Jones,	*Brittonic traces in the Lake Counties* (typescript of unpublished lecture).
J. Jones (Tegid) and W. Davies (Gwallter Mechain),	(editors) *Gwaith Lewis Glyn Cothi: the poetical works of Lewis Glyn Cothi* (Oxford 1837).
Owen Jones, William Owen ac Edward Williams,	(editors) *The Myvyrian Archaiology of Wales* (2nd edition, Denbigh 1870).
Theophilus Jones,	*History of Brecknock* (2nd edition, Brecknock 1898).
Thomas Jones,	(editor) *Brenhinedd y Saesson or The Kings of the Saxons* (Cardiff 1971). (editor) *Brut y Tywysogion, Peniarth MS 20* (Cardiff 1941). (editor) *Brut y Tywysogion or The Chronicle of the Princes, Peniarth MS 20 version* (Cardiff 1952). (editor) *Brut y Tywysogion or the Chronicle of the Princes, Red Book of Hergest version* (Cardiff 1955).
T. Gwynn Jones,	(editor) *Gwaith Tudur Aled* (2 vols. Caerdydd, Wrecsam, Llundain, 1926).
E.A. Lewis,	(editor) *Inventory of Early Chancery Proceedings concerning Wales* (Cardiff 1937).
E.A. Lewis and J. Conway Davies,	(editors) *Records of the Court of Augmentations relating to Wales and Monmouthshire* (Cardiff 1954).
E.A. Lewis,	(editor) *Welsh Port Books 1550-1603* (Cymmrodorion Record Series, London 1927).
Henry Lewis,	*Yr Elfen Ladin yn yr Iaith Gymraeg* (Caerdydd 1943).
Henry Lewis and Holger Pedersen,	*A Comparative Celtic Grammar* (Göttingen 1937).
Henry Lewis, Thomas Roberts and Ifor Williams,	(editors) *Cywyddau Iolo Goch ac eraill* (Bangor 1925) (editors) *Cywyddau Iolo Goch ac eraill* (ail argraffiad Caerdydd 1937).
Samuel Lewis,	*Topographical Dictionary of Wales* (2 vols. 4th edition, 1850).
Edward Lhwyd,	*Archaeologia Britannica* (Oxford 1707). *Parochialia* (Supplement to *Arch. Camb.* 1909-1911).
Howell A. Lloyd,	*The Gentry of South-West Wales 1540-1640* (Cardiff 1968).
J.E. Lloyd,	*A History of Wales* (2 vols. London 1911). *Owen Glendower – Owain Glyndŵr* (Oxford 1931).
J. Lloyd-Jones,	*Enwau lleoedd Sir Gaernarfon* (Caerdydd 1928). (editor) *Geirfa Barddoniaeth gynnar Gymraeg* (i, Caerdydd 1931-46; ii, Caerdydd 1950-63).
W.E. Lunt,	(editor), *The Valuation of Norwich 1254* (Oxford 1926).
Edward McLysaght,	*Irish Families, their Names, Arms and Origins* (Dublin 1953). *A Guide to Irish Surnames* (Dublin 1964).
C.M. Matthews,	*English Surnames* (London 1966).
K.B. McFarlane,	*Lancastrian Kings and Lollard Knights* (Oxford 1973).
D.P.M. Michael,	*Arthur Machen* (Cardiff 1971).
Pat Molloy,	*And they blessed Rebecca* (Llandysul 1983).
Prys Morgan,	'The Blayney Period' in *Gregynog* (edited by G.T. Hughes, P. Morgan and G. Thomas, Cardiff 1977).

T.J. Morgan,   *Y Treigladau a'u Cystrawen* (Caerdydd 1952).

John Morris-Jones,   *Cerdd Dafod* (Rhydychen 1925).
A Welsh Grammar (Oxford 1913).
Welsh Syntax (Cardiff 1931).

John Morris-Jones and   (editors) *Llawysgrif Hendregardredd* (Caerdydd 1933).
T.H. Parry-Williams,

Lord Mostyn and   *History of the Family of Mostyn of Mostyn* (London 1925).
T.A. Glenn,

M. Noble,   *Biographical History of England*, iii (London 1806).

Henry Owen,   (editor) *A Calendar of Public Records relating to Pembrokeshire* (3 vols. Cymmrodorion Record Series, London 1914-1918).
(editor) *The description of Pembrokeshire by George Owen of Henllys*, with extensive notes by Egerton Phillimore (4 vols. Cymmrodorion Records Series, London 1902-1936).

Trefor M. Owen,   *Welsh Folk Customs* (Cardiff 1959).

Thomas Parry,   (editor) *Gwaith Dafydd ap Gwilym* (1st edition, Caerdydd 1952).
(editor) *The Oxford Book of Welsh Verse* (Oxford 1962).
(editor) *Theater du Mond*, Rhosier Smyth (Caerdydd 1930).

T.H. Parry-Williams,   (editor) *Carolau Richard White* (Caerdydd 1931).
(editor) *Canu Rhydd Cynnar* (Caerdydd 1932).
The English Element in Welsh (Cymmrodorion Record Series, London 1923).

F.G. Payne,   *Crwydro Sir Faesyfed*, Rhan 2 (Llandybïe 1968).

Thomas Pennant,   *The History of the parishes of Whiteford and Holywell* (London 1796).

G.O. Pierce,   *The Place-names of the Hundred of Dinas Powys* (Cardiff 1968).

Emyr Price,   *Prentisiaeth Lloyd George a Phwllheli* (Pwllheli 1979).

T.B. Pugh,   (editor) *The Marcher Lordships of South Wales 1415-1536* (Cardiff 1963).

P.H. Reaney,   *A Dictionary of British Surnames* (London 1958).

Thomas Rees and   (editors) *Hanes Eglwysi Annibynol Cymru* (vols. I-IV, Liverpool
J. Thomas,   1871-5; vol. V, Dolgellau 1891).

William Rees,   (editor) *A Calendar of Ancient Petitions relating to Wales* (Cardiff 1975).
(editor) *A Survey of the Duchy of Lancaster lordships in Wales 1609-1613* (Cardiff 1953).
South Wales and the border in the fourteenth century (Ordnance Survey, Southampton 1933).

Melville Richards,   *Welsh Administrative and Territorial Units* (Cardiff 1969).

Thomas Richards,   *A British, or Welsh-English Dictionary* (Bristol 1753).

Thomas Richards,   *A History of the Puritan Movement in Wales* (London 1920).

John Rhŷs,   *Studies in Arthurian Legend* (Oxford 1891).
(editor) *A tour in Wales 1770-?1773*, Thomas Pennant (3 vols. Caernarfon 1883).

John Rhŷs and   (editors) *The Text of the Bruts from the Red Book of Hergest* (Oxford 1890).
J. Gwenogvryn Evans,   (editors) *The Text of the Mabinogion and other Welsh tales from the Red Book of Hergest* (Oxford 1890).

Walter Shaw-Taylor,   *Frank Brangwyn and his work* (London 1915).

Shropshire Parish Registers   (various editors, Shropshire Parish Register Society, Shrewsbury 1898-1943).

W.J. Slack,   (editor) *The Lordships of Oswestry 1393-1607* (Shropshire Archaeological Society, Shrewsbury 1951).

J.P. Steel,   (editor) *Lay Subsidy, Cumberland, Edward III* (Kendal 1912).

Taxatio Ecclesiastica   *Taxatio Ecclesiastica, Angliae et Walliae, auctoritate P. Nicholai IV, circa A.D. 1291* (Record Commission, London 1802).

D.R. Thomas,   (editor) *Y Cwtta Cyfarwydd, the chronicle written by the Famous Clarke, Peter Roberts*, with introductory chapter and pedigrees (London 1883).
                              A History of the Diocese of St Asaph (new edition, 3 vols. Oswestry 1908-13).

R.J. Thomas,   *Enwau afonydd a nentydd Cymru* (Caerdydd 1938).

Paul Vinogradoff and   *Survey of the Lordships of Denbigh 1334* (London 1914).
Frank Morgan,

D.J. Williams,   *Storïau'r Tir Glas* (Aberystwyth 1936).

G.J. Williams,   *Iolo Morganwg, y gyfrol gyntaf* (Caerdydd 1956).
                              Traddodiad Llenyddol Morgannwg (Caerdydd 1948)

Ifor Williams,   (editor) *Canu Aneirin* (Caerdydd 1935)
                              (editor) *Canu Llywarch Hen* (Caerdydd 1935).
                              (editor) *Canu Taliesin* (Caerdydd 1960).
                              (editor) *Pedeir Keinc y Mabinogi, allan o Lyfr Gwyn Rhydderch* (Caerdydd 1930).

Ifor Williams and John   (editors) *Gwaith Guto'r Glyn* (Caerdydd 1939).
Llywelyn Williams,

Ifor Williams and   (editors) *Cywyddau Dafydd ap Gwilym a'i gyfoeswyr* (Caerdydd 1935).
Thomas Roberts,

John Williams   (editor) *Annales Cambriae* (Rolls Series, London 1860).
(Ab Ithel),

John Williams   (editor) *The records of Denbigh and its Lordships* (vol. I, Wrexham 1860).
(Glanmor),

Jonathan Williams,   *A general history of the County of Radnor* (2nd edition Brecknock 1905).

Robert Williams,   *A Biographical Dictionary of Eminent Welshmen* (Llandovery 1852).

W. Ogwen Williams,   (editor) *A Calendar of Caernarvonshire Quarter Sessions Records, I, 1541-1558* (Caernarfon 1956).

Keith Williams-Jones,   (editor) *The Merioneth Lay Subsidy Roll 1292-3* (Cardiff 1976).

J.W. Willis-Bund,   (editor) *The Black Book of St David's; an extent of all the lands and rents of the lord bishop of St David's made in 1326* (Cymmrodorion Record Series, London 1902).

E.G. Withycombe,   *The Oxford Dictionary of English Christian Names* (Oxford 1945).

Patrick Woulfe,   *Irish Names and Surnames* (Dublin 1906).

Joseph Wright,   *The English Dialect Dictionary* (London 1898-1905).

Additional Articles

A.D. Carr,	'The making of the Mostyns', Cymm Trans, 1979.
C.M. Fraser,	'The Cumberland and Westmorland Lay Subsidies for 1332', TCWAAS, lxvi, 1966.
Cledwyn Fychan,	'Tudur Aled: Ailystyried ei Gynefin', NLWJ, xxiii, 1983.
John Griffiths,	'Documents relating to the early history of Conway', CaernHS, viii, 1947.
J.L. and A.D. Kirby,	'The poll-tax of 1377 for Carlisle', TCWAAS, lxvi, 1959.
T.E. Morris,	'Welsh Surnames in the Border Counties of Wales', Cy, xliii, 1932.
Bob Owen,	'Some details about the Independents in Caernarfonshire', CaernHS, vi, 1945.
T. Jones Pierce,	'Early Caernarfonshire seamen, compiled 1589', CaernHS, vi, 1945.
Melville Richards,	'The "Lichfield" Gospels (Book of "Saint Chad")', NLWJ, xviii, 1973.
D. Elwyn Williams,	'A short enquiry into the surnames in Glamorgan from the thirteenth to the eighteenth centuries', Cymm Trans, 1961.
Glanmor Williams,	'The Second volume of St David's registers', B, xiv, 1950-52.